lonely planet

Beijing

**Caroline Liou
Robert Storey**

LONELY PLANET PUBLICATIONS
Melbourne • Oakland • London • Paris

Beijing
4th edition – January 2001
First published – February 1994

Published by
Lonely Planet Publications Pty Ltd ABN 36 005 607 983
90 Maribyrnong St, Footscray, Victoria 3011, Australia

Lonely Planet Offices
Australia Locked Bag 1, Footscray, Victoria 3011
USA 150 Linden St, Oakland, CA 94607
UK 10a Spring Place, London NW5 3BH
France 1 rue du Dahomey, 75011 Paris

Photographs
All of the images in this guide are available for licensing from
Lonely Planet Images.
email: lpi@lonelyplanet.com.au

Front cover photograph
Detail of a gate in Tiantan Park (Damien Simonis)

ISBN 1 86450 144 8

text & maps © Lonely Planet 2001
photos © photographers as indicated 2001

Printed by Colorcraft Ltd, Hong Kong

Contents – Text

PLACES TO STAY

PLACES TO EAT

ENTERTAINMENT

SHOPPING

EXCURSIONS

THE GREAT WALL

LANGUAGE

GLOSSARY

INDEX

Contents – Maps

MAP LEGEND   back page

METRIC CONVERSION   inside back cover

The Authors

Caroline Liou

Caroline grew up in Michigan, the Netherlands and Louisiana. After attending university in Louisiana and Hong Kong, she escaped to New York where she worked at various publishing houses before moving to San Francisco as the guidebook publisher for Lonely Planet's US office. For the past two years she's lived in Beijing. In addition to updating this guide to Beijing, she has also contributed to Lonely Planet's guides to China and the Philippines.

From Caroline Special thanks to Amy, William, Evie and Max Soileau, for always having an open door. *Duo xie* to many others who helped out in immeasurable ways: Chris Billing, Amanda Hudson, Julia Cheung, Ingrid Dudek, Jerry Chan, Ellen Hobson and Matthew Hu. Thanks also to LP staff editor Bruce Evans and cartographer Kieran Grogan.

Robert Storey

Robert has had a number of distinguished careers, including monkeykeeper at a zoo and slot-machine repairman in a Las Vegas casino. It was during this era that he produced his first book, *How to Do Your Own Divorce in Nevada*, which sold nearly 200 copies. Since this wasn't enough to keep him in the manner to which he was accustomed, Robert decided to skip the country and sought his fortune in Taiwan as an English teacher. But writing was in his blood, and he was soon flooding the Taiwanese market with various books.

Robert's *Taiwan On Your Own* attracted the attention of Lonely Planet, and was rehashed to become LP's *Taiwan*. Since then, Robert has been involved in over a dozen LP projects, all to do with East Asian countries. His latest scheme – still a work in progress – is his first novel, *Life in the Fast Lane*.

This Book

The first three editions of Beijing were written by Robert Storey and Caroline Liou updated the text for this fourth edition. It was edited and indexed by Bruce Evans and proofed by Jocelyn Harewood and Rachael Atkinson. Layout and design were coordinated by Kieran Grogan, who also provided some text for the Arts sections. Tim Fitzgerald and Martin Heng helped in the initial stages of production, Jane Hart, Chris Love and Corie Waddell checked the layout, and Tim Uden helped out with technical difficulties. Kusnander provided the climate chart and Matt King coordinated the illustrations, which were drawn by Kelli Hamblet and Martin Harris. Maria Vallianos designed the cover. Charles Qin helped checked translations, Pinyin and Chinese script. Also thanks to Lily Chen at ASM Overseas Corporation and to Matthew Clark at Pulay Music.

THANKS

Many thanks to the travellers who used the last edition and wrote to us with helpful hints, useful advice and interesting anecdotes. Your names follow:

Adrian Lloyd, Alain Boucher, Alan Dick, Amy Edwards, Amy Leckie, Andre Amrtino, Andy Kennedy, Anthony Dapiran, Balwant Singh, Barry Blick, Beth Newman, Bob Quiggin, Bob Toomey, Brent Irvin, Bruce Connolly, C M Van Laegenigh, Caroline Villette, Cath Allen, Chantal Spleiss, Charles S Caney, Charlotte & Jim Kenney, Charlotte Martensson, Cindy Carter, Cindy Grieder, Claes Simonsen, Claire Jorrand, Claudia E Miquelon, Connie McGuire, Cornelia Zhu, Cynthia Vainstein, Danny Wongoworawat, David Barton, David Yong Kok Wei, Denise Zook, Don Trueson, E J Casey, Edward Schlenk , Ep Heuvelink, Erik Burkhardt, Frank Campbell, Frederic Vincent, Gary Heatherington, Gavin Burtonwood, Geert Desmet, Graeme Brock, Greg Savage, Gunnar de Wit, Dr Hans E Mulder, Iain Mackay, J P Richards, James Tiernan, Jamie Donahoe, Jane Stevenson, Jeroen Buiks, Joachim Bergmann, Joe Brock, Joe Carter, Johan Steurs, Johanna Court-Brown, John Bourque, John Macadam, John Parkinson, John Ruggieri, John Sheppard-Jones, Jolanda Trouwee , Jonathon Small, K Zareski, Karl-Koenig Koenigsson, Katherine Bradbury, Kathryn Kerrigan, Kees Smit, Dr Kevin J Denny, Klaus Lohrer, Kurt Straub Joho, Laura Short, Leng Goh, Leslie Ryang, Lisa A Dahl, Llana Gordon, M Hoo, Mae Rethers, Maggie Armstrong, Maria Siow, Mark Shideler, Mark Woldman, Martin Heffer, Menno Beem, Michael McColl, Michael Solarz, Michel Smit, Mikael Johansson, Mike Alcock, Milli Vayrynen, Peter Leykam, Peter Ziegel Wanger, Phil & Brenda Soffe, Philip Mason, R Brondgeest, Ren Yanqing, Richard Clark, Rick Millette, Rob Pearson, Robert Dampf, Robert F, Rogachova Irina, Ron Miller, Rose Kinnebrew, Samantha & Leigh Ebzery, Scott Ackiss, Simon Francis , Siok Han Tjoa, Steve Riley, Stuart Sugihara, Thomas Schmidt-Doerr, Tom Stahl, Tony Helga, Tracey Sutherland, Viveca Moritz, W Hardy, Willy Eriz

Foreword

ABOUT LONELY PLANET GUIDEBOOKS

The story begins with a classic travel adventure: Tony and Maureen Wheeler's 1972 journey across Europe and Asia to Australia. Useful information about the overland trail did not exist at that time, so Tony and Maureen published the first Lonely Planet guidebook to meet a growing need.

From a kitchen table, then from a tiny office in Melbourne (Australia), Lonely Planet has become the largest independent travel publisher in the world, an international company with offices in Melbourne, Oakland (USA), London (UK) and Paris (France).

Today Lonely Planet guidebooks cover the globe. There is an ever-growing list of books and there's information in a variety of forms and media. Some things haven't changed. The main aim is still to help make it possible for adventurous travellers to get out there – to explore and better understand the world.

At Lonely Planet we believe travellers can make a positive contribution to the countries they visit – if they respect their host communities and spend their money wisely. Since 1986 a percentage of the income from each book has been donated to aid projects and human rights campaigns.

Updates Lonely Planet thoroughly updates each guidebook as often as possible. This usually means there are around two years between editions, although for more unusual or more stable destinations the gap can be longer. Check the imprint page (following the colour map at the beginning of the book) for publication dates.

Between editions up-to-date information is available in two free newsletters – the paper *Planet Talk* and email *Comet* (to subscribe, contact any Lonely Planet office) – and on our Web site at www.lonelyplanet.com. The *Upgrades* section of the Web site covers a number of important and volatile destinations and is regularly updated by Lonely Planet authors. *Scoop* covers news and current affairs relevant to travellers. And, lastly, the *Thorn Tree* bulletin board and *Postcards* section of the site carry unverified, but fascinating, reports from travellers.

Correspondence The process of creating new editions begins with the letters, postcards and emails received from travellers. This correspondence often includes suggestions, criticisms and comments about the current editions. Interesting excerpts are immediately passed on via newsletters and the Web site, and everything goes to our authors to be verified when they're researching on the road. We're keen to get more feedback from organisations or individuals who represent communities visited by travellers.

Lonely Planet gathers information for everyone who's curious about the planet – and especially for those who explore it first-hand. Through guidebooks, phrasebooks, activity guides, maps, literature, newsletters, image library, TV series and Web site we act as an information exchange for a worldwide community of travellers.

Research Authors aim to gather sufficient practical information to enable travellers to make informed choices and to make the mechanics of a journey run smoothly. They also research historical and cultural background to help enrich the travel experience and allow travellers to understand and respond appropriately to cultural and environmental issues.

Authors don't stay in every hotel because that would mean spending a couple of months in each medium-sized city and, no, they don't eat at every restaurant because that would mean stretching belts beyond capacity. They do visit hotels and restaurants to check standards and prices, but feedback based on readers' direct experiences can be very helpful.

Many of our authors work undercover, others aren't so secretive. None of them accept freebies in exchange for positive write-ups. And none of our guidebooks contain any advertising.

Production Authors submit their raw manuscripts and maps to offices in Australia, USA, UK or France. Editors and cartographers – all experienced travellers themselves – then begin the process of assembling the pieces. When the book finally hits the shops, some things are already out of date, we start getting feedback from readers and the process begins again …

WARNING & REQUEST

Things change – prices go up, schedules change, good places go bad and bad places go bankrupt – nothing stays the same. So, if you find things better or worse, recently opened or long since closed, please tell us and help make the next edition even more accurate and useful. We genuinely value all the feedback we receive. Julie Young coordinates a well travelled team that reads and acknowledges every letter, postcard and email and ensures that every morsel of information finds its way to the appropriate authors, editors and cartographers for verification.

Everyone who writes to us will find their name in the next edition of the appropriate guidebook. They will also receive the latest issue of *Planet Talk*, our quarterly printed newsletter, or *Comet*, our monthly email newsletter. Subscriptions to both newsletters are free. The very best contributions will be rewarded with a free guidebook.

Excerpts from your correspondence may appear in new editions of Lonely Planet guidebooks, the Lonely Planet Web site, *Planet Talk* or *Comet*, so please let us know if you *don't* want your letter published or your name acknowledged.

Send all correspondence to the Lonely Planet office closest to you:

Australia: Locked Bag 1, Footscray, Victoria 3011
USA: 150 Linden St, Oakland, CA 94607
UK: 10A Spring Place, London NW5 3BH
France: 1 rue du Dahomey, 75011 Paris

Or email us at: talk2us@lonelyplanet.com.au

For news, views and updates see our Web site: www.lonelyplanet.com

HOW TO USE A LONELY PLANET GUIDEBOOK

The best way to use a Lonely Planet guidebook is any way you choose. At Lonely Planet we believe the most memorable travel experiences are often those that are unexpected, and the finest discoveries are those you make yourself. Guidebooks are not intended to be used as if they provide a detailed set of infallible instructions!

Contents All Lonely Planet guidebooks follow roughly the same format. The Facts about the Destination chapters or sections give background information ranging from history to weather. Facts for the Visitor gives practical information on issues like visas and health. Getting There & Away gives a brief starting point for re-searching travel to and from the destination. Getting Around gives an overview of the transport options when you arrive.

The peculiar demands of each destination determine how sub-sequent chapters are broken up, but some things remain constant. We always start with background, then proceed to sights, places to stay, places to eat, entertainment, getting there and away, and getting around information – in that order.

Heading Hierarchy Lonely Planet headings are used in a strict hierarchical structure that can be visualised as a set of Russian dolls. Each heading (and its following text) is encompassed by any preceding heading that is higher on the hierarchical ladder.

Entry Points We do not assume guidebooks will be read from beginning to end, but that people will dip into them. The tradi-tional entry points are the list of contents and the index. In addition, however, some books have a complete list of maps and an index map illustrating map coverage.

There may also be a colour map that shows highlights. These highlights are dealt with in greater detail in the Facts for the Visitor chapter, along with planning questions and suggested itin-eraries. Each chapter covering a geographical region usually begins with a locator map and another list of highlights. Once you find something of interest in a list of highlights, turn to the index.

Maps Maps play a crucial role in Lonely Planet guidebooks and include a huge amount of information. A legend is printed on the back page. We seek to have complete consistency between maps and text, and to have every important place in the text captured on a map. Map key numbers usually start in the top left corner.

Although inclusion in a guidebook usually implies a recommen-dation we cannot list every good place. Exclusion does not necessarily imply criticism. In fact there are a number of reasons why we might exclude a place – sometimes it is simply inappropriate to encourage an influx of travellers.

Introduction

For centuries, Beijing has been the promised land of China. Originally a walled bastion for emperors and officials, it remains a majestic political and architectural marvel. Today, poor peasants still flock to the city in search of the elusive pot of gold at the end of the rainbow; many wind up camped out in makeshift cardboard housing on Beijing's outskirts. The government encourages them to go home, but the lure of the capital proves too enticing. Meanwhile, down the road by the Friendship Store, smartly dressed customers clutching mobile telephones head for the nearest banquet or disco.

As the capital of the People's Republic of China (PRC), Beijing is home to bureaucrats, generals, nouveau-riche cadres, avante-garde artists and *lǎobǎixìng* (common people), and host to reporters, diplomats, students and tourists. It's a labyrinth of doors, walls, tunnels, gates and entrances, temples, pavilions, parks and museums. Beijing moves the cogs and wheels of the Chinese universe, and tries to slow them down if they're moving in the wrong direction. As far away as Xinjiang people run on Beijing's clock, and all over the land they chortle in *pǔtōnghuà*, the Beijing dialect.

Perhaps nowhere else in China is the generation gap more visible. Appalled by the current drive to 'modernise', many older people still wax euphoric about Chairman Mao and the years of sacrifice for the socialist revolution. But most youngsters disdain socialist sacrifice and are more interested in money, motorbikes, fashion, video games, sex and rock music – not necessarily in that order.

Foreigners seem to enjoy Beijing since the city offers so much to see and do. Yet up until the 1990s it was arguably one of the poorest-looking capitals in all Asia. Things have changed drastically: gone are the years of austerity and ration coupons. The Beijing of today is a forest of construction cranes, bulldozers and 24-hour work crews scrambling to build the new China. Plush shopping malls and five-star hotels rise from the rubble. Whatever one says about Beijing, it probably won't be true tomorrow – the city is metamorphosing so rapidly it makes you dizzy. Travellers of the 1980s remember Beijing as a city of narrow lanes with single-storey homes built around courtyards. These have given way to the high-rise housing estates of the 1990s. TV sets and washing machines – unimaginable luxuries in the 1980s – are now commonplace. Whereas bicycles and ox carts were the main form of transport a decade ago, both are prohibited on the new freeways and toll roads that now encompass the city.

Whatever impression you come away with, Beijing is one of the most fascinating places in China. It may be something of a showcase, but what capital city isn't? Within its environs you will find some of China's most stunning sights: the Forbidden City, the Summer Palace, Tiantan Park, the Lama Temple and the Great Wall to name just a few. During the Cultural Revolution of the 1960s these and other historical treasures of China literally took a beating. Now the damage has been repaired, the temples have been restored and everything is being spruced up.

Tourist groups are usually processed through Beijing in much the same way as the ducks are force-fed on the outlying farms – the two usually meet on the first night over the dinner table. But individual travellers will have no trouble getting around. Any effort you make to get out and see things will be rewarded. The city offers so much of interest that the main complaint of most visitors is that they simply run out of time before seeing it all.

Facts about Beijing

HISTORY

Although the area south-west of Beijing was inhabited by early humans some 500,000 years ago, the earliest records of settlement date from around 1000 BC. The city developed as a frontier trading town for the Mongols and Koreans and the tribes from Shandong Province and central China. By the Warring States Period (453–221 BC) it had grown to be the capital of the Yan Kingdom and was called Ji, a reference to the marshy features of the area. As it acquired new warlords, the Khitan Mongols and Manchurian Jurchen tribes among them, the city underwent a number of changes. What attracted the conquerors was its strategic position on the edge of the North China Plain. During the Liao dynasty (AD 916–1125) Beijing was referred to as Yanjing (Capital of Yan) – the name now used for Beijing's most popular beer.

In AD 1215 the great Mongol warrior Genghis Khan descended on the capital and razed everything in sight. From the ashes emerged Dadu (Great Capital), alias Khanbaliq, the Khan's town. By 1279 Genghis' grandson Kublai had made himself ruler of the largest empire the world has ever known, with Khanbaliq his capital. Thus was China's Yuan dynasty (1215–1368) established.

When the Mongol emperor was informed by his astrologers that the old site of Beijing was a breeding ground for rebels, he shifted his capital further north. The great palace he built no longer remains, but it was visited by the Italian traveller Marco Polo, who later described what he saw to an amazed Europe. Polo was equally dazzled by the innovations of gunpowder and paper money. History's first case of paper-currency inflation occurred when the last Mongol emperor flooded the country with worthless bills. This, coupled with a large number of natural disasters, provoked an uprising led by the mercenary Zhu Yanhang, who took Beijing in 1368. During the Ming dynasty (1368–1644) which followed, the city was rechristened Beiping (Northern Peace), though for the next 35 years the imperial capital was situated in Nanjing.

In the early 1400s Zhu's son Yongle shuffled the court back to Beiping and renamed it Beijing (Northern Capital). Millions of taels of silver were spent on refurbishing the city. Yongle is credited with being the true architect of the modern city, and many of Beijing's most famous structures, like the Forbidden City and Tiantan, were first built in his reign. The Inner City grew to encircle the imperial compound and a suburban zone was added to the south, creating a bustle of merchants and street life. The basic grid of present-day Beijing had been laid.

Under the Manchus, who invaded China and established the Qing dynasty (1644–1911), and particularly during the reigns of the emperors Kangxi and Qianlong, Beijing was expanded and renovated; summer palaces, pagodas and temples were built.

In the last 120 years of Manchu rule, Beijing and much of China were subject to invaders and rebels: the Anglo-French troops, who in 1860 marched in and burnt the Old Summer Palace to the ground; the Taiping Rebellion (1850–1868), which saw the fall of Nanking to the rebels and the death of 20 million people; and the disastrous Boxer Rebellion of 1900 against Western influence, which was supported by the corrupt regime of Empress Dowager Cixi (1834–1908; see the 'Dragon Lady' boxed text). Cixi had taken control of the dragon throne in 1860. When she died, she bequeathed power to two-year-old Puyi, who was to be China's last emperor. The Qing dynasty, brutal and incompetent at the best of times, was now rudderless and quickly collapsed. The revolution of 1911 ostensibly brought the Kuomintang (Nationalist Party) to power and the Republic of China (ROC) was declared with Sun Yatsen as president. However, real power remained in the hands of warlords who carved China up into their own fiefdoms.

One of these warlords was General Yuan Shikai, who tried to declare himself emperor in Beijing in 1915. Yuan's scheme ended abruptly when he died in 1916, but other warlords continued to control most of northern China and the Kuomintang held power in the south. The country was badly splintered by private Chinese armies, while foreigners controlled important economic zones (called concessions) in major ports like Shanghai and Tianjin.

China's continuing poverty, reluctance to adapt and control by warlords and foreigners was a recipe for rebellion. Beijing University became a hotbed of intellectual dissent, attracting scholars from all over China. Karl Marx's *The Communist Manifesto*, translated into Chinese, became the basis for countless discussion groups. One of those attending was a library assistant named Mao Zedong (1893–1976).

The Communists, including Mao, later established a power base in Shanghai and entered into an uneasy alliance with the Kuomintang to reunify China.

In 1926 the Kuomintang embarked on the Northern Expedition to wrest power from the remaining warlords. Chiang Kaishek (1886–1975) was appointed commander-in-chief by the Kuomintang and the Communists. The following year, Chiang turned on his Communist allies and slaughtered them en masse in Shanghai; the survivors carried on a civil war from the countryside. By the middle of 1928 the Northern Expedition had reached Beijing, where a national government was established with Chiang holding both military and political leadership.

In 1937 the Japanese invaded Beijing and by 1939 had overrun eastern China. The Kuomintang retreated west to the city of Chongqing, which became China's temporary capital during WWII. After Japan's defeat in 1945 the Kuomintang returned, but their days were numbered: by this time the Chinese Civil War was in full swing. The Communists, now under the leadership of Mao Zedong, achieved victory in 1949, and as the People's Liberation Army (PLA) marched into Beijing the Kuomintang leaders fled to Taiwan. On 1 October of the same year, Mao Zedong proclaimed the People's Republic of China (PRC) to an audience of 500,000 in Tiananmen Square.

After the Revolution

After 1949 came a period of urban reconstruction in Beijing. Down came the walls and commemorative arches. Blocks of buildings were reduced to rubble to widen the boulevards and Tiananmen Square. Soviet technicians poured in and left their mark in the form of Stalinesque architecture.

Progress of all kinds came to a halt in 1966 when Mao launched what became known as the Cultural Revolution. Seeing his power-base eroding, Mao officially sanctioned wall posters and criticisms of party members by university staff and students. Before long students were being issued with red arm bands and taking to the streets. The Hóngwèibāng (Red Guards) had been born. By August 1966 Mao was reviewing mass parades of the Red Guards, who chanted and fanatically waved copies of his famous *Little Red Book* in Tiananmen Square.

Nothing was sacred enough to be spared the brutal onslaught of the Red Guards. Universities and secondary schools were shut down; intellectuals, writers, artists and monks were dismissed, killed, persecuted or sent to labour camps in the countryside; the

The Mao badge: still selling like hot cakes

Dragon Lady

One of the larger-than-life figures in recent Chinese history is Empress Dowager Cixi, the Dragon Lady. Through a stroke of good fortune and some innate cunning, she managed to hold the reigns of Chinese power for more than 40 years.

Born in 1835, Cixi (given name Yehonala) was a Manchu, the daughter of a captain of the guard in the Forbidden City. At the age of 16 she was chosen to be one of Emperor Xianfeng's many concubines, so instead of marrying her sweetheart Jung Lu, a Manchu garrison commander, she went to live in the Forbidden City.

Cixi's great leap forward came when she gave birth to the emperor's only son, after which she rose in rank from third-grade concubine to secondary consort. But she also exhibited exceptional intelligence and cunning, for the emperor was said to have constantly consulted her on affairs of state.

It is hard to say how much fate played a role in Cixi's rise to power and how much was a result of her own hand, but people seemed to die conveniently for her. When Xianfeng died in 1861 (at the age of 30) and Cixi's five-year-old son, Tongzhi, became emperor, Cixi became the dowager empress. With the help of the eunuchs, who she bribed liberally, and the palace guard, with whom she had connections through her father and her former fiance (he remained loyal to her throughout his life), she seized control of the government and had her enemies beheaded.

Whether Cixi's machinations extended to deliberately causing her son, the emperor, to contract venereal disease by plying him with concubines is open to question. However, the death of one of his concubines, soon after she fell pregnant, was rumoured to be a 'forced suicide'.

After her son's death, Cixi committed the brazen act (a sure sign of her power) of choosing the next emperor: her own three-year-old nephew, Guangxu, who was not in direct line for the throne. When he became a teenager, Cixi apparently went into retirement, content to direct things from the peace and relative seclusion of the Summer Palace. But when the emperor began to show a mind of his own, initiating reforms that were unpalatable to Cixi, she returned to the Forbidden City with a vengeance. She had the emperor locked away in a pavilion, to be allowed out only on ceremonial occasions.

By this stage, the Qing dynasty of the Manchus had been in steady decline for the last hundred years. Its weaknesses had been highlighted by the Taiping Rebellion, and by the time Cixi mistakenly lent her support to the Boxer Rebellion, directed against Western influence, the dynasty's days

publication of scientific, artistic, literary and cultural periodicals ceased; temples were ransacked and monasteries disbanded; and many physical reminders of China's 'feudal', 'exploitative' or 'capitalist' past (including temples, monuments and works of art) were destroyed. Red Guard factions often battled each other and in the end the PLA was forced to bring them under control.

China was to remain in the grip of chaos for the next decade. It wasn't until around 1979 that Deng Xiaoping – a former protege of Mao who had emerged as a pragmatic leader – launched a 'modernisation' drive. The country opened up and westerners were finally given a chance to see what the Communists had been up to for the past 30 years.

Beijing saw considerable change during the 1980s – private businesses, once banned by the Communists, were allowed again. Most temples, monuments and libraries wrecked during the Cultural Revolution were repaired. Unfortunately, the decade ended on a tragic note in June 1989, when PLA troops crushed a student-led pro-democracy movement in Tiananmen Square. For a couple of years China was frozen out of the international community. These days, both the Cultural Revolution and the Tiananmen Square massacre are taboo topics among officials.

Dragon Lady

were truly numbered. The Boxers failed to oust the foreign devils and instead incurred a retaliatory attack on the capital by foreign troops.

In 1906 Cixi set about establishing yet another heir to the throne. The daughter of Cixi's former boyfriend Jung Lu married Guangxu's brother, Prince Ch'un, and had a son, Puyi, who was to be the last of the Qing emperors. When Cixi became mortally ill and realised her days were numbered, she made her moves, appointing Puyi the successor to the throne. That night Emperor Guangxu mysteriously died, thus removing any cause for doubts as to the succession, and Cixi died soon after.

Cixi wasn't a great ruler but an opportunist, and her story pales in comparison to the Tang dynasty empress Wu Hou, who was so powerful she almost succeeded in starting her own dynasty. Was her rise to power just a symptom of the times she lived in or the result of a unique and powerful character? Probably a combination of both. Certainly the blood shed in the process of her power-broking was not unusual: Chinese emperors had a habit of waiting until they were on their deathbeds before announcing an heir – a sure recipe for bloodshed – and purges in the Forbidden City were not uncommon. Cixi stands tall as the last great figure of the Qing dynasty. Palaces will always be cloaked in plot, intrigue and scandal, but Cixi's story is close enough in time to provide some detail through the shadows.

Nonetheless, in 1994 the Chinese leadership was confident that the nation had re-established its reputation on the world stage. When cities were being polled to host the 2000 Olympics, the Chinese assumed Beijing would win. They took the rebuff badly when Sydney, Australia, was chosen, although they've put in a bid for the 2008 Olympics.

Nor did the Chinese win many friends in 1995 when Beijing played host to the United Nations' Conference on Women. Having lobbied the UN hard to get the conference, the Chinese then denied visas to at least several hundred people who wanted to attend – because they were regarded as politically incorrect. About 20,000 representatives of non-governmental organisations did in fact attend, but were isolated in a fenced compound 50km from the capital because the Chinese deemed their activities potentially subversive.

China found itself at loggerheads with the West again in early 1996 when the leadership decided to fire missiles at the coastal waters just off Taiwan to 'influence' Taiwan's presidential election. The net effect was to greatly increase support for Lee Tenghui (who was re-elected with 54% of the vote), the candidate who Beijing had vilified. The crisis also brought US warships into the area and threats from China to 'nuke Los Angeles'. History repeated itself

MH

Deng Xiaoping, who pioneered China's path
to economic freedom

with the 2000 elections. The Chinese leaders' threats of war if Taiwan elected pro-independence candidate Chen Shui-bian of the Democratic Progressive Party backfired, with Chen winning the election. Despite the rhetoric, no missiles were fired.

Things have cooled down since then and Beijing has been trying to polish its tarnished image. The funeral of the paramount leader Deng Xiaoping in early 1997 was a momentous event, with huge crowds of grieving Beijingers lining the streets. There was no public talk of succession, leaving journalists to speculate on just what sort of power struggles might have been taking place behind the scenes.

China's takeover of Hong Kong in July 1997 was predictably accompanied by fireworks, parades and an orgy of nationalistic chest-thumping in Beijing, all of which seemed to delight the Chinese public and remind the West that, as always, China cannot be ignored. Macau's handover to the Mainland took place on 20 December 1999 with little fanfare.

GEOGRAPHY

Mountainous along the north and west, and flat in the south-east, Beijing municipality has a total area of 16,800 sq km. The city limits extend some 80km, including urban and suburban areas and the nine counties under its administration.

In the western corner of Beijing municipality is Ling Shan which, at 2303m, is the region's highest peak. The southern extremity of Beijing is the lowest point at 44m above sea level.

CLIMATE

Autumn (from September to early November) is the perfect time to visit: there's little rain, it's not dry or humid, and the city wears a pleasant cloak of foliage.

Winter can be interesting if you don't mind the cold. Although the temperature can dip as low as -20°C and the northern winds cut like a knife through bean curd, parts of the capital appear charming in this season. Burning coal to heat buildings produces pollution, but the resulting subdued light renders the capital oddly photogenic, with contrasting blacks and whites and some extra-sooty greys. Winter clothing is readily available – the locals tend to wear about 15 layers each.

Spring is short, dry and dusty. From April to May a phenomenon known as 'yellow wind' plagues the Chinese capital – fine dust particles, blown all the way from the Gobi Desert in the north-west, sandpaper everything in sight, including your face (see the 'Dune' boxed text). Beijing women put mesh bags over their heads to protect their smooth complexions.

In summer (June to August) the average temperature is 26°C – hot and humid, with heavy afternoon thundershowers and mosquitoes in July.

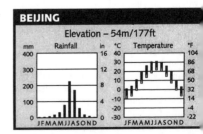

BEIJING

Elevation – 54m/177ft

ECOLOGY & ENVIRONMENT

With 12 million residents and a rapidly expanding economy, Beijing's environment has taken a beating. Before 1980 the city had a few monolithic socialist-style buildings, but it mostly consisted of *hútòng* (narrow lanes), walls and single-storey homes built in traditional *sìhéyuàn* (rectangular courtyards). For better or worse, the new Beijing is a landscape of wide boulevards, building cranes and concrete high-rises.

The consumer boom of the past few years has led to all the usual problems resulting from people using more throwaway packaging and power-hungry electrical devices. Rising affluence has led many to abandon bicycles and buses for cars and taxis.

Air pollution has been recognised as a serious health hazard and the government has made an effort to move smoke-belching factories out to rural areas. Air pollution has also been reduced by replacing coal with natural gas as a heating fuel. Unfortunately, these improvements in air quality have been sullied by the increase in motor vehicles.

In response, the municipal government has embarked on a massive road improvement scheme in the hope of reducing both traffic congestion and pollution. But as many predicted, this has simply tempted even more people to buy cars.

Super smog-emitting *miandis* (bread-box minivans), once a common sight on Beijing streets, were banned from the city in 1999 in an effort to reduce air pollution.

Mass transit should be the answer. The subway was recently expanded, and plans are afloat to build a light railway around the city, but the short-term prognosis seems to be more traffic, noise and pollution.

FLORA & FAUNA

Most of the land around Beijing has either been so heavily cultivated or urbanised that the native flora and fauna perished long ago.

However, there are two nature reserves on the far reaches of Beijing municipality. At the eastern tip of Beijing is the Wuling Shan Nature Reserve *(Wùlíngshān Zìrán Bǎohùqū)*, with a peak of 2116m. On the north-western outskirts of town is the Song Shan Nature Reserve *(Sōngshān Zìrán Bǎohùqū)*, which contains Haituo Shan (2241m). Both reserves have conifer forests and a rich assortment of migratory birds during the warmer months. Sadly, all the large animals (such as tigers) were long ago hunted to extinction.

GOVERNMENT & POLITICS

Although Beijing is the home of China's central government and thus at the apex of the Communist pyramid, it also has a mayor

---

Dune

You've heard of the Gobi and you may have heard of the Takla Makan, but did you know that Beijing may one day be another of China's deserts? Winds are blowing desert sands towards the capital at a rate of 2km a year, with dunes up to 30m high creeping ever closer.

According to the United Nations' Office to Combat Desertification and Drought (UNSO), one third of China is subject to desertification – the process by which previously semi-arable or arable land gradually becomes depleted of plant and animal life. Every year over 2600 sq km of China's arable land becomes desert. The causes are many, but even the trampling of the hooves of livestock in desert-rim areas can contribute.

The United Nations Development Programme (UNDP) is providing US$1.5 million in funds to help implement a National Action Programme in an attempt to stay the spread of the sand. On a grander scale, a green wall, which will eventually stretch 5700km – longer than the Great Wall – is being planted in north-eastern China to keep back the sand, though with dust storms more and more common in Beijing, the situation looks gloomy.

Scientists are still divided over whether desertification is a permanent process, and how and whether it can be halted or reversed. Meanwhile, the dunes are approaching Badaling. Beijingers can only hope that the green wall will prevail and prove itself more vital than its now-abandoned brick counterpart.

Model Citizen

Comrade Lei Feng was a young soldier who in 1963, one year after dying in a traffic accident at the age of 22, was lionised by the Communist Party as a model worker, warrior, Party member and all-round PRC model citizen. The masses were urged by top Party officials to 'learn from Comrade Lei Feng', whose feats included washing his fellow soldiers' laundry in his spare time, helping old ladies cross the street, and making sure everyone in his home town and army platoon was up-to-date on the latest Party doctrine.

Lei Feng was not the only model citizen dreamed up by the Communist leadership, but he certainly was (and remains) the most famous. He was made into a great hero during the Cultural Revolution of the 1960s, then forgotten for about 25 years. He resurfaced again in 1990 in a bid to counter the widespread disillusionment with the Party that followed the Tiananmen Square massacre. Soon thereafter, he disappeared from the billboards again, but in 1997 a new movie about the life and times of Comrade Lei Feng had its debut in Beijing.

Lei Feng's patriotism and sacrifices for the revolution are well known, but what about his love life? The authorities have been mum on this sensitive topic, but shortly after the movie debut, a 60-year-old woman emerged claiming to have been Lei Feng's girlfriend when she was young. If China had a tabloid press in the tradition of Fleet St, it's easy to imagine what they could have done with a story like that.

It's a great disappointment that Beijing doesn't have a museum dedicated to this national hero; however, there is one outside Lei Feng's home town – Changsha in Hunan Province – should you happen to be there.

and is an independent municipality within Hubei Province. However, like many national capitals, Beijing is directly under the control of the central government and subject to factional struggles within the Chinese Communist Party (CCP).

Villages in China with a population under 10,000 are permitted to elect local leaders, but no such elections are permitted in big cities like Beijing. Everyone from the mayor down is appointed by someone higher up the ladder.

A number of top Beijing officials fell from grace early in 1995 when the central government launched a merciless anti-corruption drive. Victims of that particular purge included Beijing's highest official, Mayor Chen Xitong, and Treasurer Wang Baosen; the latter committed suicide while under arrest.

ECONOMY

After 1949, when the Communists took over China, the Chinese could claim to be among the most devout practitioners of Marxist economic theory. All forms of capitalism were banned and foreign investors were shut out. After following this path for 30 years, China suddenly found itself behind almost every country in the region.

China started experimenting with capitalist-style economic reforms in 1980 initiated by the all-seeing Party leader Deng Xiaoping. The reforms proceeded in fits and starts for nearly a decade, and almost came to a halt with the Tiananmen incident in 1989. Since then, the economic shackles of state control have been thrown off and foreign money and technology have poured in. For the past decade economic growth has averaged a dizzying 10% a year. Flush with cash, the Chinese government has poured money into its capital city, turning it into a boom town.

After two decades of high growth, China's economy is now slowing and unemployment is on the rise. The state's current aim to restructure inefficient state-owned enterprise is costing millions of jobs and is leading to social unrest among laid-off workers – many of whom feel the government has abandoned them to the market economy. In an attempt to stimulate the economy, the government has turned to pouring money into public works projects. But consumers, worried about lay-offs, are holding on to their money. Privitisation as a means of reviving the state

Early morning massage at Houhai Lake

Taijiquan is the favoured form of morning exercise. These people are practising at Jingshan Park.

Keeping fit (clockwise from top right): ballet classes, morning exercises, taiji with Chinese sword, taijiquan, and a tango in Tiantan Park sector has also been scaled back, due to the party's fear that further privitisation would undermine its rule.

Chinese leaders hope that World Trade Organization (WTO) membership will spur the economy. In the short term, however, membership would certainly mean more factory closings and unemployment. In the longer term, it's hoped that it will increase imports and exports, force state industries into the market and revive foreign investment. Pessimists take the view that the government's hesitancy to reform its state enterprises at a faster rate and its unwillingness to nurture the private sector will drive China to crisis point. Optimists point out that China's policy of gradual economic reform has basically worked well so far and has allowed China to come out unscathed from Asia's economic crisis.

By some predictions, in another decade China will have the world's largest economy. Others are not so sure – the country's messy politics may yet again cause economic grief. Still, no-one is predicting China's imminent collapse. The pace of economic liberalisation has gone so far, so fast that it has taken on a momentum of its own. Putting the capitalist toothpaste back into the tube seems well-nigh impossible.

POPULATION & PEOPLE

The population of Beijing municipality is over 12 million, with perhaps eight million in the central city. An estimated one million people from China's countryside live illegally in Beijing. The majority of Beijingers (over 95%) are Han Chinese. The rest of China's 56 official ethnic minorities are scattered about the city, but a few have established little enclaves. Since China opened up to the outside world, the capital has acquired a fast-growing foreign business community.

ARTS
Music

Traditional Other than in conservatories, it is becoming rare to hear traditional Chinese instrumental music. More often, opera and other vocal forms tend to predominate. Such recitals as there are usually take the form of soloists or small groups of musicians performing on traditional instruments. These include the *shēng* (flute), *èrhú* (two-stringed fiddle), *húqín* (viola), *yuèqín* (guitar) and *pípa* (lute) – all used in Beijing opera. Others are the *sānxián* (three-stringed lute), *dòngxiāo* (vertical flute), *dízi* (horizontal flute), *bāngdí* (piccolo), *gǔzhēng* (zither), *suǒnà* (ceremonial trumpet) and *dàluó* (ceremonial gongs). Tapes and CDs of traditional music can be bought at places such as the Foreign Languages Bookstore in Wangfujing (see Map 4, Dongcheng).

Opera After decades in the shade of political operas like *Taking Tiger Mountain by Strategy,* Beijing opera *(jīngjù)* has made a comeback. Despite its short history it is one of opera's most famous forms, enjoying popularity since a provincial troupe performed for Emperor Qianlong's 80th birthday in 1790.

Beijing opera is more physical than its European counterpart. The mixture of singing, dancing, speaking, mime, acrobatics and dancing can go on for five or six hours, though two hours is more typical. The screeching music can be searing to Western ears, but plots are fairly simple and easy to follow.

Modern China's music market is heavily influenced by the already well-established music industries in Taiwan and Hong Kong. The advent of satellite TV and the popularity of Channel V – broadcast via Hong Kong's Star TV network – is also having an impact.

Hip young urban Chinese are into disco. Taiwanese love songs have been enormously successful in China, and Mandarin versions of Hong Kong pop music (the original songs are Cantonese) produced for the Taiwan and China markets are frequently chart hits. While Chinese tastes generally run towards soft melodies, Beijing has a nascent heavy metal and punk scene. In an attempt to show that the geriatric leadership is also hip, government officials authorised a disco version of *The East is Red,* theme song of the Mao generation – sales figures are not available!

The older generation got a jolt in 1989 with the release of *Rock & Roll for the New Long March,* by Cui Jian (see the boxed text 'Beijing Rock' in the Entertainment chapter), one of China's foremost singers. Despite being put on hold after Tiananmen, he continues to produce ambiguously worded lyrics and also featured in *Beijing Bastards,* a shoestring film by Zhang Yuan about the fringes of the city's rock scene. More jolts to the system came with heavy metal sounds by the bands Tang Dynasty and Black Panther, though the latter now look and sound like Bon Jovi. Perhaps integral to the growing influence of Chinese rock as the voice of urban youth is that most groups no longer simply copy foreign models. If you have a chance, catch Thin Man and Yao Shi – two excellent Beijing bands that are forging ahead with their own styles.

For details on venues, see the Entertainment chapter.

Painting & Calligraphy

Foreigners struggling to read shop signs might not be so impressed, but calligraphy has traditionally been regarded in China as the highest form of visual art. The basic tools, commonly referred to as 'the four treasures of the scholar's study', are paper, ink, ink-stone (on which the ink is mixed) and brush. These materials are shared by Chinese painters, reflecting the close relationship between Chinese painting and calligraphy.

Countless calligraphic styles have developed over the years. Earlier styles, such as the *zhuan* or Seal Script dating from the Western Zhou dynasty, are squarer and more formal. A more flowing, cursive style of calligraphy was later developed to cater to the desire for a speedier brush stroke.

There is also a tradition of elegant and refined porcelain, which the Chinese first began to produce during the Tang dynasty (AD 618–907). Stoneware was first produced much earlier. Bronze vessels of great sophistication have been discovered dating from around AD 1200. Silk embroidery, jade jewellery and sculpture in clay, wood and stone are other notable areas of Chinese art.

In Beijing a flourishing avant-garde art scene has emerged. The work of Chinese painters has arguably more innovative and dissident than that of writers, possibly because the political implications are harder to interpret by the authorities.

Literature

Fiction Classic works of Chinese literature now available in English translations include *Outlaws of the Marsh,* by Shi Nai'an, *The Dream of the Red Chamber* (also known as *The Dream of Red Mansions* and *The Story of the Stone*), by Cao Xueqin, and *Journey to the West,* (also known as *Monkey*), by Wu Cheng-en.

The most famous author to have called Beijing home is Lu Xun (1881–1936). Considered by many Chinese to be their greatest 20th-century writer, he first achieved fame with *A Madman's Diary*, a paranoiac fable of Confucian society. His most famous work, *The Story of Ah Q*, examines the life of a man who is chronically unable to recognise the setbacks in his life, just as China itself seemed unable to accept the apparently desperate need to modernise. Because his work reflects the need for revolution, the Communists have canonised Lu Xun and his house in Beijing has been preserved as a museum.

Lao She, another important novelist of the early 20th century, is famous for his book *The Rickshaw Boy,* a social critique of the living conditions of rickshaw drivers in Beijing.

Since the Communists came to power in 1949, writing has become a particularly dangerous occupation. During the Cultural Revolution, the safest thing a writer could do was to churn out slogans in praise of Chairman Mao. Things have eased up, but social critics are still kept on a short leash.

Some of the most interesting writers in contemporary China are Zhang Xianliang and Feng Jicai (see the 'Contemporary Chinese Writers' boxed text).

Blood Red Dusk by Lao Gui (literally 'old devil') is a fascinatingly cynical account of the Cultural Revolution years. More recently, Wang Shuo's short stories

Contemporary Art

After decades of state-dictated ideologies and social realism in the arts, China has become recognised in the last 20 years or so as home to a lively contemporary art community. Even with the return of Hong Kong to mainland sovereignty, any number of get-rich-quicker special economic zones, and the old-world charm of Shanghai, Beijing is still considered the centre of intellectual, political and cultural developments in China.

Stirrings of a modern avant-garde movement emerged as early as the late 1970s with the Stars Group, and sporadic activities throughout the country in the 1980s culminated in the infamous and ground-breaking 'China Avant-garde show' of 1989 – closed on the first day after a gun was fired during the performance of one of the pieces and reopened a few days later, only to be shut down again.

Perhaps it was this charged opening, coupled with the tragedy of the Tiananmen Square incident that followed it only a few months later, which have created the attitude that to a great extent still dominates Western expectations of Chinese contemporary art: that it should be incendiary, explosive, revolutionary, and, for whatever reason, an implicit or explicit plea for democracy. Often the absence of these traits is taken for either the depoliticising of pro-democracy impulses or their wilful repression.

But 1989 did not put an end to Chinese contemporary art. The art community has adapted alongside the rest of Chinese society to the government's fairly unpredictable stance on freedom of expression. The 'China Avant-Garde' show travelled extensively worldwide, as have other shows, including the 'Post-1989' show, 'Another Long March', and more recently, the 'Inside Out' show. Many individual artists have followed suit, with a few major notables establishing themselves securely in the international art community. These include Cai Guoqiang, Gu Wenda, Xu Bing (recent recipient of the MacArthur 'Genius' award) and Zhang Huan, all of whom came of age artistically in the 1980s. But they are not the only artists to have found audiences abroad – last year 16 Chinese artists attended the prestigious Venice Biennale.

Public attitudes and the government's stance on contemporary art, be it 'revolutionary' or otherwise, remains fairly ambivalent, but sufficiently short of indifferent to remain a little threatening should the wrong boundary be crossed. At the same time, one should not over-romanticise the plight of the Chinese artist – artists here balance their needs to make a living with maintaining a semblance of artistic integrity just like anywhere else in the world.

Artists in Beijing in the 1990s could be found setting up camp around the Old Summer Palace, or in what was Beijing's 'East Village' before it was eventually shut down by the authorities. These days artist communities seem to be moving progressively further away from the city proper in search of lower rents, bigger spaces and potentially less harassment. Even so art is more than readily accessible in Beijing if you know where to look: Red Gate Gallery (Map 7; now two locations), Chinese Art and Archives Warehouse (Map 3) and the CourtYard Gallery (Map 4; in the basement of the CourtYard restaurant) feature year-round exhibitions of contemporary and avant-garde Chinese art, by artists living in China and abroad. In any given week you might find a cross-section of experimental photography, abstract oil painting or modern re-inventions of classical Chinese painting forms. These are also the best locations to simply pull on somebody's ear about the state of contemporary art and inquire about any non-commercial, more ephemeral events.

Ingrid Dudek

have given a voice to Beijing's growing sub-class of unemployed and disaffected youth. *Playing for Thrills* is the only translation to date.

Cinema

The most dramatic development in Chinese cinema over the last 15 years has been the appearance of films made by the so-called

Contemporary Chinese Writers

Following the death of Mao in 1976, Deng Xiaoping ascended to power promising liberation of thought and the opening of China to the West. For the first time in 30 years, literature was encouraged to discover new creative boundaries. Most of the young writers who emerged were 'educated youth' who had been sent to work in the countryside during the Cultural Revolution of 1966–76. As if waking from a dream, they began to question how the turmoil of the past ten years had affected the Chinese psyche. In the liberal climate of the late 1970s, they explored previously taboo topics such as sex, individuality and social alienation in a rapidly changing society. The most interesting of these writers was Zhang Xianliang, whose *Half of Man is Woman* became controversial for its sexual content. Feng Jingcai's *Voices from the Whirlwind* encapsulates the feelings of a lost generation whose education had been halted by political campaigns.

The works of Chinese women writers were revived for the first time since the early feminist writings of the 1920s. While their Western counterparts were demonstrating for equal rights during the 1960s, many Chinese women were being swept up by the continuous stream of political campaigns. As the doors of post-Mao China began to open, women were given a fresh opportunity to re-evaluate their status in society. For the past 20 years, women writers have discussed with skill and compassion the experience of Chinese women and examined social issues with a detailed and analytical eye.

Author Zhang Jie has gained international acclaim for her controversial accounts of female experience in China's new society. Her first work *Love Must Not be Forgotten* created a storm among Chinese critics for its account of forbidden love and candid attack on the traditions of marriage. Heralded as 'China's first feminist novel' it told the story of one woman's unrequited love for a married man through the words of her disillusioned daughter. Zhang was widely criticised for her provocative opinions, but remained hugely popular among younger Chinese readers. Her second work, *The Ark*, attacked the prevalent trends of nepotism and male chauvinism in China's bureaucratic system.

One of the most diverse woman writers to emerge in the early 1980s is Wang Anyi, renowned in China for her unreserved explorations of love, sexuality and fate that would certainly have been outlawed in Mao's day. Her Love trilogy – *Love in the Mountains, Love in a Small Town* and *Love*

Fifth Generation directors. Although better known abroad than within China, their films, such as *Yellow Earth* directed by Chen Kaige, *Horse Thief* by Tian Zhuangzhuang and *Raise the Red Lantern* by Zhang Yimou, have set a new benchmark for the local film industry after the troughs of socialist propaganda. The new directors of the 1990s were dubbed the 'sixth generation' and include He Jianjun, Hu Xueyang, Lu Xuezhang, Wang Xiaoshuai and Zhang Yuan. However, the local market is given over to martial arts and historical epics copied from Hong Kong cinema.

Acrobatics

Acrobatics *(tèjì biǎoyǎn)* are pure fun. Donated pandas may soothe international relations, but it's the acrobats who are China's true ambassadors. Some people find the an-

imal acts a bit sad, but in general foreigners have reacted to the shows enthusiastically. Sometimes performing tigers and pandas (not together) show up as an added bonus.

Circus acts go back 2000 years in China. Effects are obtained using simple props – sticks, plates, eggs and chairs – and apart from the acrobatics, magic, vaudeville, drama, clowning, music, conjuring, dance and mime are thrown in to complete the performance. Happily it's an art which gained from the Communist takeover and did not suffer during the Cultural Revolution.

Acts vary from troupe to troupe. Some traditional acts haven't changed over the centuries, while others have incorporated roller skates and motorcycles. Some time-proven acts that are hard to follow are: 'Balancing in Pairs' – one man balances upside down on the head of another mimicking

Contemporary Chinese Writers

in the Valley – are fascinating accounts of narcissistic extra-marital affairs, sexual fulfilment and spiritual destiny in small-town China. Her later notable work, *Passing Time,* is the compassionate story of a woman whose life is tossed between disgrace and fortune at the whim of the country's tempestuous political tide during the Cultural Revolution. Wang Anyi is also known for her critiques of wider social issues. *Xiaobao Village* is a critical account of the prevalent but antiquated Confucian values in a rural township. *Battle Between Copper and Steel* is a remarkably moving tale of Shanghai's struggling migrant communities.

With the crackdown on arts and literature in 1989 and the materialist revolution that gripped China in the early 1990s, popular literature shifted from the 'trauma' and 'pastoral' genres of the previous decade. A new brand of commercialised 'new realist' literature emerged, reflecting the realities of modern living. Beijing writer Wang Shuo became popular for his stories of urban employment and social misfits, which struck a chord with the capital's disgruntled youth.

Liu Sola has recently achieved a cult following among Chinese and overseas readers, mostly due to the unavailability of her work on the mainland. The former Red Guard, classical pianist and rock 'n' roll rebel is now mostly known for her surrealist writings about modern living in *Reform China.* The nihilistically titled *You Have No Choice* confronted Chinese readers with the impossibility of asserting one's individuality. Not surprisingly, it was immediately banned by the government. Her later work, *Chaos and All That,* is an explicit and fascinating treatise on the debauchery and disorder in 1990s Beijing told through the eyes of a Chinese emigre exiled in London.

Awaiting translation into English is upcoming Shanghai writer Mian Mian. Her novels reflect the harsh realities faced by China's young urban MTV generation through stories about love affairs, drug addiction and promiscuity. Her first collection of short stories, *La La La,* has been published in Hong Kong, and three new volumes, *Acid Lover, Every Good Kid Deserves Candy* and *Nine Objects of Desire,* are also available for Chinese audiences. Her most recent work, *Candy,* relates more tales of sex, drugs and alcohol in today's China through the eyes of a young couple.

Ellen Hobson

every movement of the partner below, even drinking a glass of water; 'Peacock Displaying its Feathers' – an array of people balanced on one bicycle (a Shanghai troupe holds the record at 13); the 'Pagoda of Bowls' – a balancing act where the performer (usually a woman) does everything with her torso except tie it in knots, all the while balancing a stack of porcelain bowls on foot, head or both – and perhaps also balancing on a partner.

Martial Arts

Taijiquan Previously spelled 'taichichuan' and usually just called *taiji* (or t'ai chi), *taijiquan* ('slow-motion shadow boxing') has been popular in China for centuries. It is traditionally performed early in the morning. If you want to see it, visit any major park in Beijing around 6 am or so.

Gongfu Another form of the martial arts, *gōngfu* has been popular in the West mostly thanks to Hong Kong movies. Previously spelled 'kungfu', gongfu differs from taiji in that it's performed at a much higher speed and is intended to do bodily harm.

Qigong This is another variation on the gongfu theme. *Qì* represents life's vital energy, and *gōng* is from gongfu. *Qigong* is a form of energy management, and seems to work almost like magic. Through daily practice, practitioners hope to maintain good mental and physical health. The real masters take the process a step further – they try to project their qi to perform various miracles, from healing others to driving nails through boards with their bare fingers. Qigong is a standard feature of Hong Kong gongfu movies – bad guys are blown away without actually being physically touched, while mortally wounded heroes are healed with a few waves of the hands. Qigong is gaining an increasing number of fans in the West.

Beijing's Qigong Club is within the Wuta Temple grounds (near the Beijing Zoo).

SOCIETY & CONDUCT

Traditional social organisation revolved around the family, with three generations living under one roof. After 'liberation', the 'work unit' *(dānwèi)* was introduced to guarantee Chinese citizens their 'iron rice bowl'. One's work unit assigns housing, sets salaries, handles mail, recruits Party members, arranges job transfers, approves marriages, divorces, childbirth and overseas travel and keeps files on each unit member.

Theoretically, every Chinese person belongs to one. Nowadays, however, many people slip through the net by being self-employed or working in the private sector.

Family

To curb China's enormous population growth, Deng Xiaoping introduced the 'one child policy' in 1979. Often cruelly enforced, its effects are now ricocheting throughout society, particularly in urban areas. Around 70 million 'only children' have been born, in many cases to members of the 'lost generation' whose own childhoods were destroyed by the Cultural Revolution and who consequently dote on their precious youngsters. These pampered children are known as *xiǎo huángdì* or 'little emperors'.

Traditional preference for male children led to increasing infanticide, abortion and abandonment of female children, resulting in an enormous gender imbalance and a lucrative international adoption trade in Chinese baby girls. Ironically, only-child girls are better educated than their predecessors and will have their pick of the marriage market. Authorities concerned about the possibility of millions of unpartnered young males running rampant have recently begun drafting laws to deal with juvenile delinquency. Skyrocketing demand for old people's homes also prompted a bill obliging children to provide material and spiritual support to their elderly parents.

Fengshui The ancient Chinese world view included the belief that the earth, like a human body, has 'channels' or veins, along which benevolent and evil influences flowed. This belief, known as *fēngshuǐ*, or geomancy, plays an important role in the choice of sites for buildings or tombs. An example of fengshui in practice is Jing Shan, an artificial hill on the northern side of the Forbidden City. It was built specifically as a barrier to block 'evil influences' from penetrating the emperor's palace.

Although fengshui has some relevance in modern China, its practice is far less visible than in, say, Hong Kong. Nevertheless, China is still a good place to study this ancient art.

Dos & Don'ts

Dress Cynics say that the Communists are the worst-dressed people in the world. Certainly in the days of blue Mao suits there was a lot of truth to that statement, but Beijingers are now far more fashion-conscious. Suits and ties for men and flamboyant dresses for women are no longer regarded as unusual. In summer, women wear miniskirts, tank tops and shorts, which would have been scandalous a decade ago. Basically anything goes nowadays – a bleach-blonde, nose-pierced, tattoo-covered punk wouldn't turn many heads on Beijing's streets.

Face Face can be loosely defined as 'status' and many Chinese people will go to great lengths to avoid 'losing face'. For example, a foreigner may front up to a hotel desk and have a furious row with the receptionist because he or she believes that the hotel bill contains hidden charges (often true) while the receptionist denies it. The receptionist is less likely to admit the truth (and 'lose face') if the foreigner throws a tantrum.

In such situations, you can accomplish a great deal more with smiles, talking about other things for a while ('Where did you learn such good English?'), showing some of your photos from your trip etc, before putting forward your case in a quiet manner (in the case of a hotel bill, a diplomatic solution is to ask for a 'discount').

Avoid direct criticisms of people. If you have to complain about something, like the hot water not working, do so in a fairly quiet tone. Confrontation causes loss of face and that leads to trouble. Venting your rage in public and trying to make someone lose face will cause Chinese people to dig in their heels and only worsen your situation. Business travellers should take note here – a lot of westerners really blow it on this point.

Chopsticks Two chopsticks stuck vertically into a rice bowl resemble incense sticks in a bowl of ashes. This is considered a death sign in China and many other Asian countries – it's rude and should be avoided. However, younger people care less about this.

Red Ink If giving someone your address or telephone number, write in any colour but red. Red ink conveys unfriendliness. If you're teaching, it's OK to use red to correct papers, but if you write extensive comments on the back, use some other colour.

Public Etiquette While Chinese people will shake hands with westerners, they rarely do it among themselves. They will, on the other hand, often ask if you've eaten: it's not an invitation to a meal, just a form of greeting.

The Chinese are not nearly as innocent as they pretend to be when it comes to sexual matters. However, the Communist regime is one of the most prudish in the world. Walking around hand in hand is becoming more common but is still considered risque. Few people get passionate in public; refrain from it yourself. Topless sunbathing is asking for trouble.

Splitists Versus the Motherland Politics is something most Beijingers wisely avoid discussing. Ignorant foreigners sometimes offend their Chinese hosts with what seems like an innocent remark. A good way to create a near riot is to call Taiwan a country – it's firmly hammered into every Chinese head that Taiwan is part of the 'Motherland'; those who say otherwise are passionately denounced as 'splitists', which is just about the worst thing you can be called. Tibet is another sore spot – the Dalai Lama is lambasted in the Chinese press as the devil incarnate – so if you're a closet Lamaist, keep it to yourself. Indeed, it's a good idea to keep negative comments about China to a minimum (this kind of policy, of course, holds true in most countries).

RELIGION

While religions such as Islam and Christianity exist in large areas of China and in a few pockets in Beijing, Confucianism, Taoism and Buddhism dominate. Ancestor worship is also widely practised.

The three main religions have gradually combined over the centuries. Confucianism, in effect state policy for the last two millennia, advocated loyalty to the emperor and to the patriarchal structure below him. Its main tenets were set out by Confucius in the 5th century BC. Taoism has existed in two forms: firstly in the philosophical outlook advocated by the semimythical Laotzu (6th century BC), which stresses acceptance of 'the way' and 'going with the flow'; and secondly in a popular form, which has a pantheon of gods and devils. Taoism has also been a strong influence on the Chinese religious tradition. Mahayana Buddhism, imported from India during the Han dynasty (206 BC–AD 24) has had fluctuating fortunes but by the 10th century was as entrenched as the other two religions.

The Cultural Revolution devastated Chinese religion – it's yet to recover fully. Temples were destroyed, monks were sent to labour in the countryside where they often perished and believers were prohibited from worship. But the temples are now being restored and worshippers are returning.

While freedom of religion now exists in China, it's worth noting that membership in the CCP is not permitted for anyone practising religion.

LANGUAGE

The official language of the PRC is the Beijing dialect, usually referred to in the West as 'Mandarin Chinese'. The word 'Mandarin' derives from the use of the Beijing dialect as a standard language by the scholar class in centuries past. The official name for Mandarin in China is *pǔtōnghuà* (common speech).

For general use, Lonely Planet's *Mandarin phrasebook* is a handy little pocket-sized reference ideal for whipping out in an emergency. A small dictionary with English, romanisation and Chinese characters can also be very helpful. For a more thorough discussion of Mandarin Chinese and a small vocabulary, see the Language chapter at the end of this book.

Facts for the Visitor

WHEN TO GO

Summer is considered peak season, when hotels typically raise their rates and the Great Wall nearly collapses under the weight of marching tourists. Autumn has the best weather and fewer tourists. Spring is less pleasant – not many tourists but lots of wind and dust. In winter, you'll have Beijing to yourself, and many hotels offer substantial discounts – just remember it's an ice box outside. While Chinese New Year is a bad time to travel in China, since trains get mighty crowded and tickets are impossible to come by, Beijing empties out (relatively speaking, of course) during the holiday season and is nice to be around (see Public Holidays & Special Events later in this chapter).

ORIENTATION

Though it may not appear so in the shambles of arrival, Beijing is a place of very orderly design. Long, straight boulevards and avenues are crisscrossed by a network of lanes. Places of interest are either very easy to find if they're on the avenues, or impossible to find if they're buried down the *hutongs* (narrow alleys). To make sense of addresses and maps, it's useful to know just a little Chinese terminology (see the boxed text 'Map Terms' on this page).

The Forbidden City acts like a bullseye, surrounded by a chessboard of roads (with the First Ring Rd marking the outline of what was once a walled enclosure encompassing the Forbidden City). The symmetry folds on an ancient north-south axis passing through Qianmen (Front Gate).

There is a certain logic to street names in Beijing: Jianguomen Wai Dajie, for example, means 'the avenue *(dàjiē)* outside *(wài)* Jianguo Gate (Jianguomen)'; whereas Jianguomen Nei Dajie means 'the avenue inside *(nèi)* Jianguo Gate'. But this is purely an academic exercise since the gate referred to no longer exists.

Streets are also split along compass points. For example, Andingmen Dongdajie is East *(dōng)* Andingmen Avenue, and Andingmen Xidajie is the western *(xī)* part of the same street. These streets tend to head off from an intersection, usually where a gate – in this case Andingmen – once stood. A major boulevard can change names six or eight times along its length.

Then there are the *lǐ* (villages). Beijing was once surrounded by many tiny villages which over time have become neighbourhoods within the megalopolis. Thus you find addresses like Yulinli (Yulin Village). Many addresses also refer to *qiáo* (bridges) long gone, such as Anhuaqiao.

There are four 'ring roads' around Beijing, circumnavigating the city centre in concentric circles. The First (innermost) Ring Rd is a mapmaker's fiction and just part of the grid around the Forbidden City.

Map Terms

road			lane			east	
lù	路		*xiàng*	巷		*dōng*	东
street			inner			west	
jiē	街		*nèi*	内		*xī*	西
avenue			outer			village	
dàjiē	大街		*wài*	外		*lǐ*	里
boulevard			north			gate	
dàdào	大道		*běi*	北		*mén*	门
alley			south			bridge	
hútong	胡同		*nán*	南		*qiáo*	桥

However, the Second (Èrhuán) and Third (Sēnhuán) Ring Roads should be taken seriously – they are multi-lane freeways that get you around town quickly. Construction of the Fourth (Sìhuán) Ring Rd is nearly complete and a fifth is on the drawing board.

The Beijing Municipality is carved up into 10 districts and eight counties. Roughly within the Second Ring Rd are the four central districts: Xicheng (north-west), Dongcheng (north-éast), Chongwen (south-east) and Xuanwu (south-west). Outside the Second Ring Road, the so-called 'suburban' (now urbanised) districts are Chaoyang (east), Fengtai (south-west), Haidian (north-west) and Shijingshan (central-west).

MAPS

English-language maps of Beijing can be bought at the airport and train station newspaper kiosks (Y6), the Friendship Store and the Foreign Languages Bookstore, or picked up for free at most big hotels.

If you can deal with Chinese characters you'll find a wide variety of up-to-date maps to choose from. New editions printed by different companies are issued every couple of months. Street vendors hawk these maps (for about Y2) near subway stations, park entrances and other likely places.

The Foreign Languages Bookstore on Wangfujing sells several excellent atlases of Beijing, but these are entirely in Chinese characters.

Berndtson & Berndtson, the German map publisher, puts out an excellent, extremely detailed map of Beijing (it even includes hutongs), although it's not distributed in China.

TOURIST OFFICES
Local Tourist Offices

The main branch of the Beijing Tourism Group (BTG; Běijīng Lǚxíngshè), formerly known as China International Travel Service Beijing (CITS; Zhōngguó Guìjó Lǚxíngshè), is at the Beijing Tourist Building (☎ 6515 8562, fax 6515 8603) at 28 Jianguomen Wai Dajie, behind the New Otani Hotel and near Scitech Plaza. This is one of the more useful – and friendly – branches in the country. Here you can buy

Trans-Manchurian and Trans-Mongolian train tickets, purchase air tickets and find information about the city. There is an English-speaking 24-hour Beijing Tourism Hotline (☎ 6513 0828), which can answer questions and hear complaints.

Branches of BTG can be found in the Jianguo, Kunlun, Radisson SAS and Scitech Hotels (see the Places to Stay chapter for contact information for these hotels). These branches exist mainly to book tours, and don't offer much in the way of general information.

Tourist Offices Abroad

Although Hong Kong and Macau are now technically part of China, the two cities remain in limbo in most travellers' minds, so we've grouped their CTS and CITS branches below.

CITS/CNTO Note that outside China and Hong Kong, CITS is usually known as the China National Tourist Office (CNTO). CITS (or CNTO) representatives include:

Australia
  CNTO (☎ 02-9299 4057, fax 9290 1958) 19th floor, 44 Market St, Sydney NSW 2000
France
  Office du Tourisme de Chine (☎ 01 56 59 10 10, fax 01 53 75 32 88) 15 Rue de Berri, Paris, 75008
Germany
  CNTO (☎ 069-520 135, fax 528 490) Ilkenhansstr 6, D-60433 Frankfurt am Main
Hong Kong
  CITS (☎ 2732 5888, fax 2721 7154) 12th floor, Tower A, New Mandarin Plaza, 14 Science Museum Rd, Tsimshatsui East
Israel
  CNTO (☎ 03-522 6272, fax 522 6281) 19 Frishman St, PO Box 3281, Tel-Aviv 61030
Japan
  China National Tourist Administration (☎ 03-3433 1461, fax 3433 8653) 6th floor, Hamamatsu-cho Bldg, 1-27-13 Hamamatsu-cho, Minato-ku, Tokyo
Singapore
  CNTO (☎ 337 2220, fax 338 0777) 7 Temasek Blvd, #12-02A Suntec Tower One, Singapore 038987
Spain
  CNTO (☎ 01-548 0011, fax 548 0597) Gran Via 88, Grupo 2, Planta 16, 28013 Madrid

UK
CNTO (☎ 020-7935 9787, fax 7487 5842) 4 Glentworth St, London NW1
USA
CNTO Los Angeles: (☎ 818-545 7504, fax 545 7506) Suite 201, 333 West Broadway, Glendale CA 91204
CNTO New York: (☎ 212-760 9700, fax 760 8809) Suite 6413, Empire State Bldg, 350 Fifth Ave, New York, NY 10118

CTS Overseas representatives include the following:

Australia
(☎ 02-9211 2633, fax 9281 3595) Ground floor, 757 George St, Sydney, NSW 2000
Canada
Vancouver: (☎ 800-663 1126, 604-872 8787, fax 873 2823) 556 West Broadway, BC V5Z 1E9
Toronto: (☎ 800-387 6622, 416-979 8993, fax 979 8220) Suite 306, 438 University Ave, Box 28, Ontario M5G 2K8
France
(☎ 01 44 51 55 66, fax 01 44 51 55 60) 32 Rue Vignon, 75009, Paris
Germany
Frankfurt am Main: (☎ 69-223 8522, fax 223 2324) Düsseldorfer Strasse 14, D-60329
Berlin: (☎ 30-393 4068, fax 391 8085) Beusselstrasse 5, D-10553
Hong Kong
Head Office: (☎ 2853 3888, fax 2854 1383) 4th floor, CTS House, 78–83 Connaught Rd, Central
Kowloon: (☎ 2315 7188, fax 2721 7757) 1st floor, Alpha House, 27–33 Nathan Rd, Tsimshatsui
Indonesia
PT Cempaka Travelindo (☎ 21-629 4452, fax 629 4836) Jalan Hayam Wuruk 97, Jakarta-Barat
Japan
(☎ 03-3273 5512, fax 3273 2667) 103 Buyoo Bldg, 3-8-16, Nihombashi, Chuo-Ku, Tokyo
Macau
(☎ 705 506; fax 706 611) Xinhua Bldg, Rua de Nagasaki
Malaysia
(☎ 03-201 8888, fax 201 3278) Ground floor, 112–4 Jalan Pudu, 55100, Kuala Lumpur
Philippines
(☎ 02-733 1274, fax 733 1431) 801–3 Gandara St (corner Espeleta St), Santa Cruz, Manila
Singapore
(☎ 532 9988, fax 535 4912) 1 Park Rd, No

03–49 to 52, People's Park Complex, Singapore, 059108
South Korea
(☎ 02-566 9361, fax 557 0021) 8th floor, Chung Oh Bldg, 164-3 Samsung-dong, Gangnam-gu, Seoul
Thailand
(☎ 02-226 0041, fax 226 4701) 559 Yaowaraj Rd, Sampuntawang, Bangkok 10100
UK
(☎ 020-7836 9911, fax 7836 3121) CTS House, 7 Upper St Martins Lane, London WC2H 9DL
USA
San Francisco: Main Office (☎ 800-332 2831, 415-398 6627, fax 398 6669) Lower floor, 575 Sutter St, San Francisco, CA 94102
Los Angeles: (☎ 818-457 8668, fax 457 8955) Suite 303, US CTS Bldg, 119 South Atlantic Blvd, Monterey Park, CA 91754

TRAVEL AGENCIES

There are an increasing number of privately run travel agencies in Beijing, and competition is driving prices down. Unless otherwise noted, the following companies offer discounted air tickets that can be delivered to you, and also make domestic travel arrangements, accept credit cards (for a 3% to 5% surcharge) and have English-speaking staff:

Beijing Purun Air Service (☎ 6591 2283, 6503 0427, fax 6508 6480, @ bjbtcbtc@public3.bta .net.cn) 15 Dongdaqiao Lu
Beijing Tianwei Travel (☎ 6501 5289, fax 6585 7607, @ tianwei@mx.cei.gov.cn) 10 Yabao Lu (The Gateway)
BJS Holiday (☎ 8654 2608, fax 8654 2610, @ bjstour@public.fhnet.cn.net) Room 215, Zhaolong Hotel, 2 Gongti Beilu
China Travel Service (Map 5; ☎ 6461 2577 ext 6415, fax 6461 2576) CTS Bldg, 2 Beisanhuan Donglu.
Although it's not a privately run travel agent, this branch of CTS is especially helpful with domestic travel arrangements and prices are on a par with private travel agents.
Happy Holiday Travel Service (☎ 6501 3829, fax 6501 3829, @ happyday@public.bta.net.cn) Wujing Hotel, A15 Gongti Donglu (across from the east gate of Worker's Stadium), Chaoyang District. It offers a range of domestic tour packages.
Holiday Tours and Travel (☎ 6518 6888, fax 6517 1518, @ httpek@public.bta.net.cn)

7 Jianguomen Nei Dajie, T/2 Suite 6222 Bright China Chang'an Bldg. It offers domestic and international tour packages.

Sunshine Tours (☎ 6586 8069, fax 6586 8077, ✉ sunpress@public.bta.net.cn) Jinding Commercial Club, North Langjiayuan, Chaoyang District

Web site: www.sinotravel.com

Note that private-agency tour packages – from the luxury Abercrombie & Kent variety to small local travel agency tours – often use the same guides as those used by CTS and CITS (that is, if local guides are used). Before booking a tour you should clarify how the tour guides are arranged, and what they offer in comparison to CTS or CITS tours.

DOCUMENTS
Visas

A visa is required for the People's Republic of China (PRC), but at the time of writing visas were not required for most Western nationals to visit Hong Kong or Macau.

There are seven types of visas, as follows:

type	description	Chinese name
L	travel	lǚxíng
F	business or student (less than six months)	fǎngwèn
D	resident	dìngjū
G	transit	guòjìng
X	long-term student	liúxué
Z	working	rènzhí

For most travellers, the type of visa is an L, from the Chinese word for travel *(lǚxíng)*. This letter is stamped right on the visa.

Visas are readily available from Chinese embassies and consulates in most Western and many other countries. A standard 30-day, single-entry visa from most Chinese embassies abroad can be issued in three to five working days. You can get an application form in person at the embassy or consulate, or obtain one on line at Web sites such as www.cbw.com/tourism. A visa mailed to you will take up to three weeks. Rather than going through an embassy or consulate, you can also make arrangements at some travel agencies, especially Chinese

government-owned agencies (such as CITS and CTS), which have overseas representatives. Visa applications require one photo.

You can easily get a standard 30-day visa from almost any travel agency in Hong Kong. The cheapest visas are available from the Visa Office (☎ 2827 1881) at the Ministry of Foreign Affairs of the PRC, 5th floor, Low Block, China Resources Building, 26 Harbour Rd, Wanchai. For next-day service, a 30-day to three-month single-entry visa is HK$100 and a double-entry visa is HK$150. It's an extra HK$150 for same-day service. American passport holders, unless of Chinese descent, must pay an extra HK$160. There is also a photo service for HK$30. The office is open from 9 am to 12.30 pm and 2 to 5 pm Monday to Friday, and until 12.30 pm on Saturday.

If you need more than three months or a multiple-entry visa, head to one of the branches of CTS in Hong Kong or Macau. Prices range from HK$160 for a single-entry, 90-day visa issued in three days to HK$1300 for a six-month multiple-entry visa. Many Hong Kong travel agencies can also get you 60- and 90-day visas, six-month visas and multiple-entry visas at prices cheaper than CTS. On the Kowloon side, try Hung Shih Travel Service (☎ 2369 3188, fax 2369 3293), at Room 711, New East West Center, 9 Science Museum Rd, Tsimshatsui East. In Central, Four Seasons Travel Service (☎ 2523 9147) Room 102–103, Commercial House, 35 Queens Road, can get you a six-month multiple-entry F visa for about HK$500.

A 30-day visa is activated on the date you enter China, and must be used within three months of the date of issue. The 60-day and 90-day visas are activated on the date they are issued. While visas valid for more than 30 days were once difficult to obtain anywhere other than in Hong Kong, 90-day visas are now becoming easier to obtain abroad.

Multiple-entry visas allow you to enter and leave the country an unlimited number of times and are available through CTS and some travel agencies in Hong Kong and Macau. The cheapest multiple-entry visas cost HK$350 and are valid for 90 days; six-month multiple-entry visas cost HK$500 for next-day pick-up or HK$600 for same-day pick-up. The latter are business or short-term student (F) visas, which, in Hong Kong, you don't need any special documentation to obtain.

Extensions Visa extensions are handled by the Foreign Affairs Branch of the local Public Security Bureau (PSB; Gōngānjú) – the police force. In Beijing, the PSB has an office at 2 Andingmen Dongdajie (☎ 6404 7799), about 300m east of the Lama Temple. It's open from 8.30 am to noon and 1 to 5 pm Monday to Saturday. The visa office is on the 2nd floor. Extensions can cost nothing for some, but Y250 for most nationalities.

Government travel organisations, like CITS, have nothing to do with extensions, so don't bother asking.

The situation with visa extensions seems to change frequently. Recently, travellers who enter China with a 30-day visa have been able to renew their visa twice (30 days each time, so the total stay is up to 90 days) without any problem.

It's also possible to get additional visa extensions without going outside China through private visa services in Beijing. The legality of these services is questionable, and most of them seem to operate through private connections with the PSB. The typical cost for a six-month multiple-entry F visa is Y3000 and up, and can take anywhere from a couple of days to a couple of weeks to process. These services can also be useful in changing a student X visa to an F visa, which is usually difficult to do. Although some foreigners have used these services without incident, you are taking a risk. Don't hand over your payment until after your visa has been successfully extended. Look in the classified section of *City Edition* or *Metro* for listings of these services; it's wise to ask around for a personal recommendation from someone who has recently used one of the services.

The penalty for overstaying your visa in China is Y500 per day! Many travellers have reported having trouble with officials who read the 'valid until' date on their visa incorrectly. For a one-month tourist (L) visa, the 'valid until' date is the date by which you must enter the country, not the date upon which your visa expires. Your visa expires the number of days that your visa is valid for after the date of entry into China (but note that you must enter China within three months of the date the visa was issued). Sixty- and 90-day visas are activated on the day they are issued.

Travel Insurance

It's very likely that a health insurance policy that you contribute to in your home country will *not* cover you in China – if unsure, ask your insurance company. If you're not covered, it would be prudent to purchase travel insurance. The best policies will reimburse you for a variety of mishaps such as accidents, illness, theft and even the purchase of an emergency ticket home. The policies are usually available from travel agents, including student travel services. Read the small print: some policies specifically exclude 'dangerous activities', which may include motorcycling, scuba diving and even hiking. Obviously, you'll want a policy that covers you in all the circumstances in which you're likely to find yourself.

To make a claim for compensation, you will need proper documentation (hopefully in English). This can include medical reports, police reports, baggage receipts from airlines etc. Getting a police report for theft in China is next to impossible; in lieu of one try to get a signed statement from your hotel or another establishment verifying that you reported the theft.

Once in China, it's possible to obtain insurance from some Chinese insurance companies, but international companies are prohibited from selling insurance in China. It's advisable to make insurance arrangements before coming to China.

Driving Licence

Foreign tourists (those on an L or F visa) are not permitted to drive in China and an International Driving Permit is not recognised by the Chinese authorities.

It's a different story if you plan to take up residence in Beijing (an X, Z or D visa). If you have a Chinese residence certificate, you can obtain a Chinese driving licence after some bureaucratic wrangling. The process is much less complicated if you bring a valid licence from your home country – otherwise you'll have to take a driving course and test in China, which is best avoided. The procedure is basically that the Chinese authorities exchange your original driving licence for a Chinese one. They will keep your original licence until you leave China, at which time it will be returned to you in exchange for the Chinese one.

Similar procedures apply for obtaining a motorcycle licence in China.

Chinese Documents

Foreigners who live, work or study in China will be issued with a number of documents.

Student Cards A very common but not-too-useful document is the so-called 'white card'. This is a simple student ID card with a pasted-on photo that is usually kept in a red plastic holder (some call it a 'red card' for this reason). A student card can sometimes help get you a discount at hotels or on entrance fees to some sights.

Residence Permits The 'green card' is a residence permit, issued to English teachers, foreign expats and long-term students who live in China. The green card is not really a card, but resembles a small passport. Green cards are issued for one year and must be renewed annually. If you lose your card, you'll pay a hefty fee to have it replaced.

Besides needing all the right paperwork, you must also pass a health exam to obtain a resident permit. The cost of the health exam is Y350 for students or Y650 for foreigners working in China. Bring your passport and two photos. You're not supposed to eat or drink prior to the exam. Besides a general health exam, ECG and an X-ray, you will be tested for HIV. The staff use disposable syringes, which are unwrapped in front of you; if you bring your own syringe they generally refuse to use it unless you adamantly insist.

Marriage Certificates In some smaller hotels in rural areas, couples must produce marriage certificates to check into a hotel. The chance of being asked for one, especially in Beijing, is rare. If you don't have the certificates (husband's and wife's both), then you're talking about two rooms for sure. The certificate has a red cover and looks much like a passport. This practice is applied to all couples regardless of nationality.

Name Cards Business name cards are essential, even if you don't do business – exchanging name cards with someone you've just met goes down well. It's particularly good if you can get your name translated into Chinese and have it printed next to your English name. You can get name cards made cheaply in China, but it's better to have some in advance of your arrival.

In Beijing, small copy shops can usually print up name cards. See Printing under Doing Business later in this chapter for places to get high-quality name cards printed.

Copies

All important documents (passport data page and visa page, credit cards, travel insurance policy, air/bus/train tickets, driving licence etc) should be photocopied before you leave home. Leave one copy with someone at home and keep another with you, separate from the originals.

It's also a good idea to store details of your vital travel documents in Lonely Planet's free online Travel Vault in case you lose the photocopies or can't be bothered with them. Your password-protected Travel Vault is accessible online anywhere in the world – create it at www.ekno.lonelyplanet.com.

If married and travelling with your spouse, a copy of your marriage certificate can save some grief if you become involved with the police, hospitals or other bureaucratic institutions (see also Marriage Certificates in the previous Chinese Documents section). If you're thinking about working or studying in China, photocopies of college or university diplomas, transcripts and letters of recommendation could prove helpful, although they're not necessary.

EMBASSIES
China's Embassies & Consulates

Some of the addresses of China's embassies and consulates in major cities overseas include:

Australia (☎ 02-6273 4780, 6273 4781) 15 Coronation Drive, Yarralumla, Canberra ACT 2600
  Consulates: Melbourne, Perth and Sydney
Canada (☎ 613-789 3509) 515 St Patrick St, Ottawa, Ontario K1N 5H3
  Consulates: Toronto and Vancouver
France (☎ 01 47 36 77 90) 9 Avenue V Cresson, 92130 Issy les Moulineaux
Germany (☎ 0228 361 095) Kurfürstenallee 125300 Bonn 2
  Consulate: Hamburg
Italy (☎ 06-3630 8534, 3630 3856) Via Della Camilluccia 613, Roma, 00135
  Consulate: Milan
Japan (☎ 03-3403 3380, 3403 3065) 3-4-33 Moto-Azabu, Minato-ku, Tokyo 106
  Consulates: Fukuoka, Osaka and Sapporo
Netherlands (☎ 070-355 1515) Adriaan Goekooplaan 7, 2517 JX, The Hague
New Zealand (☎ 04-587 0407) 104A Korokoro Rd, Petone, Wellington
  Consulate: Auckland
Singapore (☎ 734 3361) 70 Dalvey Rd
South Korea (☎ 02-319 5101) 83 Myeongdong 2-ga, Jung-gu, Seoul
Sweden (☎ 08-767 87 40, 767 40 83) Ringvagen 56 18134 Lidings
UK (☎ 020-7636 8845) 31 Portland Place, London, W1N 5AG
USA (☎ 202-338 6688) Room 110, 2201 Wisconsin Ave NW, Washington, DC 20007
  Consulates: Chicago, Houston, Los Angeles, New York and San Francisco

Embassies in Beijing

A visit to Beijing's embassy-land is a trip in itself – sentry boxes with Chinese soldiers, fancy residences for the diplomats and snazzy stores, restaurants, discos and nightclubs for entertainment. There are two main embassy compounds – Jianguomenwai and Sanlitun.

Unless otherwise indicated, the following embassies in the Jianguomenwai area are on Map 7:

India (☎ 6532 1908, fax 6532 4684) 1 Ritan Donglu

Your Own Embassy

It's important to realise what your own embassy – the embassy of the country of which you are a citizen – can and can't do to help you if you get into trouble overseas. Generally speaking, it won't be much help in emergencies if the problem is remotely your own fault. Remember that you are bound by the laws of the country you are in. Your embassy will not be sympathetic if you end up in jail after committing a crime locally, even if such actions are legal in your own country.

In genuine emergencies you might get some assistance, but only if other channels have been exhausted. For example, if you need to get home urgently, a free ticket home is exceedingly unlikely – the embassy will expect you to have insurance. If you have all your money and documents stolen, it might assist with getting a new passport, but a loan for onward travel is out of the question.

Some embassies used to keep letters for travellers or have a small reading room with home newspapers, but these days the mail-holding service has usually been stopped and even newspapers tend to be out of date.

Ireland (☎ 6532 2691, fax 6532 2168) 3 Ritan Donglu
Israel (☎ 6505 2970, fax 6505 0328) Room 405, West Wing, China World Trade Center, 1 Jianguomen Wai Dajie
Japan (☎ 6532 2361, fax 6532 4625) 7 Ritan Lu
Mongolia (☎ 6532 1203, fax 6532 5045) 2 Xiushui Beijie
New Zealand (Map 5; ☎ 6532 2731, fax 6532 4317) 1 Ritan Dong Erjie
North Korea (Map 5; ☎ 6532 1186, fax 6532 6056) Ritan Beilu
Philippines (☎ 6532 1872, fax 6532 3761) 23 Xiushui Beijie
Singapore (Map 5; ☎ 6532 3926, fax 6532 2215) 1 Xiushui Beijie
Thailand (☎ 6532 1903, fax 6532 1748) 40 Guanghua Lu
UK (☎ 6532 1961, fax 6532 1937) 11 Guanghua Lu;
  Visa office (☎ 8529 6600, fax 8529 6080) 21st

FACTS FOR THE VISITOR

floor, North Tower, Kerry Center, 1 Guanghua
Lu
USA (☎ 6532 3831, fax 6532 6057) 3 Xiushui
Beijie
Vietnam (☎ 6532 5414, fax 6532 5720) 32
Guanghua Lu

The Sanlitun compound (Map 5) is home to
the following embassies:

Australia (☎ 6532 2331, fax 6532 6957)
21 Dongzhimen Wai Dajie
Cambodia (☎ 6532 1889, fax 6532 3507)
9 Dongzhimen Wai Dajie
Canada (☎ 6532 3536, fax 6532 4072)
19 Dongzhimen Wai Dajie
France (☎ 6532 1331, fax 6532 4841)
3 Dongsan Jie
Germany (☎ 6532 2161, fax 6532 5336)
17 Dongzhimen Wai Dajie
Italy (☎ 6532 2131, fax 6532 4676) 2 Sanlitun
Dong Erjie
Kazakhstan (☎ 6532 6182, fax 6532 6183)
9 Sanlitun Dong Liujie
Malaysia (☎ 6532 2531, fax 6532 5032)
13 Dongzhimen Wai Dajie
Myanmar (Burma; ☎ 6532 1584, fax 6532
1344) 6 Dongzhimen Wai Dajie
Nepal (☎ 6532 1795, fax 6532 3251) 1 Sanlitun
Xi Liujie
Netherlands (☎ 6532 1131, fax 6532 4689)
4 Liangmahe Nanlu
Pakistan (☎ 6532 2504) 1 Dongzhimen Wai
Dajie
Russia (☎ 6532 1267, fax 6532 4853)
4 Dongzhimen Beizhongjie, west of the
Sanlitun Compound in a separate compound
South Korea (☎ 6532 0290, fax 6532 6778)
9 Sanlitun Dong Silu
Sweden (☎ 6532 3331, fax 6532 2909)
3 Dongzhimen Wai Dajie

CUSTOMS

Chinese border crossings have gone from
severely traumatic to exceedingly easy – at
least in most cases. There are now clearly
marked 'green channels' and 'red channels',
the latter reserved for those with such everyday travel items as refrigerators, washing
machines, microwave ovens and TVs.

Take note that antiques, or even things
that look antique, could cause hassles. Objects considered to be antiques require a certificate and red seal to clear customs. Indeed,
there's a standing joke that the duty-free

shop in Beijing's airport simply 'recycles'
Chinese relics by selling them to tourists,
only to have these items seized moments
later by customs and returned to the shop.

To get the proper certificate and red seal
your antiques must be inspected by the
Relics Bureau (Wénwù Jiàndìng). Having
items appraised by an antique specialist will
not give you the proper paperwork for export. Basically anything made before 1949
is considered an antique and needs a certificate, and if it was made before 1795 or is
from Tibet it cannot legally be taken out of
the country. If you only have a few pur-
chases, take them to the Relics Bureau at the
Friendship Store for inspection from 1.30 to
4.30 pm, on Monday and Friday only. It's
located on the ground floor, at the back of
the area that sells carpets – look for the
Transportation Department sign. If you have
a large number of things to be inspected, you
must arrange for the inspectors to come to
you. The Relics Bureau can be contacted at
☎ 6401 4608; note that no English is spoken.
The inspectors will affix a red seal and give
you a receipt for all approved items.

A very peculiar restriction is the Y300
limit (Y150 if going to Hong Kong or
Macau) on herbal medicines taken out of
the country. One would think China would
like to encourage the export of Chinese
medicine, a profitable (and mostly state-run)
industry.

Duty-free, you're allowed to import 400
cigarettes or the equivalent in tobacco products, 2L of alcohol and 50g of gold or silver.
Importation of fresh fruit is prohibited. You
can legally only bring in or take out Y6000 in
Chinese currency. There are no restrictions
on foreign currency, however you should declare any cash that exceeds US$5000 (or its
equivalent in another currency).

It's illegal to import printed material,
film, tapes etc that are deemed to be 'detri-
mental to China's politics, economy, culture and ethics'. But don't be too concerned
about what you take to read. As you leave
China, any tapes, manuscripts, books etc
'which contain state secrets or are otherwise
prohibited for export' can be seized.
Mainly, the authorities are interested in

things written in Chinese – they seldom pay much attention to English publications.

MONEY
Currency

The basic unit of Chinese currency is the yuan – designated in this book by a capital 'Y'. In spoken Chinese, the word *kuai* or *kuaiqian* is often substituted for yuan. Ten *jiao* – in spoken Chinese, it's pronounced *mao* – make up one yuan. Ten *fen* make up one jiao, but these days fen are very rare because they're worth next to nothing.

Renminbi (RMB), or 'people's money', is issued by the Bank of China. Paper notes are issued in denominations of one, two, five, 10, 50 and 100 yuan; one, two and five jiao; and one, two and five fen. The one-fen note is small and yellow, the two-fen note is blue, and the five-fen note is small and green – all are hardly worth the paper they're printed on. Coins are in denominations of one yuan; five jiao; and one, two and five fen.

Exchange Rates

Exchange rates against the yuan at the time of publication include the following:

country	unit		yuan
Australia	A$1	=	4.79
Canada	C$1	=	5.58
euro	€1	=	7.48
France	1FF	=	1.14
Germany	DM1	=	3.82
Hong Kong	HK$1	=	1.06
Japan	¥100	=	7.62
UK	UK£1	=	12.44
USA	US$1	=	8.28

Exchanging Money

Foreign currency and travellers cheques can be changed at main branches of the Bank of China, the airport, China International Trust & Investment Corporation (CITIC) Bank, tourist hotels, the Friendship Store and some major department stores. Hotels usually give the official rate, but some will add a small commission. Some upmarket hotels will only change money for their own guests.

Whenever you change foreign currency into Chinese currency you'll be given a money-exchange voucher recording the transaction. Theoretically you need to show this to change Chinese yuan back to foreign currency – in practice, there is no problem. It's easier to buy and sell Chinese yuan in Hong Kong and Macau. Try not to get stuck with a lot of Chinese currency on departure, because outside China RMB is hard to unload.

Cash Australian, Canadian, US, UK, Hong Kong, Japanese and most west European currencies are acceptable in China, but US dollars are still the easiest to change.

Travellers Cheques Besides the advantage of safety, travellers cheques are useful to carry in China because the exchange rate is actually more favourable than the rate for cash. Cheques from most of the world's leading banks and issuing agencies are acceptable in Beijing – stick with the major players such as Citibank, American Express (AmEx) and Visa and you should be OK.

Some foreign banks have representative offices in Beijing, but these offices are by no means full-service banking operations. Some can issue replacements for lost or stolen travellers cheques, or at least process the paper work for you.

AmEx (☎ 6505 2888, fax 6505 4972) is in Room L115D, Shopping Arcade, China World Trade Center, 1 Jianguomen Wai Dajie (Map 7). Citibank (☎ 6510 2933, fax 6510 2932) is on the 16th floor of the Bright Chang'an Building, at 7 Jianguomen Nei Dajie (Map 7).

ATMs Most Automatic Teller Machines (ATMs) in most Chinese cities only work with the Chinese banking system and foreign cards will be rejected. Beijing, however, has several ATMs advertising international bank settlement systems such as GlobalAccess, Cirrus, Interlink, Plus, Star, Accel, The Exchange and Explore. The rear side of your ATM card should tell you which systems will work with your card. Visa, MasterCard and AmEx credit cards will work in many of these ATMs as

FACTS FOR THE VISITOR

well. Don't, however, rely solely on withdrawing cash from ATMs in Beijing as it can often be difficult to find one that is working properly. The maximum cash withdrawal per day is Y2500.

ATMs with international access can be found at the Bank of China, 2nd floor, Swissôtel, Xindong'an Plaza, Wangfujing, Sanlitun Lu (one block north of Dongzhimen Wai Dajie); the building next door (west) of Scitech on Jianguomen Wai Dajie; and the China World Trade Center.

Credit Cards Plastic money is gaining more acceptance in Beijing. Useful cards now include Visa, MasterCard, AmEx and JCB. Most four- and five-star hotels and some major department stores – the Friendship Store, Sogo, Lufthansa, Scitech – accept credit cards. Some expensive restaurants accept credit cards as well. Many travel agencies also now accept credit cards for air tickets, although they tack an extra 4% service charge onto the bill.

Expats can be issued a genuine made-in-China Peony, Jinsui or Great Wall credit card. It's possible to get a cash advance against any of these cards at CITIC Bank, 19 Jianguomen Wai Dajie, or the Bank of China (Xindong'an Plaza and Sanlitun branches), but there is a steep (4%) commission. You can also cash personal checks if you have an AmEx card at CITIC Bank. If your account is in US dollars, you can receive dollars (that way you can change your dollars on the black market for a much better exchange rate than at the bank).

International Transfers Inter-bank money transfers using China's wobbly banking system can take weeks. If you have to use a bank, try CITIC at 19 Jianguomen Wai Dajie (first open an account, then have the money wired to it).

There's also a very efficient money transfer service that is a joint venture between Western Union Financial Services in the USA and China Courier Service Corporation. There is a branch (☎ 6318 4313) at 7 Dongdanjie in Qianmen (in the post office).

Black Market The abolition of Foreign Exchange Certificates (FEC) in 1994 basically knocked China's flourishing black market on its head. But thanks to China's thriving smuggling rings (who need US dollars to carry on their business transactions), you can still change money on the black market in major cities at rates substantially better than those offered by the banks. Your best bet is to ask an expat to recommend a moneychanger. Generally speaking though, it's inadvisable to change money on the streets given the risk of short-changing, rip offs and the abundance of counterfeit currency floating about.

Costs

Beijing can be more expensive than New York or London, a ridiculous situation given that beneath its veneer, China's capital is still a poor city where most workers earn a pittance.

How much it actually costs pretty much depends on the degree of comfort you desire. Hotels are going to be the biggest expense, but food and transport can add up quickly too. Excluding the cost of getting to Beijing, ascetics can survive on as little as US$15 per day – that means staying in dormitories, travelling by bus or bicycle rather than taxi, eating from street stalls or small restaurants and refraining from buying anything. At time of writing a dorm bed was typically Y30 to Y50, and a basic meal in a run-of-the-mill street-side restaurant around Y20 to Y30.

On the opposite end of the spectrum, rooms at five-star hotels can be over US$200 per day and meals at upmarket restaurants can be US$50. And there is an increasing number of classy department stores charging Western prices.

Since the abolition of the dual-pricing system, train and plane costs have decreased about 20%. Admission fees have also substantially decreased – for example, admission to the Forbidden City was once Y85; it's now Y35.

Still, it's not uncommon for foreigners to encounter outright cheating by taxi drivers, waiters and other people in the various tourist service industries, which can substantially add to your costs.

Tipping & Bargaining

As some compensation for being frequently overcharged, Beijing is at least one of those wonderful cities where tipping is not done and almost no-one asks for it. This applies throughout China. Porters at upmarket hotels will, of course, expect a tip.

Bargaining is something else. While it is no longer a government policy to charge foreigners at least double for everything, many private businesses still charge three or four times the Chinese rate; this leaves considerable room for negotiation.

In large department stores where prices are clearly marked, there is usually no latitude for bargaining. In the smaller shops, bargaining is sometimes possible, especially where there are no price tags. At street stalls, it is expected. In all cases, there is one important rule to follow – be polite. There is nothing wrong with asking for a 'discount', if you do so with a smile. The worst they can say is 'no'. Some foreigners seem to think that bargaining is a battle of wits, involving bluff, screams and threats. This is not only unpleasant for all concerned, it seldom results in you getting a lower price – indeed, in 'face-conscious' China, intimidation is likely to make the vendor more recalcitrant and you'll be overcharged.

At hotels, there is some latitude when it comes to price. The price for hotel rooms in Beijing is ridiculously high for what's on offer, so discounts are not all that difficult to obtain. During the off season (which is the winter period, except for Chinese New Year) discounting is common, and you may be able to negotiate a better rate for a longer stay, especially at better hotels. Giving customers 50% off the rack rate is almost standard at some hotels. On the other hand, there's not much discounting at backpackers' dormitories; prices are low but firmly fixed.

You should keep in mind that entrepreneurs are in business to make money; they aren't going to sell anything to you at a loss. Your goal should be to pay the Chinese price, as opposed to the foreigners' price – if you can do that, you've done well.

Taxes

Although big hotels and fancy restaurants may add a tax or 'service charge' of 15%, all other consumer taxes are included in the price tag.

POST & COMMUNICATIONS
Post

Letters and parcels marked 'Poste Restante, Beijing Main Post Office' will wind up at the International Post Office (Map 7) on Jianguomen Beidajie, not far from the Friendship Store (about 200m south of the corner of Jianguomen Wai and Second Ring Rd). It's open from 8 am to 6 pm and from 9 am to 5 pm for international parcel pickup (be sure to bring your passport). The staff even file poste-restante letters in alphabetical order, a rare occurrence in China, but you pay for all this efficiency – there is a Y1.50 fee charged for each letter received.

Some major tourist hotels will hold mail for their guests, but this doesn't always work.

Officially, the PRC forbids certain items from being mailed to it – specifically prohibited are 'reactionary books, magazines and propaganda materials, obscene or immoral articles'. You are also considered very naughty if you mail Chinese currency abroad, or receive it by post. As elsewhere, mail-order hashish and other recreational substances will not amuse the authorities.

The international postal service seems efficient, and airmailed letters and postcards usually take around five to 10 days to reach their destinations. If possible, write the country of destination in Chinese as well as English, as this should speed up the delivery. Domestic post is amazingly fast, perhaps one day from Beijing to Shanghai. Within Beijing, same-day delivery is possible.

It is possible to post letters at the reception desks of all major hotels. In fact, even at cheap hotels you can do this – reliability varies but in general it's OK. There is a small but convenient post office in the CITIC building (Map 7), next to the Friendship Store. Another useful post office is in the basement of the China World Trade Center (Map 7).

Overseas parcels are sent and received at the International Post Office on Jianguomen Beidajie. Both outgoing and incoming packages will be opened and inspected here. Obviously, if you're sending a parcel don't seal the package until you've had it inspected. If someone sends a parcel to you, you will receive a slip of paper (in Chinese only) from the mail carrier – you must bring this and your passport to the post office and the package will be opened in front of you and the contents inspected.

Most countries impose a maximum weight limitation (20kg is typical) on packages received. This varies from country to country, but Chinese post offices should be able to tell you what the limitation is. If you have a receipt for the goods, then put it in the box when you're mailing it, since it may be opened again by customs further down the line.

Like elsewhere, China charges extra for registered mail, but offers cheaper postal rates for printed matter, small packets, parcels, bulk mailings and so on. Postage for domestic letters up to 20g is Y0.50, and domestic postcards are Y0.30. International air mail postal rates (in yuan) are as follows:

letters (weight)	international	HK, Macau & Taiwan	Asia-Pacific
0–20g	5.40	2.50	4.70
21–100g	11.40	5.00	9.80
101–250g	21.80	9.50	18.60
251–500g	40.80	17.70	34.80
501g–1kg	76.70	32.70	65.30
1–2kg	124.00	56.80	105.00
Postcards	4.20	2.00	3.70
Aerograms	5.20	1.80	4.50

EMS Domestic Express Mail Service (EMS) parcels up to 200g cost Y15; each additional 200g costs Y5. International EMS charges vary according to country. Some sample minimal rates (up to 500g parcels) are as follows:

country/region	cost (yuan)
Asia (South)	255
Asia (South-East)	150
Australia	195
Europe (Eastern)	382
Europe (Western)	232
Hong Kong & Macau	95
Japan & Korea	115
Middle East	375
North America	217
South America	262

Private Carriers There are a number of private couriers in Beijing that offer international express posting of documents and parcels. None of these private carriers is cheap, but they're fast and secure. These companies have pick-up service as well as drop-off centres, so call for the latest details. The major players in this market are:

DHL (☎ 6466 2211, fax 6467 7826) 45 Xinyuan Jie, Chaoyang District. There are also branches in the Kempinski Hotel and China World Trade Center.

Federal Express (FedEx; ☎ 800-810 2338, 6561 2003) 7 Guanghua Lu in Hanwei Bldg, Chaoyang District

United Parcel Service (UPS; ☎ 6593 3962) Unit A, 2nd floor, Tower B, Beijing Kelun Bldg, 12A Guanghua Lu, Chaoyang District

Telephone

China's phone system is undergoing a major overhaul and, given the size of the task, it has so far been reasonably successful. Both international and domestic calls can be made with a minimum of fuss from your hotel room and card phones are increasingly widespread.

Most hotel rooms are equipped with phones from which local calls are free.

Telephone Codes

International access code	☎ 00
China's country code	☎ 86
Beijing's area code	☎ 010
Guangzhou's area code	☎ 020
Shanghai's area code	☎ 021
Tianjin's area code	☎ 022

Local calls can alternatively be made from public pay phones or from privately run phone booths (there's one on every corner nowadays; cost is 3 jiao per call). Long-distance domestic calls can also be made from the phone booths, but not usually international calls. In the lobbies of many hotels, the reception desks have a system of free calls for guests, Y1 for non-guests and per-minute charges for long-distance calls.

You can place both domestic and international long-distance phone calls from main telecommunications offices. Generally you pay a deposit of Y200 and are given a card with the number of the phone booth you call from. The call is timed by computer, charged by the minute and a receipt will be provided.

Domestic long-distance rates in China vary according to distance, but are cheap. International calls are expensive, although in larger cities, with the introduction of Internet Phone (IP) cards (which work like a prepaid phone card but connect via the Internet), this is quickly changing (see Phone Cards following). Rates for station-to-station calls to most countries in the world are around Y20 per minute. There is a minimum charge of three minutes. Reverse-charge calls are often cheaper than calls paid for in China. Time the call yourself – the operator will not break in to tell you that your minimum period of three minutes is approaching. After you hang up, the operator will ring back to tell you how much it cost. There is no call-cancellation fee.

If you are expecting a call – either international or domestic – try to advise the caller beforehand of your hotel room number. The operators frequently have difficulty understanding Western names and the hotel receptionist may not be able to locate you. If this can't be done, try to inform the operator that you are expecting the call and write down your name and room number.

Phone Cards There's a wide range of local and international phone cards. Lonely Planet's eKno Communication Card is aimed specifically at independent travellers and provides budget international calls, a range of messaging services, free email and travel information – for local calls, you're usually better off with a local card. You can join online at www.ekno.lonelyplanet.com, or by phone from Beijing by dialling ☎ 800-180 0073. Once you have joined, to use eKno from Beijing, dial ☎ 800-180 0072. Check the eKno Web site for joining and access numbers from other countries and updates on super budget local access numbers and new features.

Substantially cheaper than phone cards is the recently introduced IP system. International call rates have plunged to about 25% of the old rates to Y1.50 per minute to Hong Kong, Macau and Taiwan and Y4.80 per minute to anywhere else in the world. The service is currently only available in 25 cities in China, including Beijing and Shanghai. To take advantage of these rates, you have to buy an IP card, usually available in increments of Y100. You can buy IP cards at Internet cafes, some newsstands and small stores. Basically the way they work is you dial a local number, then punch in your account number, followed by the number you wish to call (there are instructions on the back of the card). English service is usually available.

Regular card phones are also found in hotel lobbies and in most telecommunications buildings. They're about double the price of IP rates, although they've also come down substantially from former International Direct Dial (IDD) rates. Note that most phone cards can only be used in the province where you buy them. Smartcards can be used throughout China, provided you can find a Smartcard phone.

Direct Dialling & Collect Calls
The international access code in China is ☎ 00. Add the country code, then the local area code (omitting the 0 before it) and the number you want to reach. Another option is to dial the home country direct dial number (☎ 108), which puts you straight through to a local operator there. You can then make a reverse-charge (collect) call or a credit-card call with a telephone credit card valid in the destination country.

Useful Phone Numbers There's at least a 50% chance that the person answering the phone will speak no English, so you get to practise your Chinese. With that warning in mind, see the 'Useful Numbers' boxed text for a list of some numbers that may come in handy.

Rent-A-Phone You can rent a mobile phone in Beijing at Yiguang Science & Technology (☎ 6586 6667), 4th floor, Golden Bridge Building, A1 Jianguomen Wai Dajie, between China World and the Jinglun Hotel.

Mobile Phones Unless you're on the US network, your mobile phone should work in China. Chinese SIM cards cost Y2000 for one that accepts international calls or Y600 for local service. Usage rate is an additional 3 jiao per minute. If you have a Chinese

---

International Country Codes

country	direct dial	home country direct
Australia	☎ 00-61	☎ 108-61
Canada	☎ 00-1	☎ 108-1
Hong Kong	☎ 00-852	☎ 108-852
Japan	☎ 00-81	☎ 108-81
Netherlands	☎ 00-31	☎ 108-31
New Zealand	☎ 00-64	☎ 108-64
UK	☎ 00-44	☎ 108-44
USA	☎ 00-1	☎ 108-1*

* For the USA you can dial ☎ 108-11 (AT&T), ☎ 108-12 (MCI) or ☎ 108-13 (Sprint).

Useful Numbers

Unless otherwise noted, the following offer service in Chinese only:

Ambulance hotline	☎ 120
Capital Airport	☎ 2580
Fire hotline	☎ 119
General emergency	☎ 999
International directory assistance (English-speaking)	☎ 115
Local directory assistance	☎ 114
Medical (English-speaking):	
AEA	☎ 6462 9100
Beijing United Family Hospital	☎ 6433 3960
International Medical Center	☎ 6465 1561
Police hotline	☎ 110
Postal inquiries	☎ 185
Motor accident hotline	☎ 122
Taxi	☎ 6837 3399
Time	☎ 117
Tourist hotline (English-speaking)	☎ 6513 0828
Weather	☎ 121

SIM card, you can make overseas calls for Y4.8 per minute by first dialling ☎ 17901, 17911, 17921 or 17931, followed by 00, the country code then the number you want to call. You will be billed accordingly.

If you're staying in China for more than a few months and make frequent overseas calls, it's worthwhile to sign up with a call-back service. Virtually all such services are based in the USA (to take advantage of its cheap phone rates). Some of the choices available include:

Justice Technology (☎ 310-526 2000, fax 526 2100)
  Web site: www.justicecorp.com
Kallback (☎ 206-599 1992; fax 599 1982, ✉ info@kallback.com)
  Web site: www.kallback.com
Kallmart (☎ 407-676 1717; fax 676 5289, ✉ sales@kallmart.com)
  Web site: www.kallmart.com
New World Telecommunications (☎ 201-287 8400, ✉ economist@newworldtele.com)
  Web site: www.newworldtele.com

However, IP card (see Phone Cards earlier) rates are cheaper than callback services.

Pagers Those living on a budget, such as foreign students, may well find pagers a more realistic option than having a phone installed.

Pagers for use in Beijing cost Y15 a month. For a pager usable throughout

China, the price rises to Y80 per month. The paging market was opened to free competition in 1993 – there are now about 1700 paging firms in China so it's difficult to say which company is best.

Email & Internet Access

Email has taken off in China. Not only are Internet cafes found in all tourist destinations, but they're also springing up in small towns. The cheapest way to keep in touch while on the road is to sign up for a free email account with Hotmail (www.hotmail .com), Rocketmail (www.rocketmail.com) or Yahoo (www.yahoo.com) and access your account from an Internet cafe. These services are free, but you have to put up with advertising. If you're willing to spend US$15 per year, you can get all your email forwarded to any address of your choice by signing up with Pobox (www.pobox.com) – this service can also be used to block advertising and mail bombs. (Also see Lonely Planet's eKno Communication Card under Phone Cards.)

If you want to use a foreign-based Internet Service Provider (ISP; eg Compuserve), you may have trouble accessing it from China.

If you're travelling with a portable computer and modem and wish to avoid Internet cafes, you can set up a local Internet account for about Y100, plus Y4 to Y8 per hour.

Upwardly Mobile

Statistically China may still be a poor country, but you wouldn't think so judging by the number of people in the PRC toting mobile phones and pagers. Even some street vendors have them. At last count mobile phone users numbered over 60 million with the figure growing exponentially.

The other big status symbol a driving licence. Although there are only a few thousand privately owned cars in Beijing, it's everyone's aim to be ready for the day when they can afford to buy one. In the meantime, driving schools are doing great business.

Note that it can be risky to attach your modem to the phone in your hotel room and dial out through the switchboard – if the switchboard is digital (as opposed to analog) you risk frying your modem. Ironically, this is a bigger problem at newer hotels – old hotels usually have analog equipment. Konexx (Web site: www.konexx .com) sells a device called a 'mobile konnector' that not only protects the modem, but also allows you to hook up to the phone's handset cord.

You do have to put up with some censorship – the Chinese government has blocked access to sites that peddle pornography or contain political content deemed unsuitable for the masses (such as Inside China's Web site). Also, connections are often agonisingly slow. Nevertheless, you can get quite a lot of useful work done on the Internet. China Telecom offers Internet service in major Chinese cities. Internet service providers in Beijing include:

Beijing Telecommunications Administration (☎ 6306 0779) 11 Xichang'an Jie
Eastnet (☎ 6529 2268) Lufthansa Center department store (computer section)
Unicom-Sparkice (☎ 6505 2288 ext 6206, ✉ cafe@unicom.com.cn) 2nd floor, China World Trade Center

The Sparkice Internet Cafe (Shíhuá Wǎngluò Kāfēi Shì; ☎ 6833 5225), in the west wing of the Capital Gymnasium (west of Beijing Zoo), charges Y15 per hour for use of its machines. It's open from 10 am to 10 pm daily. Other branches of Sparkice are in the China World Trade Center at 1 Jianguomen Wai Dajie and within the campus of Beijing Normal University. Internet cafes can also be found outside the south gate of Qinghua University and outside the south gate of Beijing Language and Culture University. Although their computers aren't as well kept and as fast as Sparkice's, the Benk Internet cafe (☎ 6507 2814), 59 Dongdaqiao Lu, is conveniently located just around the corner from the Silk Market.

Noticeboards & Email Newsletters No discussion of communications in Beijing would be complete without some mention of the various expat noticeboards around town. This is where expats can buy used furniture and computers, find a Chinese tutor, advertise their skills (therapeutic massage anyone?) or search for flats to rent. Expat-oriented supermarkets arguably have the best noticeboards – the Wellcome supermarket in the Holiday Inn Lido shopping centre has a classic as does any Jenny Lou's grocery store on the Bar Street.

The email newsletter *Xianzai Beijing* (subscribe by emailing @ beijing@xianzai .com) has classified ads and calendar listings for what's going on around town, as does the Web site www.chinanow.com.

INTERNET RESOURCES
The World Wide Web is a rich resource for travellers. You can research your trip, hunt down bargain air fares, book hotels, check on weather conditions or chat with locals and other travellers about the best places to visit.

A good place to start is the Lonely Planet Web site (www.lonelyplanet.com). Here you'll find succinct summaries on travelling to most places on earth, postcards from other travellers and the Thorn Tree bulletin board, where you can ask questions before you go or dispense advice when you get back. You can also find travel news and updates to many of our most popular guidebooks, and the subWWWay section links you to some of the most useful travel resources on the Web.

Recommended China travel, arts and entertainment-related Web sites include:

www.66cities.com articles and entertainment listings for Beijing
www.cbw.com/tourism the Chinese Business World China travel guide. You can also book hotels at a discount and flights.
www.chinanow.com a site featuring columns, travel information, nightlife and restaurant listings and classified ads
www.chinese-art.com online modern art galleries
www.flychina.com good deals on flights to China from Canada and the US
www.surfchina.com/html/travel.html an online search engine for China with a large range of links to other China travel-related sites

Other recommended China-related Web sites include:

www.blcu.edu.cn Beijing Language and Culture University's Web site
www.caft.com Air China's Web site
www.chinadaily.com.cn the online party mouthpiece
www.chinaonline.com China business and economic news
www.insidechina.com China-related news
www.muzi.net general information and news about China
www.pku.edu.cn Beijing University's Web site
www.sinopolis.com English translations of articles from the Chinese press
www.zhaodaola.com news stories about China
www.zhaopin.com a huge database of jobs in China

You can also check out Amnesty International's informative Web site at www.amnesty.org or get its China report in print. Perhaps a more immediate Web site is run by Support Democracy in China. Their site is at www.christusrex.org/www1/sdc/sdchome.html.

BOOKS
There is enough literature on China to keep you reading for the next 5000 years, but relatively little dealing with Beijing exclusively. Ironically, Beijing itself is not a good place to find books about Beijing – the widest selection in China is in Hong Kong.

It's probably easier to find and order books in your home town before you leave than to try to buy them in Beijing. The following titles are recommended (publishing details are not included as they vary globally).

Lonely Planet
Aside from this guidebook, travellers to Beijing might also want to check out Lonely Planet's *Mandarin phrasebook,* a handy pocket phrasebook which is a good resource for finding your way around. Lonely Planet's *China* is packed with essential information on travel between Beijing and other parts of China, including the more remote areas.

Lonely Planet has also just published its *Travel Photography: A Guide to Taking Better Pictures,* written by internationally renowned travel photographer Richard I'Anson. This full-colour and travel-friendly book is packed with useful tips for getting the most out of your film and camera.

Guidebooks

The perennial guide for business travellers is the red-covered *The China Phone Book & Business Directory.* It's dry reading, but vital to those who need it. It's most easily purchased in Hong Kong (not Beijing).

The *Beijing Guidebook* is an excellent resource for expats living in Beijing. It contains information on everything from 'negotiating employment terms' to hiring an *ayi* (nanny). It's for sale at the Friendship Store.

In Search of Old Peking by Arlington & Lewisohn is one of the great classic guidebooks of the city. It's currently out of print though it can often be found in libraries or second-hand bookshops.

Biking Beijing by Diana Kingsbury has a useful selection of self-guided tours around the thoroughfares and back alleys of the capital. This book is also becoming a little difficult to find.

The Palace Museum: Peking, Treasures of the Forbidden City by Wango & Boda is a pricey hardcover guide (over US$50), but covers its subject in microscopic detail.

Beijing by Deborah Kent is part of the 'Cities of the World' series published mainly for library reference.

The *Beijing Official Guide* is published four times a year by the Chinese government. Though the information is far from complete, it's at least up to date. You can find free copies around the lobbies of various tourist hotels.

The government toots its own horn in *Places of Interest in Beijing* by the China Travel & Tourism Press – actually, it's not bad. A much slimmer volume is simply entitled *Beijing* by the China Esperanto Press. Look for both of these at the Friendship Store (Map 7) or Foreign Languages Bookstore in Beijing (Map 4).

History

An interesting aside to current intellectual history is provided by Perry Link in his *Evening Chats in Beijing.*

Dragon Lady: The Life and Legend of the Last Empress of China by Sterling Seagrave is the definitive biography of Cixi, who ruled China in the late 19th century. A fascinating read.

The Private Life of Chairman Mao by Li Zhisui offers some amazing insights into the hidden world behind the great walls of Zhongnanhai, China's so-called 'new Forbidden City'.

Rickshaw Beijing: City People and Politics in the 1920s by David Strand is, amazingly, still in print. Ditto for *The IG in Peking; Letters of Robert Hart, Chinese Maritime Customs, 1868–1907.* Also look for *Jesuits at the Court of Peking.*

Old Peking: City of the Ruler of the World by Chris Elder is a recent work (1997).

Hard to find but worth tracking down (at least in libraries) is *Twilight in the Forbidden City* by Reginald F Johnston; a British colonial official who tutored China's last emperor from 1919 to 1924.

Other books in the 'special order' category include *The Lion and the Dragon: The Story of the First British Embassy to the Court of the Emperor Qianlong in Peking 1792–1794* by Aubrey Singer; and *Old Madam Yin: A Memoir of Peking Life, 1926–1938* by Ida Pruitt.

General

China Remembers by Calum MacLeod & Zhang Lijia is an excellent collection of first-person essays by Chinese whose lives exemplify the major historical periods of the PRC.

Peking by Anthony Grey is your standard blockbuster by the author of *Saigon.* Not bad. The former should not be confused with *Peking* by Juliet Bredon, another great book.

Letter from Peking by Pearl S Buck is a classic novel currently out of print. Ms Buck lived most of her life in 19th-century China, and was a prolific writer. Her most famous book was *The Good Earth* (still in print).

Wild Swans: Three Daughters of China, by Jung Chang, is a hefty but compelling read about three generations of women living in China which provides insight into the times of Mao's Cultural Revolution.

For books published within China, see 'Literature' in the Arts section of the Facts about Beijing chapter.

NEWSPAPERS & MAGAZINES

China publishes various newspapers, books and magazines in a number of European and Asian languages. The government's favourite English-language mouthpiece is the *China Daily.* First published in June 1981, it now has two overseas editions (Hong Kong and USA). Overseas subscriptions can be obtained from the following sources:

China Daily Distribution Corporation
(☎ 212-219 0130; fax 210 0108) Suite 401, 15 Mercer St, New York, NY 10013, USA
Wen Wei Po (☎ 2572 2211, fax 2572 0441)
197 Wanchai Rd, Hong Kong

In Beijing it's easy enough to score copies of the popular imported English-language magazines including *Time, Newsweek, Far Eastern Economic Review* and *The Economist.* Occasionally you might find European magazines in French or German. Foreign newspapers like the *Asian Wall Street Journal* and *International Herald-Tribune* are available. Hong Kong's *South China Morning Post* probably has the most comprehensive coverage of news on China. Imported magazines are most readily available from the big tourist hotels and the Friendship Store.

Beijing also has a plethora of English-language rags available free at most five-star hotels and Sanlitun bars and restaurants. Unfortunately the best of the bunch, *Beijing Scene,* has been shut down by the police. Rather mainstream is *City Edition,* which has a good listings section but runs mediocre features mostly geared toward the hedonistic side of expat life in Beijing. *Metro* is a bizarre, almost unintelligible English-language rag that features a hard-to-read layout. *City Edition* and *Metro* appear every two weeks.

This Month Beijing and *Beijing Weekend* are government-run freebies that are handed out at many big hotels. They come with a basic English map of the city along with a good deal of up-to-date tourist information that can point you in the right direction, although they lack in-depth coverage.

RADIO & TV

Domestic radio broadcasting is controlled by the Central People's Broadcasting Station (CPBS). Broadcasts are made in *pǔtōnghuà,* the standard Chinese speech (Mandarin), as well as in local Chinese dialects and minority languages. Even if you can't understand what's being said, the classical music requires no translation. 'Easy FM' broadcasts in English 12 hours a day at 91.5 MHz.

If you want to hear world news broadcasts in English, a short-wave radio receiver is worth bringing with you. You can buy these in China, but Japanese-made ones are more compact and better quality.

The Chinese Central Television operates six stations (CCTV 1–6). Beijing Television (BTV) operates three channels. At the time of writing, CCTV 4 had some English-language programs including news broadcasts. Unless you want to practise your Chinese, you'll probably find most of the local stuff boring.

But the situation is not hopeless – satellite TV is all the rage in China. Hong Kong's STAR TV broadcasts via satellite to China. There are both Chinese- and English-language shows, including a range of popular American TV series – from Baywatch to Oprah˙Winfrey (well, maybe the situation *is* hopeless). CNN and HBO are also available in certain designated areas.

VIDEO SYSTEMS

China subscribes to the PAL broadcasting standard, the same as Australia, New Zealand, the UK and most of Europe. Competing systems not used in China include SECAM (France, Germany, Luxembourg) and NTSC (Canada, Japan and the USA). However, VCDs and DVDs are much more widely used in China than videotapes.

PHOTOGRAPHY & VIDEO

When the pollution isn't too thick Beijing can be a very photogenic city, and there are 13 million potential human portraits as well. Some Chinese shy away from having their photo taken and even duck for cover. Others are proud to pose and will ham it up for the camera – and they're especially proud if you're taking a shot of their kid. Nobody expects payment for photos, so don't give any or you'll set a precedent. What people would appreciate is a copy of a colour photo, which you could mail to them.

Whatever you do, photograph with discretion and manners. It's always polite to ask first and if the person says no, don't take the photo. A gesture, a smile and a nod are all that is usually necessary. Remember, wherever you are in China, the people are *not* exotic birds of paradise and the village monk is *not* a photographic model.

Many Chinese will disagree with you on what constitutes good subject matter; they don't really see why anyone would want to take a shot of a rustic street scene or an old man driving a donkey cart.

Video users should follow the same rules regarding people's sensitivities as for a photograph – having a video camera shoved in their face is probably even more annoying and offensive for locals than a still camera. Always ask permission first.

Big-name colour print film (Kodak, Fuji etc) is available almost everywhere, but is almost exclusively 100 ASA (21 DIN). Colour slide film can be bought at the Friendship Store and major hotels, who sell it at a significant mark-up. For more information on where to develop and buy film (including slide and black and white film), see Film Processing in the Shopping chapter.

Genuine Chinese brands of film are a rarity. Polaroid film is rumoured to exist, but if you know you'll need it bring your own supply. Lithium batteries can generally be found at photo shops, but it doesn't hurt to carry a spare.

Many of Beijing's scenic spots (Summer Palace, Forbidden City etc) impose special fees on video cameras or ban them outright. It's not clear if this is to prevent you from stealing state secrets, or from filming a sequel to *The Last Emperor* without paying the Chinese government.

Undeveloped film can be sent out of China and, going by personal experience only, the dreaded X-ray machines do not appear to be a problem.

Religious reasons for avoiding photographs are absent among the Han Chinese – some guy isn't going to stick a spear through you for taking a picture of his wife and stealing part of her soul – but photographing monks and the interiors of temples is generally prohibited.

Photography from planes and photographs of airports, military installations, harbour facilities, train terminals and bridges can be touchy subjects. Of course, these rules only get enforced if the enforcers happen to be around.

Taking photos is not permitted in most museums, at archaeological sites and in many temples, mainly to protect the postcard and colour slide industry. It also prevents valuable works of art from being damaged by countless flash photos.

Last but not least, if you're out on the streets of Beijing, especially in Tiananmen Square, and chance upon a protest – even if it's a single person quietly sitting in the lotus position – don't take photos. If you're spotted by plain-clothes police, not only will your film be confiscated, but you may also be detained at the police station for a few hours, if not a few days.

TIME

All of China runs on Beijing's clock, which is set eight hours ahead of GMT/UTC; daylight-saving time was abandoned in 1992. When it's noon in Beijing it's 4 am in London, 5 am in Frankfurt, Paris and Rome, noon in Hong Kong, 2 pm in Melbourne, 4 pm in Wellington, 8 pm in Los Angeles, and 11 pm in Montreal and New York.

ELECTRICITY

Electricity is 220 volts, 50 cycles AC. Plugs come in at least four designs – three-pronged angled pins (as in Australia), three-pronged round pins (as in Hong Kong), two flat pins (US style but without the ground wire) or two narrow round pins (European style). Conversion plugs are easily purchased in Beijing. Battery rechargers are widely available, but these are generally the bulky style which aren't ideal for travelling – buy a travel-friendly one in Hong Kong or elsewhere.

WEIGHTS & MEASURES

China officially subscribes to the international metric system. However, ancient Chinese weights and measures persist. The most likely ones that tourists will encounter are the *liǎng* (tael) and the *jīn* (catty).

One jin is 0.6kg (1.32 lbs). There are 16 liang to the jin, so one liang is 37.5g (1.32 oz). Most fruits and vegetables in China are sold by the jin, while tea and herbal medicine are sold by the liang.

The other unit of measure you might encounter is the *ping*. Pings are used to measure area, and one ping is approximately 1.82 sq metres (5.97 sq feet). When you buy carpet, the price will be determined by the number of pings. It's the same deal for

Chinese Medicine

Many foreigners visiting China never try Chinese herbal medicine *(zhōng yào)* because they either know nothing about it or don't believe in it. It's understandable: Western medical authorities often dismiss herbalists as no better than witch doctors, the ingredients may include exotic animal bits and the mind-boggling array of herbs on offer can make for some bitter tasting experiences.

Chinese herbs may be remarkably effective but some warnings are in order. Herbs are not miracle drugs, despite the extravagant claims sometimes made. Such medicine works best for the relief of unpleasant symptoms (such as a sore throat or toothache) and for chronic ailments like migraines and asthma.

There are relatively few side effects to herbal medicine. Nevertheless, herbs are medicine, not candy, and there is no need to take them if you're feeling fine to begin with. In fact, some herbs are mildly toxic and if taken over a long period of time can actually damage the liver and other organs. There is good advice on when to avoid common products like red ginseng (bad for the elderly or for anyone in summer) and what to avoid while taking it (such as coffee). Conversely, resist the urge to stop taking the medicine as soon as you feel a bit better – most treatments are not designed as a quick fix.

Some manufacturers falsely claim that their product contains numerous potent and expensive ingredients, such as rhinoceros horn. As the rhino is a rare and endangered species, these products are highly questionable in any case. Counterfeiting is another problem: If the herbs you take seem to be totally ineffective, it may be because you've bought sugar pills rather than medicine.

Although a tonic such as snake gall bladder may be good for treating colds, there are many different types of colds. See a doctor versed in herbal medicine and get a specific prescription; otherwise, the medicine may not suit your condition. If you can't get to a doctor, you can try your luck at a pharmacy.

Chinese medicine is often described as 'holistic': It seeks to treat the whole body rather than focusing on a particular organ or disease. A herbal doctor will almost certainly take your pulse (more than 30 kinds of pulse are considered). The doctor may then examine your tongue. Having discovered that you have, say, 'damp heat', as evidenced by a 'slippery' pulse and a 'red greasy' tongue, the doctor will prescribe the herbs that will help restore your body's yin-yang balance and *qi* (flow of vital energy).

Many Chinese deal with motion sickness, nausea and headaches by smearing liniments on their stomach or head. Look for White Flower Oil *(bái huā yóu)*, probably the most popular brand. Then there are salves, the most famous being Tiger Balm (which originated in Hong Kong). Back strain? Try 'Sticky Dog Skin Plaster'. You might be relieved to know that these days it's no longer made from real dog skin.

leasing or purchasing an apartment or house.

LAUNDRY

On just about every floor of just about every hotel in China there is a service desk. The job of the attendants at these service desks is mainly to clean the rooms, make the beds and collect and deliver laundry. Almost all tourist hotels have a laundry service, and if you should hand in clothes in the morning you should get them back the same evening or the next day. If the hotel doesn't have a laundrette, the staff can usually direct you to one. Hotel laundry services tend to be expensive and if you're on a tight budget you might wind up doing what many travellers do – hand-washing your own clothes. If you plan on doing this, dark clothes are better since the dirt's not so obvious. Laundry prices can vary widely. Budget hotels charge around Y1 or Y2 per item, while ritzier hotels can demand around Y10 per item. DIY laundrettes are not available in China, although small shops that do laundry and dry-cleaning are pretty common.

TOILETS

There has been much improvement in Beijing's toilet scene in recent years – in the not-too-distant past you basically had to squat over a very smelly hole or a ditch. However, it's still like that in public toilets around the city.

Better hotels and restaurants supply toilet paper in their public toilets, but you can't count on it in other places (public parks, department stores, train and bus stations). Always keep a stash of this vital stuff with you.

The Chinese plumbing system has problems digesting used toilet paper, and the issue of just what to do with it has caused some concern.

In general, if you see a waste basket next to the toilet, that's where you should throw the toilet paper. Even in many Beijing hotels, especially the old ones, the sewage system can't handle paper. In rural areas there's no sewage treatment at all – the waste empties into an underground septic tank and toilet paper will really create a mess if it gets thrown down the toilet. For the sake of international relations, throw the paper in the waste basket.

Remember:

| men | 男 |
| women | 女 |

HEALTH

Except for the thick layer of air pollution that sometimes blankets the city, Beijing is a reasonably healthy city – the cold climate means you needn't fear tropical bugs like malaria.

Some basic precautions are advisable. It's worth having your own medicine kit, including, for example: paracetamol, vitamins, sun screen lotion and anti-diarrhoea tablets. Tiger Balm is useful as an anti-irritant for insect bites. Other useful items are laxatives, contraceptives and a thermometer. If you wear spectacles, take a prescription with you in case they get broken. If you require a particular medication, take an adequate supply because your drug of choice may not be available locally. Also, make sure the prescription has the generic rather than the brand name, which may be unavailable; this will make getting replacements easier. See the boxed text 'Medical Kit Check List' for more suggestions.

Immunisations

There are no vaccination requirements for entry to China except yellow fever if you are coming from an area infected with yellow fever (most of sub-Saharan Africa and parts of South America; there is no risk of yellow fever in China). As a basic precaution before travelling, it's a good idea to ensure that your tetanus, diphtheria and polio vaccinations are up to date (boosters are required every 10 years). Discuss your requirements with your doctor, but other diseases you should consider having vaccinations against before you leave are hepatitis A, which is a common food- and water-borne disease, and hepatitis B, which is transmitted through sexual activity and blood (hepatitis B is highly prevalent

Medical Kit Check List

Following is a list of items you should consider including in your medical kit – consult your pharmacist for brands available in your country.

- ☐ **Aspirin or paracetamol (acetaminophen in the USA)** – for pain or fever
- ☐ **Antihistamine** – for allergies, eg, hay fever; to ease the itch from insect bites or stings; and to prevent motion sickness
- ☐ **Cold and flu tablets, throat lozenges and nasal decongestant**
- ☐ **Multivitamins** – consider for long trips, when dietary vitamin intake may be inadequate
- ☐ **Antibiotics** – consider including these if you're travelling well off the beaten track; see your doctor, as they must be prescribed, and carry the prescription with you
- ☐ **Loperamide or diphenoxylate** –'blockers' for diarrhoea
- ☐ **Prochlorperazine or metaclopramide** – for nausea and vomiting
- ☐ **Rehydration mixture** – to prevent dehydration, which may occur, for example, during bouts of diarrhoea; particularly important when travelling with children
- ☐ **Insect repellent, sunscreen, lip balm and eye drops**
- ☐ **Calamine lotion, sting relief spray or aloe vera** – to ease irritation from sunburn and insect bites or stings
- ☐ **Antifungal cream or powder** – for fungal skin infections and thrush
- ☐ **Antiseptic (such as povidone-iodine)** – for cuts and grazes
- ☐ **Bandages, Band-Aids (plasters) and other wound dressings**
- ☐ **Water purification tablets or iodine**
- ☐ **Scissors, tweezers and a thermometer** – note that mercury thermometers are prohibited by airlines
- ☐ **Sterile kit** – in case you need injections in a country with medical hygiene problems; discuss with your doctor

in China). Other vaccinations for a long-term stay might include typhoid, tuberculosis, Japanese B encephalitis and rabies. Malaria has nearly been eradicated in China and is not generally a risk for travellers visiting cities. If you will be living in Beijing for a while, a vaccination every autumn against influenza wouldn't be a bad idea, especially for seniors.

Food & Drink

Salads and fruit should be washed with purified water or peeled where possible. Ice cream is usually OK if it is a reputable brand name, but beware of ice cream that is sold on the street or has melted and been refrozen. Shellfish such as mussels, oysters and clams should be avoided as well as undercooked meat, particularly in the form of mince. Steaming does not make shellfish safe for eating.

Water supplies are fairly good, but it's still recommended that you drink only boiled or bottled water. If you don't know for certain that the water is safe, then assume the worst. Milk should be treated with suspicion as it is often unpasteurised, though boiled milk is fine if it is kept hygienically. Tea should be OK – after all, it's boiled.

Bottled water or soft drinks are fine – the main problem is that the exterior of the bottle may be encrusted in dust (or worse) as vendors don't care too much where the bottles are stored. Try to find a place to wash the bottle or can before opening it.

Diseases

Influenza (liúxíngxìng gǎnmào) The most likely illness to befall you in Beijing is influenza. China is notorious for outbreaks of nasty strains of flu and pneumonia is a possible complication. The problem is especially serious during winter, though you can catch it any time of the year. The situation is exacerbated by the Chinese habit of spitting anywhere and everywhere, which spreads respiratory illnesses. You can protect yourself to a limited extent with a flu vaccine, but 100% protection would require that you live in total quarantine or give up breathing.

Diarrhoea (lā dùzi) Travellers' diarrhoea has been around a long time – even Marco Polo had it. Simple things like a change of water, food or climate can all cause a mild bout of diarrhoea, but a few rushed trips to the toilet with no symptoms do not indicate a major problem. If you're not drinking unboiled water, the most likely way to get a bad case of diarrhoea is to eat salads (the Chinese use unprocessed faeces as fertiliser). The solution is to stick to cooked vegetables.

Dehydration is the main danger with any diarrhoea, particularly in children or the elderly in whom dehydration can occur quite quickly.

Under all circumstances *fluid replacement* (at least equal to the volume lost) is the most important thing to remember. Weak black tea with a little sugar, soda water, or soft drinks allowed to go flat and diluted 50% with clean (boiled or bottled) water are all good. With severe diarrhoea a rehydrating solution is preferable to replace minerals and salts lost. Commercially available oral rehydration salts (ORS) are very useful; add them to boiled or bottled water. In an emergency you can make up a solution of six teaspoons of sugar and half a teaspoon of salt to a litre of boiled or bottled water. You need to drink at least the same volume of fluid that you are losing in bowel movements and vomiting. Urine is the best guide to the adequacy of replacement – if you have small amounts of concentrated urine, you need to drink more. Keep drinking small amounts often. Stick to a bland diet as you recover. High-fibre or spicy foods like hot pickled chillies, raw vegetables and fruits are a disaster – you'll be running for the toilet within minutes.

Lomotil or Imodium can be used to bring relief from the symptoms, although they do not actually cure the problem. Use these drugs only if you do not have access to toilets, eg, if you *must* travel. For children under 12 years Lomotil and Imodium are not recommended. Do not use these drugs if you have a high fever or are severely dehydrated. One Chinese medication worth trying is *lăba*, available in the Friendship Store and most pharmacies.

In certain situations antibiotics may be required: these include diarrhoea with blood or mucus (dysentery), any diarrhoea with high fever, persistent diarrhoea not improving after 48 hours and severe diarrhoea. In these situations gut-paralysing drugs like Imodium or Lomotil should be avoided. Seek medical help.

Sexually Transmitted Diseases & AIDS (xing bìng) The Cultural Revolution may be over but the sexual revolution is booming in China, and Sexually Transmitted Diseases (STDs) are spreading rapidly. Therefore it pays to be cautious in sexual activity, particularly as you could be unlucky enough to catch herpes (incurable) or, worse still, Acquired Immune Deficiency Syndrome (AIDS). Apart from sexual abstinence, condoms provide the most effective protection and are available in China. The word for condom is *băoxiăn tào* – literally 'insurance glove'.

As most people know by now, AIDS can also be spread through infected blood transfusions, and by dirty needles – vaccinations, acupuncture, ear piercing and tattooing can potentially be as dangerous as intravenous drug use if the equipment is not clean. Much of the blood supply in China is *not* tested for AIDS, so if you really need a transfusion it is safest to find a healthy friend of the same blood group to donate blood to you rather than rely on the stocks in hospitals. You may choose to buy your own acupuncture needles, which are widely available in Beijing, if you're intending to have that form of treatment. Medical clinics that cater to foreigners all use disposable needles and syringes. Fear of HIV/AIDS should never preclude treatment for serious medical conditions.

Medical Facilities

Asia Emergency Assistance (AEA; ☎ 6462 9100, fax 6462 9111), at 1 Xingfu Sancunbei Jie, behind the German embassy, has the largest clientele within the foreign community. The staff are mostly expats, and emergency service is available 24 hours. AEA offers emergency evacuation from China for the critically ill.

The International Medical Centre (☎ 6465 1561, fax 6465 1560) is in the Lufthansa Center at 50 Liangmaqiao Lu.

Emergency service is available 24 hours, but it's a good idea to call first for an appointment.

Beijing United Family Hospital (☎ 6433 3960, fax 6433 3963) is at 2 Jiangtai Lu, north-east of the Hilton Hotel. It specialises in women and children's health care.

The Hong Kong International Medical Clinic (☎ 6501 2288 ext 2345, fax 6502 3426), on the 3rd floor of the Hong Kong Macau Center (also known as the Swissô-tel), has a 24-hour medical and dental clinic, including obstetrical/gynaecological services. The staff can also do immunisations. Prices here are more reasonable.

Much cheaper than foreigners clinics are Chinese hospitals that cater to foreigners. Beijing Union Medical Hospital (Xiéhé Yīyuàn; ☎ 6529 6114), at 53 Dongdan Bei-dajie, has the reputation of being the best in the country. There is a wing especially for foreigners and high-level cadres in the back building.

If you're looking for a herbal remedy to your ailment (there are cures for everything from a low sex drive to cold sores), the Beijing Traditional Chinese Medicine Hospital (Běijīng Zhōngyī Yīyuàn; ☎ 6401 6677), at 23 Meishuguan Houjie, has a foreigners clinic on the 3rd floor. There's a pharmacy on the ground floor, where thousands of herbs are stored.

WOMEN TRAVELLERS

It's often said that Beijing is one of the safest places in Asia – if not the world – for foreign women to travel solo. This may not be as true as it was a decade ago (beware of lecherous taxi drivers), but the changes are not dramatic.

Principles of decorum and respect for women are deeply ingrained into Chinese culture. Despite the Confucianist sense of superiority accorded men, Chinese women often call the shots and wield a tremendous amount of influence (especially within marriage). There is a strong sense of balance between men and women.

In general, foreign women are unlikely to suffer serious sexual harassment in Beijing; however, there have been reports of foreign women being harassed in parks or while cycling alone at night. Police tend to investigate crimes against foreigners more closely than they do crimes against locals, and more severe penalties are often imposed.

GAY & LESBIAN TRAVELLERS

Local law is ambiguous on this issue, but generally the authorities take a dim view of gays and lesbians. Certainly a scene exists in Beijing (and regular haunts are plentiful), but few dare say so too loudly.

For excellent and up-to-date information on the latest gay and lesbian hot spots in Beijing and elsewhere throughout China, have a look at the Web site www.utopia-asia.com/tipschin.htm.

See also under Gay & Lesbian venues in the Entertainment chapter.

DISABLED TRAVELLERS

While Beijing is not particularly user-friendly to disabled travellers, it's not the worst offender in this regard. Compared to the narrow lanes of other Asian cities, Beijing's wide boulevards and pedestrian footpaths make it easier to manoeuvre wheelchairs or for blind people to avoid being run over. On the down side, there are a number of streets where the only way to cross is via an underground walkway with many steps. Uneven pavements can be a hazard too. Another drawback is that the city is very spread out.

Get in touch with your national support organisation (preferably the travel officer if there is one) before leaving home. Such organisations often have travel literature to help with holiday planning and can put you in touch with travel agents that specialise in tours for the disabled.

In the UK, the Royal Association for Disability & Rehabilitation (☎ 020-7250 3222, fax 7250 0212), 12 City Forum, 250 City Rd, London EC1V 8AF, produces three holiday fact packs for disabled travellers.

In the USA, contact the Society for the Advancement of Travel for the Handicapped (SATH; ☎ 212-447 7284) 347 Fifth Ave No 610, New York, NY 10016; or Access – The Foundation for Accessibility by the Disabled

Toboggans for hire on Kunming Lake

Toffee apples

Outdoor barbers do a roaring trade.

Keeping the doctor away

A shop in Jingshan Lu

Outdoor breakfast at Wangfujing

Anyone for baozi?

Or flat bread?

Stretching a point at Panjiayuan market

(☎ 516-887 5798), PO Box 356, Malverne, NY 11565.

Australians can contact NICAN (☎ 02-6285 3713, fax 6285 3714) at PO Box 407, Curtin, ACT 2605.

In France try the CNFLRH (☎ 01 53 80 66 66) 236 bis rue de Tolbiac, Paris.

SENIOR TRAVELLERS

As already noted in the Health section, China is one vast reservoir of the influenza virus. The elderly are particularly prone, and pneumonia can be a fatal complication. Older travellers should be sure that their influenza vaccines are up to date and should not hesitate to seek medical care or leave the country if problems arise.

Aside from this, Beijing poses no particular problems for seniors.

BEIJING FOR CHILDREN

The treatment you'll receive if you're travelling with a young child or baby can often make life a lot easier in China. It opens up many more opportunities for conversing with the Chinese and therefore understanding their life, even if all they want is to have an opportunity to play with your kids. Don't be surprised if a complete stranger picks up your child or takes them from your arms: Chinese people openly display their affection for children.

Beijing is a city notable for its historical and architectural masterpieces, and while these may impress the adults, kids more likely will greet them with less interest. That is, until they spot the toboggans at the Great Wall at Mutianyu, the dinosaur park at the Old Summer Palace or the flying saucer boats at Beihai Park. These sorts of recent additions to China's tourist attractions are ubiquitous, and while they may be infinitely offensive to adults *sans* kids, they could well be the salvation of those travelling with children.

Besides this, there's no shortage of places in Beijing built to amuse China's Little Emperors. Favourites of Beijing expats include Ritan Park with its bumper cars and swings; Beijing Zoo; the Blue Zoo with its shark tunnel and next door Fundazzle, an indoor play centre with an Olympic-size pool filled with balls; the indoor ice skating rink at the China World Trade Center; and arts and crafts at Five Colors Earth in Poly Plaza. For more details on these places see the Things to See & Do chapter.

Keep in mind that Beijing's playgrounds may not be as safety conscious as similar places in your home country – a quick survey of equipment may be advantageous. It's also a good idea to take a sanitiser with you and to frequently clean your child's hands.

USEFUL ORGANISATIONS
Foreign Organisations

Several countries have full-time commercial offices in Beijing. The largest ones are:

American Chamber of Commerce (☎ 8519 1920, fax 6519 1910) Room 1903, 8 Jianguomen Beidajie, China Resources Building, Dongcheng, 100005

Australia-China Chamber of Commerce (☎ 6590 5566 ext 501) Room 314, Great Wall Sheraton Hotel, 8 Dongsanhuan Beilu, Chaoyang District, 100026

British Chamber of Commerce (☎ 6593 6611, fax 6593 6610) 31 Technical Club, 2nd floor, 15 Guanghuali, Jianguomen Wai Dajie, Chaoyang District, 100020

Canada-China Business Council (☎ 6512 6120, fax 6512 6125) 18th floor, CITIC Bldg, 19 Jianguomen Wai Dajie, Chaoyang District, 100004

Clubs

There are lots of small organisations in Beijing run by volunteers, examples being the Arts & Crafts Club, the International Choir, and Al-Anon and Alcoholics Anonymous. There are also clubs which focus on a particular nation or group of nations, such as the Dutch Club, African Solidarity Association, the Commonwealth Society and the British Club. The contact phone numbers for these organisations change frequently depending on who is willing to act as the club's liaison – it may even change several times a year. Check with your embassy to find out what is on offer and who to contact. The International Newcomers Network (see Orientation Programs later for details) also has a wealth of information on clubs in Beijing.

The Beijing International Society (BIS; ☎ 6532 2003) puts on lectures and excursions each month, from museum outings to guest speakers such as renowned Chinese writer Feng Jicai and lectures on Tibetan furniture. Membership to BIS is Y200 (Y100 for students) plus an additional fee for each outing (no additional fee for lectures).

Orientation Programs

The following organisations offer expat newcomers orientation programs that provide information on everything from choosing a school for your kids to finding housing.

Asia Pacific Access (☎ 6595 8754, 🖂 apaxess@public.bta.net.cn) Suite 115, 9 Ritan Donglu, Chaoyang District 100020. Offers a settling-in assistance program with expatriate women counsellors who provide information on everything from opening a bank account and where to shop to explaining the bureaucracy of the Chinese postal system and Beijing's social networks.

Europe Assistance (☎ 6526 0576, fax 6526 0570, 🖂 eabeijin@public3.bta.net.cn). Provides services covering a wide spectrum of expat needs: medical assistance, house searching, education for expat children, translators, travel services and paperwork handling. It's geared towards corporate accounts, though individuals can join. You can telephone or write for a brochure: Room 615, Tower B, COFCO Plaza, 8 Jianguomen Nei Dajie, Dongcheng 100005.

The International Newcomers Network (INN; 🖂 innchn@bigfoot.com). This organisation meets at 10 am every last Monday of the month in the Capital Club Athletic Center, 3rd floor (in Capital Mansions). Each meeting features a guest speaker who gives a presentation on topics ranging from where to buy furniture, carpets and jewellery to how to deal with culture shock and lectures on local traditions and festivals. INN also has a wealth of information on a wide range of services in Beijing – from schools to medical facilities to other clubs. Admission is Y30.

LIBRARIES
Chinese

The Beijing National Library (Map 3; Běijīng Túshūguǎn; ☎ 6841 5566) holds around 10 million books and four million periodicals and newspapers, over a third of which are in foreign languages. Access to books is limited and access to rare books is even more limited, though you might be shown a microfilm copy. The large collection of rare books includes surviving imperial works, such as the *Yong Le Encyclopedia* and selections from the old Jesuit library. Of interest to Ming-Qing scholars is the special collection, the *Shanbenbu* – you will not be permitted to check it out for home use. On the 3rd floor you can also access the Internet or watch Chinese and international films and listen to Chinese pop music. Foreigners aren't allowed to check books out, but you can buy a day pass for Y1 on the 3rd floor. The library is across Baishiqiao Lu west of the zoo and is open from 9 am to 5 pm every day except Sunday.

Western

Various embassies also have small libraries in English and other languages. Some of the more useful embassy libraries include the American Center for Educational Exchange (☎ 6597 3242), Room 2801, Jingguang New World Hotel, Hujialou, in Chaoyang District, and the Cultural and Educational Section of the British Embassy (☎ 6590 6903), 4th floor, British Embassy Annex, Landmark Tower, 8 Dongsanhuan Beilu, also in Chaoyang District.

UNIVERSITIES

Beijing is host to some 50 universities and colleges. The majority are in the Haidian District (north-west Beijing). If you want to make contact with foreign students, the largest concentration is to be found at the Beijing Language and Culture University (Map 2). Each campus with a foreign student population has at least one pub-restaurant where everyone goes to socialise in the evening. Finding these places isn't hard – locate the foreign student dormitory *(liúxuéshēng lóu)* on any campus and ask any likely looking person where the local hang-out is.

For making contact with the locals, the various pubs, clubs and discos (see the

Entertainment chapter) opposite Beijing University (Map 2) in the Haidian District are where students congregate after hours.

DANGERS & ANNOYANCES
Theft

Generally speaking, Beijing is very safe compared to other cities in the world its size. Crime against foreigners is seldom heard of, although some believe it is on the rise due to unemployment and the influx of people from rural areas who come to Beijing in search of work.

Some would say that the ridiculous overcharging of foreigners is the most common form of theft in China, but that happens to be legal. As for illegal crime, pick-pocketing is a problem you need to carefully guard against. In back alleys, a thief might try to grab your bag and run away, but far more common is the razoring of bags and pockets in crowded places like buses and train stations. If you want to avoid opening wallets or bags on the bus, keep a few coins or small notes ready in an accessible pocket before launching yourself into the crowd.

Hotels are usually safe places to leave your stuff; each floor has an attendant watching who goes in and out. If anything is missing from your room then they're going to be the obvious suspects since they've got keys to the rooms. Don't expect them to watch over your room like a hawk, though, because they won't.

Dormitories could be a problem: There have been a few reports of thefts by staff, but the culprits are more likely to be other foreigners! There are at least a few people who subsidise their journey by ripping off fellow travellers.

Most hotels have storage rooms where you check in your bags; some insist that you do. Obviously, do not leave your valuables (passport, travellers cheques, money, air tickets) lying around.

A money belt is the safest way to carry valuables, particularly when travelling on buses and trains. During the cooler weather, it's more comfortable to wear a vest (waistcoat) with numerous pockets, but you should wear this under a light jacket or coat since visible pockets invite wandering hands even if sealed with zips.

Perhaps the best way to avoid getting ripped off is to avoid bringing stuff you don't need – Walkmans, video cameras, expensive watches and jewellery all invite theft.

Spitting

The national sport, spitting is practised by everyone. All venues are possible – buses, trains and even restaurants. Never walk too close to a bus full of passengers, and try not to get caught in the cross fire elsewhere!

Technically, spitting is illegal in Beijing. But while anti-spitting wars (with fines for violators) are waged periodically – usually coinciding with a visit by an important foreign dignitary – in the countryside it's a free-for-all.

Queues

Basically, there are none. People tend to 'huddle' rather than queue, resembling American-style football but without the protective gear. You're most likely to encounter the situation when trying to board a bus or buy a train ticket. Good luck.

Beggars

The Beijing authorities have made an effort to reduce the number of beggars in the city (mostly by evicting them), but the destitute folks just won't disappear. While one should certainly be sympathetic to the poor, a real problem exists with professional beggars. Worst of all are the child beggars who practically have to be removed with a crowbar once they've seized your trouser leg. Child beggars are usually an organised operation, working under instructions from nearby older women who supervise them and collect most of the cash. There have even been stories of children being kidnapped, taken hundreds of kilometres from their homes and forced into these begging gangs.

LEGAL MATTERS
Crime & Punishment

Only the most serious cases are tried in front of a judge (never a jury). Most lesser crimes are handled administratively by the

Public Security Bureau. The PSB acts as police, judge and executioner – they will decide what constitutes a crime, regardless of what the law says, and they decide what the penalty will be. The ultimate penalty is execution, which serves the purpose of 'killing the rooster to frighten the monkey' or, to phrase this in official terms, 'It's good to have people executed to educate others'.

Chinese prisons generally operate at a profit. The prisoner's family often has to pay the cost of imprisonment, as well as the cost of the bullet if execution is the penalty.

Foreigners are very rarely executed, and imprisonment is only reserved for the most serious crimes. In most cases, foreigners who have had a run-in with the PSB are persuaded to write a confession and pay a fine. In some cases, foreigners are expelled from China (at their own expense).

Drugs

China takes a particularly dim view of opium and all its derivatives. The Chinese suffered severely from addiction after opium was foisted upon them by British traders in 1773 – they haven't forgotten! Marijuana is less well known by the Chinese, though some minority groups (including members of Beijing's Uyghur community) have a habit of smoking it. It's difficult to say what attitude the Chinese police will take towards foreigners caught using marijuana – they often don't care what Chinese do if Chinese aren't involved. Then again, you have to remember the old story about 'killing the rooster to frighten the monkey'. If you're planning to use drugs and don't want to become that rooster, discretion is strongly advised!

Getting caught smuggling drugs in China is bad news. Don't even think about it.

BUSINESS HOURS

China officially converted to a five-day working week in 1995, though some businesses still force their workers to put in six days. Banks, offices and government departments are normally open Monday to Friday. As a rough guide only, they open around 8 to 9 am, close for two hours in the middle of

the day, then reopen until 5 or 6 pm. Saturday and Sunday are both public holidays, but most museums stay open on weekends and make up for this by closing for one or two days mid-week. Travel agencies, the Friendship Store, foreign-exchange counters in the tourist hotels and some of the local branches of the Bank of China have similar opening hours, but are generally open on weekends as well, at least in the morning.

Many parks, zoos and monuments have similar opening hours; they're also open on weekends and often at night. Shows at cinemas and theatres end around 9.30 pm.

The restaurant situation has improved dramatically; nowadays it is always possible to find something to eat at any hour of the day.

Long-distance bus stations and train stations open their ticket offices around 5 am, before the first trains and buses pull out. Apart from a one- or two-hour break for lunch, they often stay open until midnight.

PUBLIC HOLIDAYS & SPECIAL EVENTS

Weekends and holidays aren't good for sightseeing. From the Great Wall to the shopping malls, it's like one giant phone-booth stuffing contest. Crowds thin out on Monday, but many museums are closed at that time.

Aside from Weekends, the PRC has nine national holidays during the year:

New Year's Day (Yuándàn) 1 January
Spring Festival (Chūn Jié) Otherwise known as Chinese New Year; it will fall on the following dates: 24 January 2001, 12 February 2002 and 1 February 2003
International Working Women's Day (Fúnǔ Jié) 8 March; celebrated in most Communist countries
International Labour Day (Láodòng Jié) 1 May; the closest thing the Communists have to a worldwide religious holiday
Youth Day (Qīngnián Jié) 4 May; commemorates the student demonstrations in Beijing on 4 May 1919, when the Versailles Conference decided to give Germany's 'rights' in the city of Tianjin to Japan
Children's Day (Értóng Jié) 1 June
Anniversary of the Founding of the Chinese Communist Party (Zhōngguó Gòngchǎndǎng Jiàndǎng Jié) 1 July

Anniversary of the Founding of the PLA (Jiěfàng Jūn Jié) 1 August

National Day (Guóqīng Jié) 1 October; celebrates the founding of the PRC in 1949

Spring Festival (Chūn Jié), otherwise known as Chinese New Year, is by far the biggest festival of the year. It starts on the first day of the first month according to the traditional lunar calendar. Although officially lasting only three days, many people take a week off work. Beijing pretty much empties out this time of year, as residents head to the provinces to visit relatives. Although this is not a good time of year to travel in China (trains are solidly booked), if you have accommodation in Beijing, this can be a good time of year to explore the capital. Temple fairs *(miào huì)* take place at parks and temples around Beijing. The most well-known of these are found at Ditan Park, Longtan Park, Yuyuantan, Lama Temple, Grandview Garden and White Cloud Temple. The fairs typically feature lots of food booths, arts and craft exhibits (the best paper-cuttings can be found this time of year), stilt dancers and, of course, dragon dancers. This is a great time to people-watch – Beijingers are decked out in their best new clothes and kids play with hoops and tops.

Fifteen days after the New Year is the Lantern Festival (Yuánxiāo Jié). It's not a public holiday, but it's a colourful time to visit Beijing. People take the time to walk the streets at night carrying coloured paper lanterns. It falls on the 15th day of the 1st moon, and will be celebrated on 7 February 2001, 27 February 2002 and 16 February 2003.

The birthday of Guanyin (Guānshìyīn Shēngrì), the Goddess of Mercy, is a good time to visit Taoist temples. Guanyin's birthday is the 19th day of the 2nd moon and will fall on 13 March 2001, 1 April 2002 and 21 March 2003.

Tomb Sweep Day (Qīng Míng Jié) is a day for worshipping ancestors; people visit the graves of their dearly departed relatives and clean their gravesites. They often place flowers on the tomb and burn 'ghost money' (for use in the afterworld) for the departed.

It falls on 5 April in the Gregorian calendar in most years, 4 April in leap years.

Beijing is probably at its prettiest on May Day (1 May), a holiday for Communists and officially known as International Labour Day. During this time, the whole city (especially Tiananmen Square) is decorated with flowers. Beijing also rolls out its marching bands and militaristic displays on National Day (1 October).

The Mid-Autumn Festival (Zhōngqiū Jié) is also known as the Moon Festival and is the time to eat tasty moon cakes. Gazing at the moon and lighting fireworks are popular activities, and it's also a traditional holiday for lovers. The festival takes place on the 15th day of the 8th moon, and will be celebrated on 1 October 2001, 21 September 2002 and 11 September 2003.

Special prayers are held at Buddhist and Taoist temples on full and new moon days. According to the Chinese lunar calendar, the full moon falls on the 15th and 16th days of the lunar month and the new moon on the last (30th) day of the month.

DOING BUSINESS

In bureaucratic China even simple things can be made difficult. Renting property, getting a telephone installed, hiring employees, paying taxes and so on can generate mind-boggling quantities of red tape. Many foreign business people working in Beijing and elsewhere say that success is usually the result of dogged persistence and finding cooperative officials.

If you have any intention of doing business in Beijing, be it buying, selling or investing, it's worth knowing that most urban districts *(shìqū)* have a Commerce Office *(shāngyè jú)*. If you approach one of these offices for assistance, the reaction you get can vary from enthusiastic welcome to bureaucratic inertia. In the case of a dispute (the goods you ordered are not what was delivered etc), the Commerce Office can assist you, provided it is willing.

Buying is simple, selling is more difficult, but setting up a business in Beijing is a whole different can of worms. If yours is a high-technology company, you can go into certain economic zones and register as a wholly foreign-owned enterprise. In this case you can hire people without going through the government, enjoy a three-year tax holiday, obtain long-term income tax advantages, and import duty-free personal items for corporate and expat use (including a car!).

An alternative is to list your company as a representative office, which does not allow you to sign any contracts in China – these must be signed by the parent company. To do this, first find out where you want to set up (the city or a special economic zone), then go through local authorities (there are no national authorities for this). Go to the local Commerce Office, Economic Ministry, Foreign Ministry or any ministry that deals with foreign economic trade promotion. In Beijing, the Haidian High-Technology Zone is recommended if you can qualify, but where you register depends on what type of business you're involved in. Contact your embassy staff first – they can advise you.

The most important thing to remember when you go to register a company is not to turn away when you run into a bureaucratic barrier. Bureaucrats will tell you that everything is 'impossible'. In fact, anything is possible – it all depends on your *guānxi* (relationships). Whatever you have in mind is negotiable, and all the rules are not necessarily rules at all.

Tax rates vary from zone to zone, authority to authority. It seems to be negotiable but 15% is fairly standard in economic zones. Every economic zone has a fairly comprehensive investment guide, available in English and Chinese – ask at the economic or trade section of your embassy, which might have copies of these. These investment guides are getting clearer, although even all their printed 'rules' are negotiable!

The Foreign Enterprise Service Corporation (FESCO; ☎ 6508 8287), at 14 Chaoyangmen Nandajie, is an organisation that most foreign businesses would like to avoid – it's where you are supposed to go to hire employees.

Business Services

You may find the following service-based companies handy:

Accounting

Arthur Anderson (☎ 6505 3333, fax 6505 1828) Unit 1118, 11th floor, Tower 1, China World Tower, 1 Jianguomen Wai Dajie, 100004

Price Waterhouse (☎ 6606 1155, fax 8529 9000) 18th floor, Kerry Center, 1 Guanghua Lu, Chaoyang District 100020

Advertising

Ogilvy & Mather (☎ 6443 6488, fax 6443 6498) 4th floor, Everbright Bldg, 1 Shengguzhong Lu, Dongcheng District

Saatchi & Saatchi (☎ 6510 2277, fax 6510 2278) 12th floor, Bldg 2, Bright China Chang'an Bldg, 7 Jiannei Dajie, Dongcheng District

Attorneys

Graham & James (☎ 8526 2020, fax 6500 2557) Suite 2002, CITIC Bldg, 19 Jianguomen Wai Dajie, 100004

Denton, Wilde & Sapte (☎ 6505 4891, fax 6505 4893) Room 3325, China World Trade Center, 1 Jianguomen Wai Dajie, 100004

Baker & McKenzie (☎ 6505 0591, fax 6505 2309) Room 2526, China World Trade Center, 1 Jianguomen Wai Dajie, 100004

Banking

China International Trust & Investment Corporation, main branch (CITIC; ☎ 6501 0554, fax 6500 4851), CITIC Bldg, 19 Jianguomen Wai Dajie, 100004; CITIC Headquarters (☎ 6466 0088 ext 8240), Capital Mansion, 6 Xinyuannan Lu, 100004

Computers (door to door repair services)
Hanru Tianzheng (☎ 1380 129 8900, fax 6254 9018) Room 306, Tower B Zhongke Dasha, 80 Haidian Lu, Zhongguancun; ask for David

Beijing Helping Technology Development Co Ltd (☎ 6848 6225, fax 6848 6225) Room 316, Zhongjing Tower, 72 Xisanhuan Lu, Haidian District 100037; specialises in Apple computers. Rates vary according to the problem, but expect to pay around Y200 for a home visit.

Computer rental

Jinsong Computer Company (☎ 6779 2070, fax 6775 8891) 2nd floor, Bldg 218, Zone 2, Jinsong, Chaoyang District

Insurance
Foreign companies are prohibited from selling insurance in China, so arrange insurance before you arrive.

Printing (name cards etc)
Alphagraphics (☎ 6465 1907, fax 6465 1906) S122 Lufthansa Center, 50 Liangmaqiao Lu, Chaoyang District;
(☎ 6505 2906, fax 6505 2908) 2nd floor, S206, China World Trade Center, Chaoyang District
Empire Quick Print (☎ 6592 9511, fax 6592 9510) 63 Dongdaqiao Lu, Jianguomen Wai Dajie, 100004

Translations
China Translation & Publishing Corporation (☎ 6515 6919, fax 6616 8211) 4 Taping Qiao St, Xicheng District
Sinofile (☎ 6605 9198, @ sinofile@sinofile.com) A85 Tonglinge Lu, Xicheng District

Visa Photos
Friendship Store Instant Photo 17 Jianguomen Wai Dajie
Landao Instant Photo Landao Department Store, 8 Chaoyangmen Wai Dajie
Lily Photo Ground floor, CITIC Bldg, 19 Jianguomen Wai Dajie
Lufthansa Instant Photo 4th floor, Lufthansa Center, 50 Liangmaqiao Lu

WORK

As Chairman Mao used to say, 'We all must be happy in our work'. Foreigners seeking happiness in Beijing often wind up teaching English or foreign languages. Teaching in China is not a way to get rich – pay is roughly Y2000 a month for about 12 hours of teaching per week. (This is almost twice what the average urban Chinese worker earns.) There are usually some fringe benefits like free or low-cost housing and subsidised medical care. Picking up teaching jobs that pay by the hour is usually more lucrative (although they don't provide housing). Rates are often upwards of Y150 per hour.

The main reason to work in China is to experience the country at a level not generally available to travellers. However, foreign teachers are usually forced to live in separate apartments or dormitories. Chinese students wishing to visit you at your room may be turned away at the reception desk; otherwise they may be required to register their name, ID number and purpose of visit. Since many people are reluctant to draw attention to themselves like this, they may be unwilling to come visiting at all.

In other words, teaching in Beijing can be a lonely experience unless you spend all your free time in the company of other expats, which of course deprives you of the 'China experience' you may be seeking. If you're interested in working in Beijing, contact the universities directly.

Besides teaching English, freelance writing for Beijing's expat magazines is also readily available work. Pay is usually about Y1 per word.

If you possess certain technical skills much in demand, you could possibly land a good-paying job with a foreign company in Beijing but plum jobs aren't easy to come by. The majority of foreign professionals working in Beijing are recruited from overseas; many have spent years employed in the company in their home countries. If your Chinese is fluent, your chances of finding an entry-level job in Beijing are much higher, although most likely you'll be considered a 'local hire' and earn in the range of US$1000 per month.

Most people find jobs in Beijing through word of mouth, so networking is the key. It's also worth keeping an eye on job listings in Beijing's expat rags – *City Edition* and *Metro* carry classified ads. The email newsletter *Xianzai Beijing* (see under Noticeboards & Email Newsletters earlier for subscription information) and the Web site www.chinanow.com advertise job listings. Also worth checking out are Web sites that carry job listings; try www.zhaopin.com and www.51job.com.

MOVING

If you're moving heavy stuff like furniture or all your household goods, you'll need an international mover or freight forwarder.

In Beijing, you can try any one of the following:

Asian Express (☎ 6510 1035, fax 6510 1049) Room 902, Tower 1, Bright China Chang'an Building, 7 Jianguomen Nei Dajie, Dongchneg District
Web site: www.aemovers.com.hk

Crown Worldwide Group (☎ 6585 0640; fax 6585 0648; ✉ general.cnbjg@crownworldwide .com) Room 201, West Tower, Golden Bridge Building, 1 Jianguomen Wai Dajie, Chaoyang District, 100020
Web site: www.crownworldwide.com

Global Silverhawk (☎ 6767 5566; fax 8769 4013) Chaoyang Port, 1 Dongsinanhuan Lu, Chaoyang District
Web site: www.globalsilverhawk.com

Sino Santa Fe (☎ 6514 1188, fax 6514 8080) Room 1005, COFCO Plaza, 8 Jianguomen Nei Dajie, Dongcheng District 100005
Web site: www.santafe.com.hk

TCI Worldwide Movers (☎ 6561 0575 ext 133, fax 6561 0577, ✉ tcibj@public3.bta.net.cn) Room 712, West Wing, Hanwei Plaza, 7 Guanghua Lu, Chaoyang District 100004
Web site: www.tciworldwidemovers.com

Getting There & Away

AIR
Departure Tax
International departure tax in Beijing is Y90. Domestic departure tax is Y50. This tax is not included in the price of the ticket and should be paid before check-in, in *renminbi*, at a special counter near the entrance to the airport. Make sure you have enough renminbi left over at the end of your trip to pay this tax – otherwise you'll have to revisit one of the currency exchange booths.

Other Parts of China
There is only one domestic air carrier in China (not including Hong Kong and Macau) – the Civil Aviation Administration of China (CAAC; Zhōnggúo Mínháng). From Beijing, CAAC's aerial web spreads out in every conceivable direction with something like 630 domestic air routes. Officially CAAC has been broken up into around 30 domestic and international airlines. This doesn't mean that CAAC is out of business, but it now assumes the role of 'umbrella organisation' for its numerous subsidiaries, which include China Eastern, China Southern, China Northern, China Southwest, and China Northwest.

CAAC publishes a comprehensive international and domestic timetable in both English and Chinese, which comes out in April and November each year. These can be bought in Beijing for about Y10 at the CAAC office inside the World Trade Center (Map 7). In Hong Kong the CAAC office hands them out for free.

Although it was once national policy for foreigners to pay 50% more than locals for air tickets, foreigners and Chinese now pay the same rate for domestic air travel. Children over 12 years are charged the adult fare. Legally, domestic air tickets are fixed by the government at a standard price and travel agencies catering to foreigners generally do not offer discounted domestic air tickets. However, some smaller travel agencies (illegally) offer discounted fares

(up to 20% off the standard fare). Check local Chinese-language newspapers for advertisements for discounted fares.

In theory you can reserve seats without paying for them. In practice, this often leads to disappointment: While staff at some booking offices will hold a seat for more than a week, other offices will hold seats for only a few hours so you can run to the bank and change money. Until you've actually paid for and received your ticket, nothing can be guaranteed. Usually, competition for seats is keen and people with connections can often jump the queue.

Cancellation fees depend on how long before departure you cancel. On domestic flights, if you cancel 24 to 48 hours before departure you lose 5% of the fare; if you cancel between two and 24 hours before the flight you lose 10%; and if you cancel less than two hours before the flight you lose 20%. If you don't show up for a domestic flight, you are entitled to a refund of 50%.

Even after you've purchased your ticket, it's possible to change the date or time of your flight at the airport (for example, if you miss your flight or want to get on an earlier flight) for no extra fee. After entering Capital Airport, but before entering the check-in area, there are several domestic airline counters – the agents here can help you change your ticket, buy a ticket or go on stand-by.

Other Countries
Tickets bought within China were once more expensive than those bought outside of China, but things are quickly changing. The Chinese government has loosened restrictions, resulting in increased competition and the current spate of price-slashing and deal-making by international airlines. New air carriers – Virgin Air is the latest, and negotiations were taking place with American Airlines at the time of writing – and air routes are constantly being added. The end result is that prices of tickets

57

Air Travel Glossary

Cancellation Penalties If you have to cancel or change a discounted ticket, there are often heavy penalties involved; insurance can sometimes be taken out against these penalties. Some airlines impose penalties on regular tickets as well, particularly against 'no-show' passengers.

Courier Fares Businesses often need to send urgent documents or freight securely and quickly. Courier companies hire people to accompany the package through customs and, in return, offer a discount ticket which is sometimes a phenomenal bargain. However, you may have to surrender all your baggage allowance and take only carry-on luggage.

Full Fares Airlines traditionally offer 1st class (coded F), business class (coded J) and economy class (coded Y) tickets. These days there are so many promotional and discounted fares available that few passengers pay full economy fare.

Lost Tickets If you lose your airline ticket an airline will usually treat it like a travellers cheque and, after inquiries, issue you with another one. Legally, however, an airline is entitled to treat it like cash and if you lose it then it's gone forever. Take good care of your tickets.

Onward Tickets An entry requirement for many countries is that you have a ticket out of the country. If you're unsure of your next move, the easiest solution is to buy the cheapest onward ticket to a neighbouring country or a ticket from a reliable airline which can later be refunded if you do not use it.

Open-Jaw Tickets These are return tickets where you fly out to one place but return from another. If available, this can save you backtracking to your arrival point.

Overbooking Since every flight has some passengers who fail to show up, airlines often book more passengers than they have seats. Usually excess passengers make up for the no-shows, but occasionally somebody gets 'bumped' onto the next available flight. Guess who it is most likely to be? The passengers who check in late.

Promotional Fares These are officially discounted fares, available from travel agencies or direct from the airline.

Reconfirmation If you don't reconfirm your flight at least 72 hours prior to departure, the airline may delete your name from the passenger list. Ring to find out if your airline requires reconfirmation.

Restrictions Discounted tickets often have various restrictions on them – such as needing to be paid for in advance and incurring a penalty to be altered. Others are restrictions on the minimum and maximum period you must be away.

Round-the-World Tickets RTW tickets give you a limited period (usually a year) in which to circumnavigate the globe. You can go anywhere the carrying airlines go, as long as you don't backtrack. The number of stopovers or total number of separate flights is decided before you set off and they usually cost a bit more than a basic return flight.

Transferred Tickets Airline tickets cannot be transferred from one person to another. Travellers sometimes try to sell the return half of their ticket, but officials can ask you to prove that you are the person named on the ticket. On an international flight tickets are compared with passports.

Travel Periods Ticket prices vary with the time of year. There is a low (off-peak) season and a high (peak) season, and often a low-shoulder season and a high-shoulder season as well. Usually the fare depends on your outward flight – if you depart in the high season and return in the low season, you pay the high-season fare.

bought within China compete well with those of tickets bought outside China.

Generally speaking, the free baggage allowance for an adult passenger is 20kg in economy class and 30kg in 1st class on both international and domestic flights. You are also allowed a maximum of 5kg of hand luggage, although this is hardly ever weighed. The charge for excess baggage is 1% of the full fare for each kilogram.

Hong Kong & Macau Although Hong Kong and Macau have been 'reunited' with China this doesn't apply to the airline business. Flights between Hong Kong and Macau and the rest of China are treated as international flights. This means you not only go through Immigration and Customs, but you also pay international rates (including international departure taxes). On the positive side, it also means that international standards of service and safety are maintained. That said, the government of the PRC allows only three carriers at present to fly the Beijing-Hong Kong route: Air China, China Eastern (both of which are PRC airlines) and Dragonair (Gǎnglóng Hángkōng), a CAAC-Cathay Pacific joint venture. Dragonair has better service than the others and sometimes even charges lower prices, but its flights are often fully booked. As Dragonair is closely integrated with Hong Kong's Cathay Pacific Airlines, you can book Dragonair flights from Cathay Pacific offices around the world.

The USA Discount travel agents in the USA are called consolidators (although you won't see a sign on the door saying that). San Francisco is the ticket-consolidator capital of America, although some good deals can be found in Los Angeles, New York and other big cities. Consolidators can be found through the Yellow Pages or the major daily newspapers. The *New York Times,* the *Los Angeles Times,* the *Chicago Tribune* and the *San Francisco Examiner* all produce weekly travel sections in which you will find a number of travel agency ads.

Council Travel, America's largest student travel organisation, has around 60 offices in the USA; its head office (☎ 800-226 8624) is at 205 E 42 St, New York, NY 10017. Call for the office nearest you or visit the Web site at www.ciee.org. STA Travel (☎ 800-777 0112) has offices in Boston, Chicago, Miami, New York, Philadelphia, San Francisco and other major cities. Call for office locations or visit the Web site at www.statravel.com. The Web site www.flychina.com offers good prices on air fares between the USA and China.

From the US west coast, low-season return fares to Beijing start at around US$650 with China Air, Northwest Airlines and United Airlines. Fares increase dramatically during the summer and Chinese New Year. From New York to Beijing, low-season return fares start at around US$800 with Korean Air, Northwest Airlines or United Airlines.

Canada Canadian discount air ticket sellers are also known as consolidators and their air fares tend to be about 10% higher than those sold in the USA. The *Globe and Mail,* the *Toronto Star,* the *Montreal Gazette* and the *Vancouver Sun* carry travel agent ads and are good places to look for cheap fares. Travel CUTS (☎ 800-667 2887) is Canada's national student travel agency and has offices in all major cities. Its Web address is www.travelcuts.com.

Canadian Airlines' return low-season fares from Vancouver to Beijing start at around C$1827.

Australia Quite a few travel offices specialise in discount air tickets. Some travel agents, particularly smaller ones, advertise cheap air fares in the travel sections of weekend newspapers, such as *The Age* in Melbourne and the *Sydney Morning Herald.*

Two well-known agents for cheap fares are STA Travel and Flight Centre. STA Travel (☎ 03-9349 2411) has its main office at 224 Faraday St, Carlton, Victoria, 3053, and offices in all major cities and on many university campuses. Call ☎ 13 1776 Australia-wide for the location of your nearest branch or visit STA's Web site at www.statravel.com.au. Flight Centre (☎ 13 1600 Australia-wide) has a central office at 82 Elizabeth St, Sydney, and there are dozens of offices throughout Australia. Its Web site is at www.flightcentre.com.au.

Low-season return fares to Beijing from the east coast of Australia start at around A$989.

New Zealand The *New Zealand Herald* has a travel section in which travel agents advertise fares. Flight Centre (☎ 09-309 6171) has a large central office in Auckland at National Bank Towers, corner of Queen and Darby Sts, and many branches throughout the country. STA Travel (☎ 09-309 0458) has its main office at 10 High St, Auckland, and has other offices in Auckland as well as in Hamilton, Palmerston North, Wellington, Christchurch and Dunedin. The Web address is www.sta.travel.com.au. Return low-season fares to Beijing start at NZ$1645 with Malaysia Airlines.

The UK Airline ticket discounters are known as bucket shops in the UK. Despite the somewhat disreputable name, there is nothing under-the-counter about them. Discount air travel is big business in London. Advertisements for many travel agents appear in the travel pages of the weekend broadsheets, such as *The Independent* on Saturday and *The Sunday Times*. Look out for free magazines such as *TNT*, which are widely available in London – start by looking outside the main train and underground stations.

For students or travellers under 26, popular travel agencies in the UK include STA Travel (☎ 020-7361 6161), which has an office at 86 Old Brompton Rd, London SW7 3LQ, and other offices in London and Manchester. Visit its Web site at www.statravel .co.uk. Usit CAMPUS Travel (☎ 0870 240 1010), 52 Grosvenor Gardens, London SW1WOAG, has branches throughout the UK. The Web address is www.usitcampus .com. Both of these agencies sell tickets to all travellers but cater especially to young people and students.

Other recommended bucket shops include: Trailfinders (☎ 020-7938 3939),

194 Kensington High St, London W8 7RG; Bridge the World (☎ 020-7734 7447), 4 Regent Place, London W1R 5FB; and Flightbookers (☎ 020-7757 2000), 177–178 Tottenham Court Rd, London W1P 9LF.

From the UK, low-season return fares to Beijing start at £430 with Air France and British Airways.

Continental Europe Though London is the travel discount capital of Europe, there are several other cities in which you will find a range of good deals. Generally there is not much variation in air fares from the main European cities; major airlines and travel agents usually have deals on offer, so shop around.

Reliable travel agency chains in France include: the French student travel company OTU (☎ 01-40 29 12 12), with a Web site at www.otu.fr; Nouvelles Frontieres (☎ 08 03 33 33 33), Web site www.nouvelles-frontieres .fr; and the Franco-Belgian company Wasteels (☎ 01 43 62 30 00), Web site www.voyages-wasteels.fr.

In Amsterdam, agencies with cheap tickets include the NBBS subsidiary Budget Air (☎ 020-627 1251), at Rokin 34; Web site www.nbbs.nl. In Copenhagen, STA Travel (☎ 33 141 501), Web site www.statravel .com, is at Fiolstraede 18; Kilroy Travels (☎ 33 11 00 44) is at Skindergarde 28. In Berlin, STA Travel (☎ 030-311 0950) has one of its many branches at Goethestrasse 73 (U2 stop: Ernst-Reuter-Platz).

Recommended travel agents in Rome include CTS Viaggi, whose many offices around Italy include one at 16 Via Genova (☎ 06-462 0431); and Passagi (☎ 06-474 0923), which is at Stazione Termini FS, Galleria Di Tesla. In Madrid, Usit Unlimited (☎ 902 25 25 75), Web site www .unlimited.es, is at 3 Plaza de Callao; Barcelo Viajes (☎ 91 559 1819) is at Princesa 3; and Nouvelles Frontières (☎ 91 547 4200) is at Plaza de España 18, Web site www.nouvelles-frontieres.es.

Airline Offices in Beijing

Although CAAC goes by a variety of aliases (Air China, China Eastern Airlines etc), you can purchase tickets for all of them at the Aviation Building (Map 6; Mínháng Dàshà; domestic ☎ 6601 3336; international ☎ 6601 6667). The same tickets can be bought at the CAAC office in the China World Trade Center (Map 7; ☎ 6601 7755) or from the numerous other CAAC service counters, like the one in the Beijing Hotel (Map 7) or the CITS counter in the International Hotel (Map 7).

If you speak Mandarin, you can make inquiries for all airlines at Beijing's Capital Airport (☎ 2580 from Beijing only). Other international airlines offices include:

Aeroflot (☎ 6500 2412) Jinglun Hotel, 3 Jianguomen Wai Dajie
Air France (☎ 6588 1388) 5th floor, Full Link Plaza, 18 Chaoyangmen Wai Dajie
Air Macau (☎ 6515 8988) Room 807, Scitech Tower, 22 Jianguomen Wai Dajie
Alitalia (☎ 6505 6657) 5th floor, West Tower, China World Trade Center, 1 Jianguomen Wai Dajie
All Nippon Airways (☎ 6590 9174) Fazhan Dasha, Room N200, 5 Dongsanhuan Beilu
American Airlines (☎ 6517 1788) c/o Beijing Tradewinds, 114 International Club, 11 Ritan Lu
Asiana Airlines (☎ 6468 4000) Room 134, Jianguo Hotel, 5 Jianguomen Wai Dajie
Austrian Airlines (☎ 6462 2161) S103, Lufthansa Center, 50 Liangmaqiao Lu
British Airways (☎ 6512 4070) Room 210, 2nd floor, Scitech Tower, 22 Jianguomen Wai Dajie
Canadian Airlines International (☎ 6468 2001) Unit C201, Lufthansa Center, 50 Liangmaqiao Lu
Dragonair (☎ 6518 2533) 1st floor, L107, China World Trade Center, 1 Jianguomen Wai Dajie
El Al Israel Airlines (☎ 6597 4512) Room 2906, Jingguang New World Hotel
Ethiopian Airlines (☎ 6505 0134) Room 0506, China World Trade Center, 1 Jianguomen Wai Dajie
Finnair (☎ 6512 7180) Room 204, Scitech Tower, 22 Jianguomen Wai Dajie
Japan Airlines (☎ 6513 0888) ground floor, Changfugong Office Building, Hotel New Otani, 26A Jianguomen Wai Dajie
KLM Royal Dutch Airlines (☎ 6505 3505) Suite 501, China World Trade Center, 1 Jianguomen Wai Dajie

Korean Air (☎ 6505 0088) Room 401, West Wing, China World Trade Center, 1 Jianguomen Wai Dajie
LOT Polish Airlines (☎ 6500 7215) Room 2002, Chains City Hotel, 4 Gongti Donglu
Lufthansa Airlines (☎ 6465 4488) S101, Lufthansa Center, 50 Liangmaqiao Lu
Malaysia Airlines (☎ 6505 2683) Room 1005, China World Trade Center, 1 Jianguomen Wai Dajie
Mongolian Airlines (☎ 6507 9297) 1st floor, China Golden Bridge Plaza, 1A Jianguomen Wai Dajie
Northwest Airlines (☎ 6505 3505) Room 2426, China World Trade Center, 1 Jianguomen Wai Dajie
Pakistan International Airlines (☎ 6505 1681) Room 106A, China World Trade Center, 1 Jianguomen Wai Dajie
Qantas Airways (☎ 6467 4794) Suite S120, ground floor, East Wing Office Building, Lufthansa Center, 50 Liangmaqiao Lu
Scandinavian Airlines (☎ 6518 3738) 1403 Office Tower 1, Henderson Center, 18 Jianguomen Wai Dajie
Singapore Airlines (☎ 6505 2233) Room L109, China World Trade Center, 1 Jianguomen Wai Dajie
Swissair (☎ 6512 3555) Room 201, Building 2, Scitech Tower, 22 Jianguomen Wai Dajie
Tarom (☎ 6500 2233 ext 2135) Jianguo Hotel, 5 Jianguomen Wai Dajie
Thai Airways International (☎ 6460 8899) S102B Lufthansa Center, 50 Liangmaqiao Lu
Turkish Airlines (☎ 6465 1867) Room W103, Lufthansa Center, 50 Liangmaqiao Lu
United Airlines (☎ 6463 1111) Lufthansa Center, 50 Liangmaqiao Lu
Yugoslav Airlines (☎ 6590 3388 ext 447) Room 414, Kunlun Hotel, 2 Xinyuan Nanlu

BUS
Other Parts of China

There are no international buses serving Beijing, but there are plenty of long-distance domestic buses. Although by far the majority of domestic travel is done by train, roads are improving and buses are becoming a real option. The bus journey to Tianjin, for example, is slightly faster than the train. Still, bus service is limited and good quality buses are relatively few.

In general, arriving in Beijing by bus is easier than departing, mainly because it's very confusing figuring out which bus station has the bus you need. The basic rule is that long-distance bus stations are on the perimeter of the city in the direction you want to go. The four major ones are at Beijiao (Map 2; north – also called Deshengmen), Dongzhimen (Map 5; north-east), Majuan (Map 7; east) and Haihutun (Map 2; south). Near the entrance to the Beijing-Tianjin Expressway is the Zhaogongkou bus station (Map 2), where you get buses to Tianjin. The Tianqiao bus station (Map 7) and Lianhuachi bus station (Map 6) are two places where you can get buses to sites south-west of Beijing.

There are a few small bus stations where tour buses and minibuses gather (usually just in the morning) looking for passengers heading to the Great Wall and other sites in the outlying areas. The most important of these is the Qianmen bus station (Map 7), which has two parts, just to the south-west of Tiananmen Square. Also useful is the Zhanlanguan Lu tour bus station (Map 3), which is just to the south of Beijing Zoo outside the Jishuitan subway station.

TRAIN
Domestic Trains

Most of China's railway system was blown to pieces in WWII and the subsequent civil war that brought the Communists to power. Since 1949, some 52,000km of train line has been built, a truly amazing achievement. Chairman Mao, when in power, travelled in a specially-built luxury coach – other rail traffic had to be diverted, causing chaos with the schedule. Nowadays this problem no longer exists and the trains run mostly on time.

China's trains are small towns in themselves, with populations typically well over 1000. Though crowded, trains are the best way to get around in reasonable comfort. The network covers every province except Tibet.

The safety record of the railway system is good. Other than having your bags pinched or suffering a heart attack when you see the toilets, there isn't much danger. However, the Chinese have a habit of throwing rubbish out the windows even as the train moves through a station. Avoid standing too close to a passing train, lest you get hit by flying beer bottles or chicken bones.

Stations All express trains (international and domestic) go through Beijing station (Map 7; Běijīng Zhàn) or Beijing West station (Map 6; Běijīng Xī Zhàn). Beijing West is China's largest and plushest station.

The other main stations are Beijing North (Map 2; Běijīng Běi Zhàn) and Beijing South (Map 6; Běijīng Nán Zhàn). Both these stations are served by suburban trains.

All train stations have left-luggage rooms *(jìcún chù)*, though sometimes you'll find them just outside the station itself. It usually costs about Y5 per day to store a bag.

Tickets As in the rest of China, you can purchase outbound tickets only – ie, if you're in Beijing, you can only buy tickets departing from Beijing, and not, for example, a ticket that goes from Xi'an to Beijing. Tickets can only be bought up to four days in advance, which includes the day you buy the ticket and the day you depart.

There are several places around the city to buy train tickets. It's cheapest if you buy them at the train station, but for a small surcharge you can get them at most hotel counters and ticket counters around the city or through travel agents; you can also order them by phone (☎ 6321 7188; Chinese language only) and have them delivered for a small fee. There is a train-ticket counter at the back entrance of the Great Wall Sheraton Hotel (☎ 6590 5210) that sells tickets for a small surcharge (substantially less than buying tickets from a hotel). It's open from 8 am to noon and 1 to 5 pm.

Both Beijing and Beijing West stations have special counters for foreigners to purchase tickets (the signs say 'International Passenger Booking Office'). The staff here speak passable English, but even if you can speak fluent Chinese you'll appreciate these special ticket windows as it saves you having to queue with the masses. At Beijing station (☎ 6563 3662) the foreigners ticket window is open daily from 5.30 am to 11 pm – at least those are the official times, but foreigners have often found the staff opening late and closing early. At Beijing West station (☎ 6321 4269) the foreigners ticket window is open 24 hours.

An alternative to all the above is to board the train with only a platform ticket *(zhàn-tái piào)*. These are available from the station's information booth for a few *jiao*. You then buy a proper ticket on the train. This method is usually more hassle than it's worth, but may be necessary if you arrive at the station with no time to get your ticket.

Hard-Seat Except on the trains which serve some of the branch or more obscure lines, hard-seat is in fact padded. But it's hard on your sanity – the hard-seat section tends to be spectacularly dirty, noisy and smoky, and you'll get little sleep in the upright seats.

Since hard-seat is the only thing most locals can afford it's packed to the gills. If you're lucky, you'll get a ticket with an assigned seat number, but in many cases you'll have no seat reservation and will have to battle for a seat or piece of floor space with 5000 other hopefuls.

Hard-seat can be endured for a day trip; some foreigners can't take more than five hours of it, while others have a threshold of 12 hours or even longer. A few brave, penniless souls have even been known to travel *long-distance* this way – some roll out a mat on the floor under the seats and go to sleep on top of the peanut shells, chicken bones and spittle.

Because hard-seat tickets are relatively easy to obtain, you may have to travel hard-seat even if you're willing to pay for a higher class.

Hard-Sleeper The carriage is made up of doorless compartments with half a dozen bunks in three tiers, and sheets, pillows and blankets are provided. It does very nicely as an overnight hotel. The best bunk to get is a middle one: the lower one is invaded by all and sundry who use it as a seat during the day; the top one has little headroom and loudspeakers which spew forth a cacophony of military music and pleas in Chinese not to spit or throw beer bottles out the windows. Smoking is increasingly prohibited in hard-sleeper, though attendants are generally lax

in enforcing the policy. Lights and speakers in hard-sleeper go out at around 10 pm.

Hard-sleeper tickets are the most difficult of all to buy; you almost always need to buy these far in advance.

Soft-Seat On shorter journeys (such as Beijing to Tianjin) some trains have soft-seat carriages. The seats are comfortable, overcrowding is not permitted and smoking is prohibited. If you want to smoke in the soft-seat section, you can do so only by going out into the corridor between cars. Soft-seats cost about the same as hard-sleeper and are well worth it. Unfortunately, soft-seat cars are a rarity.

Soft-Sleeper Luxury. Softies get the works with four comfortable bunks in a closed compartment – complete with straps to stop the top fatso from falling off in the middle of the night, wood panelling, potted plants, lace curtains, teacup sets, clean washrooms (or at least a higher chance of being somewhat passable), carpets (so no spitting) and often air-conditioning. As for those speakers, not only do you have a volume control, you can turn the bloody things off! Soft-sleeper costs twice as much as hard-sleeper, and almost the same price as flying – on some routes even *more* than flying! Soft-sleeper tickets are easier to come by than hard-sleeper simply because of the high price. However, with China growing more affluent, even soft-sleeper tickets are becoming elusive.

Upgrading If you get on the train with an unreserved seating ticket, you can find the conductor and upgrade *(bǔpiào)* yourself to a hard-sleeper, soft-seat or soft-sleeper if there are any available. This is sometimes the only way to get a sleeper or even a seat, but there are no guarantees.

If the sleeper carriages are full then you may have to wait until someone gets off. That sleeper may only be available to you until the next major station which is allowed to issue sleepers, but you may be able to get several hours' sleep. The sleeper price will be calculated for the distance that you used it for.

Travel Times & Train Fares from Beijing

destination	soft sleeper (Y)	hard sleeper (Y)	hard seat (Y)	soft seat (Y)	approx travel time (hours)
Baotou	316	209	131		15
Beidaihe	–	–	55	97	3
Changchun	379	249	137		11
Changsha	529	345	191		16
Chengde	–	–	41	95	4
Chengdu	642	418	231		31
Chongqing	658	430	238		32
Dalian	409	269	147		19
Dandong	400	263	143		19
Datong	159	108	54		5
Fuzhou	705	458	253		35
Guangzhou	705	458	253		24
Guilin	658	429	237		31
Hangzhou	554	363	200		16
Harbin	442	290	158		14
Hohhot	254	170	92		11
Hong Kong	1027	776	–		29
Ji'nan	205	137	73		5
Kunming	890	578	320		46
Lanzhou	600	390	215		26
Liuyuan	892	511	309		59
Luoyang	298	197	106		8
Nanjing	417	274	150		12
Nanning	770	499	276		31
Qingdao	326	215	116		10
Qinglongqiao	–	–	14	21	2
Qiqihar	529	345	191		16
Shanghai	499	327	179		14
Shenyang	286	191	103		7
Shenzhen	720	467	257		33
Shijiazhuang	139	96	21		3
Suzhou	472	309	170		15
Tai'an	241	149	92		10
Taiyuan	224	149	79		11
Tangshan	136	95	41	95	3
Tianjin	–	–	22	34	2
Turpan	985	639	354		72
Urumqi	1006	652	363		61
Xi'an	417	274	150		15
Xining	658	430	238		33
Yinchuan	458	301	165		21
Zhengzhou	264	175	94		7

The desperate may be allowed to sleep in the dining car after it closes. There is usually a small charge for this. It's not terribly comfortable but is less horrible than hard-seat.

Timetables Paperback train timetables are available, but in Chinese only. They are so excruciatingly detailed that it's a drag working your way through them; even Chinese people complain about this. Thinner versions listing the major trains can be bought at train stations for about Y2. You can also check schedules and fares for all domestic destinations throughout China on the Internet at http://train.cei.gov.cn (with Chinese-language only).

Food & Water Food is available on the trains and at stations. On all long-distance trains, railway staff regularly walk through the trains with pushcarts offering instant noodles, bread, bologna, beer and soft drinks. Boiled water is also readily available. Journeys longer than 12 hours qualify for a dining car.

Toilets The toilets in hard-seat carriages are unspeakable horrors. The facilities get a bit cleaner and nicer in hard-sleeper and soft-seat. However, all these devices are of the squat variety, and balancing yourself can be tricky. All the waste goes out a tube and straight onto the tracks, and for this reason you're not allowed to use the toilets while the train is stopped (the staff sometimes lock up the toilets if someone violates this rule).

Be sure to bring toilet paper. It's never supplied free, though you can sometimes buy it from vendors on the train. Most trains have sinks with running water, though don't be surprised if the taps don't work.

International Trains

Trans-Siberian The Trans-Siberian Railway and connecting routes comprise one of the most famous, romantic and potentially enjoyable of the world's great train journeys. Rolling out of Europe and into Asia, through eight time zones and over 9289km of taiga, steppe and desert, the Trans-Siberian makes all other train rides seem

like once around the block with Thomas the Tank Engine.

There is some confusion of terms here as there are, in fact, three railways. The 'true' Trans-Siberian line runs from Moscow to Vladivostok. But the routes traditionally referred to as the Trans-Siberian Railway are the two branches that veer off the main line in eastern Siberia to make a beeline for Beijing.

Note that these journeys cannot be 'broken' along the way: If you want to get off at, say, Ulaan Baatar you must buy a separate ticket.

Trans-Mongolian Railway The Trans-Mongolian (Beijing-Moscow, 7865km, six days) has been open since the mid-1950s and has become the route most synonymous with the 'Trans-Siberian' tag. It is marginally faster than the Trans-Manchurian but requires you to purchase an additional visa and endure another border crossing, although you do at least get to see the Mongolian countryside roll past your window. It travels north to the Mongolian border at Erenhot, 842km from Beijing; continues to Ulaan Baatar; reaches the last stop in Mongolia at Sukhe Bator; and from the Russian border town of Naushki, travels to Ulan Ude, where it connects with the Trans-Siberian line.

Trans-Manchurian Railway The Trans-Manchurian is the longer route (Beijing-Moscow, 9001km, 6½ days). The train travels north through the cities of Shanhaiguan, Shenyang and Haerbin before arriving at the border post at Manzhouli, 935km from Beijing. Zabaykal'sk is the Russian border post and it continues from here to Tarskaya, where it connects with the Trans-Siberian line.

Costs There are many things to consider in making the Trans-Siberian journey (costs, visas, accommodation in Moscow etc) and it's beyond the scope of this book. Lonely Planet's *China* guide has more information. In Beijing, you can buy tickets from CITS (☎ 6515 0093 ext 35) in the Beijing Tourist Building, across from the Gloria Plaza Hotel.

GETTING THERE & AWAY

Trans-Mongolian hard sleeper is Y1602 and Trans-Manchurian is Y1825. Tickets don't include the necessary visas; you'll need to arrange these yourself. If you want a package that includes train tickets, visas and hotel, try Moonsky Star (☎ 6356 2126, fax 6356 2127, ✉ monkeychina@compuserve.com), at the Capital Forbidden City Hotel, 48 Guanganmen Nanjie, South Building, 3rd floor, Xuanwu District, 100054.

Beijing-Vietnam There is a twice-weekly international train running between Beijing and Hanoi, which stops at Friendship Pass (the border checkpoint). You can board or exit the train at numerous stations in China. The entire Beijing-Hanoi run is 2951km and takes approximately 55 hours, including a three-hour delay at the border. Schedules are subject to change, but at present train No 5 departs Beijing on Monday and Friday, arriving in Hanoi on Thursday and Monday respectively. Going the other way, train No 6 departs Hanoi on Tuesday and Friday, arriving in Beijing on Friday and Monday respectively. Arrival and departure times are as follows:

station	to Hanoi train No 5	to Beijing train No 6
Beijing	10.51 am	5.18 pm
Shijiazhuang	1.32 pm	2.34 pm
Zhengzhou	5.25 pm	10.37 am
Hankou (Wuhan)	10.41 pm	5.26 am
Wuchang (Wuhan)	11.02 pm	4.59 am
Changsha	2.52 am	1.10 am
Hengyang	4.57 am	11.04 pm
Yongzhou	7.10 am	8.49 pm
Guilin North	10.26 am	5.33 pm
Guilin	10.52 am	5.12 pm
Liuzhou	1.26 pm	2.19 pm
Nanning	5.58 pm	10.30 am
Pingxiang	12.04 am	12.59 am
Dong Dang	3.30 am*	8.30 pm*
Hanoi	11.30 am*	2 pm*

Vietnamese Time

Beijing–Hong Kong Although Hong Kong is officially part of mainland China, the Beijing–Hong Kong train is an international route subject to Immigration and Customs controls.

This is the most luxurious train in China. It's also fast by China's standards, taking 29 hours to make the journey of 2470km (an average speed of 85km/h). There are three classes: hard-sleeper (Y776), soft-sleeper (Y1027) and deluxe soft-sleeper (Y1310).

At present, the train runs every other day. Train No 97 departs from Hong Kong's Hunghom station at 7.30 am, arriving in Beijing West station the next day at 1.10 pm. Train No 98 departs Beijing at 3 pm, arriving in Hong Kong at 8.40 pm. Note that the timetables on display in Beijing West station say 'Jiulong', the official Pinyin spelling for Kowloon.

BOAT

While Beijing is not on the ocean, there is a seaport 2½ hours away by train at Tianjin's port district of Tanggu. There are boats running between Tianjin and Kobe in Japan, and also to Incheon in South Korea.

For details on cruises between Incheon and Tianjin, ring the Tianjin Ferry Company (☎ 022-2339 4290). This popular ferry sails once every five days from Tianjin at 10 am and the journey takes a minimum of 28 hours. Expect to pay no less than US$120.

ORGANISED TOURS

China has two main government travel agencies and many smaller ones. The two biggest government-owned travel agents are China International Travel Service (CITS; Zhōngguó Guójì Lǚxíngshè) and China Travel Service (CTS; Zhōngguó Lǚxíngshè). In Beijing, CITS is known as the Beijing Tourism Group (BTG; Běijīng Lǚxíngshè). China Youth Travel Service (CYTS; Zhōngguó Qīngnián Lǚxíngshè) is smaller but known for cheaper service. For a list of China's tourist offices in China and abroad, see Tourist Offices in the Facts for the Visitor chapter. Aside from the big travel agents, there are booking counters in most of the major hotels.

Tours do ease the hassle, but that assumes your tour operator is good. There have been negative comments from travellers who have booked through CITS and CTS, but service is slowly improving.

The key players are:

Beijing Overseas Tourism Corporation (☎ 6515 8573, fax 6515 8381) 6th floor, Beijing Tourist Building, 28 Jianguomen Wai Dajie
Cathay International Tourist Corporation (☎ 6460 4813, fax 6467 7307) 19 Xinyuannan Lu, Dongzhimen Wai Dajie
Beijing Tourism Group (BTG; ☎ 6515 8562, fax 6515 8603) ground floor, Beijing Tourist Building, 28 Jianguomen Wai Dajie, behind the New Otani Hotel
China Women Travel Service (☎ 6523 1439, fax 6512 9021) 103 Dongsi Nan Dajie
China Youth Travel Service (CYTS; ☎ 6524 3388, fax 6512 0571) 23C Dongjiaomin Xiang Nei (the alley behind the Capital Hotel)
China Travel Service (Map 5; ☎ 6461 2577 ext 6415, fax 6461 2576, ✉ llf.oz@ctsho.com) CTS Building, 2 Beisanhuan Donglu. Although it's not a privately run travel agent, this branch of CTS is especially helpful with domestic travel arrangements and prices are on a par with private travel agents.
Imperial Tours (☎ 6590 1094, ✉ inquiry@ imperialtours.net) Jianhong Mansions B-18B, 13 Baijianzhuang Dongli, Chaoyang District. It's a small tour company run by expats living in Beijing. Its speciality is luxury tours of China that aim to show you an insider's view of the country.

Tour Operators Outside of China A number of travel agents in the West do China tours, although many are forced into some sort of cooperative joint venture with CITS or other government bodies. This means they use the same guides that CTS uses, and therefore your itinerary will be the same as if you took a CTS tour. However, some tour operators have foreign guides who accompany the group from home, so before booking a tour be sure to ask about this.

WARNING

The information in this chapter is particularly vulnerable to change: prices for travel are volatile, routes are introduced and cancelled, schedules change, special deals come and go, and rules and visa requirements are amended. Airlines and governments seem to take a perverse pleasure in making price structures and regulations as complicated as possible. You should check directly with the airline or travel agent to make sure you understand how a fare (and ticket you may buy) works. In addition, the travel industry is highly competitive and there are many lurks and perks.

The upshot of this is that you should get opinions, quotes and advice from as many airlines and travel agents as possible before you part with your hard-earned cash. The details given in this chapter should be regarded as pointers and are not a substitute for your own careful, up-to-date research.

Getting Around

THE AIRPORT

Beijing's Capital airport is 27km from the centre (Forbidden City area) or about 20 minutes by car (unless you get caught in a traffic jam). A spiffy new airport, built adjacent to the old one, opened just after the 50th anniversary of the PRC on October 1, 1999. Four times larger than the old terminal, the new terminal took four years to build at a cost of US$1.1 billion. It offers faster immigration services and a larger baggage claim area, not to mention a decent place to eat (at extremely inflated prices), duty-free shopping and even a beauty salon.

Generally speaking, Customs are pretty lax. Upon exiting the terminal it is very rare for your luggage to be searched.

Currency Exchange

A Bank of China, a Construction Bank and some automatic money-changing machines are located just outside the baggage claim area (after you pass through Customs). They offer a similar exchange rate as banks in the city (and probably a better rate than your hotel), so there's no need to wait till you're in the city to change your foreign currency into renminbi.

Post & Telephone

There's a small post office located in the departure hall, right as you enter the airport. If you need to make a phone call, you must buy a phone card; they are available in denominations of Y50 and Y100.

Left Luggage

Left-luggage facilities are located on the ground level of the airport. Luggage can be stored a maximum of seven days. Rates are reasonable and run to about Y10 per half-day.

Tourist Information & Hotel Booking

The arrival hall has a tourist information desk that has a hotel booking service. It can obtain substantial discounts on hotels around the city, so if you're looking to stay at a more upmarket hotel but haven't booked yet, it's worth stopping at this counter. The counter can also book CTS sightseeing tours of Beijing.

Flight Information

If you can speak Chinese, you can obtain domestic and foreign arrival and departure information by dialling ☎ 2580. Otherwise, your best bet is to call the airline representative in Beijing (see Airline Offices in Beijing in the Getting There & Around chapter).

TO/FROM THE AIRPORT

At the airport you'll be presented with a bewildering choice of buses into town: Several companies offer a service and new routes are being added all the time. The fact that the destinations are written exclusively in Chinese only adds a measure of confusion. Nevertheless, you shouldn't be intimidated as it's fairly easy to find a bus that will take you close to where you want to go; inside the airport terminal itself there's a service desk that sells tickets. All buses into town cost Y16, so just plonk down the money and tell them where you want to go. With ticket in hand, walk outside and keep muttering your destination – somebody will see that you get onto the right bus. In fact, almost any bus that gets you to a subway station will probably do. Save your ticket stub as you may have to return it to the bus driver when you disembark from the vehicle.

One company called Tongli currently operates three routes. Route A is probably the most popular with travellers. From the airport it goes to Sanyuanqiao, Yanshaqiao, Dongzhimen, Dongsishitiao and Beijing train station (Map 7; Běijīng Zhàn). Route B goes to Jinganzhuang, Xibahe, Hepingjie, Anzhenqiao, Beitaipingzhuang, Weigoucun, Zizhuqiao, Huayuanqiao, Hangtianqiao and Gongzhufen. Both of these buses can drop you at a subway station. Route C goes to Xinyuanli, Gongti, Dongdaqiao and

National Gallery (Zhōngguó Měishù Guǎn) north of Wangfujing (central area).

The Anle Bus Company offers two routes. The most popular route (route I) is to Xidan, which is close to the CAAC office (Map 6) west of the Forbidden City. It goes from the airport to Sanyuanqiao, Dongzhimen, Dongsishitiao, Chaoyangmen, Beijing train station and Xidan. Route II goes to Jinganzhuang, Xibahe, Hepingjie, Anzhenqiao, Madianqiao, Beitaipingzhuang, Jimenqiao, Weigongcun, Zizhuqiao, Hangtianqiao, Gongzhufen and Beijing West train station (Běijīng Xī Zhàn).

The official schedule for all of the above buses is once every 30 minutes between 5.30 am and 7 pm, but additional buses run during peak hours.

Some of the big hotels also run minibus shuttles. You do not necessarily have to be a guest of the hotel to use these, but you do have to pay. The price for the minibuses is higher than that for the regular airport buses.

Going from the city to the airport by bus can be quite complicated because it's hard to figure out exactly where the bus stops are. It's probably easiest to pick up the shuttle bus at the Aviation Building on Xichang'an Jie, Xidan District – this is the location of the CAAC ticket office. The bus departs on the opposite side of the street (south side of Xichang'an Jie), not from the car park of the Aviation Building. Lots of taxi drivers congregate here too. You may well have to ask someone where to find the bus stop, but don't bother asking any of the taxi drivers – they'll insist that the bus is either out of order, has gone bankrupt, or has driven off a cliff. You can also catch the bus to the airport from the building next door (north) to the Hilton Hotel. Another place to catch the bus is at the west door of the International Hotel. Buses leave every half hour from 6.30 am to 6 pm daily (Y16).

A taxi (using its meter) should cost about Y85 from the airport to the centre, including the Y15 toll for the airport expressway.

There is a well-established illegal taxi operation at the airport that attempts to lure weary travellers into a Y250 ride to the city. One man acts as a taxi pimp for a squad of drivers – he will usually solicit you while you're still inside the airport terminal building. It is advisable to ignore him, head out the doors and for the queue for the official taxis.

BUS

Sharpen your elbows, chain your wallet to your underwear and muster all the patience you can because you'll need it. Overstuffed buses are in vogue in Beijing, and you'd be wise to avoid these sardine cans at rush hours or on holidays. Given the crowds and lack of air-conditioning, you can expect the buses to be unbearably hot during summer. They're cosy in winter but difficult to exit from – try the nearest window. Fares are typically eight *jiao* depending on distance, but often it's free because you can't see (let alone reach) the conductor. Smoking is prohibited but spitting is not.

There are about 140 bus (*gōnggòng qìchē*) and electric trolley (*diànchē*) routes. This makes navigation rather tricky, especially if you can't see out of the window in the first place. Bus maps save the day.

One- or two-digit bus numbers are city core buses, 100-series buses are trolley-style, 200-series buses are night buses only, the 300 designation is for inner suburban lines and Nos 400 to 999 are for the outer suburbs. Buses run from around 5 am to 11 pm.

Minibus

These are more comfortable than the buses and definitely faster, but figuring out where the minibuses come and go from is tricky. Many simply follow the busiest bus routes and even display the same bus numbers, while others have only a sign in Chinese indicating the destination. Fares are between Y2 and Y6.

Double-Decker Bus

Special two-tiered buses for tourists and upper-crust locals, the double-deckers run in a circle around the city centre. They cost Y2 but you are spared the traumas of normal public buses – passengers are guaranteed a seat! The following routes hit major points around the city:

GETTING AROUND

1 Beijing West train station, heading east on Fuxingmen Dajie, Xichang'an Jie, Dongchang'an Jie, Jianguomen Nei Dajie, Jianguomen Wai Dajie, Jianguo Lu, Bawangfen (intersection of Jianguo Lu and Xidawang Lu)

2 Qianmen, north on Dongdan Beidajie, Dongsi Nandajie, Dongsi Beidajie, Yonghe Gong (Lama Temple), Zhonghua Minzu Yuan (Ethnic Minorities Park), Asian Games Village

3 Jijia Temple (the south-west extremity of the Third Ring Rd), Grand View Garden, Leyou Hotel, Jingguang New World Hotel, Tuanjiehu Park, Agricultural Exhibition Centre, Lufthansa Center

4 Beijing Zoo, Exhibition Centre, Second Ring Rd, Holiday Inn Downtown, Yuetan Park, Fuxingmen Dajie flyover, Qianmen Xidajie, Qianmen

6 Guofang University, Agricultural University, Beijing University, Qinghua West Gate, People's University, Weigongcun, Minzu Xueyuan, Beijing Library, Ganjiakou, Yuyuantan, Junshi Bowuguan, Beijing West train station

SUBWAY

Originally constructed as part of Beijing's botched air-raid shelter system, the east-west underground line (opened in 1969) was for a time restricted to Chinese citizens with special passes. Foreigners weren't permitted to ride on it until 1980.

The Underground Dragon now boasts three lines. Unlike most other subways, the crime rate is low (there is the odd pickpocket) and graffiti is nonexistent. Ashtrays are installed in the subway stations, just below the 'No Smoking' signs, but there are no toilets – staying dehydrated may be a smart move. The subway is less crowded than the buses, and trains run every few minutes during peak times. The carriages have seats for 60 and standing room for 200. Platform signs are in Chinese and Pinyin. The trains are *not* air-conditioned, so you suffer in summer but can enjoy a toasty ride in winter. The fare is a flat Y3 (Y2 for the Fuba line) regardless of distance. Trains run from 5 am to 11 pm.

The subway looks its age, and certainly needs upgrading. Lots of new lines are urgently needed to accommodate Beijing's ever-expanding population. The new eastern extension of the East-West Line (known as the Fuba line) is open, but unfortunately does not yet connect with the other two lines. The link between Tiananmen Xi and Xidan hasn't been completed, and to change lines at Jianguomen you need to exit the subway, pay for another ticket, then re-enter. The two lines are expected to connect by late 2000.

To recognise a subway station, look for the subway symbol, which is an English capital 'D' with a circle around it. The 'D' stands for *ditiě* (subway). Another way of recognising a subway station is to look for an enormous cluster of bicycles.

Subway Routes

The 16km Circle Line has 18 stations including Beijing Zhan and Xizhimen (the North train station and zoo).

The East-West Line has 13 stops and runs from Xidan to Pingguoyuan – a western suburb of Beijing, the name of which translates as 'Apple Orchard'. It takes about

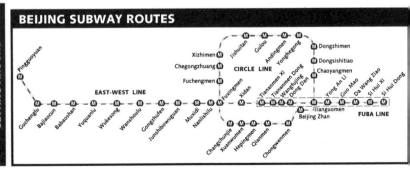

BEIJING SUBWAY ROUTES

40 minutes to travel the length of the line. Fuxingmen is where the Circle Line meets the East-West Line and there is no additional fare to make the transfer.

The new Fuba Line is an eastern extension of the East-West line. The first stop is at the north-west corner of Tiananmen Square and the last stop is in the eastern suburbs of the city (see the Subway Routes map).

CAR & MOTORCYCLE

The use of private vehicles by foreigners is tightly controlled. Resident expats with a Chinese drivers licence are allowed to drive their own cars anywhere within the environs of Beijing, Tianjin and their suburbs. They are not permitted to drive farther afield without special permission. Expats in Beijing say that the rule can be stretched a bit, but the farther from the capital you go the greater the risk of trouble with the local authorities. Foreigners busted for this particular offence have mostly been caught when checking into hotels far from Beijing.

Resident foreigners can also purchase a motorcycle, but the number of motorcycle licence plates available is tightly restricted – the Beijing municipal government wants to cut down on motorcycle use. Interestingly, these restrictions do not apply if you buy a motorbike with a sidecar – it's officially treated as a car! Sidecar or not, bikes are liable to be left lying around unused during Beijing's fierce winters, but they can be fun when the weather cooperates. In China both driver and passenger are required to wear a safety helmet; vehicles are driven on the right.

The licence plates issued to foreigners are different from those issued to the Chinese, and this is a bigger hassle than you might imagine. Since the licence plates go with the car, it means that a foreigner wanting to buy a used car must buy it from another foreigner.

Driving standards are not particularly good – nobody yields if they don't have to. Leaning on the horn is *de rigueur* – taxis might as well have a permanent siren attached. Apple cores, lit cigarette butts and spittle get unexpectedly launched out the window of the car in front of you. If you get into an accident, there is an accident hotline (☎ 122), although only Chinese is spoken.

Rather than do the driving yourself, it is much less hassle to hire a chauffeur-driven car. This can be arranged at major hotels, CITS or other travel agencies. Depending on the type of vehicle, a chauffeur-driven car could cost you as much as Y1000 per day. It's far cheaper to hire a *xiali* ('bullet taxi') by the day for about Y350 (see the following Taxi section).

Beijing Car Solutions (☎ 6501 1388, ✉ fresh@public.gb.com.cn), at Suite 304, Beijing Yatken, 22 Goan Dongdian Jie, Chaoyang District, offers a range of car-related services, including car rental, assistance in buying or selling a car, guidance in getting a Chinese drivers licence and help with all the accompanying paperwork, help with paying taxes and advice on insurance. New Concept Car Rental (☎ 800-810 9001, fax 6457 2035) rents cars to foreigners with a valid Chinese drivers licence. It has a rental counter at the airport.

TAXI

In 1986 there were fewer than 1000 taxis in the capital, so if you wanted one it had to be booked hours in advance. By 2000, the number of taxis exceeded 100,000. So finding a cab is seldom a problem, though during rush hours you may have to battle it out with 12 million residents. Taxis are always scarce during heavy rainstorms, and at such times the drivers often won't even take you if you want to go far afield.

One government brochure claims that 80% of Beijing taxi drivers can speak English. Perhaps they meant 80 drivers, since out of the total 100,000 that would be just about the right number. If you don't speak Chinese, bring a map or have your destination written down in characters. It helps if you know the way to your destination; sit in the front with a map. If you seem totally ignorant, you could be taken for quite a long ride.

The vehicles usually have a sticker on the window indicating their per-kilometre charge, which varies all the way from Y1.20 to Y2 with a Y10 minimum. If you don't get one with a meter, be sure to negotiate the fare for the trip in advance. Cabs can be hired for distance (use the meter), by the hour, or by the day (a minimum of Y350 for the day). You can usually get a cheaper rate if you say in advance, 'I don't need an official receipt' *(wǒ búyào fāpiào)*.

The yellow microbuses – affectionately called 'bread taxis' *(miàndī)* by the Chinese because they're shaped like a loaf of bread – have sadly been phased out of Beijing (due to their super-smog emitting exhaust pipes). They've been replaced by xialis, which cost Y10 for the first 4km or less, after which you pay Y1.20 for each additional kilometre.

Next up in the pecking order are the more sturdy Citroen cars that cost Y1.60 per kilometre. Top of the line are the petrol-guzzling limousine taxis which cost Y12 for the first section up to 4km and Y2 for each kilometre thereafter. Between 11 pm and 6 am a 20% surcharge is added to the metered fare.

Taxis can be hailed in the street or summoned by phone. For phone bookings, contact Beijing Taxi (☎ 6837 3399) or Capital Taxi (☎ 6487 2387). There is also a number to call for making taxi complaints (☎ 6835 1180; 6837 3320 for Beijing Taxi only).

If you're staying for a long time and you meet a taxi driver you like, ask for a name card. Most drivers have home phones, mobile phones or pagers (or all three) and can be hired for the day.

PEDICAB

Three-wheeled bicycles can accommodate one or two passengers in the back plus the driver up front. These look like a charming way to get around, but often they're not. What ruins it is that the drivers are aggressive and almost universally dishonest. The government should put meters on these things, because whatever fare you've agreed on in advance almost always gets multiplied by 10 when you arrive at your destination (or the driver will stop halfway and refuse to continue unless you agree to pay more). As a rule, it's almost never cheaper to take a pedicab than a taxi. Still, if you have the patience to spend some time good-naturedly bargaining, pedicabs can be a fun way to get around. They also come in handy because they can take you down small hutongs or routes otherwise difficult for cars to access.

BICYCLE

The scale of Beijing is much reduced on a bike, and bikes can also give you a great deal of freedom. Beijing's rush hour can be rather astounding, consisting of a roving population of more than three million bicycles – a fact explained by the agony of bus rides.

Hotels, especially budget hotels, often have bike hire. Bike-hire agencies tend to congregate around hotels and tourist spots – look for signs in English. Costs vary wildly, depending on the type of bike and where you rent it. Around the Jinghua Hotel you can score a heavy workhorse bike for Y10 per day, but a spiffy mountain bike can go for Y100 per day over at the Palace Hotel. One conveniently located rental shop, though, is the Dazhalan Bicycle Rental Shop (Dàchìlàn Zìxíngchē Shāngdiàn; ☎ 6303 5303) at the western end of Dazhalan (Dàchìlàn), right next to the gate at the end of the street. You can rent a bike here for Y10 per day plus a Y100 to Y300 deposit (depending on the type of bike you rent). The shop is open from 9 am to 6.30 pm daily.

If you're looking to buy a bike, good-quality ones can be bought from Giant (☎ 6403 4537) at 77 Jiaodaokou Dongdajie. Much cheaper are Flying Pigeons, which can be found at any of the numerous bicycle shops around the city. Giants start at around Y500, whereas Flying Pigeons can be had for around Y250.

Bike theft is a big problem. You might want to consider using your own cable lock (they can be bought in department stores, rather than the ones provided by bike vendors.

Several shopping areas are closed to cyclists from 6 am to 6 pm; Wangfujing is an important one. Bike parks are everywhere and cost peanuts (1 to 2 jiao) – compulsory peanuts since your trusty steed can be towed away if you're not careful. Roadside puncture repair kits cost around Y5.

On Your Bike

It's Beijing's broad avenues, tree-lined side streets and narrow hutongs (winding alleyways, some of which date back 500 years) that lend the city its unique character. A taxi goes either too quickly for you to catch the details, or too slowly to sustain interest. Chronic traffic jams can make bicycle travel not just more adventurous, but more efficient as well.

Beijing city is a sprawling metropolis with six million inhabitants, but it is flat and ideal for cycling. Much of Beijing life is lived on the street, too. For an evening's entertainment, people fly kites or throw Frisbees in Tiananmen Square. Elsewhere, under the Imperial Palace walls, young people dance to rock, and older ones gather for ballroom dancing. Clusters of neighbours squat under streetlights to gossip and play cards. Street stalls offer kitchenware, silk, vegetables, noodles and even banquets. Repairmen, upholsterers and house painters jostle on footpaths with their tool boxes.

You may cycle past dentists extracting teeth, barbers doing short-back-and-sides, teenage boys shooting pool, old men taking constitutionals, caged birds in hand. Magicians, 'miracle medicine' salesmen and all sorts of other street performers compete for attention. Tables spill out of restaurants onto the pavement, and brawlers tumble out of bars and karaoke clubs.

Cars, trucks, motorcycles and buses caught in the hideous traffic jams of the inner city rev their motors impatiently. Tempers flare and great bouts of cursing and counter-cursing add to the commotion.

The bustle can seem daunting. But you quickly work out how to weave around the horse-drawn carts and negotiate the buses and trams that seem to dip into the bike lanes from nowhere. You learn that crossing large intersections is best done in clusters; opportunistic alliances that are tight as the traffic policemen's white gloves. You find that, unless it's very late, there's almost nowhere you can break down, or get a flat, that's too far from the roadside stand of an itinerant bicycle repairman. With luck, you won't discover that the easiest way to get into a fight in Beijing is to run into another bicycle.

There are places in Beijing that really only ought to be seen by bicycle; places of such magic that only the breeze on your face convinces you they're for real. One is the moat around the Forbidden City, traversable around the eastern side of the palace. On one side of the path the clay-red wall of the Imperial Palace, with its crenellated battlements, rears up. Ornamental guard towers with flying eaves and roofs of gold jag into view at each corner. On the other, through weeping willows, you see lotuses and fishermen lounging as pleasure boats stir up ripples on the still water of the moat. Fabulous by day, the moat is enchanting by night. If you start at the front of the palace, by Tiananmen Square, when you come out the back you're just a short ride to the even more spectacular 'back lakes' – Houhai and Shishahai.

Villas that once belonged to princes (now the abodes of the communist nomenklatura) line these man-made lakes, along with sprawling *dazayuar,* labyrinthine courtyard houses shared by dozens of families. The majestic Drum Tower, where once imperial timekeepers beat out the hours of the day, looms over the scene. In summer, the paths are lively with strollers, lovers and locals trying their luck with rod and reel. In winter, a blanket of snow freshens the Beijing grey; no sooner does the lake freeze over than it swarms with skaters.

Linda Jaivin

Linda Jaivin is a writer and translator. Her books include Confessions of an S&M Virgin, Eat Me *and* Rock n Roll Babes from Outer Space.

Billboards around Beijing depict the gory results of cyclists who didn't look where they were going. They also give tips on how to avoid accidents and show 're-education classes' for offenders who have had several accidents.

To avoid becoming a feature in the next billboard display, take care when you're on your bike. Beijing in winter presents special problems, like slippery roads (black ice) and frostbite. The fierce winds during springtime present another challenge –

cycling conditions aren't exactly optimum, but if you follow the example of the hardy locals nothing will deter you. Riding at night can also be hazardous, in large part because few Chinese bikes are equipped with lights.

Bringing your own bike to China is not recommended, because local ones are cheap and good enough for all but long-distance tours. However, consider bringing your own helmet, as they aren't worn in China.

Dragon Tours

Tour BS-701
Badaling Great Wall and Ming Tombs; departs 8.30 am, returns 5.30 pm daily (Y320).

Tour BS-702
Tiananmen, Forbidden City and Temple of Heaven; departs 8.30 am, returns 3.30 pm Tuesday, Thursday and Saturday (Y300).

Tour BS-703
Summer Palace, Lama Temple and Beijing Zoo; departs 8.30 am, returns 3.30 pm Monday, Wednesday and Friday (Y280).

Tour BS-704
Tiananmen Square, Forbidden City, Summer Palace and Temple of Heaven; departs 8.30 am, returns 5.30 pm Monday, Wednesday, Friday and Sunday (Y350).

Tour BS-705
Mutianyu Great Wall; departs noon, returns 5 pm Tuesday, Thursday and Saturday (Y230). Departs from the Jianguo Hotel (11.40 am), Beijing Tourism Building (11.50 am), Great Wall Sheraton (12.15 pm), Kunlun Hotel (12.20 pm), Radisson SAS Hotel (12.30 pm).

Tour BS-706
Old Beijing on Rickshaw (explore the hutongs by pedicab); departs 8.30 am, returns 11.30 am daily (Y180). Departs 200m west of the north entrance of Beihai Park.

Tour BS-707
Half Day City Tour: Tiananmen Square and Gate Tower, Mao Mausoleum, CCTV Tower; departs noon, returns 4 pm Monday, Wednesday and Friday (Y230). Departs from SAS Hotel (11.40 am), Kunlun Hotel (11.50 am), Landmark Hotel (11.55 am), Jianguo Hotel (12.10 pm), Scitech and Tourism Building (12.15 pm), Wanfujing Grand Hotel (12.30 pm).

Tours BS-701 to 704 depart between 8.10 and 9 am from the following hotels: Holiday Inn Crowne Plaza, Radisson SAS, Landmark, Kunlun, Hilton, Jingguang, China World, Jianguo and Scitech, as well as the Beijing Tourism Building. Call ahead for the exact times of departure.

Tickets can be purchased from the Tourism Building (☎ 6515 8566), Jianguo Hotel, Scitech Hotel, Kunlun Hotel, Landmark Hotel, Radisson SAS Hotel and the Wangfujing Grand Hotel.

ORGANISED TOURS

CITS offers a number of 'Dragon Tours' – the name refers to the cute logo on the side of the tour bus (see the boxed text 'Dragon Tours').

Bookings can be made at the Beijing Tourist Group (BTG; ☎ 6515 8562, fax 6515 8603) at 28 Jianguomen Wai Dajie, behind the New Otani Hotel and near Scitech Plaza, or from the service counters at the Jianguo, Scitech, Kunlun and Radisson SAS Hotels. On tours that extend past noon, lunch is thrown in 'free'. There are pick-up points for these tours at many hotels, so inquire when you book.

Many travellers have recommended the BS-706 tour – guests are transported by pedicab around the hutongs, with stops at the Drum Tower, a local family's courtyard house and Prince Gong's Palace.

GETTING AROUND

Things to See & Do

HIGHLIGHTS

There is so much to see in Beijing it's difficult to know where to begin. Many people start with Qianmen, Tiananmen Square and the Forbidden City, followed by a jaunt through nearby Jingshan and Beihai Parks. Another busy day could be spent at the Summer Palace. And a bike ride or pedicab tour through Beijing's fast-disappearing *hutong* is well worth the time.

SQUARES, GATES & HALLS
Tiananmen Square (Map 7)
Tiān'ānmén Guǎngchǎng 天安门广场

Though it was a gathering place and the site of government offices in the imperial days, Tiananmen Square is Mao's creation, as is Chang'an Jie, the street leading onto it. It's the world's largest square, a vast desert of pavement and photo booths. Major rallies took place here during the Cultural Revolution when Mao, wearing a Red Guard armband, reviewed parades of up to a million people. In 1976 another million people jammed the square to pay their last respects. In 1989 PLA tanks and soldiers cut down pro-democracy demonstrators here. Today the square is a place for people to wander and fly kites or buy balloons for the kiddies.

Surrounding or studding the square is a mishmash of monuments past and present: Tiananmen (Gate of Heavenly Peace), the Chinese Revolution History Museum, the Great Hall of the People, Qianmen (Front Gate), the Mao Mausoleum and the Monument to the People's Heroes.

If you get up early you can watch the **flag-raising ceremony** at sunrise, performed by a troop of PLA soldiers drilled to march at precisely 108 paces per minute, 75cm per pace. A flag-lowering ceremony is similarly performed at sunset, but you can hardly see the soldiers for the throngs gathered to watch. Most foreigners don't find it all that inspiring, but the Chinese queue for hours to get a front-row view.

Tiananmen (Map 7 & Forbidden City Map)
Tiān'ānmén 天安门

Tiananmen (Gate of Heavenly Peace) is a national symbol which pops up on everything from airline tickets to policemen's caps. The gate was built in the 15th century and restored in the 17th. From imperial days it functioned as a rostrum for dealing with or proclaiming to the assembled masses. There are five doors to the gate, and in front of it are seven bridges spanning a stream. The use of each of these bridges was restricted to certain people and only the emperor could use the central door and bridge. The dominating feature is now the gigantic **portrait of Mao**. To the left of the portrait is a slogan in Chinese 'Long Live the People's Republic of China' and to the right is another, 'Long Live the Unity of the Peoples of the World'.

You pass through Tiananmen Gate on your way into the Forbidden City (assuming you enter from the south side). There is no fee for walking through the gate, but to go upstairs and look down on the square costs Y15. It's open 8.30 am to 4.30 pm daily.

Qianmen (Map 7)
Qiánmén 前门

Qianmen (Front Gate) sits on the south side of Tiananmen Square. Qianmen guarded the wall dividing ancient Inner City and outer suburban zone, and dates back to the reign of Emperor Yongle, who ruled in the 15th century. With the disappearance of the city walls that once extended from it, the gate has had its context removed, but it's still an impressive sight.

There are two gates – the southern one is known as the Arrow Tower (Jiàn Lóu) and the northern (or rear) one is called the Main Gate (Zhèngyángmén), or the City Building (Chéng Lóu). You can go upstairs into the Main Gate for Y3.

Great Hall of the People (Map 7)

Rénmín Dàhuì Táng 人民大会堂

The Great Hall of the People is the venue of the rubber-stamp legislature, the National People's Congress. It's open to the public when the Congress is not sitting, and to earn some hard currency it's even rented out occasionally to foreigners for conventions! As you tramp through the halls of power, many of them named after provinces and regions of China and decorated appropriately, you can see the 5000-seat banquet room and the 10,000-seat auditorium with the familiar red star embedded in a galaxy of lights in the ceiling. The hall was completed over a 10-month period from 1958 to 1959.

The hall is on the western side of Tiananmen Square and admission costs Y15. When there aren't any special events taking place it's open from 9 am to 2 pm daily. Photography *is* permitted so you needn't check in cameras or bags.

MONUMENTS & MAUSOLEUMS
Monument to the People's Heroes (Map 7)

Rénmín Yīngxióng Jìniàn Bēi
人民英雄纪念碑

On the site of the old Outer Palace Gate at the southern end of Tiananmen Square, the Monument to the People's Heroes was completed in 1958. The 36m obelisk, made of Qingdao granite, bears bas-reliefs of key revolutionary events (one depicts opium being destroyed in the 19th century) as well as appropriate calligraphy from Mao Zedong and Zhou Enlai.

Mao Zedong Mausoleum (Map 7)

Máo Zhǔxí Jìniàn Táng 毛主席纪念堂

The '*Mao*soleum' (as expats call it) was opened in 1977 and is where Mao's body is kept on display.

Mao died on 8 September 1976; the ruling Politburo voted just hours later to preserve his body for two weeks, then extended the mandate to 'perpetuity'. Mao's personal physician, Dr Li Zhisui, was most alarmed about this as he had no idea how to preserve a dead body permanently. In his book, *The Private Life of Chairman Mao,* Dr Li reveals that a wax Mao figure was constructed just in case the preservation techniques didn't work. According to Dr Li, both the real Mao and the wax dummy are stored in a vault below the public viewing area, and a lift is used to move the body (or the wax, as the case might be) to where it can be seen by the public.

However history will judge Mao, his impact on its course was enormous. Easy as it now is to vilify his deeds and excesses, many Chinese show deep respect when confronted with his physical presence. CITS guides freely quote the old 7:3 ratio on Mao that first surfaced in 1976 – Mao was 70% right and 30% wrong (what, one wonders, are the figures for CITS itself?) and this is now the official Party line.

The atmosphere in the inner sanctum is one of hushed reverence. Foreigners are advised to avoid loud talk, and not to crack jokes or indulge in other behaviour that will get you arrested.

The mausoleum is open from 8.30 to 11.30 am daily; entry is free but bags and cameras must be left at a booth across the street which charges Y10. Join the enormous queue of Chinese sightseers, but don't expect more than a quick glimpse of the body as you file past the sarcophagus. At certain times of year, the body (or wax) requires maintenance and is not on view.

Whatever Mao might have done to the Chinese economy while he was alive, sales of Mao memorabilia are certainly giving the free market a boost these days. At the souvenir stalls near the mausoleum you can pick up Chairman Mao key rings, thermometers, face towels, handkerchiefs, sun visors, address books and cartons of cigarettes – a fitting tribute to the chain-smoking Mao.

MUSEUMS

As far as travellers are concerned, Beijing's museums are worthwhile visiting but pretty poorly presented: Signs and other information in the museums are very rarely in English.

Chinese Revolution History Museum (Map 7)

Zhōngguó Gémìng Lìshǐ Bówùguǎn
中国革命历史博物馆

Housed in a sombre building on the east side of Tiananmen Square, the Chinese Revolution History Museum was for a long time made impenetrable by special permission requirements. From 1966 to 1978 the museum was closed so that history could be revised in the light of recent events.

The presentation of history poses quite a problem for the Chinese Communist Party, which has failed to publish anything of note on its own history since it gained power. This is due to the reams of carefully worded revision that would be required according to what tack politics (here synonymous with history) might take, making it best left unwritten.

There are actually two museums here combined into one – the Museum of History and the Museum of the Revolution. The Museum of History has English explanations for about a third of the displays (although you can rent an audio guide in English for Y40 plus a Y400 deposit), whereas the Museum of the Revolution has simple English explanations throughout.

The Museum of History contains artefacts and cultural relics (many of them copies) from year zero to 1919, subdivided into early human societies, slavery, feudalism and capitalism/imperialism, laced with Marxist commentary.

The Museum of the Revolution is divided into five distinct sections: the founding of the Chinese Communist Party (1919–21), the First Civil War (1924–27), the Second Civil War (1927–37), resistance against Japanese forces (1937–45) and the Third Civil War (1945–49). There are English explanations throughout the museum.

It's open from 8.30 am to 3.30 pm daily except Monday, and admission costs Y5 for the Museum of Chinese History and Y3 for the Museum of the Revolution.

Military Museum (Map 6)

Jūnshì Bówùguǎn 军事博物馆

The Military Museum traces the genesis of the PLA from 1927 to the present and has some interesting exhibits: pictures of Mao in the early days, astonishing socialist-realist artwork, captured American tanks from the Korean War and other tools of destruction.

The museum is on Fuxingmen Wai Dajie on the western side of the city; to get there take the subway to Junshibowuguan station. The museum is open from 8.30 am to 4 pm daily and admission is Y5.

Natural History Museum (Map 7)

Zìrán Bówùguǎn 自然博物馆

The four main exhibition halls of the Natural History Museum are devoted to flora and fauna, ancient fauna and human evolution. Some of the more memorable exhibits include a human cadaver cut in half to show the insides and a complete dinosaur skeleton. There are also displays of animal specimens preserved in bottles. Some of the exhibits were donated by the British Museum, the American Museum of Natural History and other foreign sources.

The Natural History Museum is located at 126 Tianqiao Nandajie, just north of Tiantan Park's west gate. It's open from 8.30 am until 5 pm daily, and admission is Y15.

China Art Gallery (Map 4)

Zhōngguó Měishù Guǎn 中国美术馆

During the Cultural Revolution one of the safest occupations for an artist was to retouch classical-style landscapes with red flags, belching factory chimneys or bright red tractors. Nowadays things have loosened up a lot and artists in China are finding much more freedom of expression (see the 'Contemporary Art' boxed text in the Facts about Beijing chapter). You can get some idea of the state of the arts in China at the China Art Gallery. At times very good exhibitions of current work, including photo displays, are held in an adjacent gallery.

The gallery is just north-east of the Forbidden City on Chaoyangmen Nei Dajie. It's open from 9 am to 4 pm Tuesday to Sunday. Admission is Y4.

continued on page 93

THE PALACES OF BEIJING

As China's capital, Beijing has acquired many imperial residences over the centuries, including housing for the emperors' eunuchs, consorts, concubines and servants. It should not be forgotten that this is still the capital, and the construction of 'palaces' continues, albeit in different forms.

Forbidden City

Zĭjìn Chéng 紫禁城

The Forbidden City, so called because it was off limits to commoners for 500 years, is the largest and best-preserved cluster of ancient buildings in China. It was home to two dynasties of emperors, the Ming and the Qing, who didn't stray from this pleasure dome unless they absolutely had to.

The Beijing authorities insist on calling the complex the Palace Museum (Gùgōng). It's open from 8.30 am to 5 pm daily and last admission tickets are sold at 3.30 pm. Tickets cost Y30; for another Y30 you can rent a cassette tape for a self-guided tour narrated by none

Right: Thomas Allom travelled through China in the mid-1800s, recording what he saw. This etching, showing the Qing dynasty Emperor Daoquang reviewing his palace guards in the Forbidden City, is from his 1843 book, *China, its Scenery, Architecture & Social Habits*.

other than Roger Moore (of James Bond fame). Tape players are available free but you need to give a refundable Y300 (or your passport) for deposit – you can use your own Walkman instead. For the tape to make sense you must enter the Forbidden City from the south gate and exit from the north. Tapes are available in a myriad of languages. Watch out for unscrupulous characters who will do their best to convince you that you must have an official guide to see the palace: It isn't true.

It's worth mentioning that many foreign tourists get the gate at Tiananmen confused with the Forbidden City entrance because the two are physically attached and they're not labelled with signs in English. As a result, some people wind up purchasing the Tiananmen admission ticket by mistake, not realising that this only gains you admission to the upstairs portion of the gate. To find the Forbidden City ticket booths, keep walking north until you can't walk any further without paying.

History

The basic layout of the city was established between 1406 and 1420 by Emperor Yongle, who made use of battalions of labourers and craftspeople – by some estimates there may have been up to a million of them – to build it. From this palace the emperors governed China, often rather erratically as they tended to become lost in this self-contained little world and allow real power to wind up in the hands of the court officials, eunuchs and whoever else was close to the halls of power.

Most of the buildings you can see now are post-18th century, as are a lot of restored or rebuilt structures around Beijing. The largely wooden palace was a pyromaniac's dream and was constantly going up in flames – a lantern festival combined with a sudden gust of Gobi wind would easily do the trick, as would a fireworks display. Fires were also deliberately lit by court eunuchs and officials who could get rich off the repair bills. In 1664 the Manchus stormed in and burned the palace to the ground.

It was not just the buildings that went up in smoke, but also rare books, paintings, calligraphy and anything else that was flammable. In the 20th century there were two major lootings of the palace: first by Japanese forces, and second by the Kuomintang, who on the eve of the Communist takeover in 1949 removed thousands of crates of relics and carted them off to Taiwan, where they are now on display in Taipei's National Palace Museum (worth seeing). Perhaps this was just as well, since the Cultural Revolution turned much of China's precious artwork into confetti. The gaps left by the removal of these treasures have been filled by other treasures, old and newly manufactured, from other parts of China. Of these, only a small percentage is on display. Plans are afoot to construct an underground museum in order to exhibit more of the collection.

Top: The Summer Palace mixes the cooling elements of water, gardens and hills.

Middle: Enjoying Jasper Pavilion reflects a little of the Old Summer Palace's former glory.

Bottom: The Marble Boat was Empress Dowager Cixi's response to China's need for a navy.

The Palaces of Beijing

DIANA MAYFIELD

GLENN BEANLAND

Left: Two views from the Forbidden City

GLENN BEANLAND

GLENN BEANLAND

GLENN BEANLAND

Top: Hall of Preserving Harmony, Forbidden City

Middle: Long Corridor, Summer Palace

Bottom: Hall of Benevolence and Longevity, Summer Palace

The Palaces of Beijing

DAMIEN SIMONIS

HILARY SMITH

Top: Detail of the painted ceiling in the Long Corridor, Summer Palace (Northern Area)

Bottom: Near the entrance to Prince Gong's Palace

Layout

The palace is so large (720,000 sq metres, 800 buildings, 9000 rooms) that a permanent restoration squad moves around repainting and repairing. It's estimated to take about 10 years to do a full renovation, by which time they have to start repairs again. The complex was opened to the public in 1949.

Whatever you do, try not to miss the delightful courtyards, pavilions (and mini-museums within them) on each side of the main complex. Allow yourself a full day for exploration, or perhaps several separate trips if you're an enthusiast. The information given here can only be a skeleton guide; if you want more detail then tag along with a tour group for explanations of individual artefacts.

There are plenty of Western tour groups around – the Forbidden City has 10,000 visitors a day. Tour buses drop their groups off at Tiananmen and pick them up again at the north gate; you can also enter the palace from the east or west gates. Even if you had a separate guidebook on the Forbidden City, it would be rather time-consuming to match up and identify every individual object and building, and a spoken guide has more immediacy.

On the north-south axis of the Forbidden City, from Tiananmen at the south to Shenwumen at the north, lie the palace's ceremonial buildings.

Restored in the 17th century, **Meridian Gate** (Wǔmén) is a massive portal which in former times was reserved for the use of the emperor. Gongs and bells would be sounded upon imperial comings and goings. Lesser mortals would use lesser gates – the military used the west gate, civilians the east gate. The emperor also reviewed his armies from here, passed judgement on prisoners, announced the new year's calendar and surveyed the flogging of troublesome ministers.

Across the Golden Stream, which is shaped to resemble a Tartar bow and is spanned by five marble bridges, is **Supreme Harmony Gate** (Tàihémén). It overlooks a massive courtyard which could hold an imperial audience of up to 100,000.

Raised on a marble terrace with balustrades are the Three Great Halls (Sān Dàdiàn), the heart of the Forbidden City. The **Hall of Supreme Harmony** (Tàihédiàn) is the most important and the largest structure in the Forbidden City. Built in the 15th century and restored in the 17th century, it was used for ceremonial occasions such as the emperor's birthday, the nomination of military leaders and coronations. Flanking the entrance to the hall are bronze incense burners. The large bronze turtle in the front is a symbol of longevity and stability – it has a removable lid and on special occasions incense was lit inside so that smoke billowed from the mouth.

To the west of the terrace is a small pavilion with a bronze grain-measure and to the east is a sundial; both are symbolic of imperial justice. On the corners of the roof, as with other buildings in the city, you'll see a mounted figure with his retreat cut off by mythical and actual animals, a story that relates to a cruel tyrant hanged from one such eave.

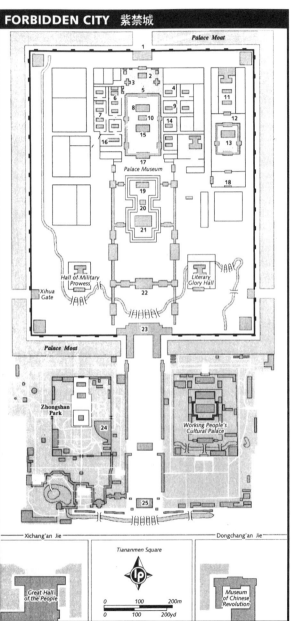

FORBIDDEN CITY 紫禁城

1 Divine Military Genius
   Gate
   神武门
2 Imperial Peace Hall
   钦安殿
3 Thousand Autumns
   Pavilion
   千秋亭
4 Arts & Crafts Exhibit
   明清工艺美术馆
5 Imperial Garden
   御花园
6 Western Palaces
   宫廷史迹陈列
7 Eternal Spring Palace
   长春宫
8 Earthly Tranquillity Pal
   坤宁宫
9 Ceramics Exhibition
   陶瓷馆
10 Hall of Union
   交泰殿
11 Jewellery Exhibition
   珍宝馆
12 Character Cultivation
   养性殿
13 Imperial Supremacy H
   (Painting Exhibit)
   绘画馆
14 Bronzes Exhibition
   青铜器馆
15 Palace of Heavenly Pu
   乾清宫
16 Mental Cultivation Hall
   养心殿
17 Heavenly Purity Gate
   乾清门
18 Nine Dragon Screen
   九龙壁
19 Hall of Preserving Har
   保和殿
20 Hall of Middle Harmon
   中和殿
21 Hall of Supreme Harm
   太和殿
22 Supreme Harmony Ga
   太和门
23 Meridian Gate
   午门
24 Beijing Music Hall
   北京音乐厅
25 Tiananmen Gate
   天安门

Inside the hall is a richly decorated **Dragon Throne** (Lóngyǐ) where the emperor would preside (decisions final, no correspondence entered into) over trembling officials. The entire court had to touch the floor nine times with their foreheads (this was the custom known as kowtowing); combined with the thick veils of incense and the battering of gongs, it would be enough to make anyone dizzy. At the back of the throne is a carved Xumishan, the Buddhist paradise, signifying the throne's supremacy.

Behind the Hall of Supreme Harmony is the smaller **Hall of Middle Harmony** (Zhōnghédiàn) which was used as a transit lounge for the emperor. Here he would make last-minute preparations, rehearse speeches and receive close ministers. On display are two Qing dynasty sedan chairs, the emperors' mode of transport around the Forbidden City. The last of the Qing emperors, Puyi, used a bicycle and altered a few features of the palace grounds to make it easier to get around.

The third hall is the **Hall of Preserving Harmony** (Bǎohédiàn) used for banquets and later for imperial examinations. It now houses archaeological finds. The Hall of Preserving Harmony has no support pillars, and behind it is a 250-tonne marble block carved with dragons and clouds which was moved into Beijing on an ice path. The outer housing surrounding the Three Great Halls was used for storing gold, silver, silks, carpets and other treasures.

The basic configuration of the Three Great Halls is echoed by the next group of buildings, smaller in scale but more important in terms of real power, which in China traditionally lies at the back door, or in this case, the back gate.

The first structure is the **Palace of Heavenly Purity** (Qiánqīng Gōng), a residence of Ming and early Qing emperors, and later an audience hall for receiving foreign envoys and high officials.

Immediately behind it is the **Hall of Union** (Jiāotàidiàn), which contains a clepsydra – a water clock with five bronze vessels and a calibrated scale. Water clocks date back several thousand years; this one was made in 1745. There's also a mechanical clock on display, built in 1797, and a collection of imperial jade seals.

At the northern end of the Forbidden City is the **Imperial Garden** (Yùhuā Yuán), a classical Chinese garden of 7000 sq metres of fine landscaping with rockeries, walkways and pavilions. This is a good place to take a breather, with snack bars, toilets and souvenir shops. Two more gates lead out through the large **Divine Military Genius Gate** (Shénwǔmén).

The western and eastern sides of the Forbidden City are the palatial former living quarters, once containing libraries, temples, theatres, gardens and even the tennis court of the last emperor. These buildings now function as museums requiring extra admission fees. Opening hours are irregular and no photos are allowed without prior permission. Special exhibits sometimes appear in the palace museum halls, so check the *Beijing Weekend* or *Beijing This Month* for details.

Behind the Wall

If ceremonial and administrative duties occupied most of the emperor's working hours, it was the pursuit of pleasure behind the high walls of the Forbidden City which occupied much of his attention during the evenings. With so many wives and consorts to choose from, a system was needed to help the emperor choose his bed-time companions. One method was to keep the names of royal wives, consorts and favourites on jade tablets near the emperor's chambers. By turning the tablet over the emperor made his request for the evening, and the eunuch on duty would rush off to find the lucky lady. Stripped naked and therefore weaponless, the little foot-bound creature was gift-wrapped in a yellow cloth, piggybacked over to the royal boudoir and dumped at the feet of the emperor, the eunuch recording the date and time to verify legitimacy of a possible child.

Aside from having fun, all this activity had a more serious purpose – prolonging the life of the emperor. An ancient Chinese belief that frequent sex with young girls could sustain one's youth even motivated Mao Zedong to follow the same procedure.

Financing the affairs of state probably cost less than financing the affairs of the emperor, and keeping the pleasure dome functioning drew heavily on the resources of the empire. During the Ming dynasty there were an estimated 9000 maids of honour and 70,000 eunuchs serving the court. Apart from the servants and the prize concubines, there were also the royal elephants to maintain.

While pocketing the cash was illegal, selling elephant dung for use as shampoo was not – it was believed to give hair that extra sheen. Back in the harem the cosmetic bills piled up to 400,000 liang of silver. Then, of course, the concubines who had grown old and were no longer in active service were still supposed to be cared for. Rather than cut back on expenditure, the emperor sent out eunuchs to collect emergency taxes whenever money ran short.

As for the palace eunuchs, the royal chop was administered at the Eunuch Clinic near the Forbidden City, using a swift knife and a special chair with a hole in the seat. The candidates sought to better their lives in the service of the court, but half of them died after the operation. Mutilation of any kind was considered grounds for exclusion from the next life, so many eunuchs carried their appendages around in pouches, believing that at the time of death the spirits might be deceived into thinking them whole.

The archives of the Ming and Qing empires, formerly housed in a separate museum, have recently been moved back into the Forbidden City. Some of the books and documents here go back 450 years, which is about as long as you can expect paper to hold up under less than ideal conditions. To their credit, the Ming and Qing emperors were good at keeping notes. Then, like now, it was necessary to make accurate records of whatever laws, edicts and rantings emanated from the imperial palace. This monumental task was given to a small army of eunuchs who did their tedious work with ink and brush pens.

Keeping the imperial family tree up to date was an especially complex affair given the level of marital activity within the Forbidden City. The family archives is the most amazing book in the entire collection, a mind-boggling tome 1m thick and weighing in at 150kg. You won't be allowed to casually flip through the pages, but it's still incredible to see.

Zhongshan Park (Zhōngshān Gōngyuán), otherwise known as Sun Yatsen Park, is in the south-west of the Forbidden City and was laid out at the same time as the palace. Here you'll find the **Altar of Land and Grain**, which is divided into five sections, each filled with earth of a different colour (red, green, black, yellow and white) to symbolise all the earth belonging to the emperor. You can also rent boats here to paddle around the moat.

The **Working People's Cultural Palace** (Láodòng Rénmín Wénhuà Gōng), in the south-eastern sector of the Forbidden City, is a park with halls dating from 1462 which were used as ancestral temples under the Ming and Qing; they come complete with marble balustrades, terraces and detailed gargoyles. The park is now used for movies, temporary exhibits, cultural performances and the odd mass wedding.

Right: The ornate surrounds of Beijing's palaces and official residences were often as impressive as the buildings themselves.

Zhongnanhai

Zhōngnánhǎi 中南海

Just west of the Forbidden City is China's new forbidden city, Zhongnanhai. The interior is off-limits to tourists, but you can gawk at the entrance. The name means 'The Central and South Seas', after the two large
lakes in the compound. The southern entrance is via Xinhuamen (Gate of
New China), which you'll see on Chang'an Jie; it's guarded by two PLA
soldiers and fronted by a flagpole with the red flag flying. The gate was
built in 1758 and was then known as the Tower of the Treasured Moon.

The compound was first built between the 10th and 13th centuries as
a sort of playground for the emperors and their retinues. It was expanded
during Ming times but most of the present buildings date from the Qing
dynasty. Empress Dowager Cixi once lived here; after the failure of the
1898 reform movement she imprisoned Emperor Guangxu in the Hall of
Impregnating Vitality where, ironically, he later died. Yuan Shikai used
Zhongnanhai for ceremonial occasions during his brief presidency of the
Chinese Republic, after the overthrow of the imperial government; his
vice-president moved into Guangxu's death-house.

Since the founding of the People's Republic in 1949, Zhongnanhai
has been the site of the residence and offices of the highest-ranking
members of the Communist Party.

Summer Palace

Yíhé Yuán 颐和园

One of Beijing's most visited sights, the Summer Palace is an immense
park containing some newish Qing architecture. The site had long been
a royal garden and was considerably enlarged and embellished by Emperor Qianlong in the 18th century. He deepened and expanded Kunming Lake with the help of 100,000 labourers, and reputedly surveyed
imperial navy drills from a hilltop perch.

Anglo-French troops badly damaged the buildings during the Second
Opium War (1860). Empress Dowager Cixi began rebuilding in 1888
using money that was supposedly reserved for the construction of a
modern navy – but she did restore a marble boat that sits immobile at
the edge of the lake.

In 1900 foreign troops, annoyed by the Boxer Rebellion, had another go at roasting the Summer Palace. Restorations took place a few
years later and a major renovation occurred after 1949, by which time
the palace had once more fallen into disrepair.

A garage on the palace grounds houses the first car ever imported
to China, a Mercedes-Benz.

As its name implies, the original palace was used as a summer residence. The residents of the Forbidden City packed up and decamped here
for their holidays, so the emphasis was on cool features – water, gardens,
hills. It was divided into four sections: court reception, residences, temples and strolling or sightseeing areas.

Three-quarters of the park is occupied by **Kunming Lake** (Kūnmíng Hú), and most items of structural interest are towards the east or north gates. The main building is the **Hall of Benevolence and Longevity** (Rénshòudiàn), just off the lake toward the east gate. It houses a hardwood throne and has a courtyard with bronze animals. In it the emperor-in-residence handled state affairs and received envoys.

Along the north shore is the 700m **Long Corridor** (Cháng Láng), which is decorated with mythical scenes. If the paint looks new it's because a lot of pictures were whitewashed during the Cultural Revolution.

On artificial Longevity Hill (Wànshòu Shān) are a number of temples. The **Precious Clouds Pavilion** (Bǎoyún Gé) on the western slopes is one of the few structures to escape destruction by the Anglo-French forces. It contains some elaborate bronzes. At the top of the hill sits the Buddhist **Temple of the Sea of Wisdom** (Zhì Huìhǎi), made of glazed tiles; good views of the lake can be had from this spot.

Other sights are largely associated with Empress Cixi, like the place where she celebrated her birthdays, and exhibitions of her furniture and memorabilia.

The **Tingliguan** (Listening to the Orioles) **Restaurant** serves imperial banquet food – fish from Kunming Lake, velvet chicken and dumplings – on imperial tableware lookalikes. It has a splendid alfresco location and

1 Site of the Zhijing
    Pavilion
    治镜阁址
2 Jade Belt Bridge
    玉带桥
3 Mirror Bridge
    镜桥
4 Changguan Hall
    畅观堂
5 Zaojian Hall
    藻鉴堂
6 Chain Bridge
    练桥
7 Knowing in the
    Spring Pavilion
    知春亭
8 17-Arch Bridge
    十七孔桥
9 Bronze Ox
    铜牛
10 Phoenix Mound
    凤凰墩
11 Willow Bridge
    柳桥
12 Xiuyi Bridge
    绣漪桥

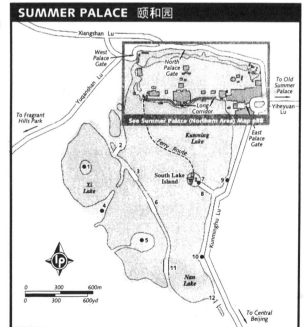

SUMMER PALACE 颐和园

SUMMER PALACE – NORTHERN AREA

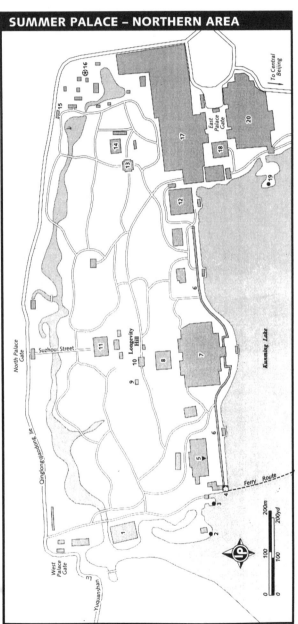

1 Boathouse
船坞

2 Rowing Boat Dock
划船码头

3 Marble Boat
清晏船

4 Ferry Dock
码头

5 Tingliguan
Restaurant
听鹂馆

6 Long Corridor
长廊

7 Cloud Dispelling Hall
排云殿

8 Buddhist Virtue
Temple
佛香阁

9 Precious Clouds
Pavilion
排云殿

10 Wisdom Sea Temple
智慧海

11 Buddhist Tenants
Hall
香崇宗印之阁

12 Renshou Hall
仁寿殿

13 Jingfu Pavilion
景福楼

14 Yishou Hall
益寿堂

15 Tiaoyuan House
眺远斋

16 Harmonious Interest
Garden
谐趣园

17 Theatre Stage
戏楼

18 Hall of
Benevolence &
Longevity
仁寿殿

19 Rowing Boat Dock
划船码头

20 Wenchang Pavilion
文昌殿

exorbitant prices, and is housed in what was once an imperial theatre; nowadays there are attached souvenir shops (see also the Places to Eat chapter).

Another noteworthy feature is the **17-arch bridge** spanning 150m to South Lake Island; on the mainland side is a beautiful bronze ox. Also note the **Jade Belt Bridge** (Yùdài Qiáo), on the mid-western side of the lake, and the **Harmonious Interest Garden** (Xiéqù Yuán), a copy of a garden in Wuxi, at the north-eastern end.

You can get around the lake by rowing boat, or on a pair of ice skates in winter. As with the Forbidden City moat, it used to be a common practice to cut slabs of ice from the lake in winter and store them for summer use.

The park is about 12km north-west of the centre of Beijing. The easiest way to get there is to take the subway to Xizhimen (close to the zoo), then a minibus or bus No 375. Bus No 332 from the zoo is slower but will get you there eventually. There are lots of minibuses returning to the city centre from the Summer Palace, but get the price and destination settled before departure. You can also get there by bicycle; it takes about 1½ to two hours from the city centre. Rather than taking the main roads, it's far more pleasant to bike along the road following the Beijing-Miyun Diversion Canal.

Tickets are Y8. This ticket does *not* get you into everything – there are some additional fees inside. Opening times are 7 am to 5 pm. Be sure you don't visit on a weekend or the only things you'll see will be camera flashes, candyfloss and 'I Love Beijing' T-shirts.

ght: The doomed Hall of Audience in the grounds of the Old ⌐mmer Palace. The hall ⅂s destroyed by British and French troops in 1860.

Old Summer Palace

Yuánmíng Yuán 圆明园

The original Summer Palace was laid out in the 12th century and by the reign of Emperor Qianlong it had developed into a set of interlocking gardens. Qianlong set the Jesuits to work designing European palaces for the gardens, adding elaborate fountains and baroque statuary.

In the Second Opium War (1860), British and French troops torched the place and sent the booty abroad. Since the Chinese pavilions and temples were made of wood they did not survive the fires, but a marble facade, some broken columns and traces of the fountains remain.

Once a favourite picnic spot for foreigners living in the capital and Chinese couples seeking a bit of privacy, the Old Summer Palace is nowadays more a tourist circus – crowded and blasted with music from loudspeakers over the entire grounds. There's even a dinosaur park.

The site is enormous – 2.5km from east to west – and divided into three separate compounds. The western section is the main area, **Perfection and Brightness Garden** (Yuánmíng Yuán). The southern compound is the **10,000 Springs Garden** (Wànchūn Yuán). The eastern section is the **Eternal Spring Garden** (Chángchūn Yuán). It's here that

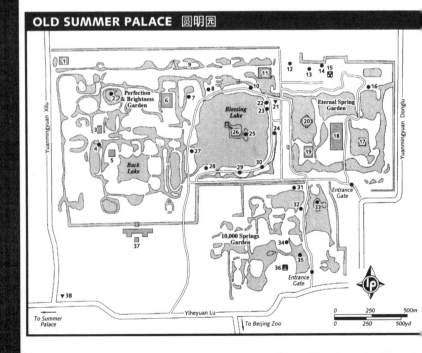

you'll find the **Great Fountain Ruins** (Dàshuǐfǎ), considered the best-preserved relic in the palace and featured prominently in tourist brochures. Here is also the fully restored **10,000 Flowers Maze** (Wànhuā Zhèn).

Minibuses connect the new Summer Palace with the old one, for about Y5, but a taxi on the same route only costs Y10. Bus No 375 from Xizhimen Subway Station (on the circle line) will get you there.

There are some slower but pleasant trips you can do around the area by public transport. Take bus No 332 from the zoo to the Old Summer Palace and to the Summer Palace; change to bus No 333 for the Fragrant Hills; change to bus No 360 to go directly back to the zoo.

Another route is to take the subway to Pingguoyuan (the last stop in the west) and from there take bus No 318 to the Fragrant Hills; change to No 333 for the Summer Palace, and then No 332 for the zoo.

Admission is Y10; the grounds are open from 7 am to 7 pm daily.

OLD SUMMER PALACE

1 Purple Blue Lodge
紫碧山房

2 Library Pavilion
文源阁

3 Wuling Spring Beauty
武陵春色

4 Universal Peace
万方安和

5 Apricot Blossoms in Spring Lodge
杏花春馆

6 Guards' Citadel
舍卫城

7 Open World to the Public
皓然大公

8 Autumn Moon Over the Calm Lake
平湖秋月

9 Far North Mountain Village
北远山村

10 Collecting Mysteries Tower
藏密楼

11 Square Pots Wonderland
方壶胜境

12 10,000 Flowers Maze
万花阵

13 Oceanic Banquet Hall
海宴堂

14 Exhibition Hall
展览馆

15 Great Fountain Ruins (European Gardens)
西洋楼

16 Lion's Forest
狮子林

17 Exquisite Jade Hall
玉玲珑馆

18 Containing Scriptures Hall
含经堂

19 Everlasting Thoughts Studio
思永斋

20 Open Sea Hill
海岳开襟

21 Fuhai Restaurant
福海酒家

22 Rowboat Dock
船台

23 Clear Reflection of the Void
涵虚朗鉴

24 Grace & Beauty Lodge
接秀山房

25 Blessing Sea Fairy Hill Hall
瀛海仙山亭

26 Jade Terraces on Penglai Isles
蓬岛瑶台

27 Body Bathed in Virtue
澡身浴德

28 Lakes & Hills View
湖山在望

29 Broad Nutrient Palace
广育宫

30 New Fairyland
别有洞天

31 Pine Moon Pavilion
松月亭

32 Contain Autumn Hall
涵秋馆

33 Phoenix & Unicorn Isles
凤麟洲

34 Boat Dock
船台

35 Enjoying Jasper Pavilion
槛碧亭

36 Awareness Temple
正觉寺

37 Great Palace Entrance Gate
大宫门

38 Xiyuan Restaurant
西苑饭店

Prince Gong's Palace

Gōngwáng Fŭ 恭王府

As palaces go, this is a small one. Prince Gong was the son of a Qing emperor and the father of Puyi, the last of China's emperors. The palace was his former residence.

This compound is one of the largest residential compounds in Beijing, with a nine-courtyard layout, high walls and elaborately laid out gardens.

To find the palace, you have to search in the small alleys running around the Shisha Hai Lakes. It's more or less at the centre of the arc created by the lakes running from north to south. It is open 8.30 am to 4.30 pm daily. Admission costs Y5.

Left: Thomas Allom's etching of a scene in the Forbidden City, showing nobles gathered at an imperial ceremony *continued from page 78*

Xu Beihong Museum (Map 3)
Xú Bēihóng Jìniàn Guǎn 徐悲鸿纪念馆
This place displays oil paintings, gouaches, sketches and assorted memorabilia of the famous artist Xu Beihong (1895–1953), noted for his galloping horse paintings. Albums of paintings are on sale, as well as reproductions and Chinese stationery.

The Xu Beihong Museum (☎ 6225 2265) is at 53 Xinjiekou Beidajie, Xicheng District. It's open from 9 am to 5 pm Tuesday to Sunday (but closed noon to 1 pm for lunch), and admission is Y5.

Museum of Ancient Architecture (Map 7)
Gǔdài Jiànzhú Bówùguǎn 古代建筑博物馆
Housed on the site of the Xiannong Altar, where Ming and Qing emperors once made sacrifices to the gods, this museum houses displays in a large courtyard-style building. Exhibits give overviews (with English explanations) of architectural features of cities, palaces, temples, mosques, gardens and mausoleums. Stone and wood carvings and architectural pieces are on display, along with photos of Chinese masterpieces in each of these categories. The museum (☎ 6301 7620) is just south-east of the Qianmen Hotel at 21 Dongjinglu. It's open from 9 am to 4 pm daily except Monday.

FORMER RESIDENCES
Unless you are pursuing an historical interest, most of the famous former residences are of little interest. A notable exception is the Song Qingling Former Residence.

Song Qingling Former Residence (Map 3)
Sòng Qìnglíng Gùjū 宋庆龄故居
Madam Song was the wife of Sun Yatsen, founder of the Republic of China. In 1981 her large residence was transformed into a museum dedicated to her memory and to that of Sun Yatsen. On display are personal items and pictures of historical interest such as clothing and books. The Song Qingling Museum is on the northern side of Shicha

Houhai Lake at 46 Beiheyan Lu. It is open from 9 am to 4 pm daily except Monday and admission is Y8.

Lu Xun Museum (Map 3)
Lǔ Xùn Bówùguǎn 鲁迅博物馆
Dedicated to the nation's 'No 1 Thinking Person's Revolutionary', the Lu Xun Museum has manuscripts, diaries, letters and inscriptions by the famous writer. Lu Xun was the pen name of Zhou Shuren (1881–1936), often regarded as the father of modern Chinese literature. Before his time, Chinese authors saw themselves as scholars and insisted on writing in a literary style which was all but unintelligible to the masses. Lu Xun broke this tradition once and for all. His most famous work is *The True Story of Ah Q*.

The museum (☎ 6616 4168) is off Fuchengmen Nei Dajie, west of the Xisi intersection. It is open from 9 am to 4 pm daily except Monday and admission is Y5.

Mei Lanfang Former Residence (Map 3)
Méi Lánfāng Jìniàn Guǎn 梅兰芳纪念馆
Beijing opera was popularised in the West by the actor Mei Lanfang (1894–1961) who played *dàn* or female roles, and is said to have influenced Charlie Chaplin. Mei Lanfang's former residence (☎ 6618 0351) at 9 Huguosi Lu, Xicheng District, has been preserved as a museum. It's closed during winter and also every Monday; admission is Y5.

Guo Moruo Former Residence (Map 3)
Guō Mòruò Gùjū 郭沫若故居
Born Guo Kaizhen, Guo Moruo (1892–1978) was one of Communist China's most politically correct writers. From a wealthy landlord family, he received an elite education in Japan but in spite of his ruling-class roots he founded the Marxist-inspired Creation Society in 1921. In the same year, a collection of Guo Moruo's poetry, *The Goddesses* (*Nǚshén*), was partially translated into English. In 1927 he wrote an article criticising Chiang Kaishek and as a result was forced to flee to Japan in 1928. With the outbreak of the Sino-Japanese War, he returned to China

THINGS TO SEE & DO

and wrote anti-Japanese tracts. When the Communists came to power in 1949, Guo was made director of the Chinese Academy of Sciences. In 1951 he was awarded the Stalin Peace Prize (an oxymoron if ever there was one). He was given several other high-level posts during his twilight years. Unlike many other writers, he survived the Cultural Revolution with barely a scratch.

Guo lived in a garden-like compound in Beijing. His house has been preserved along with many of his books and manuscripts. You'll find it at 18 Qianhai Xijie in the Xicheng District. The house (☎ 6612 5392) is open from 9 am to 4 pm, but is closed during the winter months and on Monday during the other seasons. Admission is Y6.

Mao Dun Former Residence (Map 4)
Máo Dùn Gùjū 茅盾故居
Mao Dun was the pen name of Shen Yanbing (1896–1981). He was born into an elite family in Zhejiang Province but was educated in Beijing. In 1916 he worked in Shanghai as a translator for the Commercial Press (a major state-run publishing operation which is still in business today – check out its store in Hong Kong, which is a brilliant source of books about China). In 1920 he helped found the Literary Study Society (the earliest literary society of the New Literature Movement). The society advocated literary realism. Mao Dun joined the League of Left Wing Writers in 1930 and became active in Communist worker activities in Shanghai. He became solidly entrenched in the bureaucracy after the Communists came to power. He laid low during the Cultural Revolution, but briefly returned to writing in the 1970s.

The Mao Dun Former Residence (☎ 6404 0520) is at Jiaodakou Nandajie, 13 Haoyuan Anshi Hutong. It's open to the public from 9 am to 4 pm on Tuesday, Thursday and Saturday only. Admission costs Y1.

Lao She Former Residence (Map 4)
Lǎo Shě Jìniàn Guǎn 老舍纪念馆
Lao She was the pen name of Shu Sheyu (1899–1966), an early 20th-century novelist. He's most famous for *The Rickshaw Boy,* also known as *Camel Xiangzi,* a social critique of the living conditions of Beijing rickshaw drivers. Lao She's other works include *Cat City* and the play *Teahouse.*

For his efforts he was severely persecuted during the Cultural Revolution and died from wounds inflicted by Red Guards.

Lao She lived for 16 years in an undistinguished house with courtyard at 19 Fengfu Hutong, Dengshi Xijie (☎ 6514 2612). There really isn't all that much to see here. The museum is open from 9 am to 5 pm daily except Monday. Admission is Y5

TEMPLES
Lama Temple (Map 4)
Yōnghé Gōng 雍和宫
This is the most colourful temple in Beijing with beautifully landscaped gardens, stunning frescoes and tapestries and incredible carpentry.

The Lama Temple was once the official residence of Count Yin Zhen. In 1723 the count became emperor and moved to the Forbidden City. His name was changed to Yong Zheng, and his former residence became Yonghe Palace. The green tiles were changed to yellow (the imperial colour) and – as was the custom – the place could no longer be used except as a temple. In 1744 it was converted into a lamasery and became home to large numbers of monks from Mongolia and Tibet.

In 1792 the Emperor Qianlong, having quelled an uprising in Tibet, instituted a new administrative system involving two gold vases. One was kept at the Jokhang Temple in Lhasa, where it was intended to be used for determining the reincarnation of the Dalai Lama (under the supervision of the Minister for Tibetan Affairs). The other was kept at the Lama Temple for the lottery for the Panchen Lama. The Lama Temple thus assumed a new importance in ethnic minority control.

The lamasery has three richly-worked archways and five main halls, each taller than the preceding one. Styles are mixed – Mongolian, Tibetan and Han – with courtyard enclosures and galleries.

The first hall, **Lokapala**, houses a statue of the future Buddha, Maitreya, flanked by celestial guardians. The statue facing the back door is Weituo, the guardian of Buddhism, made of white sandalwood. Beyond, in the courtyard, is a pond with a bronze mandala depicting Xumishan, the Buddhist paradise.

The second hall, **Yonghedian**, has three figures of Buddha – past, present and future.

The third hall, **Yongyoudian**, has statues of the Buddha of Longevity and the Buddha of Medicine (to the left). The courtyard beyond the hall features galleries with some *yandikesvaras,* or joyful Buddhas, tangled up in multi-armed close encounters. These are coyly draped lest you be corrupted by the sight, and are to be found in other discreet locations.

The **Hall of the Wheel of Law** (Fǎlún Diàn), further north, contains a large bronze statue of Tsong Khapa (1357–1419), founder of the Gelukpa or Yellow Hat sect, and frescoes depicting his life. This Tibetan-style building is used for study and prayer.

The last hall, **Wanfu Pavilion**, has an 18m-high statue of the Maitreya Buddha in its Tibetan form, clothed in yellow satin and said to have been sculpted from a single piece of sandalwood. The smoke curling up from the yak-butter lamps transports you momentarily to Tibet, which is where the wood for this statue came from.

In 1949 the Lama Temple was declared protected as a major historical relic. Miraculously it survived the Cultural Revolution without scars. In 1979 large amounts of money were spent on repairs and it was restocked with several dozen novices from Inner Mongolia, a token move on the part of the government to back up its claim that the Lama Temple is a 'symbol of religious freedom, national unity and stability in China'. The novices study Tibetan language and the secret practices of the Gelukpa sect.

The temple is active again, though some question whether the monks in tennis shoes are really monks or Public Security Bureau officials. Prayers take place early in the morning and are not for public viewing, but if you inquire discreetly of the head lama you might be allowed to return the following morning. No photography is permitted inside the temple buildings, but the postcard industry thrives.

The temple is open from 9 am to 4 pm daily. Take the subway to Yonghegong station or double-decker bus No 2. Entry costs Y15.

Confucius Temple & Imperial College (Map 4)

Kǒng Miào; Guózǐjiān 孔庙、国子监

Just down the hutong opposite the gates of the Lama Temple is the former Confucius Temple (the largest in China after the one at Qufu) and the Imperial College. It was reopened in 1981 after some mysterious use as an official residence. It's now a museum, in sharp contrast to the Lama Temple.

The **steles** in the temple courtyard record the names of those successful in the civil service examinations (possibly the world's first) of the imperial court. It was the ambition of every scholar to see his name engraved here, but it wasn't easy. Each candidate was locked in one of about 8000 cubicles, measuring roughly 1.5m square, for a period of three days. Many died or went insane during their incarceration. Imagine that.

The Imperial College was the place where the emperor expounded the Confucian classics to an audience of thousands of kneeling students and professors; this was an annual rite. Built by the grandson of Kublai Khan in 1306, the former college was the only institution of its kind in China. It's now the Capital Library. In the 'collection' are the **stone tablets** commissioned by Emperor Qianlong. These are engraved with 13 Confucian classics – 800,000 characters (12 years' work for the scholar who did it). There is an ancient 'Scholar-Tree' in the courtyard.

The easiest way to get to the Confucius Temple is to take the subway to Yonghegong station. The temple (☎ 8401 1977) is located at 13 Guozidian. It is open from 8.30 am to 5 pm daily and admission is Y10, Y3 for students (admission includes the Capital Museum).

Dongyue Temple (Map 5)
Dōngyuè Miào 东岳寺

Built in the Yuan dynasty, Dongyue Temple is a recently restored Taoist temple in the middle of the Chaoyang District.

The huge courtyard is surrounded on all sides by 'heavenly departments', each in charge of different aspects of existence. Worried about your finances? Make a deposit at the Department for Bestowing Material Happiness. Concerned about China's environment? Pay a visit to the Department for the Preservation of Wilderness. Life-size painted clay figures – many of which are half animal and painted in garish colours, bearing menacing expressions and brandishing painful-looking weapons – depict each department. There are also English explanations of each department's function.

Dongyue Temple is located on Chaoyangmen Wai Dajie, about 200m east of Full Link Plaza on the opposite side of the street. Admission is Y10.

Great Bell Temple (Map 2)
Dàzhōng Sì 大钟寺

The bell at the Great Bell Temple, the biggest in China, weighs a hefty 46.5 tonnes and is 6.75m tall. It is inscribed with over 227,000 Chinese characters of Buddhist sutras.

The bell was cast during the reign of Ming Emperor Yongle in 1406 and the tower was built in 1733. Getting the bell from the foundry to the temple proved problematic: A shallow canal was built, and when it froze over in winter the bell was moved across the ice by sled.

Within the grounds are several buildings in addition to the one housing the bell. They include the Guanyin Hall (Guānyīn Diàn), the Sutra-keeping Tower (Cángjīng Lóu), the Main Buddha Hall (Dàxióng Bǎo Diàn) and Four Devas Hall (Tiānwáng Diàn). This monastery was reopened in 1980, and is one of the most popular temples in Beijing.

The Great Bell Temple is almost 2km east of the Friendship Hotel on Beisanhuan Xilu.

White Dagoba Temple (Map 3)
Báitǎ Sì 白塔寺

The White Dagoba Temple can be spotted from the top of Jingshan, and is similar (and close) to the one in Beihai Park. It was used as a factory during the Cultural Revolution but reopened after restoration in 1980. The *dagoba* dates back to Kubla Khan's days though the halls date only from the Qing dynasty. It lies off Fuchengmen Nei Dajie.

Wuta Temple (Map 3)
Wǔtǎ Sì 五塔寺

The Indian-style Wuta (Five Dagoba) Temple has five pagodas and was first constructed in 1473 from a model presented to the imperial court. The temple has been renovated and sits in a small park filled with stone turtles and inscribed stone **steles**. For this reason, it's also known as the Carved Stone Museum (Shíkē Bówùguǎn). The temple is no longer an active place of worship but it's a delightful place. The compound currently houses the China Life Sciences Research Institute and the Qigong Club.

The temple is easily found by crossing the canal bridge directly opposite the rear exit of the Beijing Zoo.

Guangji Temple (Map 3)
Guǎngjì Sì 广济寺

The Guangji (Universal Rescue) Temple is on the north-west side of Xisi intersection and east of the White Dagoba Temple. It's the headquarters of the Chinese Buddhist Association.

Fayuan Temple (Map 6)
Fǎyuán Sì 法源寺

In a lane just east of Niujie Mosque is the Fayuan (Origin of the Law) Temple. The temple was originally constructed in the 7th century and is still going strong. It's now the China Buddhism College. A visit here is like going to a college campus, with students playing ping pong during the breaks, hanging out and chatting – except the students are monks dressed in Buddhist saffron robes. Don't miss the hall at the very back of the temple, which houses a

iantan Park's Hall of Prayer for Good Harvests

Urn outside the Hall of Prayer for Good Harvests

iew from Jingshan Park, just north of the Forbidden City

DAMIEN SIMONIS

One of Tiantan Park's gates

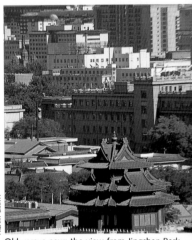

HILARY SMITH

Old versus new: the view from Jingshan Park

GLENN BEANLAND

The north shore of Kunming Lake

unusual **copper-cast Buddha** seated upon a thousand-petal lotus flower throne. From the entrance of Niujie Mosque, walk left 100m then turn left into the first hutong. Follow the hutong for about 10 minutes and you'll arrive at Fayuan Temple. The temple (☎ 6353 4171) is open from 8.30 to 11.20 am and 1.30 to 3.30 pm every day except Wednesday. Admission to the temple is Y5.

White Cloud Temple (Map 6)
Báiyúnguàn 白云观
The White Cloud Temple was once the Taoist centre of North China and the site of temple fairs. Inside you'll find several courtyards containing a pool, bridge, several halls of worship and Taoist motifs. Walk south on Baiyun Lu and cross the moat; continue south along Baiyun Lu, turn into a curving street on the left and follow it for 250m to the temple entrance. The temple is open 8.30 am to 4.30 pm daily; Y8 admission.

Zhihua Temple (Map 5)
Zhìhuà Sì 智化寺
Notable for its deep blue tiling, the Zhihua Temple is a pretty example of Ming architecture (dating from 1443), but there's nothing else of note. The temple is north of Beijing train station in the Yabao Lu area, down a hutong called Lumicang which runs east off Chaoyangmen Nanxiaojie (about 1.5km north of the station). The temple is at the eastern end of Lumicang. The coffered ceiling of the third hall of the Growth of Intellect Temple is not there – it's in the USA. Lumicang hutong had rice granaries in the Qing dynasty but these days it's mostly got traffic.

MOSQUES & CATHEDRALS
Dongsi Mosque (Map 4)
Dōngsì Qīngzhēn Sì 东四清真寺
The Dongsi Mosque is one of two functioning mosques in Beijing, the other being Niujie Mosque (see following). The mosque is at 13 Dongsi Nandajie, just south of the intersection with Chaoyangmen Nei Dajie.

Niujie Mosque (Map 6)
Niújiē Lǐbài Sì 牛街礼拜寺
Beijing is estimated to have some 180,000 ethnic-Chinese Muslims (now officially labelled the 'Hui' minority). There are some 40 mosques in town, and the largest and oldest of them all is the Niujie Mosque, which was built in AD 996. It's in the south-west of Beijing, south of Guang'anmen Nei Dajie (Beijing's largest Hui neighbourhood).

Bare legs are a no-no inside the compound, but if you show up in shorts or a miniskirt you can borrow a pair of trousers. Although anyone can go into the compound, only male Muslims are permitted to enter the main hall of worship. The women's worship area is in the north-east corner of the compound.

Near the mosque is Niu Jie (Ox St), the heart of Beijing's Muslim Quarter. The mosque is open from 8 am to sunset daily. Admission is free for Muslims, Y10 for everyone else.

South Cathedral (Map 6)
Nántáng 南堂
The South Cathedral (also known as St Mary's Church) is Beijing's main functioning cathedral, and the city's other cathedrals are in a sorry state. This one was built on the site of the house of Matteo Ricci, the Jesuit missionary who introduced Christianity into China. Since it was built in 1703 it has been destroyed three times.

The cathedral is on Qianmen Dajie at the Xuanwumen intersection (north-east side) above the subway station.

Mass is held daily in Latin and Chinese beginning at 6.30 am. English mass is at 10 am on Sunday.

North Cathedral (Map 3)
Běitáng 北堂
Also called the Cathedral of Our Saviour, this church was built in 1887 but was badly damaged during the Cultural Revolution before being converted into a factory warehouse. It was reopened at the end of 1985 when restoration work was completed. The cathedral is at Xishiku in the Xicheng District.

PARKS

In imperial days the parks were laid out at the compass points: to the west of the Forbidden City lies Yuetan Park; to the north lies Ditan Park; to the south lies Taoranting Park and to the east is Ritan Park. To the south-east of the Forbidden City is the showpiece, Tiantan Park.

All of these parks were venues for ritual sacrifices offered by the emperors. Not much remains of the shaman structures, bar those of the Temple of Heaven in Tiantan Park, but if you arrive early in the morning you can witness *taijiquan*, fencing exercises, or even opera-singers and musicians practising their arts. It's well worth experiencing the very different rhythms of the city at this time.

Temporary exhibitions take place in the parks, including horticultural and cultural ones, and there is even the odd bit of open-air theatre as well as some worthy eating establishments. If you take up residence in Beijing, the parks become very important for preserving sanity. They are open late too, typically until 8 pm.

Tiantan Park (Tiantan Park Map & Map 7)

Tiāntán Gōngyuán 天坛公园

The perfection of Ming architecture, Tiantan (Temple of Heaven) has come to symbolise Beijing. Its lines appear on countless pieces of tourist literature and its name serves as a brand name for a wide range of products from balm to plumbing fixtures. In the 1970s the complex got a face-lift and was freshly painted after pigment research. It is set in a 267-hectare park, with four gates at the compass points, and bounded by walls to the north and east. It originally functioned as a vast stage for the solemn rites performed by the Son of Heaven, who came here to pray for good harvests, seek divine clearance and atone for the sins of the people.

With this complicated mix in mind, the unique architectural features will delight numerologists, necromancers and the superstitious – not to mention acoustic engineers and carpenters. Shape, colour and sound combine to take on symbolic significance. Seen from above, the temples are round and the bases square, a pattern deriving from the ancient Chinese belief that heaven is round and earth is square. Thus the northern end of the park is semicircular and the southern end is square – the Temple of Earth, also called Ditan (see Ditan Park later), is on the northern compass point and the Temple of Heaven on the southern compass point.

Tiantan was considered sacred ground and it was here that the emperor performed the major ceremonial rites of the year. Just before the winter solstice, the emperor and his enormous entourage passed down Qianmen Dajie to the Imperial Vault of Heaven in total silence. Commoners were not permitted to view the ceremony and remained cloistered indoors. The procession included elephant chariots, horse chariots and long lines of lancers, nobles, officials and musicians, dressed in their finest, flags fluttering. The next day the emperor waited in a yellow silk tent at the southern gate while officials moved the sacred tablets to the Round Altar, where the prayers and sacrificial rituals took place. It was thought that this ritual decided the nation's future, thus the least hitch in any part of the proceedings was regarded as an ill omen. This was the most important ceremony although other excursions to the Temple of Earth took place.

Tiantan, it should not be forgotten, is still an important meeting place. Get there at 6.30 am (before the ticket booth opens) to see taijiquan, dancing to Western music and some other games people play. This is how Beijing awakens. It becomes just another Chinese park by 9 am. Tiantan is open 8.30 am to 4.30 pm daily and admission is Y14.

Round Altar The 5m-high Round Altar (Yuán Qiū) was constructed in 1530 and rebuilt in 1740. It is composed of white marble arrayed in three tiers, and its geometry revolves around the imperial number nine. Odd numbers were considered heavenly, and nine is the largest single-digit odd number. The top tier, thought to symbolise heaven, has nine rings of stones, each ring composed of multiples of nine stones, so that the ninth ring has 81 stones. The middle tier – earth – has the 10th to 18th rings. The bottom tier – man – has the 19th to 27th rings, ending with a total of 243 stones in the largest ring, or 27 times nine. The number of stairs and balustrades are also multiples of nine. If you stand in the centre of the upper terrace and say something, the sound waves bounce off the marble balustrades, making your voice appear louder (by nine times?).

Echo Wall Just north of the altar, surrounding the Imperial Vault of Heaven, is the Echo Wall (Huíyīn Bì), 65m in diameter. This enables a whisper to travel clearly from one end to your friend's ear at the other – that is, if there's not a tour group in the middle.

In the courtyard are the **Triple-Sounds Stones** (Sānyīn Shí). It is said that if you clap or shout standing on the stones, the sound is echoed once from the first stone, twice from the second stone and thrice from the third stone. Four echoes is a sure sign of misfortune!

TIANTAN PARK 天坛

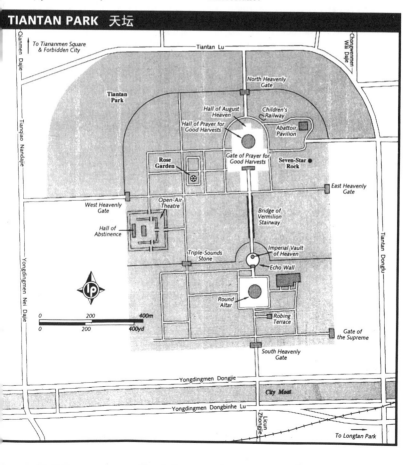

To Tiananmen Square & Forbidden City

Tiantan Lu

North Heavenly Gate

Tiantan Park

Hall of August Heaven

Children's Railway

Hall of Prayer for Good Harvests

Abattoir Pavilion

Rose Garden

Gate of Prayer for Good Harvests

Seven-Star Rock

East Heavenly Gate

West Heavenly Gate

Open-Air Theatre

Bridge of Vermilion Stairway

Hall of Abstinence

Triple-Sounds Stone

Imperial Vault of Heaven

Echo Wall

Round Altar

Robing Terrace

Gate of the Supreme

South Heavenly Gate

Qianmen Dajie

Tianqiao Nandajie

Yongdingmen Nei Dajie

Chongwenmen Wai Dajie

Tiantan Donglu

Licun Zhonglu

0   200   400m
0   200   400yd

Yongdingmen Dongjie

City Moat

Yongdingmen Dongbinhe Lu

To Longtan Park

Imperial Vault of Heaven The octagonal Imperial Vault of Heaven (Huáng Qióng Yŭ) was built at the same time as the Round Altar, and is structured along the lines of the older Hall of Prayer for Good Harvests, though it is smaller. It used to contain tablets of the emperor's ancestors, which were used in the winter solstice ceremony.

Proceeding up from the Imperial Vault is a walkway: to the left is a molehill composed of excess dirt dumped from digging air-raid shelters and to the right is a rash of souvenir shops.

Hall of Prayer for Good Harvests The crown of the whole complex is the Hall of Prayer for Good Harvests (Qínián Diàn), which is a magnificent piece mounted on a three-tiered marble terrace. Built in 1420, it was burnt to cinders in 1889 and heads rolled in apportioning blame. The cause seems to have been lightning. A faithful reproduction based on Ming architectural methods was erected the following year, using Oregon fir for the support pillars.

The four central pillars symbolise the seasons, the 12 in the next ring denote the months of the year, and the 12 outer ones represent the day, broken into 12 'watches'. Embedded in the ceiling is a carved dragon, a symbol of royalty. The patterning, carving and gilt decoration of this ceiling and its swirl of colour is a dizzying sight.

All this is made more amazing by the fact that the wooden pillars ingeniously support the ceiling without nails or cement – for a building 38m high and 30m in diameter, that's quite an accomplishment. Capping the structure is a deep blue umbrella of tiles with a golden knob and two complementary eaves.

Jingshan Park (Map 4)

Jīngshān Gōngyuán 景山公园

North of the Forbidden City is Jingshan Park, which contains an artificial mound made of earth excavated to create the palace moat. The mound is known as Jing Shan (Prospect Hill), but was formerly called Mei Shan (Coal Hill). It was the highest point in Beijing during the Ming dynasty, but it's fair to say the city has grown a bit since then

and numerous higher hills have now been incorporated into the megalopolis.

If you clamber to the top pavilions of this regal pleasure garden you get a magnificent panorama of the capital and a great overview of the russet roofing of the Forbidden City. On the eastern side of the park is a locust tree (not the original) where the last of the Mings, Emperor Chongzhen, hanged himself (after slaying his family) rather than see the palace razed by the Manchus. The hill supposedly protects the palace from the evil spirits – or dust storms – from the north, but it didn't quite work for Chongzhen.

Entrance to Jingshan Park is a modest Y2 or you can pay over 5 times as much for an optional souvenir 'tourist passport ticket'. The park is open 6 am to 7.30 pm daily.

Beihai Park (Beihai Park Map & Map 4)

Běihǎi Gōngyuán 北海公园

Just north-west of the Forbidden City, Beihai (North Sea) Park is the former playground of the emperors. It's also said to have been the private domain of the great dragon-lady/witch Jiang Qing, widow of Mao who, until her death in May 1991, was serving a life sentence as No 1 member of the Gang of Four. Half of the park is a lake. The island in the lower middle is composed of the heaped earth dug to create the lake – some attribute this to the handiwork of Kublai Khan.

The site is associated with the Great Khan's palace, the navel of Beijing before the creation of the Forbidden City. All that remains of the Khan's court is a large jar, made of green jade, in the Round City near the south entrance. A present given in 1265 and said to have held the Khan's wine, the jar was later discovered in the hands of Taoist priests who used it to store pickles. In the Light Receiving Hall (Chéngguāng Diàn), the main structure nearby, is a 1.5m high **white jade Buddha** inlaid with jewels, a gift from Myanmar (Burma) to Empress Dowager Cixi.

From the 12th century on, Beihai Park was landscaped with artificial hills, pavilions, halls, temples and covered walkways.

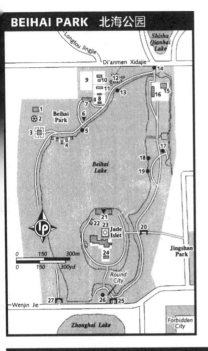

BEIHAI PARK 北海公园

During the present era the structures have been massively restored and Beihai Park is now one of the best examples of a classical garden found in China. Dominating Jade Islet on the lake, the 36m-high **White Dagoba** (Bái Tǎ) originally dates from 1651, when it was erected for a visit by the Dalai Lama, and was rebuilt in 1741. It's believed that Lamaist scriptures, robes and other sacred objects are encased in this brick-and-stone landmark.

On the north-east shore of the islet is the handsome double-tiered **Painted Gallery** (Huàfǎng Zhāi), with unusual architecture for a walkway. Near the boat-dock is the Fangshan Restaurant, dishing up recipes favoured by Empress Cixi. She liked 120-course dinners with about 30 kinds of desserts. The restaurant is expensive and high class, and reservations are necessary (but check out the decor!). Off to one side, however, is a snack bar that dispenses royal pastries much more cheaply.

The big attraction on the northern side of the park is the **Nine Dragon Screen** (Jiǔlóng Bì), 5m high and 27m long, made of coloured glazed tiles. The screen, standing

BEIHAI PARK

PLACES TO EAT
6 Beihai Restaurant
北海餐厅
21 Fangshan Restaurant
仿膳饭庄

OTHER
1 Wanfulou
万福楼
2 Gardens
植物园
3 Miniature Western Paradise
小西天
4 Five Dragon Pavilion
五龙亭
5 Rowboat Dock
游船码头
7 Nine Dragon Screen
九龙壁

8 Tianwang Hall
天王殿
9 Beihai Playground
北海体育场
10 Glazed Pavilion
琉璃阁
11 Hall
大慈真如殿
12 Jingxin House
静心斋
13 Rowboat Dock
游船码头
14 North Gate
北门
15 Qincan Hall
亲蚕殿
16 Kindergarten
北海幼儿园
17 Painted Boat Studio
画舫斋

18 Boat House
船坞
19 Rowboat Dock
游船码头
20 East Gate
东门
22 Pavilion of Calligraphy
阅古楼
23 White Dagoba
白塔
24 Falun Hall
法轮殿
25 South Gate
南门
26 Light Receiving Hall
承光殿
27 West Gate
西门

at the entrance to a temple which is no longer there, was meant to scare off evil spirits. To the south-west of the boat dock on this side is the Five Dragon Pavilion dating from 1651.

Over on the eastern side of the park are the **Gardens Within Gardens**. These waterside pavilions, winding corridors and rockeries were summer haunts of the imperial family, notably Emperor Qianlong and Empress Cixi. They date back some 200 years, with structures like the Painted Boat Studio and the Studio of Mental Calmness. Until 1980 the villas were used as government offices.

Beihai Park is a relaxing place to stroll around, grab a snack, sip a beer, rent a rowing boat (Y10, with a Y100 deposit) or, as the locals do, cuddle on a bench in the evening. It's crowded on weekends. Swimming in the lake is not permitted, but in winter there's skating. This is nothing new in China – ice skating apparently goes back to the 18th century when Emperor Qianlong reviewed the imperial skating parties here. It's open 7 am to 7 pm daily. Admission is Y5.

Fragrant Hills Park (Fragrant Hills Park Map & Map 2)
Xiāngshān Gōngyuán 香山公园
Within striking distance of the Summer Palace and often combined with it on a tour are the Fragrant Hills. The hills were formerly a resort for Communist Party brass, but now that most of the leadership is elderly they prefer to stay in the Zhongnanhai compound.

You can scramble up the slopes to the top of Incense Burner Peak, or take the crowded chairlift. From the peak you can enjoy an all-embracing view of the countryside. The chairlift is a good way to get up the mountain, and from the summit you can hike further into the Western Hills and leave the crowds behind. Beijingers love to flock here in the autumn when the maple leaves carpet the hillsides in hues of red.

The Fragrant Hills area was razed by foreign troops in 1860 and 1900 but a few bits of original architecture still poke out. A glazed tile pagoda and the renovated **Temple of Brilliance** (Zhāo Miào) – a mock Tibetan temple built in 1780 – are both in the same area. The surrounding heavily wooded park was a hunting ground for the emperors and once contained a multitude of pavilions and shrines, many of which are being restored. It's a favourite strolling spot for Beijingers and destined to become another Chinese Disneyland – the chair lift and souvenir shops are signs of horrors to come. It's possible to stay the night here at the four-star *Fragrant Hills Hotel (Xiāngshān Fàndiàn;* ☎ 6259 1166, fax 6259 1762), Xiangshan Gongyuan Nei, Haidian District, 100093. Standard twins cost Y580.

Within walking distance of the north gate of Fragrant Hills Park is the **Azure Clouds Temple** (Bìyún Sì), the landmark of which is the Diamond Throne Pagoda (Jīngāng Bǎozuò Tǎ). Of Indian design, it consists of a platform with a central pagoda and stupas. Built in 1366 and expanded in the 18th century with the addition of the Hall of Arhats, it holds 500 statues of Buddha's disciples. Dr Sun Yatsen's coffin was placed here in 1925 before being moved to Nanjing. The memorial hall still has a picture display of Sun's revolutionary activities.

There are a couple of ways to get to the Fragrant Hills by public transport: bus No 333 from the Summer Palace, bus No 360 from the zoo, and bus No 318 from Pingguoyuan (the westernmost stop on the East-West Line).

Ditan Park (Map 4)
Dìtán Gōngyuán 地坛公园
Although 'ditan' sounds just like the Chinese word for carpet, in this case it means Temple of Earth. Ditan Park was built around 1530 as a place for the emperors to sacrifice lesser beings to keep on good terms with the Earth God. The park experienced many years of neglect, but reopened in 1984 as a sort of activity centre for the elderly. It is just north of the magnificent Lama Temple.

Ritan Park (Map 5)
Rìtán Gōngyuán 日坛公园
Ritan means Temple of the Sun. Ritan Park is one of Beijing's older parks and was built

FRAGRANT HILLS PARK 香山公园

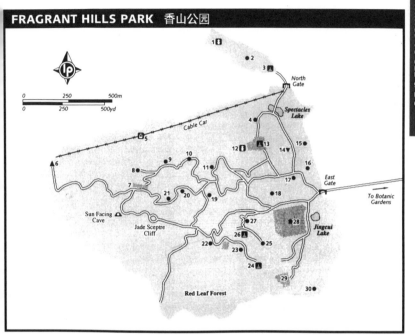

FRAGRANT HILLS PARK

1 Diamond Throne Pagoda
金刚宝座塔

2 Sun Yatsen Memorial Hall
孙中山纪念堂

3 Azure Clouds Temple
碧云寺

4 Unbosoming Chamber
见心斋

5 Middle Station
中站

6 Incense Burner Peak
香炉峰

7 Platform
平台

8 Stele of Western Hills Shimmering in Snow
西山晴雪

9 Tiered Cloud Villa
梯云山馆

10 Fourth Jade Flower Villa
玉花四院

11 Hibiscus Hall
芙蓉馆

12 Glazed Tile Pagoda
琉璃塔

13 Temple of Brilliance
昭庙

14 Pine Forest Restaurant
松林餐厅

15 Fragrant Hills Villa
香山别墅

16 Administrative Office
管理处

17 Peak Viewing Pavilion
望峰亭

18 Scattered Clouds Pavilion
多云亭

19 Jade Flower Villa
玉花山庄

20 Varied Scenery Pavilion
多景亭

21 Moonlight Villa
栖月山庄

22 Jade Fragrance Hall
玉香馆

23 White Pine Pavilion
白松亭

24 Fragrant Hills Temple Site
香山寺遗址

25 Halfway Pavilion
半山亭

26 Red Glow Temple
洪光寺

27 Eighteen Turns
十八盘

28 Fragrant Hills Hotel
香山宾馆

29 Twin Lakes Villa
双清别墅

30 See Clouds Rise
看云起

in 1530 as an altar for ritual sacrifice to the Sun God. Practically in the middle of Jianguomenwai embassy-land, it's a big hit with the diplomatic corps, their families and other notables who like to rub elbows with important foreigners. Admission is just Y1.

Ritan Park has two courtyard-style restaurants, both of which serve Sichuan cuisine and are very popular with westerners.

Taoranting Park (Map 6)

Táorántíng Gōngyuán 陶然亭公园

Taoranting (Happy Pavilion) Park is in the southern part of Beijing. The park dates back to at least the Qing dynasty (which began in 1644), when it gained fame chiefly because it was one of the very few leafy city areas accessible to the masses (most of the others were the private playgrounds of the emperors). While it's one of the less inspiring parks in Beijing, it does have a good public swimming pool complete with water slides.

Beijing Botanic Gardens (Map 2)

Běijīng Zhíwù Yuán 北京植物园

About halfway between the Fragrant Hills and the Summer Palace are the Beijing Botanic Gardens. While not spectacular, the gardens are a botanist's delight and certainly a pleasant place for a stroll, although on weekends the place gets very crowded.

At the northern end of the gardens is the **Sleeping Buddha Temple** (Wòfó Sì). This reclining Buddha is 5.2m long and cast in copper. Its weight is unknown but could be up to 50 tonnes. The history books date it to 1331 but it's more likely to be a later work in the style of that period. Pilgrims used to make offerings of shoes to the barefoot statue. During the Cultural Revolution the Buddhas in one of the halls were replaced by a Mao statue (since removed).

On the eastern side of the gardens is the **Cao Xueqin Memorial** (Cáo Xuěqín Jìniànguǎn), the former residence of Cao Xueqin (1715–1763). Cao is credited with authoring the classic *The Dream of Red Mansions* (also translated as *The Dream of the Red Chamber* and *The Story of the Stone*), a sort of complex Romeo and Juliet

saga set in the early Qing period. The official address of the memorial is 39 Zhengbaiqi.

Zizhuyuan Park (Map 3)

Zǐzhúyuàn Gōngyuán 紫竹院公园

The park's name means Purple Bamboo, a reference to some of what has been planted here. This place doesn't have much history to distinguish it, being mainly former paddy fields, but during the Ming dynasty there was a Temple of Longevity here. Zizhuyuan Park is pleasant enough and there is a reasonably large lake which is good for ice skating in winter. It is in a prestigious neighbourhood just west of the zoo.

Longtan Park (Map 7)

Lóngtán Gōngyuán 龙潭公园

Longtan (Dragon Pool) Park is just east of the Temple of Heaven; visit the park at dawn to see taiji performances.

The western side of Longtan Park has been converted into the Beijing Amusement Park, a world of balloons, candy floss and nauseating rides (don't eat Sichuan food before getting on the 'Spider').

Grand View Garden (Map 6)

Dàguānyuán Gōngyuán 大观园公园

Unlike most of Beijing's parks, which date back to imperial days, this one is new. Construction started in 1984 and was completed four years later. The park was built as a replica of the family gardens described in the classic Chinese novel *The Dream of Red Mansions*, written by Cao Xueqin in the late 18th century. While the park is not steeped in history, it could be of interest if you've read the novel. Otherwise, just relax and enjoy the birds, trees and colourful pavilions. The Grand View Garden (☎ 6354 4994) is in the south-west corner of town just inside Second Ring Rd. You can get there on bus No 59 from Qianmen. Admission costs Y10.

Jade Spring Mountain (Map 2)

Yùquán Shān 玉泉山

About 2.5km west of the Summer Palace is Jade Spring Mountain. The spring's name is derived from its waters' jade-like, crystalline appearance. During the Ming and Qing dynasties water from this spring was sent daily to the Forbidden City to quench the emperor's thirst – it was believed the water had a tonic effect, an essential consideration with so many concubines to satisfy.

In the 1950s villas were built here for China's top five leaders at the time: Mao Zedong, Liu Shaoqi, Zhou Enlai, Zhu De and Ren Bishi. Mao seldom stayed in his villa because he was said to be unhappy with the size of the swimming pool (it was made small to make drowning impossible).

It wasn't until the 1990s that this hallowed area was opened to the public as a park. The area is now dressed up with all the usual temples, pagodas and pavilions. At the base of the mountain is the **Garden of Light and Tranquillity**.

THEME PARKS

If you want to avoid being smothered by candy floss and blinded by popping camera flashes, it's important to avoid Beijing's theme parks on weekends and holidays. On more sedate weekdays, you are far more likely to be able to enjoy what's on offer.

World Park (Map 2)

Shìjiè Gōngyuán 世界公园

A monument to kitsch, Beijing's World Park has miniaturised reproductions of world-famous architectural wonders. Exhibits include France's Eiffel Tower, the pyramids of Egypt, America's Statue of Liberty and the White House. Since most Chinese are unable to travel abroad, this is as close as they can come to an overseas holiday.

The park is south-west of the centre, about 3km due south of Fengtai train station. If you don't plan to travel by taxi, you'll have to take a bus to Fengtai train station and a minibus from there to the park. Bus Nos 309 and 406 also get you there.

China Ethnic Minorities Park (Map 2)

Zhōnghuá Mínzú Yuán 中华民族园

Far more hallucinogenic than World Park, this is where you get to see China's 55 nationalities in their native habitat – or

rather, Han Chinese dressed up in minority costumes. Actually, 56 nationalities are represented if you count the highly dubious 'Gaoshan' nationality which is what China calls Taiwan's nine aboriginal tribes (the Taiwanese aborigines vehemently reject this label of course).

The park is also dressed up with small-scale imitations of famous Chinese scenic spots such as a fake Jiuzhaigou Dragon Waterfall. Ethnic holidays are re-enacted on the appropriate dates – the Water-Splashing Festival of the Dai minority, for example. Perhaps the best thing about the place is the opportunity to sample some ethnic minority speciality foods.

The China Ethnic Minorities Park is to the west of the Asian Games Village. Double-decker bus No 2 goes there. The park is open from 8 am to 10 pm daily and admission costs Y60.

Lakeview Water Park

Hújǐng Shuǐshàng Lèyuán 水上乐园

This immense, newly opened water park gets rave reviews from Beijing expats. It features a tangled web of twisting and turning water slides, an inner tube courseway and man-made beach.

The park is north of Huairou. Tourist bus Nos 1 and 3 leave at 7.25 and 8.32 am respectively each day from Beijing train station. Bus Nos 2 and 4 return to Beijing at 4.01 and 6.40 pm respectively. Admission is Y80 for adults and Y40 for children under 1.2m tall. The park is open 9 am to 6.30 pm daily from the end of May to the end of September.

ZOOS
Beijing Zoo (Map 3)

Běijīng Dòngwùyuán 北京动物园

With the exception of the well-catered to pandas, the Beijing Zoo is mostly a downer – no attempt has been made to re-create natural environments for the animals, which live in tiny cages with little shade or water.

The zoo got its start as a private garden for a Qing dynasty aristocrat. Credit for creating the zoo goes to Empress Dowager Cixi – she imported 700 animals from Germany for her own amusement. The quality of the zoo hasn't improved much since Cixi's time, though the number of animals has increased nearly 10-fold, making this the largest zoo in China.

Admission is a modest Y7, but there is an extra charge for the Panda House and other surcharges for special exhibits.

Getting to the zoo is easy enough: Take the subway to the Xizhimen station. From there it's a 15-minute walk to the west or a short ride on any of the trolley buses.

Next to the zoo is the Beijing Planetarium (Běijīng Tiānwén Guǎn) and the bizarre Soviet-style Beijing Exhibition Hall (Map 3; Běijīng Zhǎnlǎn Guǎn).

At the south gate of the Worker's Stadium near Sanlitun, the Blue Zoo (☎ 6591 3397) is a New Zealand joint venture that features a smallish but well-executed underwater zoo complete with baby sharks – great entertainment for kids. Admission is Y80 for adults and Y50 for children.

OTHER SIGHTS
Ancient Observatory (Map 7)
Gǔ Guānxiàngtái 古观象台
One interesting perspective on Beijing is the Ancient Observatory mounted on the battlements of a watchtower, once part of the city walls. Dwarfed by embassy housing blocks, it's surrounded by traffic loops and highways just west of the Friendship Store, on the south-west corner of Jianguomen Nei Dajie and Second Ring Rd. The views themselves are worth the visit. There are some English explanations. The observatory dates back to Kublai Khan's days, when it was north of the present site. Khan – like later Ming and Qing emperors – relied heavily on the predictions of astrologers to plan his military moves.

The present Beijing Observatory was built between 1437 and 1446, not only to facilitate astrological predictions but also to aid seafaring navigators. Downstairs are displays of some of the navigational equipment used by Chinese ships. On the 1st floor are replicas of five 5000-year-old pottery jars, unearthed from Henan Province in 1972 and showing painted patterns of the

sun. There are also four replicas of Han dynasty eaves tiles representing east, west, north and south. There is a map drawn on a wooden octagonal board with 1420 stars marked in gold foil or powder; it's a reproduction of the original, which is said to have been made in the Ming dynasty but based on an older map from the Tang dynasty. Busts of six prominent astronomers are also displayed.

On the roof is a variety of astronomical instruments designed by the Jesuits. The Jesuits, scholars as well as proselytisers, found their way into the capital in 1601 when Matteo Ricci and company were permitted to work with Chinese scientists. The emperor was keen to find out about European firearms and cannons from them.

The Jesuits outdid the resident Muslim calendar-setters and were given control of the observatory, becoming the Chinese court's official advisers.

Of the eight bronze instruments on display (including an equatorial armillary sphere, celestial globe and altazimuth), six were designed and constructed under the supervision of the Belgian priest Ferdinand Verbiest, who came to China in 1659 as a special employee of the Qing court.

The instruments were built between 1669 and 1673, and are embellished with sculptured bronze dragons and other Chinese handiwork – a unique mix of east and west. The azimuth theodolite was supervised by Kilian Stumpf, also a missionary. The eighth instrument, the new armillary sphere, was completed in 1744 by Ignaz Kögler. It's not clear which instruments on display are the originals.

During the Boxer Rebellion, the instruments disappeared into the hands of the French and Germans. Some were returned in 1902 and others came back under the provisions of the Treaty of Versailles (1919).

More recently, government officials were caught off guard when local and foreign rock bands got together and staged a dance party in the ancient tower. The observatory (☎ 6512 8923) is open 9 am to 5 pm daily; admission is Y10.

Central TV Tower (Map 3)

Zhōngyāng Diànshìtái 中央电视台

Though westerners tend to be less than thrilled by TV towers, these appear to be a major drawcard for Chinese tourists. At 238m, Beijing's Central TV Tower is the tallest structure in the city. For a steep Y50, you can be whisked to the top for a meal at a pricey restaurant with a bird's-eye view. Unfortunately, even the birds look depressed by Beijing's smoggy skyline. With this in mind, the trip is more rewarding at night.

The Central TV Tower (☎ 6845 0715) is on the western side of Yuyuantan Park. Bus Nos 323 and 374 stop there.

Drum Tower (Map 4)

Gǔlóu 鼓楼

The tower is an impressive structure with a solid brick base. It was built in 1420 and has several drums which were beaten to mark the hours of the day, making it in effect the Big Ben of Beijing. Time was kept with a water clock. Most cities in ancient China had similar drum towers, and not too surprisingly they were either torn down or allowed to decay once clocks and watches came into fashion.

During the Cultural Revolution, drum towers were scornfully regarded as yet another reminder of the feudal past – now they are treasured as ancient artefacts and are being restored. Local artisans are particularly keen on Beijing's Drum Tower and exhibitions are occasionally held here. It is open from 9 am to 4.30 pm daily. Admission is Y10.

Bell Tower (Map 4)

Zhōng Lóu 钟楼

Not to be confused with the Great Bell Temple in north-west Beijing (see Temples earlier), the Bell Tower sits just behind the Drum Tower (down an alley directly north). It was originally built at the same time as the Drum Tower but burnt down. The present structure is 18th century. The gigantic bell was moved to the Drum Tower for a while but has now been returned to its original location. Legend has it that the bell maker's daughter plunged into the molten iron before the bell was cast. Her father only managed to grab her shoe as she did so, and the bell's soft sound resembled that of the Chinese for 'shoe' (xié). The same story is told about a couple of other bells in China – seems like committing suicide in molten iron was a serious social problem. The tower is open from 8.30 am to 5 pm daily.

WALKING TOURS

Walking tours are close to impossible in sprawling Beijing. You can walk a bit in certain neighbourhoods like Wangfujing, Dazhalan, Qianhai Lake, Jianguomenwai and Sanlitun, but the city is so spread out that the obvious way to go is by bicycle.

BLOCKBUSTER BICYCLE TOUR

Tiantan Park (west side) – Natural History Museum – Dazhalan – Qianmen – Tiananmen Square – Chinese Revolution History Museum – Great Hall of the People – Mao's Mausoleum – Tiananmen Gate – Forbidden City – Zhongnanhai – Beihai Park – Jingshan Park – Prince Gong's Palace – Song Qingling Museum – Drum Tower – Bell Tower – Confucius Temple – Lama Temple – China Art Gallery – Wangfujing – Tiantan Park (east side) – Home?

Obviously this tour only gives you a cursory glance at Beijing's many fine sights; indeed, you could spend a full day in the Forbidden City alone. But if you start out early (such as at dawn) you can see a good chunk of town and take in some of Beijing's many moods, and you can always continue the tour the next day if your schedule permits.

For the following tour, cycling time is about two hours – Chinese bike, western legs, average pace. The starting point is the western side of Tiantan Park. The finishing point is the eastern side of the same park.

The southern end of Qianmen Dajie is called Yongdingmen Dajie; it's here that you'll find the west entrance of **Tiantan Park**. The park is certainly worth exploring, but you can do that on the way back. Right now, our goal is just a little to the north, the **Natural History Museum** on the eastern side of Yongdingmen Dajie.

After you've had your dose of natural history, continue north to where Yongdingmen

Dajie becomes Qianmen Dajie. Coming up on your left is **Dazhalan**, one of Beijing's most intriguing hutongs. Bikes cannot be ridden into this particular hutong, though you can explore most others on two wheels.

Slightly more than a stone's throw to the north is **Qianmen**, the front gate to the vast expanse of **Tiananmen Square**. Traffic is one way for north-south avenues on either side of the square. If you want to go to Tiananmen, dismount after the archway and wheel the bike to the parking areas along the sidewalk. Bicycles cannot be ridden across Tiananmen Square (apparently tanks are OK), but you can walk the bike. Nearby are the **Chinese Revolution History Museum**, **Great Hall of the People**, **Mao's Mausoleum**, **Tiananmen Gate** and the **Forbidden City** itself.

Over to the western side of the Forbidden City you're heading into the most sensitive part of the capital, the **Zhongnanhai** compound. On the right, going up Beichang Jie, you pass some older housing that lines the moat. On the left is a high wall which shields from view the area where top Party members live and work (it was decided not to rip down this section of the old walls). In 1973, when the new wing of the Beijing Hotel shot up, the police realised that guests with binoculars could observe activity in Zhongnanhai, so a fake building was erected along the western wall of the Forbidden City to block the hotel guests' line of sight. Mysterious buildings abound in this locale – as do rumours of a network of clandestine tunnels connecting such buildings.

Next is **Beihai Park**, which by this time of day should be bustling with activity. You can exercise your arms as well as your legs by hiring a rowing boat. There's a cafe near the south gate overlooking Beihai Lake, where you can refresh yourself with beer, coffee, tea or cold drinks.

Back on the bike, you'll soon bump into **Jingshan Park**. There's bicycle parking by the entrance. Jingshan Park is a splendid place to survey the smog of Beijing, get your bearings with 360° views and enjoy a good overview of the russet roofing of the Forbidden City opposite.

North of Jingshan Park it gets a bit tricky. You want to get off the main road into the small alleys running around the Shisha Hai Lakes. In this area, and worth checking out for a taste of literary history, is **Prince Gong's Palace**, thought to be the house used by Cao Xueqin as a model in his classic *The Dream of Red Mansions*.

The lake district is steeped in history; if you consult a Beijing map you will see that the set of lakes connects from north to south. In the Yuan dynasty, barges sailed through various canals to the top lake (Jīshuǐtán), a sort of harbour for Beijing. Later the lakes were used for pleasure-boating, and were bordered by the homes of high officials.

The larger lake to the north-west is the Shisha Houhai (Lake of the Ten Back Monasteries). Below that is the Shisha Qianhai (Lake of the Ten Front Monasteries). On the western side of Shicha Qianhai is the Blue Lotus Cafe, where you can have a rest and quench your thirst.

Also around the lakes you'll find the **Song Qingling Museum**, the retirement residence of Sun Yatsen's respected wife.

Make a small detour here. If you go north-east through the hutongs you will arrive at the **Bamboo Garden Hotel**, which is a wonderful example of the surprises that hutongs hold. This place was originally the personal garden of Sheng Xuanhuai, an important Qing official. There are exquisite landscaped gardens and courtyards, renovated compound architecture and a fancy restaurant with an English menu (alfresco in summer). It's a quiet place to sip a drink.

Another small detour brings you to the Kaorouji Restaurant – not necessarily the cheapest place to get your roast lamb, but the balcony dining in summer is pleasant enough. If you're here after 5 pm next door to Kaorouji is a small, as yet unnamed bar that is worth a stop. Its bamboo-adorned interior captures the feel of a hip South-East Asian beachside cafe.

Back on the main drag you come to the **Drum Tower**, which originally held 24 drums. Only one remains. Directly to the north down an alley is the **Bell Tower** – the bell no longer tolls but it's still impressive

Gong, but not Forgotten

Prince Gong is known for being the last emperor's father, but he also earned an unflattering footnote in history as a failed negotiator with the British. The issue was over who might live in Beijing's splendid courtyard houses: With the forced signing of the infamous Tianjin Treaty (1858), China was expected to permit foreign ambassadors to reside in the capital.

Most clauses of the treaty – tolerance of Christian missionaries, more 'open' trade and the continued sale of opium (illegal in China) – could be conceded. But while the British were no longer to be referred to as *yi* (barbarians), allowing them to live in the Son of Heaven's city was too much.

Unimpressed, British troops pushed the issue by force, attacking seaside forts east of Beijing. When this didn't work, the British sent negotiators to the capital, some of whom were promptly arrested and executed. By now the situation was critical; the emperor (who had fled to Manchuria) sent his brother Prince Gong to negotiate, but the Prince's efforts were doomed. The leader of the British delegation was the son of the same Lord Elgin who had removed the Parthenon's famous statuary ('Elgin's marbles') to England 'for safekeeping'. After allowing British and French troops to pillage what they could, the younger Elgin ordered the Summer Palace burned.

This act was distressing enough to the Qing, but it might have been worse: the Forbidden City was only spared because its destruction would have brought down the entire dynasty, and the British considered this a little bad for business. Prince Gong immediately agreed to all the Tianjin Treaty's terms, and further pledged a large payment of silver plus part of Kowloon to British Hong Kong. In exchange, the British agreed to protect their new gains by supporting the Qing against the dangerous Taiping rebellion.

Russ Kerr

Back on the road you'll reach the former **Confucius Temple and Imperial College**. Unless you can read stele-calligraphy, you probably won't want to spend much time here. A **stele** standing in the hutong ordered officials to dismount at this point but you can ignore this unless of course you happen to be travelling on horseback.

Just down the road is the **Lama Temple**, one of Beijing's finest temples. Along the way to the Lama Temple you might pass through several decorated lintels; these graceful *páilóu* (archways), which commemorate mandarin officials or chaste widows, were ripped out of the thoroughfares of Beijing in the 1950s. The reason given was the facilitation of traffic movement. Some have been relocated in parks. The ones you see in this hutong are rarities.

This is the northernmost point of today's journey (you're still with us, aren't you?). Head south, and if you're ready for yet another museum there's the **China Art Gallery**, a slight detour to the west at the northern end of Wangfujing. Unfortunately, Wangfujing itself is closed to cyclists.

Launch yourself into the sea of cyclists, throw your legs into cruising speed and cycle the length of Dongdan south to the east entrance of **Tiantan Park**. If this is still day one of your bike tour, you're probably too exhausted to walk inside to see the Temple of Heaven – well, there's always tomorrow. From this point, you're well positioned to head back to where you started from.

ACTIVITIES
Health Clubs

Guests at major hotels can generally use all facilities for free, while nonguests must pay additional requisite fees. A one-day pass for nonguests is about Y100 to Y150, but you can also pay by the month. Most hotels offer substantial discounts if you pay on a biannual or annual basis. Beijing's best-equipped health clubs include:

Kerry Sports Center (☎ 6499 3401) 1 Guanghua Lu. This is Beijing's most luxurious health club, with a basketball court, tennis and squash courts, an indoor pool plus a full range of weight and cardio equipment; Y6000 joining fee plus a monthly fee of Y1100.

China World Fitness Center (☎ 6505 2266) 1 Jianguomen Wai Dajie. After the Kerry Center, China World is considered Beijing's next best place for a work-out; Y500 joining fee plus a monthly fee of Y920.

Kempinski Hotel (☎ 6465 3388) 50 Liangmaqiao Lu. Smaller than the above two clubs, but also a favourite of Beijing expats, the club is split into two sections: the main one at basement level and a smaller part on the top floor of the hotel, where there's a small but attractive pool. It also offers aerobic classes for Y250 for 10 sessions; no joining fee, Y950 per month.

Swissôtel (☎ 6501 2288) Dongsishitiao. In addition to cardio and weight equipment, the Swissôtel has a swimming pool and regular aerobic classes; Y1500 joining fee plus Y850 monthly.

In addition to the above, the Hilton, Harbor Plaza, Great Wall Sheraton, Traders, Movenpick and New Otani Hotels also have health clubs.

Reflexology

Dating back to the fourth century BC, foot reflexology *(zúdǐ ànmó)* is acknowledged for both its diagnostic and healing properties. Reflexologists believe that every organ in the body is connected to a point on the sole of the foot. Using this approach ailments can not only be diagnosed but also cured. No matter what your beliefs, a foot massage is undeniably a stress-reliever and a pick-me-up.

Some of the city's best reflexologists can be found at the Beijing Tianhe Liangzi Healthy Company (☎ 6506 4466 ext 6087), at 1A Jianguomen Wai Dajie, in the building next door (west) of the China World Trade Center. A 90-minute session costs Y138. There is another branch in Rainbow Plaza, on Dongsanhuan Lu where it meets Gongti Beilu.

Bowling

Bowling *(gǔnmùqiú)* has taken off in China, and you'll have no trouble finding a neighbourhood bowling alley wherever you may be staying. Many hotels also have bowling

alleys, including the Friendship and International Hotels, Holiday Inn Lido and Scitech. You can also find a bowling alley at the Beijing Recreation Centre, north of the Asian Games Village.

Golf

Golf *(gāoěrfūqiú)* enjoys high prestige in face-conscious China. If you want to keep your swing in form, check out the Beijing International Golf Club (Běijīng Guójì Gāoěrfūqiú Jùlèbù; ☎ 6076 2288). This Sino-Japanese joint venture is considered the best course in Beijing. The 18-hole course is 35km north of Beijing, close to the Ming Tombs. Pushing that little ball around is not cheap, but the course is in top condition and the scenery is spectacular. Green fees are Y650 on weekdays and Y1100 on weekends and public holidays. You can rent a set of golf clubs and spiked golf shoes for an additional fee. The course is open from 8 am to 5 pm, March to November.

There is a 36-hole golf course which goes by a variety of names at Shunyi, north-east of the capital airport. Officially it's the Beijing Golf Club (Běijīng Gāoěrfūqiú Jùlèbù; ☎ 8947 0005). Green fees and equipment will set you back Y350 (women) or Y1000 (men) on weekdays, Y1400 (men and women) on weekends. It's open 8 am to 5 pm.

In the city itself is the nine-hole Chaoyang Golf Club (Cháoyáng Gāoěrfūqiú Chǎng; ☎ 6500 1149), at Tuanjiehu Beikou. It includes a driving range, but the course leaves much to be desired. Green fees are Y240 on weekdays and Y350 on weekends.

Miniature Golf Mark Twain used to say that golf was a good walk ruined. If you agree, you might find miniature golf more suitable.

Beijing's best miniature golf course can be found in the Beijing Dongdan Sports Center (☎ 6528 8495), at 108 Chongwenmen Nei Dajie, on the south-west corner of Dongdan and Chang'an. One 18-hole round costs Y25 for adults and Y10 for children.

continued on page 117

A STROLL DOWN MEMORY LANE

Off the wide avenues with their high-rises, fast-food outlets and relentless traffic, an increasingly rare Beijing phenomenon lingers on. Known as *hutong*, these fast-disappearing narrow side alleys, which form the skeleton of old Beijing, give a fascinating glimpse into the ancient capital.

Hutong History

The story of Beijing's hutongs is almost as fascinating as a visit to the lanes themselves. The original meaning of the word 'hutong' is uncertain. It is based on the Mongolian, and derives from the time when the Khan's horsemen camped in the new capital of the Yuan dynasty. It may have referred to a passageway between *gers* (or 'yurts', the Russian term). Or it may come from *hottog*, meaning a well – wherever there was water in the dry plain around Beijing, there were inhabitants.

This being China, lots of commerce takes place on hutongs. In a city with abundant labour, specialisation is the rule – lanes dedicated to cotton-jacket padding or taxi-sign repair thrive just out of sight of state department stores. Many hutongs were named after the markets (fish, rice, sheep) or trades (hats, bowstrings, trousers) once conducted along them. Others took their names from the seats of government offices or specialised suppliers to the palace (granaries, red lacquer, armour). Yet others were named after dukes now entombed in history books.

Around the Forbidden City there were some rather unusual industries. Wet-Nurse Lane was full of young mothers who breast-fed the imperial offspring. They were selected from around China on scouting trips four times a year. Clothes-Washing Lane was where the women who did the imperial laundry lived. The maids, grown old in the service of the court, were packed off to faraway places until their intimate knowledge of royal undergarments was out of date.

Wind-Water Lanes

Following *fengshui* and the precepts of the classic *Zhou Li* text, hutongs ideally run east-west, since compound entrances should face south. This maximises sunny, southern Yang (left side; heavenly forces) vibes while minimising northern Yin (right side; earth forces) ones. These 'regular' hutongs intersect with broader north-south streets and avenues to form a grid, in accordance with the symbolism of the earth as a square.

Strict rules for the width of lanes, streets and avenues were relaxed over the centuries, and hutongs ranging from the claustrophobic (50cm wide) to the relatively capacious (10m) emerged. Hutong directions vary as well: some are slanted to the south-east, others run north-south. Entering some neighbourhoods is like stepping into a maze.

Courtyard Houses

Behind the walls which define the orderly chaos of hutongs lie Beijing's courtyard houses *(siheyuan)*, where now only a fraction of the city's population lives. Until 'modernisation' got going in a big way and sky-scrapers started turning a long-time horizontal city into a vertical eyesore, these one-storey structures formed a dignified, slate-grey backdrop to the auspicious vermilion and yellow imperial palaces.

Make sure you see life on both sides of the solid courtyard gates while you still can – the siheyuan are disappearing fast. Countless generations of Beijing families rich and poor have lived and died here. Only a hard-hearted real estate developer would deny that something more than traditional architecture is disappearing along with the siheyuan.

Like hutongs, siheyuan were built according to a plan hardly changed since the Han dynasty (206 BC–AD 220). Order and harmony are key values – a siheyuan's four-walled enclosure (as opposed to the three-walled *sanheyuan* found in some parts of China) is a model of symmetry. Like Beijing itself, courtyard houses are oriented to a north-south axis.

Confucian ideals of joining heaven and earth through *jen* ('human-heartedness') and proper filial relations can be seen in the way the si-heyuan is laid out. Courtyard arrangements can form heavenly characters on the ground, like the sun (the outer rooms and central guest hall in the floor plan illustration form the 'sun' character).

In a common, one-courtyard house (shaped like the character *kou*, symbolising 'right speech'), ancestral tablets and family shrines are carefully placed to receive first morning light through the south-east entrance. Ancestor tablets aren't decorations: the most honoured people in the house (eg, the grandparents) sleep closest to them. And mirrors aren't just for vanity: they're used to ward off demons and help direct a healthy flow of *qi* through the house. Ideal arrangements of rooms and courtyards also depend on the Yin and Yang balance of elements in the compound.

Courtyards have some less esoteric aspects too: they provide ventilation and light, and if there's a small courtyard off one of the main halls (as in the upper left corner of the illustration), even a little privacy.

The size and number of courtyards in a siheyuan originally depended on the owner's status (so a 'seeing clearly' layout, with its three

CAROLINE LIOU

Right: A hutong during the celebration of the PRC's 50th anniversary

A Trip Down Memory Lane

GLENN BEANLAND

GLENN BEANLAND

GLENN BEANLAND

Left: Beijing's fast-disappearing hutongs offer a glimpse of times gone by.

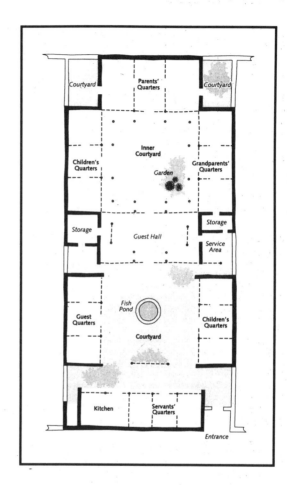

Right: Courtyard houses have been built to a traditional design hardly changed since the Han dynasty.

main courtyards, was more prestigious than a 'sun' plan). Nonetheless, aside from the structure's scale, even a humble siheyuan (with a fence and low gate rather than high walls) shared the same layout as the Son of Heaven's living quarters in the Forbidden City.

The inner and outer aspects of the Forbidden City were repeated in the surrounding siheyuan. The courtyard nearest the entrance was open to just about anyone, while the far courtyard had limited access (the guest hall in the floor plan illustration marks the transition area between the two).

From the Ming dynasty onwards, four main siheyuan pockets were distinguished around the Forbidden City: to the east mainly lived the aristocracy, to the west were officials, while the north and south was largely occupied by labourers, traders and those eking out a marginal living in the capital, often with squalid housing to match.

Beijing's often violent, earthquake-prone history means that most of the courtyard houses you'll see date from the 19th century. The 1976 earthquake destroyed some of these; bureaucrats are taking care of what's left.

The Housing Freeze

Though they're damn cold in winter (coal braziers and/or space heaters make life bearable, and Chinese babies aren't wrapped like arctic mummies for nothing), given the choice between a high-rise block and a traditional compound, most residents of Beijing would probably opt for the latter. The compounds have a lot more character – and provide space to grow vegetables. On the other hand, with running water, heating, electricity and toilets (all or most of which siheyuan lack), life in new high-rise flats may look tempting to some. Many young Beijingers are also willing to sacrifice a lot of traditional living for a little bit of modern privacy.

Originally built to house one more-or-less extended family (with servants when possible), a siheyuan can be pretty cramped. Some compounds now hold 30 people – halls have been divided into smaller rooms and add-ons built to satisfy the allocation of housing space. Rental subsidy policies, connections and free-booting capitalism dictate

KH

who can afford the luxury of having a courtyard house to themselves. Desirable courtyard houses are now astronomically expensive, ranging from US$2000 to US$10,000 per month.

The Fate of Hutongs

The motto of Beijing's developers might be 'Planning grows out of the blade of a bulldozer'. How best to preserve the old city while developing modern infrastructure has been debated for years. Meanwhile, the practice has been to preserve a few worthy siheyuan (which may then be walled in by new high-rises), recreate 'old Beijing' on some gentrified lanes (eg Liulichang), and plough through as many others as possible for new streets and housing.

Exploring Hutongs

Beijing's remaining traditional lanes have become a tourist attraction, but happily tour buses (thus far) don't fit in them. Hutongs are best explored by bicycle (see the boxed text 'On Your Bike' in the Getting Around Chapter and the Blockbuster Bicycle Tour section in the Things to See & Do chapter), either self-powered or pedalled for you.

Hutongs can be found in pockets all around Beijing. Some of the more well-known and better-preserved hutong areas are: on the eastern side of the Forbidden City (nanchizi and beichizi); the area to the west of Qianhai and Houhai Lakes (just north of Beihai Park); Liulichang and Dazhalan (in Qianmen); and the area north of Jingshan Park up to the Drum Tower. The area west of Qianhai and Houhai in particular is an excellent place to explore on bike or on foot. On the shore of the lake you can catch Beijing *laotou* (old folks) quietly passing the time fishing or playing Chinese chess. On the western shore of Qianhai is the Blue Lotus Cafe (see Cafes in the Places to Eat chapter), the perfect place for a rest after your wanderings. A 10-minute walk north-east from the Blue Lotus is a small as yet unnamed bar located just next door to Kaorouji (see the Places to Eat chapter). If you're in the area in the late afternoon or evening, this lakeside hut also makes for a nice place to relax and take in your surroundings.

KH

As you roam today's hutongs, several characteristics give you clues to the wealth and status of the original resident. Look at the outside gate: You'll notice beams or knobs protruding from above the doorway. Two knobs indicate the home of a commoner, merchant or scholar, while four knobs indicate the home of a high-ranking official or perhaps even a member of the imperial household. Also an indication of a wealthy household is a gate that is set back from the street, with two small walls protruding before either side of the doorway.

On both sides of the base of the door lie carved door stones. Door stones are typically round with two flat sides or rectangular blocks into which flowers or animals are carved. Households of high-ranking officials are flanked with door stones in the shape of lions.

If the gate happens to be ajar, you might catch a glimpse of a 'spirit wall,' placed just inside the gate. The wall is meant to protect residents from ghosts, which are traditionally believed to walk only in straight lines. Thus a ghost trying to enter a courtyard house would bump into the spirit wall and, unable to turn right or left, would be prevented from entering.

A pedicab tour plies some of the more memorable lanes along a three-hour route that includes the Drum Tower and a stop at Prince Gong's Palace, a fine example of an aristocrat's siheyuan. There are two tours daily; see the Dragon Tours boxed text in the Getting Around chapter. Tours can be arranged at the travel desk (call or drop in) at most large hotels, or ring the Beijing Hutong Tourist Agency (☎ 6615 9097). Be on time, as pedicabs wait for no-one.

Russ Kerr & Robert Storey

continued from page 110

Hiking

If you're interested in hiking less-trodden areas of the Great Wall, contact the Great Wall Hikers (☎ 6307 4009) for a schedule of their outings.

Horse Riding

If horse riding *(qímǎ)* is your interest, there are several clubs on the outskirts of Beijing or farther afield. The following are worth trying:

Beijing Green Equestrian Club (☎ 6457 7166)
1km east of Lijing Garden Villa on Jichang-fulu; Y150/180 adults/children
Beijing Horseman Club (☎ 8575 0149) 6km east of the Jingguang New World Hotel; Y120 per hour
Daoxianghu Horse Grounds (☎ 6261 9158) north-west of the Summer Palace at Daoxi-anghu Park; Y150 per hour
Kangxi Grasslands (see the Excursions chapter for more details); Y120 per hour.

Ice Skating

Beijing's best indoor rink for ice skating *(liū bīng)* is in China World (☎ 6505 3551, basement level). The 800-sq-metre rink is open year round, and best of all, you can rent skates in big shoe sizes; Y20 to Y40 per hour.

There are heaps of outdoor venues, and the usual warnings apply about making sure it's damned cold and the ice thick enough to support your bulk. Popular spots include Beihai Lake, Kunming Lake, Zizhuyuan Park and the moat around the Forbidden City. Kunming Lake has a marked-off area where the ice is considered safe (is it really?) and there are skate rentals there.

Kite Flying

Kite flying *(fēngzhēng)* is an old tradition in China and Beijing's favourite venue is Tiananmen Square. Kites are for hire in the square itself, or you can buy one at the Friendship Store (or other department stores).

Paintball

A good way to let out your frustrations, paintball *(pītèbó)* can be played at a number of places, including the Caidanbo Jichang (Cáidànbō Jīchǎng) Paintball Center. Also worth trying is the Wanfangting Paintball Grounds (Wànfāngtíng Pītèbó Yùndòng Chǎng), in Wanfangting Park on the southern part of Third Ring Rd.

Shooting

If being ripped off by street vendors and pedicab drivers is getting you down, you can work out your aggressions with some shooting *(shèjī)* at the Beijing Shooting Range (Běijīng Shèjī Chǎng; ☎ 6886 2277) on the west side of town (near Badachu). Run by the PLA, it has Chinese 'Red Star' pistols and AK-47s. If this doesn't crank your tractor, west of the Ming Tombs is the International Shooting Range where you can play with bazookas and anti-aircraft guns! Cost is around US$1 per bullet – much more for artillery shells.

Swimming

For swimming *(yóuyǒng)*, you can take a dip at most of the big-name tourist hotels, but large Olympic-sized pools are harder to find. Perhaps the cheapest and best place for the more hard-core swimmer would be the Olympic-size pool at the 21st Century Hotel complex. Worthwhile hotel pools can be found at the China World Hotel, Kerry Center, Hotel New Otani, Swissôtel, the Great Wall Sheraton and the Hilton. The Friendship Hotel has a beautiful outdoor swimming pool where you can relax on lounge chairs and while away a sweltering Beijing summer day.

Squash

For squash *(xiǎo xiàngpí qiú)*, the Kempinski (☎ 6465 3388) has three courts; the Kerry Center (☎ 6561 8833) and Hilton (☎ 6466 2288) each have two.

Tennis

Known to the Chinese as *wǎng qiú* ('net ball'), tennis has an enthusiastic following and all public facilities are very crowded. It's much easier to find a vacant court at an upmarket hotel or club, but such places charge Y120 to Y200 per hour. Even then, reservations are usually mandatory. You can try any of the following venues:

Chaoyang Tennis Club (☎ 6501 0959) south gate of Chaoyang Park; Y200 per hour for nonmembers

Friendship Hotel (☎ 6849 8888 ext 32) Baishiqiao Lu (Third Ring Rd); outdoor courts for Y60 per hour on weekdays, Y80 per hour on weekends

International Club (☎ 6532 2046 ext 3015) 21 Jianguomen Wai Dajie; indoor courts for Y150 per hour, Y200 per hour after 5pm and on weekends

International Tennis Centre (☎ 6714 2374) 50 Tiantan Lu (south-east of the Temple of Heaven); indoor and outdoor courts for Y300 per hour, Y100 if you're a member

Olympic Sports Center Tennis Courts (☎ 6491 2233 ext 218) 1 Anding Lu (head north from Andingmen and it's just before you reach the Asian Games Village); outdoor courts for Y40 per hour weekdays, Y50 weekends

Sino-Japanese Youth Centre (☎ 6466 3311 ext 3185) 40 Liangma Lu; outdoor courts for Y60 per hour

The China World Fitness Center, Kerry Center, Shangri-La Hotel and Movenpick Hotel (with outdoor courts) also have excellent tennis facilities.

COURSES
Martial Arts

For martial arts *(wǔshù)* enthusiasts, the Yuanmingyuan Ruyi Martial Arts School (☎ 6257 1596, 6258 7485) is at Qinghuaxi Lu, 152 Yuanmingyuan Lu, next to the Old Summer Palace. This is the place to go if you want to study *gongfu* and *qigong*; Y600 for three months.

The Martial Arts Community Club (☎ 6418 1099), Culture Club, 29 Dongzhong Jie, at East Gate Plaza (next to Poly Plaza off Second Ring Rd), offers *jujitsu* and taiji classes. It's Y500 per month; classes start at 7.30 pm and take place two to three times per week.

Traditional Medicine

Despite the language, one subject which continues to draw large numbers of foreign students is traditional Chinese herbal medicine and acupuncture. However, it's difficult (if not impossible) to find classes with English-language instruction. The following offer classes:

The Beijing University of Chinese Medicine (Zhōngyā Xuéyuàn; ☎ 6421 3458, fax 6422 0858) 11 Beisanhuan Donglu, Chaoyang District. This is the most well-known traditional Chinese medicine school, and the most popular with foreigners. To gain admission one must pass the middle-band C level HSK (Chinese-language proficiency exam). On offer are courses in Chinese medicine, acupuncture and Chinese pharmacology. Tuition is US$3500 per year.

Hua Tuo School of Traditional Chinese Medicine Institute (☎ 6401 4411 ext 2481) 18 Beixincang Hutong, Dongzhimen Nei; classes in acupuncture and massage.

Music

There aren't many places in the West where you can learn to play traditional Chinese musical instruments such as the two-stringed fiddle or three-stringed lute. In Beijing the following schools offer such courses:

Central Music Conservatory (Zhōngyāng Yīnyuè Xuéyuàn; ☎ 6642 5702) 43 Baojia Jie, Xuanwu District

China Music Conservatory (Zhōngguó Yīnyuè Xuéyuàn; ☎ 6487 4884) Deshengmen Wai Dajie, Weizikeng, Chaoyang District

Sino-Japanese Youth Exchange Center (☎ 6466 3311 ext 502) 40 Liangmaqiao Lu, Chaoyang District.

Cooking

More and more travellers are interested in learning to cook Chinese cuisine. Chang's Club (☎ 6416 0377,✆ cchang@unet.net.cn), at the southern end of Bar Street (just north of Gongti Beilu) near the Butterfly Bar, offers instruction in English and also allows you to choose the dishes you want to learn to cook.

Language

Many foreigners take the opportunity to study Mandarin while they're staying in Beijing. For details of schools, see the boxed text 'Language Schools' on the facing page.

Language Schools

Beijing is a good place to study Chinese, but prices and the quality of instruction vary widely. A budget quote for four hours of instruction per day, five days a week is US$500 per month. Some schools charge by the semester, with rates typically US$1100 to US$1300 per semester, and about two-thirds that for the summer session. Dormitory housing starts at around US$15 a day for a shared dorm room with private bath, air-con and TV. The lower range is about US$4 a day for a shared room, no air-con and shared bath. It's probably to your advantage to sign up for a short semester and extend later if you like it.

Most language schools (as well as other college campuses) are in Haidian, the far north-west edge of Beijing. The spring semester usually starts just after Chinese New Year (February or March) and ends in early July, and is followed by a short summer semester (six to nine weeks). The fall semester starts in mid-September and ends in early January. Class hours for full-time students are generally 8 am till noon, Monday to Friday. Following are some of the more well-known language schools:

The Beijing Language and Culture University (BLCU; Yǔyán Xuéyuàn; admissions ☎ 8230 3088, short courses ☎ 8230 3928, fax 8230 3902), at 15 Xueyuan Lu, Haidian, has the largest number of liúxuéshēng (foreign students). In fact, you could easily go through this course and never speak much Chinese because there are so many foreign students here. Still, this is considered the best language school in Beijing, with about 20 to 25 students per instructor. It has a Web site at www.blcu.edu.cn.

Beijing Normal University (Běishīdà; ☎ 6220 7986, fax 6220 0567), at 19 Xinjiekouwai Dajie, also attracts many foreign students. One advantage of studying here is that it's closer to the centre of Beijing than other Haidian language schools. Classes fill quickly, so register as early as possible. Class size is about 25 students per instructor.

Classes at Beijing University (Běidà; ☎ 6275 1230, fax 6275 1233, @ cqlb@pku.edu.cn), at 5 Yiheyuan Lu, are generally smaller (about five to 10 students) than at other schools. While this is China's premier university, the language school here doesn't have as good a reputation as BLCU.

People's University (Rénmín Dàxué; ☎ 6251 1588, @ rmdxwsc@public.bta.net.cn), at 175 Haidian Lu, also attracts a sizable population of foreign students (though not nearly as many as those mentioned earlier). Classroom and dorm conditions are on the shabby side.

Beijing Second Foreign Language University (Èrwài; ☎ 6577 8564, fax 6576 2520) attracts mostly Japanese and Korean students. Unlike most other college campuses, it is in the Chaoyang District. However, because it's so far east it still takes over an hour to get here from the city centre.

Other universities that offer Chinese-language courses are Qinghua University (Qīnghuá Dàxué), considered China's second-most prestigious university after Beida; the Film Academy (Diànyǐng Xuéyuàn); the University of International Business and Economics (Jīngmào Dàxué); Beijing Foreign Studies University (Běiwài) and Capital Normal University (Shǒushīdà).

If you want to study part-time, Beijing's two best-known language schools are Bridge School (Qiáo Yǔyán Xuéyuàn; @ bridge.school@mailcity.com) and Taiwan Language Institute. Bridge School has branches at Cofco Plaza (☎ 6526 0818, fax 6526 4051), Tower B, Suite 622, 8 Jianguomen Nei Dajie, and at Room 1308 (☎ 6468 0290, fax 6468 0287), 3rd floor, Guangming Hotel, Liangmaqiao Lu.

The Taiwan Language Institute (TLI; ☎ 6466 3311 ext 3509, @ tli@bj.col.com.cn), at 40 Liangmaqiao Lu, has mostly one-on-one classes. TLI's teaching methods and books emphasise conversation, and give the student the option not to learn Chinese characters. TLI has a good reputation and is popular with Beijing journalists and embassy staff. However, tuition (about US$13 per hour) is very costly.

Other language schools that offer after-hours, one-on-one instruction are the Island Chinese Language School (☎ 6505 1226), at Room 3532, 15th floor Consultec Building, China World Trade Center, and the Beijing Chinese Language and Cultural Center for Diplomatic Missions (LCC; ☎ 6532 3005, @ zhongxin@public2.east.cn.net), at 7 Sanlitun Beixiaojie, on the northern side of the German Embassy. Rates for both these schools are about Y70 per hour.

Places to Stay

PLACES TO STAY

In China, you can't simply stay in any hotel with a vacancy – the hotel must be designated a 'tourist hotel'. There's not much use trying to charm your way into a Chinese-only hotel; even if the staff would love you to stay they dare not break the rules, which are enforced by the Public Security Bureau (PSB).

During the summer peak season, hotels (especially the cheaper ones) tend to fill up quickly and you may have to scramble to find something affordable. If you arrive in town without hotel reservations and are planning to stay in a mid-range or top-end hotel, stop by the airport hotel reservations counter, which has been known to get discounts of up to 50% off rack rates. The counter is located just outside the arrivals area, after you pass through customs.

Bargaining for a room is usually possible – politely ask for a 'discount'. Many travellers negotiate discounts of 30% or more.

Hotel reservation Web sites can also be useful in getting reductions on standard rates. Try www.sinohotel.com or www.cbw.com.

For more information on the taxes and discounts applicable to hotels in Beijing, see under Costs and Taxes in the Facts for the Visitor chapter.

PLACES TO STAY – BUDGET

The good news is that dormitory hotels in Beijing seem to be proliferating; the bad news is that they're still mostly only found in the southern part of town, far from the city centre. For the sake of definition, any hotel where a double can be had for less than Y200 in the high season is considered 'budget'. Dorm beds in the high season average around Y35.

Beijing (Map 2)

The *Jinghua Hotel* (*Jīnghuá Fàndiàn;* ☎ *6722 2211, Nansanhuan Zhonglu, Yongdingmen Wai*) is on the southern part of Third Ring Rd, far from the city centre, and despite complaints of exceptionally unfriendly service, it's a good place to get travel information, rent bicycles and book trips to the Great Wall. Dorm beds cost Y35 in a four-bed room, or Y26 in a 30-bed room. Twins are Y180. Bus Nos 2 and 17 from Qianmen stop nearby. For many years this was *the* backpacker haven in Beijing, although things look set to change with the newly opened Zhaolong International Youth Hostel, a much better option (see Map 5).

Just around the corner are the *Sea Star Hotel* (*Hǎixīng Dàjiǔdiàn;* ☎ *6721 8855, fax 6722 7915, 166 Haihutun, Yongwai*) and the *Lihua Hotel* (*Lìhuá Fàndiàn;* ☎ *6721 1144, 71 Yangqiao, Yongdingmen Wai*). Dorm beds at both are Y35. Bus No 14, from Xidan and Hepingmen subway stations, is the easiest way to get there.

A kilometre north of the east gate of Beijing Language and Culture University (Yuyan Xueyuan) is *Yujing Dasha* (☎ *6234 0033, Xueqing Lu*), which has doubles with shared bath starting at Y160. The hotel has a dorm-like atmosphere, as many foreign students studying at nearby universities rent rooms here by the month.

West of the university, near the south gate is the *Xijiao Hotel* (*Xījiāo Bīnguǎn;* ☎ *623. 2288, 18 Wangzhuang Lu*), located in Wudakou where Beijing's Korean students hang out. The hotel has a luxurious lobby, and rooms are well kept. Doubles start at Y192. It has a Web site at www.xijiao-hotel.com.cn

Inside Beijing University's campus is the *Shaoyuan Hotel* (*Sháoyuán Bīnguǎn,* ☎ *6275 2218, fax 6256 4095*). The hotel is next to the foreign students' dormitory. Standard doubles are Y250; if there's an empty dorm room it can be had for Y180. Rooms are clean, but the atmosphere is drab.

Just outside the south-west corner of Beijing University is the large *Resource Yanyuan Hotel* (*Zīyuán Yànyuán Bīnguǎn,* ☎ *6275 0869, fax 6275 0858, 1 Yiheyuan Lu*). Standard doubles start at Y360, although you can get a windowless room for Y240. This hotel doesn't have much atmosphere, but rooms are clean.

Dongcheng (Map 4)

Built by a Mongolian general in the Qing dynasty, the *Lüsongyuan Hotel* (*Lǚsōngyuán Bīnguǎn;* ☎ 6401 1116, 6404 0436, fax 6403 0418, 22 Banchang Hutong), north of the Forbidden City, is a superb courtyard hotel. Its location among the *hutong* makes it a good base for exploring the city, and the staff are very friendly. You can also rent bikes here for Y30 per day. Dorm beds are Y100, singles are Y250 and doubles Y450. If you want a double bed book ahead as the hotel only has two (the rest of the rooms have two single beds). There is a small sign (in English) on Andingmen Nei Dajie. The hotel is about 50m down the alley. Take bus No 104 from Beijing train station to the Beibingma Si bus stop. Walk a short distance south then turn right down the first alley.

The *Beijing International Youth Hostel* (*Běijīng Guójì Qīngnián Bīnguǎn;* ☎ 6512 6145, fax 6522 9494, 10th floor, 9 Jianguomen Nei Dajie*), in the building behind the International Hotel, is a short distance east of Tiananmen Square. Facilities and prices are the same as for the Zhaolong International Youth Hostel (see under Chaoyang later), although this branch markets itself more to groups and is more likely to be booked solid during peak season.

The *Fangyuan Hotel* (*Fāngyuán Bīnguǎn;* ☎ 6525 6331, fax 6513 8549, 36 Dengshikou Xijie*) deserves a plug even though it's relatively undiscovered by westerners. Its very central location off Wangfujing Jie is a big plus. The staff are pretty friendly and the hotel is well run. Twins cost Y217 and Y248.

Chaoyang (Map 5)

Clean, comfortable and conveniently located is the recently opened *Zhaolong International Youth Hostel* (*Zhàolóng Fàndiàn Guójì Qīngnián Bīnguǎn;* ☎ 6597 2299, fax 6597 2288, ✉ zlh@zhaolonghotel.com.cn, 2 Gongti Beilu*), in the building directly behind the Zhaolong Hotel. Just around the corner from Beijing's premier nightlife area, this is hands down your best bet for budget accommodation in Beijing. A dorm bed is Y60 per night for nonmembers and Y50 for members.

The hostel has 140 beds. Amenities include a laundry, kitchen, air-con and 24-hour hot water.

The *Red House Hotel* (☎ 6416 7500, ✉ redhouse@ht.rol.cn.net, 10 Chun Xiu Lu*) has rooms with kitchenettes starting at Y300. The best thing about this place is its location, in the middle of Sanlitun (heading north on Gongti Xilu, cross Gongti Beilu and it's on the right). It also has a bar downstairs. Red House is owned by the same folks who started Poachers Bar (*the* place to go a couple of years ago). Dormitory space (Y95) was in the works at the time of writing.

An OK budget option also in Sanlitun is the *Gongti Hotel* (*Gōngtǐ Bīnguǎn;* ☎ 6501 6655), located in the eastern side of Worker's Stadium. Doubles with shared bath start at Y140. The hotel is a bit run down, but it's conveniently located in the heart of Beijing's bar scene. Of course, if a sports match or concert is taking place in the stadium prepare for lots of noise.

The foreign students dormitory of the *21st Century Hotel* (*Èrshíyī Shìjì Fàndiàn;* ☎ 6460 9911 ext 6101, 40 Liangmaqiao Lu*), near the Lufthansa Center, has also been known to rent rooms out to travellers. Dorm rooms here are pretty comfortable, with air-con and private bath, but cost Y166 for a double room in a suite.

Fengtai & Xuanwu (Map 6)

The *Qiaoyuan Hotel* (*Qiáoyuán Fàndiàn;* ☎ 6301 2244, fax 6303 0119, 135 Youanmen Dong Binhe Lu*) offers dorm beds for Y30 in a 10-bed room or Y60 in a two-bed room with bath. Although the rooms are passable, its location gives it a feeling of isolation.

The *Far East Hotel* (*Yuǎndōng Fàndiàn;* ☎ 6301 8811, fax 6301 8233, 90 Tieshuxie Jie, Qianmen Wai*) has a fine location among Beijing's hutongs. Tieshuxie Jie is in fact the western end of Dazhalan (south-west of Qianmen). Twins cost Y298 to Y398. There are also cheerless doubles in the basement for Y160 (shared bath). To get here head south on Nanxinhua Jie. About 200m after you pass Liulichang you'll see a sign (in English) on the right-hand side of the street saying Far East Hotel. Follow the hutong for about 50m; the four-storey hotel is on the right. The Y298 rooms are often fully booked so try to call ahead.

Chongwen & Chaoyang (Map 7)

It's sometimes possible to stay in foreign student dormitories if there are empty rooms. The *Central Academy of Arts Dormitory* *(Zhōngyāng Měishù Xuéyuàn Liúxuéshēng Sùshè;* ☎ *6513 0926, 8th floor, 5 Xiaowei Hutong)* is very centrally located behind the Palace Hotel in Wangfujing and has been known to rent out doubles (shared bath) for Y120. As space is very limited, it's a good idea to call ahead. From the Palace Hotel walk west and turn left down the first small street (if you've hit Xindong'an Plaza you've gone too far). The dormitory is about 50m down on the right. Enter the second door.

PLACES TO STAY – MID-RANGE

The following are hotels with twin rooms in the Y200 to Y600 range. It's worth considering staying in a courtyard hotel, most of which fall in this range. Staying in one of these is a good way to experience a more traditionally Chinese atmosphere; all of the courtyard hotels are located amid Beijing's few remaining hutongs and offer a quiet escape from the city.

Dongcheng (Map 4)

The *Haoyuan Guesthouse (Hàoyuán Bīnguǎn;* ☎ *6512 5557, fax 6512 5557, 53 Shijia Hutong)* is a quiet courtyard hotel close to Wangfujing's main drag. Comfortable, clean rooms are Y360 for a double (all rooms have two single beds). To get here go north on Dongdan Dajie. About 25m before Dengshikou Dajie you'll see a small alley – Shijia Hutong – leading off to the right. The hotel is about 50m down the alley on your left. You can't miss the big red gates guarded by two stone lions.

In a hutong just off Jiaodaokou, the *Youhao Hotel (Yǒuhǎo Bīnguǎn;* ☎ *6403 1114, fax 6401 4603, 7 Houyuansi)* was once the residence of Chiang Kaishek, and after 1949 the site of the Yugoslav Embassy. Today it's a nice but slightly run-down courtyard hotel. Singles/doubles are Y288/380.

West of the Drum Tower, the *Bamboo Garden Hotel (Zhúyuán Bīnguǎn;* ☎ *6403 2229, fax 6401 2633, 24 Xiaoshiqiao Hutong)* is a largish hotel surrounding four interconnected courtyards with a traditional Chinese rock garden and bamboo groves. Small doubles are Y380, while more spacious doubles with a balcony overlooking the garden are Y580. Y1200 will get you the suite decorated with Ming-style furniture.

Fengtai & Xuanwu (Map 6)

The *Qianmen Hotel (Qiánmén Fàndiàn;* ☎ *6301 6688, fax 6301 3883, 175 Yong'an Lu),* south-west of Qianmen, has standard twins for Y630. This large hotel is a favourite of package-tour groups.

Chongwen & Chaoyang (Map 7)

A well-kept courtyard hotel, a short distance south of the east gate of Tiantan Park, *Tiantan Haoyuan Hotel (Tiāntán Hàoyuán Bīnguǎn;* ☎ *6701 4499, fax 6701 2404, 9A Tiantan Donglu)* has recently renovated doubles for Y480 and suites for Y880. Of Beijing's courtyard hotels, this is the best maintained and most stylish, and considering the location it's excellent value.

Near the Temple of Heaven, the *Tiantan Sports Hotel (Tiāntán Tǐyù Bīnguǎn;* ☎ *6701 3388, fax 6701 5388, 10 Tiyuguan Lu)* was recently renovated. Clean, good-value (though characterless) doubles are Y268.

The *Beiwei Hotel (Běiwěi Fàndiàn;* ☎ *6301 2266, fax 6301 1366, 13 Xijing Lu),* on the western side of Tiantan Park, has recently renovated clean rooms. Singles/doubles are Y180/232.

Also in the area, very close to the west gate of the Temple of Heaven, the newly opened *Xiao Xiang Hotel (Xiǎoxiāng Dàjiǔdiàn;* ☎ *8316 1188, fax 6303 0690, 42 Beiwei Lu)* is a standard hotel, but as rooms are new it's extremely clean. Doubles start at Y480, but staff are quick to offer a 40% discount.

Just around the corner from Panjiayuan (aka the Dirt Market), the small *Leyou Hotel (Lèyóu Fàndiàn;* ☎ *6771 2266, fax 6771 1636, 13 Dongsanhuan Nanlu)* is nothing special, but rooms are clean and in good shape. Standard doubles start at Y288.

PLACES TO STAY – TOP END

Keeping up with the top-end hotels in Beijing is like skiing uphill. No sooner does one extravaganza open its doors than the ground-breaking ceremony is held for an even more luxurious pleasure palace. For definition purposes, anything costing over Y700 for a standard twin room is called 'top end'. Listed are a selection of Beijing's top five-star hotels and good-value, centrally located three- or four-star hotels. As rates for five-star hotels are given in US dollars, that's what we've listed here. Keep in mind that there is usually a 15% service charge on top of the room rate. As with mid-range hotels, discounts of 30% or more are often available if you ask.

It's worth noting that while many government-run tourist hotels rate themselves as four- and five-star (with prices to match), service is often not up to international standards. A good example of this is the state-owned Beijing Hotel, which continues to 'win awards'.

Beijing's top luxury hotels can be narrowed down to three: the St Regis, the Grand and the Palace. The China World, the Kerry Center and the Kempinski are also considered among Beijing's most opulent.

Beijing (Map 2)

The *Holiday Inn Lido* (*Lìdū Jiàrì Fàndiàn;* ☎ 6437 6688, fax 6437 6237, Jichang Lu, Jiangtai Lu) is on the road to the airport. Standard twins cost Y1450 to Y1632, superior rooms are Y1824 and suites are up to Y7864.

The *Friendship Hotel* (*Yǒuyì Bīnguǎn;* ☎ 6849 8888, fax 6849 8866, 3 Baishiqiao Lu) was built in the 1950s to house 'foreign experts'. The sprawling garden-style hotel has managed to retain its old-style charm and boasts Beijing's nicest outdoor swimming pool. Doubles start at Y468.

Haidian & Xicheng (Map 3)

The *Shangri-La Hotel* (*Xiānggélǐlā Fàndiàn;* ☎ 6841 2211, fax 6841 8006, 29 Zhizhuyuan Lu, Haidian District) has rooms from Y1980 to Y3600.

Dongcheng (Map 4)

Considered by many to be Beijing's top hotel is the *Palace Hotel* (*Wángfǔ Fàndiàn;* ☎ 6512 8899, fax 6512 9050, 8 Jinyu Hutong, Wangfujing Dajie). It's right around the corner from Beijing's first indoor shopping mall, Xindong'an Plaza. The published rate for doubles starts at US$320, but there is usually a 'promotional price', bringing the price down to around US$192.

The four-star *Peace Hotel* (*Hépíng Bīnguǎn;* ☎ 6512 8833, fax 6512 6863, 3 Jinyu Hutong, Wangfujing Dajie) has twins starting at Y580.

Chaoyang (Map 5)

The following six hotels are rated five star and won't disappoint.

The *Great Wall Sheraton* (*Chángchéng Fàndiàn;* ☎ 6500 5566, fax 6590 5398, 10 Dongsanhuan Beilu) has standard twins for US$220, although it usually has a promotional rate of US$150. This is one of the city's first international hotels – when it was built, wide open spaces surrounded it. Now the Hard Rock Cafe is next door and other upmarket hotels, shops and restaurants sprawl in all directions.

The *Hilton Hotel* (*Xīěrdùn Fàndiàn;* ☎ 6466 2288, fax 6465 3052, 1 Dongfang Lu, Dongsanhuan Beilu) has twins from Y2072 to Y2986. This typical upmarket hotel has a well-equipped gym and an excellent Cajun restaurant, Louisiana.

At the *Kempinski Hotel* (*Kǎibīnsījī Fàndiàn;* ☎ 6465 3388, fax 6465 3366, Lufthansa Center, 50 Liangmaqiao Lu) standard twins begin at Y1370. The hotel has a great location, next door to the Lufthansa Center and across the street from a string of small but excellent local restaurants – choose from Italian, Japanese, Korean, Sichuan or Hunan. The hotel also has one of Beijing's best gyms and a good deli and bakery.

The five-star *Kunlun Hotel* (*Kūnlún Fàndiàn;* ☎ 6500 3388, fax 6506 8424, 2 Xinyuan Nanlu) has standard twins for Y2155. The top floor has a revolving restaurant and bar with excellent views of the city (when the air is clear!).

PLACES TO STAY

The **Swissôtel** (*Ruìshì Jiǔdiàn;* ☎ *6501 2288, fax 6501 2501,* ✉ *swissotel@ chinamail.com*) is just outside the Dong-sishitiao subway stop. Standard doubles start at US$220.

At the **Jingguang New World Hotel** (*Jīngguǎng Xīn Shìjiè Fàndiàn;* ☎ *6597 8888, fax 6501 3333, Hujialou*) twins start at Y1660. This was once Beijing's tallest building, with 52 floors.

The four-star **Zhaolong Hotel** (*Zhàolóng Bīnguǎn;* ☎ *6597 2299, 2 Gongti Beilu*) offers the usual amenities, but its best feature is its location a short walk from the Sanlitun Bar Street. You can get doubles here from Y774.

The three-star **City Hotel** (*Chéngshì Bīnguǎn;* ☎ *6500 7799, fax 6500 7668, 4 Gongti Donglu*) is next to The Den, one of Beijing's most popular nightclubs. Singles/doubles are Y680/800.

The **Ritan Hotel** (*Rìtán Bīnguǎn;* ☎ *6512 5588, fax 6512 8671,1 Ritan Lu*) is next to the Russian fur market, near Ritan Park. This hotel is a favourite of Russian businesspeople. Standard twins cost Y660.

The **Radisson SAS Hotel Beijing** (*Huángjiā Dàfàndiàn;* ☎ *6466 3388, 6A Beisanhuan Donglu*) is another upmarket hotel. Its location in north-west Beijing is a little inconvenient unless you're attending a convention at the Exhibition Hall next door. Prices start at US$90.

Fengtai & Xuanwu (Map 6)

The three-star **Minzu Hotel** (*Mínzú Fàndiàn;* ☎ *6601 4466, fax 6601 4849, 51 Fuxingmen Nei Dajie*) is west of CAAC and Fuxingmen subway station. Twins cost US$85 to $128 and suites are US$144 to $198.

Chongwen & Chaoyang (Map 7)

Among Beijing's swanky five-star hotels, you couldn't do better than the **Grand Hotel Beijing** (*Guìbīnlóu Fàndiàn;* ☎ *6513 0057, fax 6513 0050,* ✉ *sales@mail.grandhotel beijing.com.cn, 35 Dong Chang'an Jie*). Standard twins are US$275, while rooms overlooking the Forbidden City start at US$300. Rooms are decorated with Chinese-style furniture, with an East-meets-West theme. The hotel boasts the bar with the best view of the city – the 10th floor has outdoor tables overlooking Chang'an Jie and the Forbidden City. Also, the hotel couldn't be more centrally located, just a few minutes' walk from Tiananmen Square and the Forbidden City to the east and Wangfujing, Beijing's premier shopping area, to the west.

The **St Regis Hotel** (*formerly called the International Club Hotel; Guójì Jùlèbù Fàndiàn;* ☎ *6460 6688, 21 Jianguomen Wai Dajie*) rivals the Grand as Beijing's most luxurious hotel. Rooms are on the small side but are elegantly decorated and include a huge jacuzzi-style bathtub. The hotel has a small British-style bar called the Press Club, one of Beijing's best Italian restaurants – Danieli's – and a scrumptious Sunday brunch. Rooms start at US$225.

The **Kerry Center Hotel** (*Jiālǐ Fàndiàn;* ☎ *6561 8833, fax 6561 2626, 1 Guanghua Lu*) is the latest addition to Beijing's collection of five-star hotels. Standard rooms start at US$170. Located next to the China World Trade Center, it boasts Beijing's most well-equipped gym.

The **China World Hotel** (*Zhōngguó Dàfàndiàn;* ☎ *6505 2266, fax 6505 4323, 1 Jianguomen Wai Dajie*), inside the China World Trade Center, is another five-star hotel in contention for the title of Beijing's most upmarket lodging. Standard double rooms start at US$205.

The **Traders Hotel** (*Guómào Fàndiàn;* ☎ *6505 2277, 1 Jianguomen Wai Dajie*), just behind the China World Hotel, is another four-star hotel with well-kept rooms that start at the bargain rate of US$99.

The **Beijing Hotel** (*Běijīng Fàndiàn;* ☎ *6513 7766, fax 6513 7307,* ✉ *business @chinabeijinghotel.com.cn*) is at 33 Dongchang'an Jie. At the time of writing a new west wing, slated to open at the end of 2000, was under construction. Opened in 1900, this hotel is Beijing's oldest. Famous guests include Zhou Enlai and Edgar Snow. Hotel conditions are up to par, but there isn't much in the way of charm or style. Twin rooms start at US$160 and suites are US$300 to US$350.

The *Jianguo Hotel (Jiànguó Fàndiàn;* ☎ *6500 2233, fax 6500 2871, 5 Jianguomen Wai Dajie)* has standard twins starting at US$192. This is one of Beijing's best four-star hotels. It has a cosy atmosphere, houses one of Beijing's top-rated restaurants (Justine's) and has a great Sunday morning brunch accompanied by live classical music.

Right next door to the Jianguo Hotel is the four-star *Jinglun Hotel (Jīnglún Fàndiàn;* ☎ *6500 2266, fax 6500 2022,* ✉ *jinglun@public3.bta.net.cn, 3 Jianguomen Wai Dajie).* Twins are US$180 to $220 and suites are US$230 to $480. Its standards are disappointing; for the price you'd be better off staying elsewhere.

The four-star *Scitech Hotel (Sàitè Fàndiàn;* ☎ *6512 3388, fax 6512 3542,* ✉ *sthotel1@sw.com.cn, 22 Jianguomen Wai Dajie)* has twins for US$160 and suites starting from US$260. The rooms here are clean and comfortable. The best thing about staying here is its convenient location, within a short walk of some of Beijing's top restaurants and shopping.

A short walk from the southern end of Tiananmen Square is the *Capital Hotel (Shǒudū Bīnguǎn;* ☎ *6512 9988, 3 Qianmen Dong Dajie),* a well-kept four-star hotel. Standard rooms start at US$108.

Airport
The four-star *Mövenpick Hotel (Guódū Dàfàndiàn;* ☎ *6456 5588, fax 6456 5678)* is at Capital Airport. Twins start at Y1144. Amenities include excellent tennis courts, a great gym and a big outdoor pool.

LONG TERM ACCOMMODATION
Accommodation options for those planning to live, work or study in Beijing are increasing. Years ago, foreigners had little choice but to live in luxury hotels. However China's housing market is anything but free. Although it's easing, regulations still govern where a foreigner can live.

The two basic rules are that government policy is to ensure Chinese and foreigners are separated, and that foreigners must pay the earth for apartments. But very recently the separating line has begun to blur. New housing laws have been introduced, stipulating that foreigners can live in Chinese housing as long as the owners of the apartment register the foreign resident with the local police department. However, locals are still mostly unwilling to do this – either they haven't heard about the changes or are suspicious of them.

Foreigners who live in Chinese housing can be subject to periodic 'raids'. Usually the owner of the apartment gets wind that the PSB will be doing a sweep, and will tell you to stay away for a few days. If you live in Chinese housing, you can expect a raid at least a couple of times a year. If you are caught, you will be kicked out and the owner fined. These raids happen mostly in Chinese housing areas where relatively large numbers of foreigners live, such as around the Beijing Language and Culture University, Maizidian (near the Sheraton Hotel) and Huajiadi (in the vicinity of the Lido Hotel).

The advantage of living in Chinese housing, of course, is that rent is easily ten times less than for 'foreign' housing. But besides having to put up with being homeless every so often, Chinese housing leaves much to be desired. Chinese plumbing can't handle toilet paper flushed down the toilet, there's no hot water (you need to buy your own hot water heater), floors are concrete, everything from door knobs to leaking faucets is in constant need of repair – the list goes on.

If you're coming to study, your school will probably have some sort of dormitory. It's also possible to live long-term in a hotel, such as Yujing Dasha, near the Beijing Language and Culture University. Rates here are about Y3000 per month. It's possible to move in with a Chinese family and simply pay rent, but unless you are officially registered, you face the prospect of being kicked out at any moment. Families typically charge Y1000 per month for a room. If you teach or work for the government, your housing will likely be provided free or at the Chinese price (next to nothing).

Most foreigners are exiled to special high-priced compounds. Foreigners' apartments tend to be in big residential and office towers on Jianguomen Wai and the

PLACES TO STAY

Sanlitun area in north-east Beijing – examples would include the Capital Mansion or the China World Trade Center. Because of intense competition (after a building boom there's now a housing glut), prices for these apartments are dropping – they're now down to about the rate of New York City rental rates. An average two-bedroom is about US$2000 per month. Villas cost about double this rate.

A very new emergence is upmarket Chinese housing. Rents are substantially lower than foreign housing, and while standards are lower than typical foreign housing, they're much higher than average Chinese housing (tiles on the floor, decent plumbing etc).

Foreigners expecting to make Beijing their permanent home can buy property (at astronomical prices), and by so doing also gain a residence permit. In most cases, buying actually means leasing the property for 75 years, after which it converts to state ownership.

Besides word of mouth, the best way to find housing in Beijing is through a real estate agent or by checking housing ads. *City Edition* carries listings. Also try the Web site www.rooffinder.com which has rental listings around Beijing.

Places to Eat

Although in 1949 Beijing had an incredible 10,000 snack bars and restaurants, by 1976 that number had rocketed down to less than 700. Restaurants, a bourgeois concept, were all to have been phased out and replaced with dispensaries dishing out rice. The free enterprise reforms of the past two decades have changed all that with an explosion of privately owned eateries. Gone are the famines and ration cards. Nowadays, almost any kind of cuisine can be had in Beijing – from the cuisine of the farthest corners of China to French, Thai, African or Middle Eastern.

FOOD

Eating out in Beijing is a true adventure, one that should be seized with both chopsticks. But pay careful attention to opening times, as most restaurant staff insist on taking their *xiuxi* (afternoon nap) between 2 and 5 pm.

The northern capital has always been supplied with an abundance of produce from the rest of China, and this is reflected in the spectrum of restaurants. From quick snacks at a street stall to a 12-course (or larger) imperial banquet, you're not going to be stuck for variety. You could spend months working through all Beijing's variants of Chinese regional cooking.

However, prices are escalating rapidly. The days are gone when a budget traveller could afford to visit an upmarket restaurant and rub elbows with Beijing's big shots. On the other hand, just about every neighbourhood is packed with a choice of very reasonably priced restaurants serving *jiācháng cài* (homestyle food).

Despite the relatively small variety of produce which can be grown in the north, Beijing has still developed its own distinctive cuisine, centred on the cold northlands of China. Since this is the country's wheat belt, steamed breads, dumplings and noodles figure more prominently than rice. The other local grain, millet, supplies Beijingers with a hearty winter gruel, usually eaten with beef and pickles, and is very filling.

Beef, chicken and pork are the most common meats. The Chinese also do interesting things with fungi (more politely called 'truffles') of which there are numerous species with different tastes. There are relatively few local vegetables, cabbages being the main exception. Others are tomatoes, shallots and leeks.

In general, Beijingers like their food relatively bland and less spicy than elsewhere in China. However, you'll find a wide variety of pickled side dishes to go with your noodles.

One of the most common ways of cooking Chinese food is the *bào* ('explode-frying') method. Food is deep fried (with all the usual popping, sizzling, crackling noises, hence the name) in smoking hot peanut oil for about 60 seconds, to seal in the nutrients and flavours.

Representative dishes in a Beijing-style restaurant might include cold spiced pork as an appetiser, then a choice of at least a dozen chicken recipes. Among these, look for the famed *qǐgàijī* (beggar's chicken), supposedly created by a beggar who pinched the emperor's chicken and had to bury it in the ground to cook it. The dish is wrapped in lotus leaves and baked all day in hot ashes.

The standard Beijing budget fare is *jiǎozi* (dumplings), which can be steamed, boiled or fried. They're normally prepared in small bamboo steamers, stacked on top of each other, and sold on street stalls. Buy them by the *jin* – half a jin is plenty for one person. Smaller alternatives are called *bāozi* and *shāomài*. The good old *chūn juǎn* (spring roll) is also common and it comes with a variety of fresh fillings.

Hóngshǔ (baked sweet potatoes) are a cheap (about Y2), filling snack sold at street stalls throughout the city during winter. Vendors attach oil drums to their bikes, which have been converted into mobile ovens. Choose a nice soft sweet potato and the vendor will weigh it and tell you how much it costs.

Jiān bǐng (Chinese crepes with egg) are another big favourite on the streets of Beijing. The crepes are made with a millet flour batter and cooked on a round griddle with a spicy sauce poured on top. The whole thing is then wrapped in brown paper. Look for the glass-topped three-wheeled carts, and expect to pay about Y3 for this delicious morsel.

DRINKS
Non-alcoholic Drinks

Tea is the most common beverage in Beijing. Indian tea is not generally available in restaurants, but if you need the stuff, large supermarkets stock well-known brands like Lipton and Twinings.

Coffee addicts will be pleased to know they can satisfy their addiction almost anywhere in the city. Starbucks and Bella's outlets are found around the city and serve decent coffee. You can also buy good ground coffee, roasted in Yunnan, for about Y24 per half kilo.

Coca-Cola, introduced into China by US troops in 1927, is now manufactured in Beijing. Fanta and Sprite are widely available in both genuine and copycat versions. Sugary Chinese soft drinks are cheap and sold everywhere – some are so sweet they'll turn your teeth inside out. Jianlibao is a Chinese soft drink made with honey rather than sugar, and is one of the better brands. Lychee-flavoured fizzy drinks have received rave reviews from foreigners. Fresh milk is rare in Beijing but you can buy imported UHT milk from Western-style supermarkets.

Boxed ice tea is another very popular drink. Chinese manufacturers experienced a big surge in sales after NATO's bombing of the Chinese embassy in Belgrade, after which American products (like Coke) were briefly boycotted.

A surprising treat is fresh sweet yoghurt, available from street stalls and shops everywhere. It's usually sold in what look like small milk bottles and is consumed by drinking with a straw rather than eating with a spoon. This is excellent stuff and makes a great breakfast.

Alcoholic Drinks

If tea is the most popular drink in Beijing then beer must be number two. By any standards the top brands are great stuff. The best known is Tsingtao, made with a mineral water which gives it its sparkling quality. It's really a German beer since the town of Qingdao (formerly spelt 'Tsingtao') where it's made was once a German concession and the Chinese inherited the brewery. Some claim that draft Tsingtao tastes much better than the bottled stuff.

Beijing has several local beers. The best is said to be Yanjing, while another, Beijing Beer, is like coloured water. Cheaper than bottled drinking water, a big bottle (355ml) of these local brews will set you back Y2.5. A wide range of foreign brands is also readily available – Beck's, Carlsberg, Heineken, Corona, San Miguel and Budweiser are commonly found at grocery stores around the city.

China has probably cultivated vines and produced wine for over 4000 years. The word 'wine' *(jiǔ)* gets rather loosely translated; many Chinese 'wines' are in fact spirits. *Báijiǔ* or *máotái* is a spirit made from sorghum (a type of millet). It's used for toasts at banquets and has a similar texture to Jagermeister because of its acutely alcoholic and syrupy texture. Rice wine – a favourite with Chinese alcoholics because of its low price – is intended mainly for cooking rather than drinking. Lizard wine is produced in the southern province of Guangxi; each bottle contains one dead lizard suspended perpendicularly in the clear liquid. Wine with dead bees or pickled snakes is also desirable for its alleged tonic (or aphrodisiac) properties. In general, the more poisonous the creature, the more potent are the alleged tonic effects.

China also produces its own *pútao jiǔ* (red and white wines), which unanimously get the thumbs down from westerners. Dragon Seal and Great Wall are the brands to watch out for. Imported wines are at least twice as expensive as domestic brands, with the least expensive bottles (imported from Bulgaria) starting around Y68.

It's not uncommon to see Chinese women drink in public in Beijing, though it's not as accepted as in Western countries. Western women need not worry about breaking some social taboo when it comes to drinking. As a rule Chinese men are not big drinkers, but toasts are obligatory at banquets. If you really can't drink, fill your wine glass with tea and say you have a bad stomach. In spite of all the toasting and beer drinking, public drunkenness is strongly frowned upon.

Imported alcohol – like XO, Johnny Walker, Kahlua, Napoleon Augier Cognac etc – is highly prized by the Chinese for its prestige value rather than exquisite taste. The snob appeal and steep import taxes translates into absurdly high prices. If you can't live without Western spirits, take advantage of your duty-free allowance on arrival.

In the following rundown of places to eat in Beijing, budget is considered to be any place where you'd pay less than Y50 per person at time of writing, mid-range is Y50 to Y100, and top end is Y100 and upwards.

PLACES TO EAT – BUDGET

Every street and hutong is so packed with small eateries and food stalls that it would take a book many times larger than this to list them.

A special mention should go to the *Dong'anmen Night Market (Map 4),* which gets going from around 6 to 9 pm daily. All sorts of exotic eats from street stalls are available, including deep-fried scorpion, grasshopper or caterpillar kebabs. It's also a good place to try typical street food, like *málà tāng* (spicy soup), *zòngzi* (sticky rice in lotus leaves) or jianbing. The night market is at the northern end of Wangfujing near Xindong'an Plaza.

Northern Chinese

Beijing *Tangenyuan (Map 4; Tángēnyuàn;* ☎ *6427 3356, A1 Ditan Dongmen Wai)* serves up some of Beijing's most authentic local food – try the *má dòufǔ* (tofu paste), *mènsūyú* (fried and pickled fish), and *zǐmǐ zhōu* (purple porridge). Patrons spit on the floor and smoke while they're eating as they watch cross-talk, Peking opera and acrobats

on stage at this not-to-be-missed restaurant just outside Ditan Park's east gate. They even have rickshaws waiting at the park gate to take customers up to the front door. Yes, it's a tourist trap, but prices are extremely reasonable and its noisy and crowded atmosphere makes for a fun night out if you go with the flow.

The *First Floor Restaurant (Map 7; Diyīlóu Fàndiàn;* ☎ *6303 0268, 83 Qianmen Dajie)* has the best *tāng bāo* (soup buns) around, and for only Y9 per bamboo steamer. Other typical, simple Beijing fare to try include *xiǎo cōng bàn dòufu* (scallion tofu; Y3) and *liáng bàn huáng guā* (cold cucumber; Y4).

Nearby, at 36 Qianmen Dajie *(Map 7),* on the corner of Dazhalan, is **Duyichu** *(Dūyīchù Fànzhuāng;* ☎ *6702 1555),* where delicious steamed baozi have been served for over 100 years. A steamer of 10 costs Y10 to Y18, depending on the filling. You can also get *sùcài* (vegetarian) baozi (Y12).

A couple of blocks south of Liulichang, the *Huji Noodle House (Map 6; Hǔjì Miànguǎn;* ☎ *6304 3078, 58 Nan Xinhua Jie)* serves up typical hearty, heavy Beijing fare in a boisterous atmosphere. The waiters are decked out in Qing-dynasty costumes and greet you with a yell when you enter and again when you leave. Red lanterns, bird cages and hard wooden benches add to the theme atmosphere. Besides delicious noodles like *zhájiàngmiàn* (see next paragraph for description), try the *hú bǐng* (thin egg pancake with vegetables) and *sōngshǔ yú* (sweet-and-sour Mandarin fish).

Just north of the east gate of the Temple of Heaven and across from Hongqiao market, *Beijing Noodle King (Map 7; Lǎo Běijīng Zhájiàngmiàn Dàwáng;* ☎ *6705 6705, 29 Chongwenmen Wai Dajie)* is *the* place to try zhajiang mian – thick noodles mixed with thin slices of cucumber, scallions, turnip and beans along with black bean sauce (Y8 per bowl). The waiters make a ruckus with the clanging of plates as they mix the vegetables into the noodles at your table.

PLACES TO EAT

Geng Wu Mess (Map 5; Gēngwǔ Càiwū;
☎ *6416 5186, Xin Donglu),* a hole-in-the-wall
eatery with wooden benches and tables, is a
cosy little place that serves up typical Beijing
fare. Excellent are its *cài tuánzi* (cornbread
rolls stuffed with cabbage and pork) and
bōcài wánzi (spinach and meatballs). This is
also a good place to try *zhōu* (rice porridge),
bǐng (pancake) or *mántou* (steamed bread).

If you're in the mood for dumplings day or
night, *Golden Cat Dumpling City (Map 5;
Jīn Māo Jiǎozichéng;* ☎ *8598 5011),* next to
the east gate of Tuanjiehu Park, serves over a
dozen varieties of dumplings, from pumpkin
to donkey meat to the standard pork-filled.
Order dumplings by the *liang* (Y3.5 per liang,
about five dumplings). The restaurant is in a
courtyard house, so you can sit outside when
the weather cooperates. It's open 24 hours.

Also open 24 hours, and conveniently located near Sanlitun's Bar Street on Gongti
Donglu, is a branch of *Da Cheng Yong He
(Map 5; Dà Chéng Yǒng Hé),* where you
can get typical Chinese breakfast fare. The
fluorescent lighting is a bit glaring at 3 am,
but the *dòujiāng* (soybean milk; Y2), *yóutiáo* (fried dough stick; Y2), *zòngzi* (sticky
rice in lotus leaves; Y4), *húntun* (won ton
soup; Y8) and jiaozi (Y6) taste great. There
is also an English menu. Other branches of
this chain are scattered around town.

The basement floor of the Beijing Arts
and Crafts Central Store (Map 7) on Wangfujing Dajie has a *food court* with all types
of local snacks at very reasonable prices.
Decide what you want to eat then buy the
appropriate amount of tickets to give the
server. The food court is open 9 am to 9 pm.

You could do worse than spending a hot
summer evening in the courtyard of *Jinghua
Shiyuan (Map 7; Jīnghuá Shíyuán;* ☎ *6711
5331, 1 Longtan Lu),* at the east gate of Longtan Park. Rising out of the centre of the courtyard is a 150-year-old *yuánbāo* tree, from
which hang illuminated red lanterns. The speciality here is Beijing *xiǎochī* (snacks). Try
the baby corn cakes (Y8), wine sauce chicken
silk threads (Y7) and fried duck meat with
bread (Y40). For dessert, try the steamed
glutinous rice and pear (Y15). All, of course,
washed down with bottles of Yanjing *píjiǔ...*

Mongolian Hotpot Hotpot in Beijing i
so good that it's hard to believe it can be s
bad in Mongolia. Nothing like a casserol
hotpot in the Western sense, it was origi
nally prepared in the helmets and shields o
Mongol warriors. Using a brass pot with
flame inside, you get to cook strips of mut
ton and vegetables yourself, fondue fashion
spicing as you like.

Standard hotpot fare includes *yángrò*
(mutton), *fěnsī* (rice noodles), *bōcà*
(spinach), *báicài* (cabbage), *tǔdòu* (potato)
dòufu (tofu) and *mógū* (mushrooms). Som
patrons swear hotpot restaurants add popp
seeds *(fàng yào;* literally 'add medicine') t
the soup, an illegal practice created to hoo
customers into coming back for more.

Beijing's most renowned hotpot restaur
ant is *Nengrenju (Néngrénjū;* ☎ *660
2560, 5 Taipingqiao, Baitasi, Xicheng).* I
winter this place is packed with loyal pa
trons so come early. Also very popular wit
locals is *Donglaishun (Dōngláishù
Fànzhuāng;* ☎ *6528 0501, 5th floor Xin
dong'an Plaza).*

Just south of the China World Trade Cen
ter is *Huangcheng Laoma Hot Pot (Map 7*
☎ *6779 8801, 39 Qingfengzha Houlu*
which serves fiery Sichuanese hotpo
Sichuan hotpot has two sections (makin
the pot look like a Yin-Yang symbol) – wit
one side spicy and the other not. The mix o
modern decor with traditional touches give
this place an upbeat atmosphere.

Uyghur Belonging to a Muslim ethni
group from Xinjiang, Uyghur cuisine is di
cheap if you know the right place to look
and the right place is Weigongcun, in Haid
ian, just north of the Beijing Library. Thi
is where Beijing's Uyghur minority con
gregates. Ganjiakou, south of here, wa
once the centre of Uyghur activity, bu
sadly the restaurants here were demolishe
for street' widening (part of the city'
scheme to fix the city up in preparation fo
the PRC's 50th anniversary in 1999). Al
though there are some signs of life emerg
ing from the rubble, at the time of writin
only a couple of small restaurants had re
opened. Lacking the aggressive restaura

teurs of Ganjiakou, Weigongcun is a pleasant little street lined with tiny, family-owned restaurants serving up the usual Uyghur fare: *náng* (flatbread), *xīnjiāng shālā* (spicy tomato and lettuce salad), *lāmiàn* (noodles) and *yángròu chuàn* (lamb kebabs).

Hunan
This style of cooking is similar to Sichuan cuisine, but also borrows the Cantonese concept of making anything palatable. Hunan menus typically include onion dog, dog soup (reputed to be an aphrodisiac) and dog stew.

But for those a little sensitive to the culinary culling of canines, perhaps a switch to Hunan-style duck spiced with hot pepper, or some seafood, and several styles of noodles would be better.

Across the street from the Kempinski hotel, *Ban Cheng Xiang Jiulou (Map 5; Bàn Chéng Xiāng Jiǔlóu; ☎ 6464 1820)* serves up spicy cuisine from Mao's home province in a no-frills atmosphere. Its specialities include *máo jiā hóngshāo ròu* (red-cooked pork in a clay pot; Y26), *zhá mántou* (fried bread with condensed milk; Y7) and *duòjiāo yútóu* (fish head in hot peppers; Y28). Tip: the best part of the fish head is the cheek.

Just outside the Lama Temple is the *Mao Family Restaurant (Map 4; Máo Jiā Cài; ☎ 8401 7173, 30 Yonghegong Dajie)*, where you will be greeted by a giant porcelain bust of Mao as you enter. Don't let the kitschy decor – bamboo alcoves with beads hanging in the doorway – put you off. The food here is authentic Hunanese. Try the *hóngshāo ròu* (red-cooked pork; Y30), *huā pèi yú* (smoke-dried fish fried with onions; Y20) and *nánguā bǐng* (deep-fried pumpkin bread; Y5).

Nostalgia
Peasant murals and photos of fallen revolutionary leaders decorate the walls of *Sunflower Village (Xiàngyángtún; ☎ 6256 2967, 51 Wanquanhe Lu, Haidian)*. The cuisine here recalls the Cultural Revolution, when people ate simply – or whatever they could get their hands on. Cornbread, eggplant stuffed with garlic and chillies and chicken dishes are on offer, as are more exotic fare such as fried silkworms and ant soup, all served from crude crockery reminiscent of the era.

Similar restaurants include the Mao Family Restaurant (see Hunan, earlier), Fangshan (see Imperial, later), the Red Capital Club (see Fusion, later), Tangenyuan and Huji Noodle House (see Beijing, earlier).

Shanxi
Flour-based and carbohydrate heavy, Shanxi cuisine is based on a foundation of brown vinegar. One of the best places to try it is *Jinyang Restaurant (Map 6; ☎ 6303 7637, 241 Zhushikou Xidajie)*. Try the *māo ěrdūo* (cat ears – short noodles loosely resembling the shape of cat ears) and *dāo xiāo miàn* (long noodles with vegetables and a healthy dash of vinegar). Another speciality of the house is *guò yóu ròu* (oiled pork).

Other Asian Cuisine
There are lots of Korean students at the Beijing Language and Culture University in the Haidian District, and they've staked out an ethnic cuisine enclave in the nearby neighbourhood of Wudaokou (Map 2). You'll find dozens of great Korean restaurants here. Look for the picture of a hotpot (Korean barbecue).

Western Cuisine
If you've a hankering for Western food, there's no shortage of American fare to be had in Beijing. The American fast-food chain *Schlotsky's Deli (Map 5; ☎ 6504 1246, Gongti Donglu)*, located a half block south of Gongti Nanlu, has some of the best sandwiches in Beijing – from pastrami to vegetarian. After 8 pm its rather mediocre-tasting pizzas go at half-price. *Sammie's (Map 2; ☎ 6506 8838)*, in the Beijing Language and Culture University campus, serves up good sandwiches, muffins and cookies. If you're not studying at BLCU, it also can make deliveries.

PLACES TO EAT – MID-RANGE
Northern Chinese

Beijing Refined in atmosphere and light on the grease, the *Sihexuan Restaurant (Map 7; Sìhéxuān Fàndiàn;* ☎ *6500 2266, Jinglun Hotel, 4th floor, 3 Jianguomen Wai Dajie)* serves fresh and delicious street fare such as baozi, jiaozi and zhou at reasonable prices in a restaurant designed to look like a courtyard house. It's also open till 2.30 am, a rarity in Beijing.

Beijing Duck This is made on the same principle as that other great delicacy, paté de foie gras, namely by force-feeding ducks. By the time they get to your table, the birds have been plucked, blown up like a balloon (to separate the skin from the flesh), basted in honey and vinegar, wind-dried, and grilled. The duck is served in stages. First comes boneless meat and crispy skin with a side dish of shallots, plum sauce or sweet flour paste, and crepes. This is followed by duck soup made of bones and all the other parts except the quack.

There are plenty of places which specialise in Beijing duck, but you can also order it from almost any major hotel restaurant that does Chinese cuisine.

Tucked in a hutong in East Qianmen, *Lichun Roast Duck Restaurant (Map 7; Lìchún Kǎoyā Diàn;* ☎ *6702 5681, Beixiangfeng Hutong, Zhengyi Lu Nankou)* is a tiny restaurant squeezed into a typical Beijing courtyard house. It's worth it to come here for the atmosphere alone, and the duck isn't bad either. There are only a few tables and the owners insist that you make reservations. From Qianmen Dongdajie, walk east till you hit Zhengyi Lu, then turn right. At the end of Zhengyi Lu turn right, then take your first left. Follow the alleyway to the end, then turn right, then take your first left. Take the next left, and the duck restaurant is at the end of this alley. If all the zigzagging gets you lost, ask the locals to point you in the right direction – just ask for the *kǎoyādiàn*. A duck here will set you back Y68.

Jiuhua Shan Roast Duck Restaurant (Map 3; Jiǔhuāshān; ☎ *6848 3481, 55 Zhengguang Lu),* behind the Ziyu Hotel, serves hands down the Capital's most delicious roast duck. *Kǎoyā* lovers say this is how roast duck should be done: crispy skin cooked just right so all the fat has dripped out. Although it's in Haidian, a bit of a trek from the city centre, and the atmosphere is nothing special (a brightly lit cavernous hall with big tables), the duck here is worth the effort. A whole duck is Y88.

Tuanjiehu Roast Duck Restaurant (Map 5; Běijīng Kǎoyā Diàn; ☎ *6582 2892, 3 Tuanjiehu Beikou),* on the opposite side of Dongsanhuan Lu from the Zhaolong Hotel, is another favourite of Beijing expats. Its convenient location and low-key atmosphere – as well as delicious duck – make it worth a try. Besides the usual onions, cucumber and plum sauce that accompany the duck and pancakes, a small dish of sugar is served, which, according to the restaurateur, is the way refined women traditionally ate duck (sans onions and garlic). Mashed garlic is also served with the duck, another condiment with which duck is traditionally eaten (by men and unrefined women).

Uyghur Beijing's most popular Uyghur restaurant is *Afanti (Map 5;* ☎ *6527 2288, 2 Houguaibang Hutong, Chaoyangmen Nei Dajie).* It's famous for its table dancing (by patrons, not staff), which astoundingly takes place every night of the week. Xinjiang folk music and traditionally dressed dancers get the atmosphere going. It's best to come here in a big group, and to make reservations.

Muslim Near Silver Ingot Bridge (Yíndìng Qiáo) close to the Drum Tower, *Kaorouji (Map 4; Kǎoròujì;* ☎ *6404 2554, Dianmen Wai Dajie, 14 Qianhai Dongye)* is an old Beijing stand-by. Its speciality is *kǎoròu hè zhīmà shāobǐng* (roast lamb in sesame bread; Y38). The atmosphere here is decidedly state-run (ie, pretty drab), but its lakeside location among some of Beijing's nicest hutongs makes it worth a stop. Note that the food here differs from Uyghur (Xinjiang Muslim).

Shandong Shandong cuisine hails from one of the coldest parts of China. Since this is China's wheat belt, steamed bread and noodles are the staples rather than rice, and as it's a coastal province, seafood figures prominently in the dishes. Shandong cuisine combines simple cooking techniques (stir-frying and steaming) with soy sauce, garlic and scallions for flavouring. It is similar to Beijing style, but with more focus on vegies and seafood. 'Confucian food' is considered Shandong style, since Confucius was born in Qufu, in Shandong Province.

A Beijing institution, *Fengzeyuan (Map 7; Fēngzéyuán Fànzhuāng; ☎ 6318 6688 ext 125, 83 Zhushikou Xidajie)* is where locals go to celebrate a special occasion. Don't be surprised if the next table is busy toasting round after round of snake wine. This is a good place to try Shandong delicacies like sea cucumber with scallion (Y60), sauteed fish slices (Y40) and for dessert, toffee apple. There is an English menu.

Dim sum (Cantonese)

No self-respecting tourist hotel in Beijing would be without a Cantonese restaurant dishing up dim sum to its Hong Kong clientele. Remember that dim sum is for breakfast and lunch only – at night meals are mostly seafood. Dim sum consists of all sorts of little delicacies served from pushcarts wheeled around the restaurant. It's justifiably famous and highly addictive stuff.

Sampan (Map 7; ☎ 6515 8855 ext 3166, Gloria Plaza Hotel) serves excellent dim sum every day from 11.30 am to 2 pm. Another popular place is *Full Moon (Map 5; Huadu Hotel)*, next to the Kunlun Hotel – but expect to wait for a table. *Windows on the World (Map 7; ☎ 6500 3335)* offers reasonably priced dim sum with a great view (smog permitting). This place is on the 28th floor of the CITIC building on Jianguomen Wai Dajie. *Sui Yan (Map 5; Suí Yuán; ☎ 6466 2288)*, in the Hilton Hotel, also has a good reputation for dim sum.

Sichuan

Sichuan food is China's spiciest cuisine – we're talking chillies that can do damage here. One speciality is smoked duck cooked in peppercorns, marinated in wine for 24 hours, soaked in tea leaves and cooked again on a charcoal fire. Also worth a try is the salted shrimp with garlic, dried chilli beef, and eggplant with garlic.

Famous for its fiery *làzi jī* (pepper chicken), *Golden Hill City Restaurant (Map 5; Jīnshānchéng Chóngqìng Càiguǎn; ☎ 6464 0945, 52 Lingmaqiao Lu)*, across from the Kempinski Hotel, is a great place to eat Sichuan food. Other excellent dishes include *sōngshǔ guìyú* (deep-fried squirrel fish topped with a sweet-and-sour sauce), *zhútǒng féiniú* (steamed beef in a bamboo tube), *gānbiǎn sìjì dòu* (crispy-fried green beans) and, if you still have room after all that, the *básī píngguǒ* (toffee apples).

A favourite of Beijing expats, *Xihe Yaju Restaurant (Map 5; also known as Ritan Park Restaurant; ☎ 6506 7643)*, on the north-east corner of Ritan Park, serves up reliably tasty dishes in a courtyard-style setting. Try some of the standard Sichuan fare like *mápó dòufu* (tofu) and *gōngbào jīdīng* (chicken with peanuts). The eclectic menu also has Shandong and Cantonese food.

Reliable and convenient sums up *Berena's Bistro (Map 5; ☎ 6592 2628, 6 Gongti Donglu)*, a few doors down from the City Hotel in Sanlitun. This place is squarely aimed to attract the foreign crowd (a local is yet to be spotted here), and the English menu makes ordering easy. Mapo doufu, crispy rice dishes and sweet-and-sour pork are reliable staples, and the dried green beans with garlic are excellent.

Sichuan Fandian (Map 3; Sìchuān Fàndiàn; ☎ 6615 6924, Gongwangfu, 14A Liuyin Jie) is Beijing's oldest and most famous Sichuan restaurant. While the food here is tasty, the real reason to come here is to soak up the atmosphere of the surrounding area, near the banks of Shicha Qianhai Lake in one of Beijing's best-preserved hutong neighbourhoods.

PLACES TO EAT

Shanghai

Need a break from greasy Beijing fare? The large **Shanghai Moon** (Map 5; Yè Shànghǎi; ☎ 6506 9988, 4 Gongti Beilu) has excellent Shanghai cuisine and also has plenty on the menu for vegetarians. House specialities include sùyā (vegetarian duck), songshu guiyu and cuìpí dòufu (crunchy skin tofu). It's open till 3.30 am.

Vegetarian

In the heart of Qianmen, **Gongdelin Vegetarian Restaurant** (Map 7; Gōngdélín Sùcàiguǎn; ☎ 6511, 2542, 158 Qianmen Nandajie) serves up Buddhist-style vegie food (ie, vegetables dressed up to look and taste like meat) in a slightly dank atmosphere typical of a state-owned enterprise. Still, it's a Beijing institution and well worth a try. If you ask nicely you'll even get the English menu. It's open 10.30 am to 8.30 pm.

The **Green Angel Vegetarian Restaurant** (Map 4; Lùtiānshí Sùshí Guǎn; ☎ 6524 2476, 57 Dengshikou Dajie) serves similar fare but in cleaner, brighter, more peaceful surroundings (and with slightly higher prices). A crystal shop and small vegetarian grocery occupy the first floor. Mount the staircase to the restaurant on the second floor and you will be greeted by photos of famous vegetarians: Socrates, Einstein, Plato, Darwin – and Paul Newman. Specialities include Beijing duck, meatballs and broccoli, and sweet-and-sour fish with pine nuts (all fashioned from vegies only). Be sure to check the prices on the menu (in English) before letting them make suggestions for their best dishes.

Other Asian Cuisine

Indian Big points here for the **Asian Star Restaurant** (Map 5; Yàzhōu Zhīxīng Xīnmǎyìn Cāntīng; ☎ 6591 6716), an excellent combination eatery with a busy and jovial atmosphere. Cuisine includes dishes from Malaysia, Singapore and India – a delight for curry enthusiasts. Dinner comes to about Y125 per head and reservations are recommended on the weekend.

Golden Elephant (Map 5; Jīn Xiàng; ☎ 6417 1650), down the alley across from Jenny Lou's (see Supermarkets later), off

Sanlitun Jiuba Jie, is actually a Thai and Indian restaurant, though its Indian food is far superior to the Thai.

The **Omar Khayyam Restaurant** (Map 5; Wèiměijiā Yìndù Cāntīng; ☎ 6513 9988 ex 20188) can be found in the Asia Pacific Building at 8 Yabao Lu, near Ritan Park. Naan (Indian bread), tikka (fish) and the many vegetarian dishes are all good choices here. Expect to pay about Y125 per person.

Japanese Guarded by two big ceramic dogs, **Matsuko** (Map 5; ☎ 6582 5208), of East Third Ring Rd, across the street from TGI Friday's and just south of the Zhaolong Hotel, is a favourite of Japanese expats. It food ingredients are flown in daily. Well worth the Y68 is the lunch buffet (11 am to 3 pm daily), where you can indulge in all you-can-eat sushi, sashimi, tempura, Asahi beer and more.

Sansi Lang (Map 5; ☎ 6464 5030), directly across from the Kempinski Hotel, is another reliable place for good Japanese cuisine. Look for the two red lanterns and wooden sign above the door. This cosy two storey restaurant has a warm atmosphere and is always bustling.

Jazz-ya (Map 5; ☎ 6415 1227, 18 Sanlitun Jiuba Jie) has a small Japanese restaurant off to the side. The food here is decidedly mediocre, although it's a nice place to linger over a meal followed by rounds of drinks.

Korean Excellent Korean food can be found at **Sorobol** (Map 5; ☎ 6465 3388 ex 5720), in the basement of the Lufthansa Center. Try its bànfàn (rice with egg, vegetables, meat and hot pepper sauce) or páigǔ (roast spare ribs).

Thai Phrik Thai (Map 5; ☎ 6586 9726, Guandongdian Lu, Lane 3), a short distance west of the Jingguang Hotel on Chaoyangmen, is a tiny restaurant that serves the best Thai food in Beijing, and at reasonable prices. Try its pomelo salad or kale (a green leafy vegetable) with salted fish. Its red and green curry dishes are also excellent.

With a more chic atmosphere is **Serve the People** (Map 5; Wèi Rénmín Fúwù, ☎ 641:

3242), down the alley across from Jenny Lou's, off Sanlitun Jiuba Jie. Besides good, reliable Thai food, it has a reasonably priced imported wine list.

Western Cuisine

American Considered Beijing's original expat hang-out, *Frank's Place (Map 5; ☎ 6507 2617, Gongti Donglu)*, next to the City Hotel, serves hamburgers and fries, club sandwiches and other standard American fare that you can wash down with beer on tap.

German Consistently packed with *laowai* (foreigners) is *Kebab Kafe (Map 5; ☎ 6415 5812, Sanlitun Jiuba Jie)*, across from No 46 Sanlitun Lu. Outdoor tables make this a nice place to while away a weekend afternoon, although the food here is pretty bland.

Italian If you're craving Italian food, *Metro Cafe (Map 5; ☎ 6552 7828, 6 Gongti Xilu)* won't let you down. It has a fine selection of delicious homemade pastas and sauces, and while the atmosphere is upmarket, prices are very reasonable.

The best reason to come to *Adria (two locations: Map 5; ☎ 6460 0896, across from the Kempinski Hotel; Map 7; ☎ 6500 6186, 14 Dongdaqiao Lu)* is for its delicious pizzas – made in wood-burning ovens. It also delivers.

Peter Pan (Map 5; ☎ 6595 1414, Maizi Dian), near the Great Wall Sheraton Hotel, is another popular spot for Italian food in a casual atmosphere. Despite its popularity, the pastas and pizzas are a letdown.

Middle Eastern

Just across from the Zhaolong Hotel, *1,001 Nights (Map 5; ☎ 6532 4050, Gongti Beilu)* serves excellent Middle Eastern food around the clock, including *baba ganoush, hummous* and *schwarma*. Similar fare, in a less ostentatious atmosphere, is served just around the corner from the Friendship Store at *Once Upon a Time (Map 7; ☎ 6591 3100, 17 Jianguomen Wai Dajie)*.

Pub Grub

Mainly a bar, *Hidden Tree (Map 5; ☎ 6509 3642, 12 Sanlitun Nanlu)* also serves tasty Mediterranean fare. It's a fine place to come for a dinner with Beijing's best selection of imported beers (mainly Belgian), both on tap and bottled.

Brunch

Not including expensive five-star hotel brunches, *The Den (Map 5; ☎ 6509 3833, 4 Gongti Donglu)*, next to the City Hotel, serves the best Western brunch around (weekends only). Y80 will get you a glass of juice (try the carrot – it's the only one that's prepared fresh) or milk shake, a cup of strong coffee, and a scrumptious main dish – from eggs Benedict with home-style potatoes to pancakes, bagels or English muffins.

Mexican

Craving refried beans, guacamole, fajitas and burritos? Look no further than *Mexican Wave (Map 7; ☎ 6506 3961, Dongdaqiao Lu)*, a half block north of Jianguomen Wai Dajie.

Russian

The *Baikul (Map 5; ☎ 6405 2380, 2 Dongzhimen Beizhongjie)*, 50m from the Russian embassy, is the place to come for Russian food and a favourite gathering spot of expats. The interior is reminiscent of an old ship, and the atmosphere is livened up by musicians who belt out old Russian tunes each night. Try the beet salad (Y20) and *pirozhki* (Y10). And of course, don't forget the vodka – the vodka menu is more extensive than the food menu.

PLACES TO EAT – TOP END
Northern Chinese

Beijing Duck Otherwise known as the 'Old Duck', the *Qianmen Quanjude Roast Duck Restaurant (Map 7; Qiánmén Quànjùdé Kǎoyā Diàn; ☎ 6511 2418, 32 Qianmen Dajie)* is one of the oldest restaurants in the capital, dating back to 1864, and Beijing's most famous duck restaurant. The atmosphere here is definitely touristy, complete with duck souvenirs such as stuffed animals and baseball caps with big duck bills for sale at the entrance. It's still a good place to try roast duck. Now there's a dozen or so branches across the city. Price depends on which section of the restaurant you sit in. Ducks here go for Y108 or Y168.

Imperial Imperial food *(gōngtíng cài* or *mǎnhàn dàcān)* is food fit for an emperor and will clean your wallet out very quickly. In 1982 a group of Beijing chefs set about reviving the imperial pastry recipes, and even went so far as to find the last emperor's brother to try out their products on.

Beijing's most elaborate Imperial cuisine is served up in the *Fangshan Restaurant (Behai Park Map; Fángshān Cānkè; ☎ 6401 1889, Beihai Park)* located in a pavilion overlooking the lake – enter through either the west or south gate of the park. Set menus range from Y100 to Y500 per person. All dishes are elaborately prepared, and range from delicately filled pastries to dishes such as sea cucumber with deer tendon, peppery inkfish's egg soup and camel paw with scallion (no, it's not a real camel paw). The Y500 menu will get you rare delicacies such as bird's nest soup, abalone and turtle meat. Reservations are a must (last reservations at 7.30 pm).

The Summer Palace houses a similar restaurant – the *Tingliguan Imperial Restaurant (Summer Palace Northern Area Map; Tīnglìguǎn Fànzhuāng; ☎ 6288 1955).* The restaurant is open 11 am to 2 pm daily, with a set lunch for around Y200. Reservations are a must for dinner, and will set you back a hefty Y500 per person.

The *Li Family Restaurant (Map 3; Lì Jiā Cài; ☎ 6618 0107, 11 Yangfang Hutong)* is off Deshengmen Wai Dajie on the scenic south bank of Shisha Houhai Lake. There's a Y200 per-head set menu which includes delicious appetisers. Take note: this place is tiny – in summer, reservations are required two weeks in advance!

Cantonese

Cantonese dinners can be somewhat adventurous for Western palates. The Cantonese are said to eat anything with four legs but the table, though they aren't limited to quadrupeds – specialities are 1000-year eggs (traditionally made by soaking eggs in horse's urine), shark's fin soup, snake soup and dog stew.

Summer Palace (Map 7; Xiàgōng Cāntíng; ☎ 6505 2266 ext 34), in the lobby of the China World Hotel, has excellent Cantonese cuisine in a refined atmosphere typical of what you'd expect in a top five-star hotel. For more Cantonese restaurants, see Dim Sum earlier.

Fusion

If you're looking for upmarket dining, Beijing has a few exceptional restaurants. The following restaurants all serve Chinese-influenced food, but with a modern twist (hence the subheading). Reservations are necessary; expect to pay around Y200 per person.

Beijing's most chic restaurant is *The Courtyard (Map 4; Sìhéyuán; ☎ 6526 8881, 95 Donghuamen Dajie).* It has a stunning view of the Forbidden City (the restaurant is just outside the east gate) and its surrounding moat. There's also a modern art gallery downstairs (see the 'Contemporary Art' boxed text in the Facts about Beijing chapter) and a cosy cigar room upstairs.

Hidden away down a quiet hutong is the *Red Capital Club (Map 5; Xīnhóng Zī Jùlèbù; ☎ 6402 7150–2 daytime, ☎ 8401 8886 evenings and weekends, 66 Dongsi Jiu Tiao).* It's in a meticulously restored courtyard house, with traditional Chinese decor. Every dish has an accompanying myth, so be prepared to spend at least a half hour reading the menu (it's in English). Look for the big red doors with no sign.

A beautiful little place to go for lunch or dinner is the *Green Tea House (Map 5; Zǐyúnxuān; ☎ 6468 5903, 54 Tayuancun, Sanlitun).* This tiny Chinese-style teahouse is lavishly decorated and its refined dishes and teas are gastronomical delights. But the real reason to come here is to see the presentation of the foods, which are truly works of art.

Other Asian Cuisine

Indian Beijing's best Indian food can be had at *Taj Pavilion (Tàijī Lóu Yìndù Cāntīng; ☎ 6505 5866)*, in the China World Trade Center, on the same side as Henry J Beans. Enjoy your sizzling Tandoori in bright, clean, almost upmarket surroundings. It also has a large range of vegetarian dishes and various types of naan.

Thai The *Red Basil Restaurant (Map 5; ☎ 6460 2342, Beisanhuan Donglu)*, in north-east Beijing, has the usual fiery hot Thai dishes. A relatively new place, it has high ceilings, beautiful decorations and an atmosphere that is decidedly un-Chinese.

Western Cuisine

American Complete with wrought iron decor, *Big Easy (Map 2; ☎ 6508 6776, Chaoyang Park, South Gate)* looks like a Bourbon Street transplant, but its Cajun cuisine disappoints. Unauthentic ingredients infiltrate the dishes – chickpeas make their way into the red beans and rice and tomato sauce serves as the base for the gumbo. Still, jazz bands from the American South liven up the atmosphere and can make this a fun place to party.

Italian Posh *Danieli's (Map 7; ☎ 6460 6688 ext 2440, 2nd floor, St Regis Hotel)* has the best home-made pasta in Beijing. Its lunch set menu (Y98) is good value and includes a salad, pasta and drink.
Roma (Map 4; ☎ 6559 2888, Palace Hotel) is another excellent, and expensive, Italian restaurant serving a range of pastas. This is also a good place to come for a scrumptious weekend brunch.

French A true Parisian bistro (complete with chain-smoking patrons), *La Galopin (Map 5; ☎ 6595 8380)*, tucked behind Dance Agogo on Dongsanhuan Lu, just north of Gongti Beilu, offers a wide selection of French fare as well as a decent wine list at reasonable prices. Try the grilled salmon or the veal – both served up in hearty portions.
A cosy little French bistro French expats swear by is *Bleu Marine (Map 7; ☎ 6500 6704, 5 Guanghua Xilu)*. It's said to serve up authentic country-style French fare. In summer there's the added benefit of outdoor seating.
One of Beijing's poshest restaurants is *Justine's (Map 7; ☎ 6500 2233, Jianguo Hotel)*. The French fare is the real thing, and well worth the top, top-end prices. If you're looking to splash out for a special meal, this is the place.

German The *Paulaner Brauhaus (Map 5; ☎ 6465 3388)*, in the Kempinski Hotel, is a great place for micro-brewed beer and big servings of German food (meat, meat and more meat). At about Y200 per person, it's not cheap – but with the huge all-you-can-eat rolls and liverwurst that come with each meal, you won't have to eat for a week after this.

Spanish Sip *sangria* at chic *Ashanti (Map 5; ☎ 6416 6231, 168 Xinzhong Jie)*, a few doors west of the corner of Xinhong Jie and Gongti Beilu, where modern Chinese art adorns the walls. The menu features several tapas dishes and even paella.

Brunch Looking to while away a weekend afternoon basking in five-star luxury? Your salvation lies at the St Regis (formerly the International Club), Palace or Jianguo Hotels, where Beijing's best weekend brunches are to be found. The Jianguo features a live orchestra from 10.30 am to 12.30 pm. An all-you-can-eat brunch at any of the places costs about Y180.

SELF CATERING
Supermarkets

The quality and range of goods on offer in Beijing's supermarkets has improved enormously in the past few years.
Certainly one of the best-stocked supermarkets is in the basement of Scitech Plaza (Map 7), a department store on the southern side of Jianguomen Wai. On the eastern fringe of Jianguomen Wai is the China World Trade Center (Map 7) – head for the basement to find a fully fledged Wellcome supermarket, imported lock, stock and

shopping carts from Hong Kong. Just north of the Great Wall Sheraton Hotel is the Lufthansa Center (Map 5). Yes, it *is* a German airline office, but it also has a shopping mall with a great supermarket in the basement packed with imported goods.

While the above supermarkets are conveniently located and carry just about anything you could be craving for, the mark-up on some items can be mind-boggling. If you're not looking for anything special, head to a regular Chinese grocery store, or even the Friendship Store or Jenny Lou's, where the mark-up is nominal.

The Friendship Store (Map 7; Yǒuyí Shāngdiàn) also carries a good selection of groceries. Although the fresh produce here is outrageously priced it's a good place to stock up on dried fruits and nuts and other train snacks.

Although not a supermarket, tiny Jenny Lou's somehow manages to carry just about all the groceries a westerner looks for – from muesli and feta cheese to a good selection of red wine and reasonably priced fruits and vegetables (it even sells basil plants). Jenny Lou's is located on Sanlitun's Jiuba Jie, at the northern end of the clothing market.

Delicatessens

Chinese bread is about as tasty as a dried-out sponge, but a few entrepreneurs in Beijing have started to introduce edible baked goods to the masses. One fine effort in this direction is *Bella's (Map 5)*, where you can get freshly baked bread and pastries (try the cinnamon ring), along with a pretty decent cafe latte or espresso. There are outlets on Sanlitun's Bar Street and next to Kylin Plaza on Gongti Beilu.

Another place to look is in some of the big hotels – a few have sent the staff off to Europe for a winter crash course in making German black bread and Danish pastries. Unfortunately, hotel prices tend to be high. The deli in the *Holiday Inn Lido (Map 2)* stocks delectable chocolate cake, sourdough bread and other requisite baked goods, but it's certainly not cheap. The *Kempinski Hotel Deli* (Map 5) and the

Swissôtel Deli (Map 5) are also good places to look for yummy fresh bread. Cakes and breads are half-price after 8 pr at the Kempinski.

Mrs Shannon's Bagels (☎ 6435 956 A3 Zhaojiu Road, Jiuxianqiao), in the vicin ity of the Holiday Inn Lido, makes fres bagels daily, along with fresh cream chees and lox. You can find its bagels for sale a Jenny Lou's and the Friendship Store.

The *Green House* (☎ 6506 197 @ greenhse@mail.sparkice.com.cn) has catering service and does deliveries. It of fers a range of sandwiches, dips and finge foods – a great service if you're planning picnic.

TEAHOUSES

Teahouses are experiencing a revival i Beijing. Tranquil oases, they are the perfec antidote to brash Beijing and offer a fine al ternative to sitting in Starbucks (hey, wh leave home?).

One of the most beautifully decorated i the Green Tea House (see Fusion, earlier You can experience a complete traditiona tea ceremony at the *Purple Vine Tea Hous (Map 4; Zǐténglú Cháyúguǎn,* ☎ 660 6614, 2 Nanchang Jie), where you'll b greeted with the gentle sounds of *guzhen* music and the smell of incense. Traditiona Chinese furniture and century-old Shanx wooden screens decorate this tiny oasis jus outside the west gate of the Forbidden City Choose from the menu of jasmine, black green or oolong teas; a pot ranges in pric from Y40 up to Y250 for oolong.

Not far from the Silk Market is the *Bei jing Qingxin Court Tea House (Map 7 Qīngxīnjū;* ☎ 6507 0487, 53 Dondaqia Lu), across the street from Bleu Marine where you can sip tea in tranquil surround ings. In Liulichang, the *Ji Gu Ge Teahous (Map 6; Jígǔgé Cháyuán,* ☎ 6301 784 2nd floor, 132–136 Liulichang) infuses i teas with mineral water. A pot of humbl jasmine will set you back Y15. It also sell loose tea – but at super-inflated prices You're better off buying it from a small te shop or even the Friendship Store. It's ope 9 am to 11 pm.

CAFES

Finding a good cup of coffee in Beijing is not nearly as elusive as it was even a year ago. The coolest cafe in Beijing is *Blue Lotus (Map 4; Lánliánhuā;* ☎ *6618 2542, 11 Shicha Qianhai North Bank)*. In a restored courtyard house on the banks of Qianhai Lake, it's owned by local artists Qing Qing and Huizi. Its mellow atmosphere and dim lighting make it the perfect place to spend all day and all night drinking coffee (or tea, which they also serve). It's open 10 am to 2 am.

Back in Sanlitun, *Bella's (Map 5)* is where to watch the comings and goings of Beijing's expat community. *Starbucks* (with outlets in the Friendship Store and the China World Trade Center) is another spot unfailingly inundated with laowai. On Sanlitun Nanlu, across the street from Durty Nellie's, is *Rainbow (Map 5)*, a sweet little coffee shop with only enough space for three stools pulled up to a narrow counter. You can get a strong cup of Italian espresso or cappuccino here for Y10 (a bargain)!

PLACES TO EAT

Entertainment

Back in the days of Mao, 'nightlife' often meant revolutionary operas featuring evil foreign and Kuomintang devils who eventually were defeated by heroic workers and peasants inspired by the *Little Red Book*. Fortunately, options have widened immensely. These days, you can see jazz, rock, punk, classical or Peking opera almost any night of the week.

To get the latest information on what's on, check out *City Edition* (see Newspapers & Magazines in the Facts for the Visitor chapter). The Web site www.chinanow.com has continuous updates of what's going on around the city.

BARS
Jiǔbā

The Chinese government may be claiming sovereignty, but the Chaoyang District of north-east Beijing appears to have been taken over by expats. The Sanlitun area, considered the centre of expat life in Beijing, accounts for about 75% of the expat bar-cafes in town. There are two main bar streets in Sanlitun – the main one that runs between Gongti Beilu and Dongzhimen Wai (Sanlitun Lu), and a smaller alleyway that runs south from Gongti Beilu (Sanlitun Nanlu). There are also several bars adjacent to the City Hotel, just off Gongti Donglu. While at the time of writing the bars here are going strong, darkening the horizon are rumours that the area is scheduled for major redevelopment. If this comes to pass, all of the following pubs could disappear overnight.

Sanlitun (Map 5)
Sanlitun Lu Beijingers refer to Sanlitun Lu as the *jiǔbā jiē* (Bar Street). The reason will be obvious when you come here – the east side of the street is lined with bar after bar. In summer, outdoor tables are set up on the sidewalk (although authorities periodically ban them).

Right in the middle of the street is *Public Space* (☎ 6416 0759, 50 Sanlitun Lu), a popular place that plays good music and attracts a hip crowd. You can also grab a late dinner here – try the warm salmon salad (Y45) or couscous (Y35). *Jazz-ya* (☎ 641 1227) is a relatively long-standing bar that i frequented by expats. The official address i 18 Sanlitun Beilu though it's actually hidden in a small alley just to the east of the main road; open 10.30 am to 2 am (but only get busy after 8 pm). *Boys & Girls* (☎ 641 4697, 52 Sanlitun Lu) packs in a mostly Chinese crowd that comes to hear live music - usually Canto-pop.

Sanlitun Nanlu This narrow lane is to the east of the Workers Stadium but west o Sanlitun Lu (and runs parallel to it). The lane runs south from Gongti Beilu – look for the neon green 'Nashville' sign across from Kylin Plaza. This little strip is the most popular nightlife area for Beijing expats. Most of the bars here do not open until after 7 pm, but stay open till dawn.

Enter the alley from the northern side and walk south. The first place you encounter is *Minders* (☎ 6500 6066). One o the liveliest spots on this alley is *Hidden Tree* (☎ 6509 3642), a restaurant-pub with a Mediterranean menu. The Belgian owner keeps a wide variety of mostly Belgian beers to choose from, including some on tap. *Jam House* (☎ 6506 3845) has a nice rooftop space, and live music downstairs Although it bills itself as an Irish pub *Durty Nellie's* (☎ 6502 2808) attracts an American fraternity-boy type crowd, and packs them in on weekends.

Around Workers Stadium & Gongti Donglu There is another row of bars along a side street near the corner of Gongti Donglu and Gongti Beilu, next to the City Hotel. Although its heyday may be fading with the onset of newer, trendier clubs, *The Den* (☎ 6592 6290) is still a popular place to go. It's nicely appointed in stylish chinoiserie-style decor and there's also a small dance floor upstairs.

A few doors down is ***Downtown Cafe*** *(☎ 6507 3407)*. The decor is more or less British (there's even a dartboard hidden in a corner). The cafe's owner is very friendly, and both food (Western-style) and service are excellent here.

Just a hop, skip and a jump to the south is ***Frank's Place*** *(☎ 6507 2617)*, a beer-garden setting popular with expats. Steaks, burgers and big-screen TV are major attractions. Like the Downtown Cafe, it's open 11.30 am to 2 am.

A half block north of Gongti Beilu on the western side of Gongti Donglu is the very chic ***Club Vogue*** *(☎ 1300-113 5089)*, the place to be seen if you're a Chinese model, artist or musician. Vogue often plays host to foreign DJs who spin techno on weekends. It's owner, Henry Lee, is a well-known man about town – if you want to know what's hip in Beijing, he's the man in the know.

At the east gate of Workers Stadium is ***Maggie's*** *(☎ 6501 6655, ext 5293)*, popular with Western men looking for prostitutes. Its small dance floor and musty red-velvet booths create atmosphere though, and it can be a fun place even for those not looking to partake.

Havana Cafe *(☎ 6586 6166)*, at the north gate of Workers Stadium on Gongti Beilu, is a great place to come in the summer. It has a beautiful outdoor space at the back complete with sangria bar. Inside, the packed dance floor attracts dancers well versed in the art of salsa.

The latest club to take Beijing by storm is ***The Loft*** *(☎ 6501 7501)*, down a small street off Gongti Beilu, next to the monstrous Pacific Place office and apartment complex. On weekends it attracts just about every walk of life – from the hip artsy crowd to frat boys to businesspeople. Its colossal interior is decorated with a combination of traditional-style wooden Chinese furniture and gleaming steel chairs and bar stools.

North-East Third Ring Road The north-east section of Third Ring Rd is called Dongsanhuan Beilu. On the 1st floor of the huge Lufthansa Center is the ***Paulaner Brauhaus*** *(☎ 6465 3388 ext 5732)*, an excellent German pub-cum-restaurant. Open 10 am until midnight, this place brews its own genuine German beer and has a spacious outdoor patio in the summer.

About a kilometre east of the Kempinski Hotel on Liangmaqiao Lu, a new string of tacky bars that mostly attract a Chinese crowd has recently sprung up.

The ***Island Club*** *(☎ 8597 8391)* is in the middle of Tuanjiehu Park, which is on Third Ring Rd in east Beijing (enter from the park's west gate). It serves mostly as a venue for special functions. It has a small British-style bar that's nice for a quiet drink.

Jianguomenwai

Jianguomenwai embassy-land is on the northern side of Jianguomen Wai Dajie, though some of the nightlife action spills out onto the south side of the boulevard. It's here you'll find good restaurants, bars and the worst traffic jams in Beijing.

A favourite of expat families who live in the surrounding apartments, the ***Goose & Duck Pub*** *(Map 2; ☎ 6538 1691)*, at the west gate of Chaoyang Park, serves pub grub like bangers and mash and fish and chips in a sports bar setting, complete with pool table and darts.

On the southern side of the park is Guanghua Lu, where you'll find the ***John Bull Pub*** *(Map 7; ☎ 6532 5905)*, which looks like it was cloned out of London. On the northern side of the park at 17 Ritan Beilu is the ***Elephant Bar*** *(Map 5; ☎ 6502 4013)* which features Russian food and has outdoor rooftop space. Inside the St Regis (formerly International Club) Hotel is the sophisticated ***Press Club*** *(Map 7; ☎ 6460 6688)*, where you can sip scotch surrounded by dignified dark-wood panelling.

Around the Forbidden City

On the 10th floor of the Grand Hotel Beijing (Map 7) is Beijing's best bar with a view, ***Palace View*** *(☎ 6515 7788)*. Except in winter, outdoor tables graced by a string of palm trees make this a wonderful place to escape the city as you enjoy the view overlooking Chang'an Avenue, Forbidden City and Tiananmen Square.

The upstairs of *The Courtyard (Map 4;* ☎ *6526 8883)*, opposite the east gate of the Forbidden City, is a tiny cigar room, with a perfectly framed view of the gate and the surrounding moat. Here you can sip your port in a cracking leather chair and contemplate times gone by.

Haidian District

Most of Beijing's big universities are in the Haidian District. With lots of students, it has a colourful collection of low-cost night spots. The most popular are *Solutions (Map 2;* ☎ *6255 8877)*, opposite the west gate of Beijing University and, next door, *First Avenue (*☎ *6264 0702)*. There are also other bars and a teahouse along this strip.

DISCOS
Dísīkè

Some of Beijing's discos are open daily but the vast majority are either closed o very quiet except on Friday and Saturday nights, when they rage.

Sanlitun Area

The monolithic *Rock 'n Roll (Map 2 Yáogǔnyuè;* ☎ *6592 9856)* is part of a huge neon-lit strip of clubs and bars at the south gate of Chaoyang Park. If you want to party with the locals, this is the place to come.

Owned by the PLA, *Hot Spot (Map 5; Re Diǎn;* ☎ *6501 9955)* is a long-standing haven for Beijing clubbers. It's most well known for its cage dancers, who appear nightly.

Beijing Rock

In 1986 during a 'World Peace' music concert in Beijing, a young trumpet player named Cui Jian walked on stage, strapped on a guitar and played a song that would forever change the sound and look of Chinese popular music. With its distinctly abrasive vocal style and lyrics describing loneliness and alienation, *Nothing to My Name (Yi Wo Suo You)* was unlike any song ever performed by a mainland Chinese musician. Up until that time even pop music was relatively new to China and Taiwan's Teresa Teng (Deng Lijun) was virtually the only 'pop' star who had achieved any notable success on the mainland. Since that audacious performance, the prolific singer/songwriter has released a number of influential albums (including 1989's *Rock and Roll for the New Long March* and most recently 1998's *Power of the Powerless*), blending influences that range from punk to jazz and hip-hop, and his name has become synonymous with Chinese rock.

Cui Jian was introduced to rock music through tapes of the Beatles, Rolling Stones and Talking Heads brought over by foreigners living in Beijing. For other early Chinese rock bands like Tang Dynasty and Black Panther, the pounding riffs and power chords of heavy metal from the 1970s and 1980s (ie, Led Zeppelin, Rush) provided the inspiration to pick up guitars, grow long hair, and start a band. This 'First Generation' of Chinese rock bands not only took inspiration from classic rock and heavy metal, but from punk's aggression and abrasiveness as well. Chinese proto-punk He Yong's song *Garbage Dump* blazed a trail for later Chinese punk acts with its angry lyrics describing Beijing's urban decay in the early 1990s, while China's first all-female band Cobra, and Tian Zhen, the lead singer of Compass, gave Chinese fans an early glimpse of Riot Grrrl power.

Since those early days Chinese rock has continued to flourish and Beijing has gained the reputation of China's rock music mecca. A new generation of musicians has built on the legacy left by China's rock pioneers. These younger acts, often labelled the Dakou Generation after the bounty of foreign surplus CDs sold in underground shops around town, draw their influences from today's ever-expanding range of styles and tastes – from the slow syncopated beats of Trip Hop to Digital Hardcore's aural assault. Newer acts like hardcore punks Wuliao Contingent, Jesus Lizard disciples The Fly, ambient break-beaters Supermarket, and Primus and Pixies scions Yao, and the Nirvana- and Doors-influenced Cold Blooded Animals share the stage at Beijing's numerous live music venues (see the Bars and Discos sections in this chapter) with older and more established acts like Cui Jian,

Banana (Map 5; ☎ 6599 3351, 5th floor, ? Chaoyangmen Wai Dajie) is another ng-standing Beijing disco. The crowd ucks the dance floor as techno blasts from e massive speakers.

In addition to the above discos, *Havana afe*, *The Den*, *Vogue* and *The Loft* (when ey have live DJs) all pack them in on the ance floors (see under Bars for more tails).

The latest addition to the Beijing club ene is *Club Orange (☎ 6515 7413)*, down e small alley across the street from the avana Cafe. Here you can dance as if oating on clouds as manufactured fog afts over the dance floor. If you're into ypnotic rhythms of techno, this is the place o be.

Haidian (Map 2)

NASA (☎ 6203 2906) advertises 'advanced designed style appealing to radicals'. It's another typical warehouse-style Chinese disco, featuring old jeeps and other strange decor. It's opposite the Jimen Hotel at the corner of Xueyuan Lu and Xitucheng Lu, just north of Third Ring Rd.

Solutions (see earlier) is another popular place to go on weekends if you're in the mood for dancing.

LIVE MUSIC

In the beginning, real culture shock struck when East met West over the music score – China's leadership had a hard time deciding how to react. Western music was vehemently denounced by the government as yet

Beijing Rock

pop-rock king Zang Tiansuo, and the shoe-gazing Dou Wei (former lead singer of Black Panther), while a number of Beijing-based record labels (Modern Sky/Badhead, New Bees, Red Star, Jingwen) put out ever-expanding catalogues of rock and dance releases.

DJ culture has also come to China with clubs like Vogue, The Loft, Solutions and Orange (see the Bars section for more details) featuring DJs from Beijing and abroad. Clubgoers can now get their grooves on to the booming sounds of Hip Hop, House, Drums & Bass, Techno and Trance in addition to the popular sounds of home-grown Chinese house music.

This infusion of new styles and sounds has left an indelible impression on Chinese society, especially its youth culture. Today the sight of a long-haired Beijing gemen'r (homeboy) with a guitar strapped to his back is about as common as that of a cigarette vendor or cab driver. Television music programs and radio shows play songs by rock acts almost as frequently as they do pop crooners and divas while even hotel bars feature rock bands on a regular basis. Indeed, with such an infusion of new sounds and styles in Chinese popular music it appears that Chinese rock is here to stay.

Jerry Chan

COURTESY BEIJING EASTWEST PRODUCTIONS

Chinese rock legend Cui Jian

ENTERTAINMENT

another form of 'spiritual pollution'. China's first concert featuring a foreign rock group was in April 1985, when the British group Wham! was allowed to perform. The audience remained deadpan – music fans who dared to get up and dance in the aisles were hauled off by the PSB. Since then, things have become considerably more liberal, and China has produced some notable bands (see Music in the Facts for the Visitor chapter). Still, it'll be a while before bands of the Sex Pistols ilk are allowed to perform in China. The international roster mostly includes bands of the innocuous variety. On the schedule to perform in China in 2000 are Wynton Marsalis, Sheryl Crow and Kenny G, among others.

Rock

There are several clubs around town where you can behold Beijing's thriving rock scene. The newly opened *Friends (Map 5; Péngyou;* ☎ *6597 1166 ext 8082),* in the Huadu Hotel, next door to the Kunlun Hotel, is owned by one of Cui Jian's former band members. It's an excellent place to see some of Beijing's top bands, including the awesome Yao Shi, whose lead singer is called by some the 'next Cui Jian.' It occasionally hosts a 'Screaming Punk Night'.

In Haidian, near the NASA disco, is *Sound Stage (*☎ *8208 9579),* which also puts on live music.

On Sanlitun Nanlu, *Riders (*☎ *6508 9439), Jam House* and *Minders* (see earlier for more details) are laid-back dives with live music, from jazz to African to folk, most nights of the week.

Jazz

If you're in the mood for jazz, try *CD Cafe (Map 5;* ☎ *6501 8877 ext 3032).* Red velvet curtains frame the stage at this bordering-on-swanky jazz joint. The Liuyuan Jazz Quartet plays most Saturday nights and the Rhythm Dogs usually perform on Sunday. Both acts are worth catching. Performances start at 9.30 and cover is Y20.

In front of Rock 'n Roll, *Big Easy (Map 2;* ☎ *6508 6776),* at the south gate of Chaoyang Park, features a house jazz band night brought over from the American south. The is also an extensive cocktail menu.

Beijing hosts an international jazz festival every November. Jazz bands play venues around town and are announced shortly before the festival.

Classical

Sanwei Bookstore (Map 6; ☎ *6601 320 60 Fuxingmen Nei Dajie),* opposite the Minzu Hotel, has a small bookshop on the ground floor and a teahouse on the second It features traditional Chinese music on Saturday night. Business hours are from 9.30 am until 10.30 pm, but the live music begins at around 8 pm. Cover charge is Y3

Blue Lotus Cafe (Map 4; ☎ *6618 254,* on the west side of Qianhai Lake, occasionally has live classical Chinese music. The coffeehouse, open till the wee hours, is in small, elegantly decorated courtyard hous The surrounding neighbourhood is a gre place for a stroll and to soak up the traditional atmosphere.

Among Beijing's larger venues hosting classical music is the *Beijing Concert H (Běijīng Yīnyuè Tīng;* ☎ *6605 5812, 1 Be inhua Jie, Liubukou, Xuanwu),* which h regular performances of both Western a Chinese classical music. Other venues th occasionally host concerts are the *Centu Theatre (*☎ *6462 8470, 40 Liangmaqiao Lu* next to the 21st Century Hotel, the *Gre Hall of the People,* on the west side Tiananmen Square, the *Beijing Exhibitio Hall Theatre (Map 3;* ☎ *6835 1383, 1. Xizhimen Wai Dajie, Haidian)* and *Po Plaza* (see later under Acrobatics for conta details).

GAY & LESBIAN VENUES

Beijing's gay and lesbian scene keeps a lo profile. Still, a couple of openly gay ba have managed to stay around for som years. Off Gongti Beilu, heading north the alley to the east of Kylin Plaza, is *Ha & Half (Map 5;* ☎ *6416 6919),* Beijing most popular gay bar.

Lesbian venues are a bit more elusiv with no open meeting places to report of

KARAOKE
<ǎlā OK

Karaoke bars in Beijing are mostly frequented by businessmen on big expense accounts. The attraction isn't merely the ability to hear your melodic voice amplified across the room – the draw is to entertain business associates with the 'hostesses,' many of whom double as prostitutes, who frequent these joints. The cost of 'talking to the hostesses' can be outrageous: The bill for a couple of Cokes could amount to six months wages for the average Chinese worker.

CINEMAS

Chinese movies *(diànyǐng)* are starting to delve into contemporary issues, even verging on Cultural Revolution aftershock in a mild manner (see Film in the Facts about Beijing chapter). There are about 50 cinemas in the capital, but they show mostly Chinese films and these are seldom subtitled. The Chinese government limits imported foreign films to just 10 a year (although this could change to 40 to 50 with China's entry into the World Trade Organization), which rather puts a damper on variety. On the other hand, films made in Hong Kong usually have English subtitles and Mandarin dialogue. If you really want to see foreign films, you may have to content yourself with STAR TV or VCDs.

Cherry Lane Theatre (Map 5; ☎ 6522 4046, 40 Liangmaqiao Lu), next to the 21st Century Hotel, has Chinese films with English subtitles. The place is very popular with expats, but there is only one screening every two weeks (always on a Friday night). Admission is Y50.

Owned by Zhuang Songlie, a graduate of the Beijing Film Academy, *Sculpting in Time (☎ 6252 1746, 45 Chengfujie)*, near the small east gate of Beijing University, shows-international videos every Tuesday and Thursday night. It's best to call ahead to make reservations as this tiny place gets packed.

Every Friday afternoon at 6 pm and Saturday afternoon at 2 pm, the *Number 50 Bar (☎ 6203 3051)*, next to the main gate of the Beijing Film Academy (Diànyǐng Xuéyuàn) in Taiping Zhuang off Beisanhuan Lu, holds screenings of Chinese independent arthouse films. The small bar gets so packed you're lucky if you can get a place to stand, so come early – or better still, call ahead and make reservations. Most of the films even have English subtitles.

One cinema that generally shows most of the 10 imported foreign films screening in Beijing is the *Star Cinema (Map 4; Míngxīng Diànyǐng Yuàn; ☎ 6405 8939, 537 Dongsi Beidajie)*, near Wangfujing. This little theatre has big, comfortable seats (and even cup holders) and is a very pleasant place to see a film. Premiers of foreign films are shown at many other theatres, though they rarely have English subtitles. The current line-up of cinemas in Beijing includes:

Dahua Cinema (Map 7; Dàhuá Diànyǐng Yuàn; ☎ 6527 4420) 82 Dongdan Dajie, Dongcheng District
Honglou Theatre (Hónglóu Diànyǐng Yuàn; ☎ 6605 1908) 156 Xisi Dingzi Jie, Xicheng
Shoudu Cinema (Map 6; Shǒudū Diànyǐng Yuàn; ☎ 6605 5510) 46 Xichang'an Jie
Victory Theatre (Běijīng Yuàn; ☎ 6617 5091) 55 Xisi Dongdajie
Ziguang Cinema (Map 5; Zǐguāng Diànyǐng Yuàn; ☎ 6500 3868) 168 Chaoyangmen Wai Dajie, Chaoyang District

ACROBATICS
Tèjì Biǎoyǎn

Two thousand years old, and one of the few art forms condoned by Mao, acrobatics is the best deal in town. Most of today's acrobatic repertoire originates from the works of Zhang Heng (AD 25–220), who is credited with creating acts including 'Balancing on a High Pole', 'Jumping through Hoops', 'Swallowing Knives' and 'Spitting Fire'. Wuqiao County in Hebei Province is said to be the original bastion of Chinese acrobatics.

Good places to catch an acrobatics show are *Poly Plaza (Bǎolì Dàshà Guójìjùyuàn; ☎ 6500 1188 ext 5127, 14 Dongzhimen Nandajie)*, where the China Acrobatics Troupe takes to the stage nightly at 7.15 pm. The venue is being renovated but should be open by the time you read this. The **Chaoyang Theatre** *(Map 5; Cháoyáng Jùchǎng;* ☎ *6507 2421, 36 Dongsanhuan Beilu)*, at Chaoyang Beilu in north-eastern Beijing, runs shows from 7.15 to 8.45 pm. Tickets to either venue are Y80.

BEIJING OPERA
Jīngjù
Originally an ancient temple, the ornately decorated **Zhengyici Theatre** *(Zhèngyǐcí Jùchǎng; Map 6;* ☎ *6303 3104, 220 Xiheyan Dajie, Hepingmen Wai)* is the oldest wooden theatre in the country and the best place in the city to experience this traditional art form. The theatre was restored

by a private businessman and re-opened in 1995 after a long period of disrepair. Three years later the theatre was summarily closed after the owner couldn't afford its hefty rent. It reopened under new management a few months later. The theatre has nightly performances from 7.30 to 9 pm; tickets are Y50.

Similarly decorated, with balconies surrounding the canopied stage, the **Huguang Guild Hall** *(Map 6; Húguǎng Huìguǎn* ☎ *6351 8284, 3 Hufangqiao Lu)* stages performances nightly from 7.15 to 8.40 pm. The theatre is the site where the Kuomintang, led by Dr Sun Yatsen, was established in 1912. Tickets range from Y20 (for a back table) up to Y150.

Beijing Opera

It used to be the Marx Brothers, the Gang of Four and the Red Ballet, but it's back to the classics these days. Beijing opera has been revived, and is still regarded as the *creme de la creme* of all the opera styles prevalent in China. Traditionally it's been the opera of the masses. The themes are usually inspired by disasters, natural calamities, intrigues or rebellions. Many have their source in the fairy tales and stock characters and legends of classical literature. Titles like *The Monkey King*, *A Drunken Beauty* and *A Fisherman's Revenge* are typical.

The music, singing and costumes are products of the opera's origins. Formerly, opera was performed mostly on open-air stages in markets, streets, teahouses or temple courtyards. The orchestra had to play loudly and the performers had to develop a piercing style of singing which could be heard over the throng. The costumes are a garish collection of sharply contrasting colours because the stages were originally lit by oil lamps.

The movements and techniques of the dance styles of the Tang dynasty are similar to those of today's opera. Provincial opera companies were characterised by their dialect and style of singing, but when these companies converged on Beijing they started a style of musical drama called *kunqu*. This developed during the Ming dynasty, along with a more popular variety of play-acting with pieces based on legends, historical events and popular novels. These styles gradually merged by the late 18th and early 19th centuries into the opera we see today.

The musicians usually sit on the stage in plain clothes and play without written scores. The *èrhú* is a two-stringed fiddle which is tuned to a low register, has a soft tone and generally supports the *húqín*, a two-stringed viola tuned to a high register. The *yuèqín*, a sort of moon-shaped four-stringed guitar, has

The *Lao She Teahouse* (Map 7; *Lǎo Shě Cháguǎn;* ☎ 6303 6830, *3rd floor, 3 Qianmen Xidajie*) has nightly shows although they're mostly in Chinese. The performance here is a combination of Peking Opera, cross-talk and acrobatics. Prices depend on the type of show and where you sit – typically from about Y60 to Y130. Show time is usually from 7.30 to 9.30 pm. Sometimes there are also afternoon performances starting at 3 pm, but call ahead for the schedule.

The *Liyuan Theatre* (Map 6; *Líyuán Jùchǎng;* ☎ 6301 6688 ext 8867, *175 Yong'an Lu*), in the Qianmen Hotel, and the *Chang'an Grand Theatre* (Map 7; *Cháng'ān Dàjùchǎng; 7 Jianguomen Nei Dajie),* just west of the International Hotel, also put on regular opera performances. Though nice, these theatres are of the sterile, movie-theatre variety; it's much more interesting to see Beijing opera performed in a traditional setting.

SPECTATOR SPORTS
Yùndòng Huì

The main places to see national (and rarely international) athletic competitions is *Workers Stadium* (Map 5; *Gōngrén Tǐyù Guǎn;* ☎ 6502 5757) in the Sanlitun area. The *Asian Games Village* (Map 2), otherwise known as the National Olympics Sports Centre, sometimes hosts events as well.

Beijing Opera

a soft tone and is used to support the erhu. Other instruments are the *shēng* (a reed flute) and the *pípa* (lute), as well as drums, bells and cymbals. Last but not least is the *ban,* a time-clapper which virtually directs the band, beats time for the actors and gives them their cues.

There are four types of actors' roles: the *shēng, dàn, jìng* and *chǒu.* The sheng are the leading male actors, and they play scholars, officials, warriors and the like. They are divided into the *lǎoshēng* who wear beards and represent old men, and the *xiǎoshēng* who represent young men. The *wénshēng* are the scholars and the civil servants. The *wushēng* play soldiers and other fighters, and because of this are specially trained in acrobatics.

The dan are the female roles. The *lǎodàn* are the elderly, dignified ladies such as mothers, aunts and widows. The *qīngyī* are aristocratic ladies in elegant costumes. The *huādàn* are the ladies' maids, usually in brightly coloured costumes. The *dǎomǎdàn* are the warrior women. The *cǎidàn* are the female comedians. Traditionally, female roles were played by male actors, but now they are almost always played by females.

The jing are the painted-face roles, and they represent warriors, heroes, statesmen, adventurers and demons. Their counterparts are the *fújìng,* ridiculous figures who are anything but heroic.

The chou is basically the clown. The caidan is sometimes the female counterpart of this male role.

Apart from the singing and music, the opera also incorporates acrobatics and mime. Few props are used, so each move, gesture or facial expression is symbolic. A whip with silk tassels indicates an actor riding a horse. Lifting a foot means going through a doorway. Language is often archaic Chinese, music is ear splitting (bring some cotton wool), but the costumes and make-up are magnificent. The only action that really catches the Western eye is a swift battle sequence – the female warriors involved are trained acrobats who leap, twirl, twist and somersault into attack.

There are numerous other forms of opera. The Cantonese variety is more 'music hall', often with a 'boy meets girl' theme. Gaojia opera is one of the five local opera forms from Fujian province and is also popular in Taiwan, with songs in the Fujian dialect but influenced by the Beijing opera style.

When you get bored after the first hour or so, and are sick of the high-pitched whining, the local audience is with you all the way – spitting, eating apples, plugging into a transistor radio (important sports match?) or breast-feeding an urchin on the balcony. It's a lively prole-audience entertainment fit for an emperor.

ENTERTAINMENT

It's Just a Game

Dictatorships have long recognised the potential of international sporting events to drum up nationalism and support for the government. China's government only seems to have become aware of this around 1990. Since then, millions of yuan have been poured into crash programs to outfit China with an Olympic team. When the Eastern Bloc collapsed in 1991, the PRC government brought East Germany's famous (and infamous) Olympic coaches to China. From virtually nowhere, Chinese athletes have sprung onto the world stage and now typically walk away with a sizable percentage of the medals at all international sporting events.

What the Chinese public doesn't get to hear are the accusations about their athletes using steroids. The Chinese government claims their teams use nothing stronger than traditional herbal medicines, but they've been caught with their pants down on several occasions.

However, it takes more than drugs to make a star athlete – training is rigorous. Potential Olympic stars are identified at around age eight to 12, and are then subjected to five or more years of harsh round-the-clock training. Despite the promise of big rewards, the dropout rate is high and sometimes results in embarrassing defections and revelations when the team goes abroad.

China's big dream is to host the Olympic Games, but the dream has been frustrated by protests over China's human rights record. China didn't win any friends in 1993 when the International Olympic Committee rolled into Beijing to check out China's bid for hosting the year 2000 games – locals had their heat and hot water turned off because the government didn't want the committee to see the pollution caused by burning coal. Street urchins were bussed out of town during the three-day visit; workers were stopped and fined for gobbing on the footpaths; streets were cleaned, potholes were patched and squatters' shacks were bulldozed; and most people were prohibited from driving their vehicles so the committee would see no traffic jams. These tactics backfired – the foreign press soon picked up on how the visit was stage-managed and the committee finally chose Sydney, Australia. China has now put in a bid for the 2008 games.

Soccer
Zú Qiú

If there is any spectator sport the Chinese have a true passion for, it's soccer. Games are devoutly covered in the mass media and during the season live matches are often held at **Workers Stadium**, in Gongti Donglu. China has dreams of taking the World Cup eventually, and the government has been throwing money into the project by importing players and coaches. The season runs approximately from April to November. Tickets are available from the Workers Stadium box office (near the north gate).

Basketball
Lán Qiú

Basketball hasn't quite fired the Chinese imagination the way soccer has, but there's a professional basketball league and players have been recruited from the USA. Games are sometimes held in the Workers Stadium in Sanlitun.

Shopping

The consumer boom has arrived in China, though there is a marked difference between the goods on offer and what gets exported. Goods here are often of inferior quality – zips that break the first time you use them, imitation discmans that last a week and electrical appliances that go up in smoke the first time they're plugged in. Keep in mind the Latin expression caveat emptor (let the buyer beware). Always test zips, examine stitching and, in the case of electrical appliances, plug them in and make sure they won't electrocute you before handing over the cash. Chinese sales clerks expect you to do this; they'll consider you a fool if you don't.

A word about antiques – most are fakes. There is, of course, nothing wrong with buying fakes as long as you're paying the appropriate prices. Remember that you need special certificates to take genuine antiques out of China (see Customs in the Facts for the Visitor chapter). If you buy a real antique, ask the seller for a guarantee of authenticity that will let you return the item if you find out it's a fake. True antiques also should bear a red wax seal, which allows the owner to export it; if it doesn't have one, you must get one issued by the Cultural Relics Bureau. Some shipping companies can help you obtain one. For fakes, be sure you have receipts to prove that they are fakes, otherwise the goods may get confiscated.

There are several notable Chinese shopping districts offering abundant goods and low prices: Wangfujing, Qianmen (including Dazhalan hutong) and Xidan. More luxurious shopping areas can be found in the embassy areas of Jianguomenwai and Sanlitun. Shopping at an open-air market is an experience not to be missed. Beijing's most popular markets are the Silk Market, Panjiayuan, the market at Sanlitun and Hongqiao Market. There are also some specialised shopping districts such as Liulichang (see later under Where to Buy for details).

Good buys are silk, stationery (chops, brushes, inks), prints, handicrafts, clothing and antiques. Small or light items to buy are silk scarves, embroidered purses, paper cuttings, wooden and bronze Buddhas, fold-up paper lanterns and kites. Down jackets are one of the best bargains you can find in Beijing and are essential survival gear if you visit during winter.

Stores are generally open 9 am to 7 pm seven days a week; some are open 8 am to 8 pm. Open-air markets are generally open 10 am till sunset. New department stores have been springing up all around the capital. Most are open from 9 am to 9 pm daily. While prices at department stores are generally fixed (sometimes you can get a 10% discount if you ask), bargaining is a must pretty much everywhere else.

WHAT TO BUY
Arts, Crafts & Antiques
Hands down the best place to shop for arts, crafts and antiques in Beijing is Panjiayuan (Map 7), also known as the Dirt Market or the Sunday Market. The market only takes place on Saturday and Sunday, beginning at dawn and winding down around 2 pm. It has everything from calligraphy, cultural revolution memorabilia and cigarette ad posters to Buddha heads, ceramicware and Tibetan carpets.

Serious collectors arrive at dawn and start on the periphery of the market, where their hope is that some poor country bumpkin with family possessions spread out on a worn blanket will have some precious relic which he'll unwittingly let go for Y10. Early Sunday morning is said to be the best time to come for this particular type of hunting. However, finding a real antique here is extremely rare. Almost everything is a reproduction: A coin collector bought several 'old' coins here, only to find when he went home that they were all fakes.

Keep in mind that this market is chaos – if you're intimidated by crowds or hard bargaining, then you'd be much better off in a more orderly department store or boutique. Also, forget about the 'don't pay more than half' rule here – vendors here may start at 10 times the real price. If you don't have at least a basic idea about what the price should be, it's worth browsing in a department store with fixed prices first, such as the Friendship Store, to get a feel for the ranges. You should also make a few rounds at Panjiayuan before actually buying anything, to see what items are for sale vendor after vendor and what items are unique.

Panjiayuan is located east of the Temple of Heaven, just off east Third Ring Rd. Head south on Third Ring Rd from China World, and exit just before the sign for Panjiaqiao. The market is about a block down on the left (look for the tangled mass of three-wheeled motorbikes parked in front).

Another excellent market with a large variety of arts, crafts and antiques is the Liangmaqiao Market, across the street from the Kempinski Hotel. Although it's a bit desolate and the vendors a little pushy, there's a wide range of items for sale, including Ming-style Chinese furniture, and there's a shop in the back that sells Tibetan carpets.

Across from the east gate of the Temple of Heaven, Hongqiao Market (Map 7) is another good place to browse for Chinese arts, crafts and antiques. You'll find them on the third floor, on either side of the vendors that sell pearls. The market is open daily from 9 am to 6.30 pm.

Not far from Panjiayuan is Curio City, just off east Third Ring Rd a short way from Huaweiqiao. This massive building houses stall after stall of all manner of arts and Chinese furniture.

Yet another place to shop for arts and crafts is the market directly across from the Holiday Inn Lido Hotel, which also has clothes and other everyday items.

Liulichang is a fun place to wander the streets and look for arts and crafts. It's worth an excursion even if you're not interested in shopping. See under Where to Shop for more information.

In addition to the above markets, the Friendship Store and the Arts and Crafts store in Wangfujing are department stores that carry a good range of wares. However you pay for the convenience, as prices are on the high side. Also, if you're looking for something unique, you won't find it here - forget about buying a life-size Mao bust here – these places are stocked to the ceiling with tacky cloisonne vases and bronzeware. Prices are generally fixed, although you can sometimes get a 10% discount if you ask.

Pearls & Jewellery

Buyers from around the world flock to the Pearl Market, on the third floor of Hongqiao Market, for fantastic bargains on pearls. Here you can buy a pair of pearl earrings or a necklace for as little as Y15. There's a huge range of pearls available - freshwater and seawater, white pearls and black pearls – and prices vary incredibly with quality. You can also buy other types of jewellery here, such as garnet and amber.

Dragon House (☎ 6595 9796), at 59 Dongdaqiao Lu, sells silver and gold jewellery, including pendants with Chinese characters for good luck, double happiness, longevity, love, money and harmony. Prices vary according to material, but start at Y50. You can have jewellery custom made here. Dragon House also has a counter on the third floor of the Friendship Store.

Furniture

If you're interested in buying traditional Chinese furniture, Zhaojia Chaowai Market (Map 7) is a good place to start. This huge four-storey warehouse is packed with vendor after vendor and traditional Chinese furniture – from opium beds to barrel-stools to ornately carved side tables. Prices are very reasonable (Y250 for a wooden chest to Y800 for a large cabinet), but rise considerably with quality. Many vendors claim their wares are actually from the Ming or Qing dynasty, but unless you're an expert it's hard to tell. Most of the furniture has, however, been collected from rural households across China and restored. The stalls get fancier the higher the floor, and prices rise accordingly. The fourth floor contains ceramics and other antiques. Vendors are happy to arrange for you to visit their workshop or warehouse, where you can see more of their wares and watch furniture being made or refurbished. They can also custom-make furniture and arrange for shipment. The market is located on the southern part of east Third Ring Rd at Panjiaqiao, a short distance south of Curio City.

The Liangmaqiao Market and Curio City (see earlier, under Arts, Crafts & Antiques) also house several furniture dealers.

Carpets

Beijing is an excellent place to shop for rugs from all over China – from Xinjiang and Ningxia to Gansu and Tibet. Carpet shops sell both antique and new carpets. Antique carpets are often preferred for their richness in colour, attained through the use of natural dyes, and because they are hand made, although some people prefer new ones (well, they're cleaner).

Located deep in a hutong at 35 Juzhang Lu is Yihong Carpet Factory (Map 7; ☎ 6712 2195, 6714 3307), a small, very dusty little warehouse stocked with a great selection of antique carpets from all around China. Prices for a small Tibetan carpet start around Y600 and rise to the thousands for a higher quality, larger one. Yihong is located east of the Temple of Heaven. It's difficult to find, so you're best off calling the place first and then having someone write down directions in Chinese for a taxi driver.

Like Yihong, the Qianmen Carpet Company (☎ 6715 1687), at 44 Xingfu Dajie, 50m north of the Tiantan Hotel, stocks a good selection of carpets from Tibet and Xinjiang. Its warehouse is larger and better organised, but prices are steeper.

The Linxia Flying Horse Carpet Co (☎ 6302 2029), at 66 Zhushikou Xidajie, near Qianmen, has a small outlet where new hand-woven rugs from Gansu Province are sold at reasonable prices. Carpets from here incorporate Chinese elements, such as dragons and phoenixes, as well as Tibetan elements, like lotus flowers.

Gangchen Carpets (☎ 6465 3388) in the Kempinski Hotel has a beautiful selection of new, high-quality Tibetan carpets.

You can also find carpet vendors at Panjiayuan, Curio City, Liangmaqiao Market and Zhaojia Chaowai Market (see earlier for details).

Silk

Qianmen is *the* place to buy silk in Beijing. Even if you're not interested in textiles, Ruifuxiang (Map 7; ☎ 6303 2808), at 5 Dazhalan, is worth a browse. An incredible selection of Shandong silk, brocade, satin-silk and more is available at this century-old shop for Y65 per metre (Y29 for satin-silk). Brocade silks incorporate traditional Chinese designs such as dragons, bamboo and the *shòu* ('long life') symbol. Ruifuxiang recently opened a branch at 190 Wangfujing Jie. Nearby, the Beijing Silk Store (☎ 6301 6658), at 5 Zhubaoshi, off Qianmen Dajie, carries a similar selection.

Other places that carry a good selection (but not as much and with slightly higher prices) are Yuan Long (☎ 6702 4059), at 15 Yong Nei Dong Lu, near the south gate of the Temple of Heaven, the Friendship Store, the Lufthansa Center, Landao Department Store and Kylin Plaza (see under Shopping Centres & Department Stores later).

Clothing & Accessories

The Xiushui Silk Market (Map 7; Xiùshuǐ Dōngjiē) is on the northern side of Jianguomen Wai between the Friendship Store and the Jianguo Hotel. Because of the prestigious location surrounded by luxury hotels, this place is elbow-to-elbow with foreign tourists at times – go early to avoid crowds but forget it on Sundays. This market is one of the best places to pick up good deals in 'upmarket' clothing. However, most of the brand-name clothing is either fake or has defects, so inspect carefully before buying your Northface jacket or cashmere scarf – if you suspect it's fake, pay accordingly. As in all other markets in Beijing, bargaining is expected here, although it can sometimes be difficult because of all the foreign tourists willing to throw money around like water. Prices are marked, but the real price is sometimes only a quarter of the marked price.

Also very popular with foreigners is the Sanlitun Market (Sānlǐtún Jiǔbājiē), where stalls carry similar stock to those at the Silk Market. This market is smaller and vendors a little easier to bargain with. The opposite side of the street is lined with bars and cafes, making a nice place to relax when you get tired of shopping.

If you're looking for fake brand-name bags, purses and wallets, the second floor of Hongqiao Market is the place to go. Prada, Gucci, Fendi, Burberry's – you name it (see under Arts, Craft & Antiques for details).

Tailor-Made Clothes If you have the time, tailor-made clothing, including traditional Chinese *qipao* (or *cheongsam* in Cantonese) and Mao suits, is a bargain in Beijing. Most tailors can supply material, or you can supply your own. Staff at fabric shops can tell you how much material to buy if you say what you plan to make (or draw them a picture). Most fabric shops and department stores also have tailors on staff, although results are hit and miss. You're better off paying a little more and going to a proper tailor who can ensure a good fit.

Beijing's most famous qipao maker is the Moo Jen Liao store: even Beijing's most frugal locals will save up to get a qipao made from here for once-in-a-lifetime occasions. They have to save for quite a while though, as prices start at Y1300 with material included, or Y800 if you bring your own. It usually takes about two weeks, including a fitting after the first week. Moo Jen Liao has outlets in Xin Dong'an Plaza in Wangfujing, the Lufthansa Center and Sogo Department store.

Beijing has very few traditional qipao makers left. One is Cao Senlin (☎ 6526 4515), at Shijia hutong. Go north on Dongdan Dajie, then about 25m before Dengshikou Dajie you'll see a small alley (Shijia hutong) leading off to the right. Cao Senlin is about 150m down the alley on your left. Cao has been making qipaos the traditional way – hand sewn – since 1938. A qipao here costs Y700 (or Y500 if you bring your own material) and takes three weeks.

If you're looking for a more funky version of the qipao try Bing Bing (☎ 138-0132 2646) at 15 Gonti Donglu, or Dreamweavers (☎ 6466 3449) – heading north on Sanlitun Bar Street, take the first left after you pass the Friendship Supermarket. Both are owned by graduates of Beijing's prestigious Central Academy of Arts. Qipaos here cost around Y650 including material and take about a week. Red Phoenix (☎ 6416 4423) on the corner of Sanlitun Bar Street and Dongzhimen Wai, is where Beijing celebrities have their avant-garde silkware tailored (at celebrity prices).

If you're after a Mao suit, Hongdu's (☎ 6513 6644), at 28 Dongjiao Mingang, just east of Tiananmen Square, once fitted Mao and Deng themselves. You'll pay for the privilege though with Mao-style or Western suits starting at Y4000.

Cashmere Cashmere from Inner Mongolia is another good buy in Beijing. The Silk Market is a good place to hunt for bargains on cashmere; however, as with other things here, look at it carefully as some stalls sell synthetics posing as the real thing. The Friendship Store has a huge selection of cashmere scarves and shawls in a wide variety of colours and sizes. Large shawls sell for around Y900. If you're in Beijing in November or December, check the China World Convention Center, which is host to a large cashmere market each year. King Deer brand is well known for its quality.

Books

Gone are the days when bookstores in Beijing sold only a measly selection of poorly printed English-language books published by the People's China Publishing House. Nowadays you can buy Daniel Steele and Stephen King novels, and even Lonely Planet guides. But don't come expecting to find a wide range of interesting literature – while growing, the selection is still extremely limited, as are bookshops that carry English-language books.

The Friendship Store (Map 7), the Foreign Languages Bookstore (Map 4) in Wangfujing and the Lufthansa Center (Map 5) carry the widest range of English-language books, with textbooks for students studying Chinese, fashion magazines and coffee-table books about everything from traditional Chinese clothing to furniture. The Foreign Languages bookstore also has a wide selection of Chinese music (although, like books, music is produced and distributed by the government, so selection is limited). The China World shopping centre also has a small bookstore that carries some English-language books, including some Lonely Planet guides.

If you can read Chinese, the Beijing Xinhua Book Center (☎ 6607 8477), at 17 Chang'an Jie on the corner of Xidan Dajie, is Beijing's largest bookstore. Hip young Chinese head to the New Ark Bookstore (Fāng Zhōu; ☎ 6835 0801), at Zhanlanlu Building 24, A1, independently owned by rock writer Hao Fang. Fang, who has written books about the history of rock and a biography of Kurt Cobain, specialises in Chinese translations of counter-culture Western classics like *Catcher in the Rye*, Chinese literary magazines and the more pragmatic *Principles and Tactics of American Visa Application*.

Pirated Goods

Pirated CDs, VCDs and DVDs are a booming business in China. Quality varies – CDs are generally OK, but with VCDs sound quality is often poor, you get to watch people walking up and down the aisles of the theatre where the movie was illegally filmed, or the VCD suddenly cuts off just before the last clinching minutes of the movie. Sanlitun and the area between the Friendship Store and CITIC building are swarming with hawkers whispering 'CD, VCD.' If your conscience allows you to indulge, CDs go for Y10 while VCDs are Y15.

Beijing is also the land of fake Prada bags (and other luxury name brands). Hongqiao Market and the Silk Market have a large selection (see above for details). The Silk Market and the Sanlitun Market are good places to pick up fake Armani ties and Northface jackets.

Computers & Electronics

Buried within the Haidian District is a neighbourhood called Zhongguancun, south of the Old Summer Palace. In the vicinity of the Zhongguancun bus stop (Map 2), this area is Beijing's hi-tech answer to California's Silicon Valley. The big attractions are the computer shops and some fledgling Internet cafes. If you're ready to put your money where your mouse is, Zhongguancun is Beijing's best venue for finding cheap knock-off PCs. While prices are reasonably low, so is the quality, and it's only recommended you buy a machine in Beijing if you'll be staying a while so that you can take advantage of the one-year warranty. Buy only desktop PCs in Beijing – if you need a portable machine, you'll do better to pick one up in Hong Kong, Taiwan or elsewhere.

Much of the world's Chinese-language software originates in Zhongguancun, and if Chinese computing is something you plan to do then check out the racks of CD ROMs. Pirating software is a big local industry too, but it's kept low-key because of China's international promises (usually broken) to protect intellectual property rights.

Film Processing

You can find Kodak shops on every other corner in Beijing, and while some are just fine, others produce poor quality photos. Your China photos probably need all the help they can get (to make up for shooting through smog); following are where the pros get their film developed. Prices here are very reasonable and comparable to regular photo-developing shops.

About 20m down a small street directly opposite Beijing West train station, Jinri Jicheng Tupianshe (☎ 6395 4874) offers print and slide (unmounted only) development and sells a wide variety of film (including black-and-white and 6cm-x-6cm film). The Tibet Dipper Photo Service (☎ 6416 3046), opposite the north gate of Workers' Stadium, also offers professional-quality film and slide development, as does Lily Photo (☎ 6500 2255 ext 31100), on the ground floor of the CITIC Building. It can mount slides and develop film in an hour.

Camping & Travel Gear

You're best off bringing your own gear into China, but if for some reason you need to pick up a few things, the Silk Market carries waterproof jackets, hiking boots and backpacks. However, most of the merchandise here is fake, and therefore probably unreliable in extreme situations (the backpacks will fall apart after a week). Some say a few of the stalls sell real brand-name merchandise, but you'll have to hunt around and then they'll charge accordingly.

Extreme Beyond (☎ 6505 5121), at 15 Gongti Donglu, is a small shop that has a good selection of real brand-name hiking boots, waterproof jackets, backpacks and sleeping bags. Some of the merchandise is defective, so inspect carefully. Prices here are not cheap (eg, Y650 for hiking boots) but you can bargain.

Worth checking out is the PLA Military Supply Shop (☎ 6585 9312), at 23 Donsanhuan Beilu. Outlets are scattered around town, but one of the best is on Dongsanhuan Lu, south of the Jingguang Hotel. Need a headlamp, compass, canteen, hiking boots, leather gloves, sleeping bag? You can pick up all this and more for very, very reasonable prices. Be sure to check out its collection of PLA watches – the perfect souvenir of the PRC.

Xindong'an Plaza, Sogo and the Lufthansa Center also carry decent selections of sports equipment.

WHERE TO SHOP
Wangfujing & Dongdan

This prestigious shopping street is just east of the Beijing Hotel – it's a solid block of stores and a favourite haunt of locals and tourists seeking bargains. For a while it became known as 'McDonald's St' because of the restaurant which once occupied the southern intersection (it was torn down in 1996 to make way for the massive Oriental Plaza). In pre-1949 days it was known as Morrison St and catered mostly to foreigners. The name Wangfujing derives from a 15th-century well.

Wangfujing recently underwent an extensive renovation, and is now a pedestrian walkway (well, sort of – buses are still allowed here, so watch out).

Xindong'an Plaza (Map 4), an enormous shopping mall, dominates Wangfujing. The Bank of China is on the ground floor. Across the street is the Beijing Department Store (Map 7; Běijīng Bǎihuò Dàlóu). Of prime interest to foreigners is the Foreign Languages Bookstore (Map 4; Wàiwén Shūdiàn) at shop No 235. This is not only *the* place to buy English-language books, but also has a pretty impressive music section upstairs. A branch of Ruifuxiang, Beijing's famous silk emporium, is at No 190. Next door is the Beijing Arts and Crafts Central Store (Map 7; Běijīng Gōngyì Měishù Fúwùbù), where you can find a good selection of jade (which comes along with a certificate of authenticity) along with cloisonne vases, carpets and other arts and crafts. There's a great food court in the basement, where you can fill up on *jiaozi*, *baozi* and noodles for less than Y10.

A few blocks east of the Forbidden City in the Wangfujing area is Dongdanbei Dajie. This is another area for fashionable clothes and small speciality shops.

Dazhalan (Map 7)

If Wangfujing is too organised for you, the place to go and rub shoulders with the proletariat is Dazhalan, a hutong running west from the top end of Qianmen. It's a heady jumble of silk shops, tea shops, department stores, theatres, herbal medicine, food and clothing specialists and some unusual architecture.

Dazhalan has a definite medieval flavour to it, a hangover from the days when specialised products were sold in hutongs – lace in one, lanterns in another, jade in another. This particular one used to be called 'Silk Street'. The name Dazhalan actually refers to a wicket-gate that was closed at night to keep prowlers out.

In imperial Beijing, shops and theatres were not permitted near the city centre, and the Qianmen-Dazhalan District was outside the gates. Many of the city's oldest shops can be found along or near this crowded hutong.

Just off the beginning of Dazhalan at 3 Liangshidian Jie is Liubiju, a 400-year-old pickle-and-sauce emporium patronised by discriminating shoppers. Nearby is the Zhimielou Restaurant, which serves imperial snacks. On your right as you go down Dazhalan is a green concave archway with columns at No 5; this is the entrance to the century-old Riufuxiang, one of the better-known material and silk stores.

Another famous shop is the Tongrentang at No 24, selling Chinese herbal medicines. It's been in business since 1669, though it doesn't appear that way from the renovations. It was a royal dispensary in the Qing dynasty, and creates its pills and potions from secret prescriptions used by royalty. All kinds of weird ingredients – tiger bone, rhino horn, snake wine – will cure you of anything from fright to encephalitis, or so they claim. Traditional doctors are available on the spot for consultation; perhaps ask them about fear of Chinese train ticket offices (patience pills?).

Dazhalan runs west off Qianmen Dajie. At the far end where the hubbub dies down there's a bunch of Chinese hotels. Dazhalan was once the gateway to Beijing's red-light district; folklore has it that the Tongzhi emperor would frequently disguise himself as a peasant, slip out of the Forbidden City at night and patronise the brothels. In 1949 the brothels were shut down and the women packed off to factories.

Qianmen Dajie, and Zhushikouxi Dajie heading off to the west, are interesting places to wander around. On Qianmen Dajie there's a tea shop at No 118, a herbal medicine shop and pharmacy at No 128, a Beijing opera costume shop at No 130 and a pottery store at No 149. Almost a century old, Duyichu (☎ 6702 1555), at 36 Qianmen Dajie where Dazhalan meets Qianmen, serves delicious steamed dumplings.

Liulichang (Map 6)

Not far to the west of Dazhalan is Liulichang, Beijing's antique street. Although it's been a shopping area for quite some time, it's only in the past decade that it's been dressed up for foreign tourists. The stores here are all designed to look as if they're straight out of an ancient Chinese village, and this makes for good photographs even if you don't want to buy anything.

Liulichang (meaning glazed tile factory) shops specialise in antiques (most are fakes), Chinese ink and watercolour scroll paintings, brushes, ink and paper. This is also the place to get a chop made. Chops start as low as Y15, and can be carved for around Y10 per character.

A few of the shops here are state-run, such as Rongbaozhai (☎ 6303 6090), at 19 Liulichang Xijie. Rongbaozhai has an excellent selection of scroll paintings, woodblock prints, paper, ink and brushes. Because it's state-run, prices are generally fixed although you can usually get 10% off. Also worth checking out is the Cathay bookshop, which carries a wide variety of colour art books (in Chinese) on Chinese painting, ceramics, furniture – you name it. The Ji Gu Ge Teahouse (see Teahouses in Places to Eat), is a nice place to take a break.

Jianguomenwai (Map 7)

The Friendship Store (Yǒuyì Shāngdiàn), at 17 Jianguomen Wai Dajie, is the largest store in the land – this place stocks both touristy souvenirs and practical everyday items. Not long ago, the Friendship Store was *the* place to shop in Beijing – so exclusive that only foreigners and cadres were permitted inside – but these days anyone can go in. The touristy junk is upstairs, but the ground floor is where the really useful items are – tinned and dried foods, tobacco, wines, spirits, coffee, Chinese medicines and film. The book and magazine section is a gold mine for travellers starved of anything to read. To the right are a supermarket and deli. It's open 9 am to 9 pm daily.

Just down the street from the Friendship Store is the newer Guiyou Department Store (Guìyǒu Dàshà).

Scitech Plaza (Sàitè Gòuwù Zhōngxīn) is a huge department store with an enormous selection – pragmatic shoppers will probably most enjoy the supermarket in the basement. Upstairs is where you'll find the more upmarket items: the latest fashions,

SHOPPING

Making a Name for Yourself

The traditional Chinese name chop or seal has been used for thousands of years. It's likely that people began using name chops because Chinese characters are so complex and few people in ancient times were able to read and write.

A chop served both as a unique personal statement and as a valid signature. All official documents in China needed a chop to be valid. Naturally, this made a chop quite valuable, for with another person's chop it was possible to sign contracts and other legal documents in their name.

Today, most Chinese are literate, but the tradition lives on. In fact, without a chop it is difficult or impossible to enter into a legally binding contract in China. A chop is used for bank accounts, entrance to safe-deposit boxes and land sales. Only red ink is used for a name chop

If you live in China for work or study, you will almost certainly need to have a chop made. On the other hand, if you're staying a short time a chop makes a great souvenir. A chop can be made quickly, but first you will need to have your name translated into Chinese characters.

There are many different sizes and styles of chops. Inexpensive small chops can be carved from wood or plastic, while expensive ones can be carved from ivory, jade, marble or steel. Most Chinese people have many chops to confuse a possible thief, though they run the risk of confusing themselves as well. One chop might be used for their bank account, another for contracts and another for a safe-deposit box. Obviously, a chop is important and losing one can be a big hassle.

Since the people who carve chops don't check your ID, it might occur to you that obtaining a fake or forged chop would be very easy. Indeed, it is. It's also a very serious crime in China.

cosmetics and perfumes. Kitchen wares are in basement No 2. Scitech Plaza is on the southern side of Jianguomen Wai, opposite the CITIC building.

The Xiushui Silk Market (see Clothing & Accessories earlier) is on the northern side of Jianguomenwai between the Friendship Store and the Jianguo Hotel. Besides clothing, fake Beanie Babies (about Y10 each) are a popular buy.

Sanlitun (Map 5)

The Sanlitun embassy compound is in north-east Beijing, close to the Great Wall Sheraton Hotel. Like Jianguomenwai, the stores here are decidedly upmarket.

The gigantic Lufthansa Center (Yānsha Shāngchǎng), also known as the Kempinski Hotel (Kǎibīnsījī Fàndiàn), falls into a category by itself, being Beijing's first flashy multi-storey shopping mall. You can buy everything here from floppy disks to bikinis. A supermarket is in the basement.

Xidan (Map 3)

Officially known as Xidan Beidajie, this street (west of the Zhongnanhai compound) aspires to be a little Wangfujing. It's certainly a popular place with the locals, but for foreign tourists it's a bit disappointing. There is no shortage of things to buy, but it's mostly of the 'cheap junk that breaks easily' variety. However, it's a good street for budget travellers in search of practical everyday items. The major store is the highrise Xidan Shopping Centre (Xīdān Gòuwù Zhōngxīn).

Shopping Centres & Department Stores

The biggest and shiniest of Beijing's new malls is Xindong'an Plaza (Map 4) in the heart of Wangfujing. You can find just about anything here – a Nike store, the best shoe stores, several clothing boutiques, a qipao maker. There's also a food court. Other shopping malls include China World (Map 7), Cofco Plaza (Zhōng Liáng Guǎngchǎng), at 8 Jianguomen Nei Dajie, and Full Link Plaza (Map 5; Fēng Lián Guǎngchǎng), at 18 Chaoyangmen Wai Dajie. Full Link has a

Internet cafe and a Park 'n Shop supermarket in the basement, as well as a Watson's (Qūchénshì) on the ground floor. This place sells every vitamin known to humankind, plus sunscreen (UV) lotion, beauty creams, balms, tampons and scented toilet paper.

The soon-to-be-opened megacomplex Oriental Plaza (Map 7), at 1 Chang'an Dajie (corner of Wangfujing), is also slated to have a shopping arcade.

One of the newest additions to Beijing's collection of upmarket department stores is Sogo (Map 6; ☎ 6310 3388, Xuanwu), a Japanese department store. It has huge se-

lections of cosmetics, shoes, clothing and sporting equipment, and also an excellent supermarket and food court in the basement. The Lufthansa Center (Sanlitun), Scitech (Jianguomenwai) and Parkson (Map 6; ☎ 6601 3377), at 101 Fuxingmen Nei Dajie, in Xidan, are other fully-stocked upmarket department stores. More typical Chinese department stores are Landao (Blue Island; Lándǎo Dàshà), at 8 Chaoyangmen Wai Dajie, north of Jianguomenwai, and Kylin Plaza (Qílín), Gongti Beilu, in Sanlitun, although they're much better than typical state-run department stores.

Excursions

All the places in this chapter can be visited as day trips from Beijing, although in some cases you might find it worth your while to stay overnight.

TOMBS

Death and its rituals have always played a big role in Chinese culture. For emperors, the ceremonies reached epic proportions, as did the wealth and attention spent on their tombs. Around Beijing there are three major tomb sites, and each tomb holds (or held) the body of an emperor, his wives, concubines and funerary treasures. All the tombs have been plundered at one time or other, but recent efforts at restoration have benefited China's cultural pride, not to mention the tourist industry.

The three tomb sites open to tourists are the Ming Tombs, the Western Qing Tombs and the Eastern Qing Tombs. Of the three, the Ming Tombs are by far the most frequently visited.

Ming Tombs (Ming Tombs Map & Map 1)

Shísān Líng 十三陵

The 7km road known as the Spirit Way starts with a triumphal arch then goes through the Great Palace Gate, where officials had to dismount, and passes a giant tortoise (made in 1425) bearing the largest stele in China. This is followed by a guard of 12 sets of stone animals. Every second one is in a reclining position, legend has it, to allow for a 'changing of the guard' at midnight. If your tour-bus driver whips past them, insist on stopping to look. Beyond the stone animals are 12 stone-faced human statues of generals, ministers and officials, each distinguishable by headgear. The stone figures terminate at the Lingxing Gate.

Unfortunately, the Chinese drivers don't care much about the statues and usually prefer to spend half an hour at the Shisanling Reservoir. The reservoir itself is pretty dull, though the history behind it is interesting. It

was Mao's brainchild, constructed in 1958 as part of a massive nationwide water conservancy project. The reservoir was constructed entirely by hand using armies of 'volunteers' working around the clock. Mao himself showed up and shovelled dirt for 30 minutes while the event was recorded for the world news media. Even some foreign embassy staff based in Beijing lent a hand while the cameras rolled. It was a great

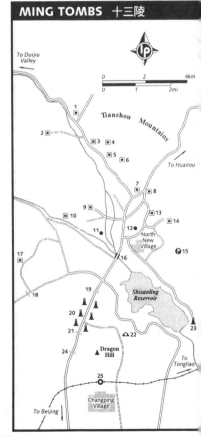

MING TOMBS 十三陵

demonstration of socialist solidarity, and a precursor to the disastrous 'Great Leap Forward' launched later that year.

Thirteen of the 16 Ming emperors are buried in this 40-sq-km area, hence its other name: the Thirteen Tombs. Ding Ling was the first of the tombs to be excavated and opened to the public. Two others, Chang Ling and Zhao Ling, are now open to the public.

Ding Ling, the tomb of Emperor Wan Li (1573–1620), is the second-largest tomb (Chang Ling is the largest). It took the emperor six years, half a million workers and a heap of silver to build his necropolis. It was excavated between 1956 and 1958 and you can now visit the underground passageways and caverns. The underground construction, entirely of stone, covers 1195 sq metres and is sealed with an unusual lock stone. The tomb yielded 26 lacquered trunks of funerary objects; some originals are on site, while others have been removed to Beijing's museums and replaced with copies.

Wan Li and his royal spouses were buried in double coffins surrounded by chunks of uncut jade. The jade was thought to have the power to preserve the dead, or so the Chinese tour literature relates. Meanwhile experts on cultural relics as well as chefs are studying the ancient cookbooks unearthed from Ding Ling with a view to serving Wan Li's favourite dishes to visitors, using replicas of imperial banquet-table ware.

Another of the tombs is Chang Ling, the final resting place of Emperor Yongle. Construction began in 1409 and took 18 years to complete. According to the story, 16 concubines were buried alive with Yongle's corpse. This was the second of the Ming Tombs to be excavated and opened to the public. It consists mainly of displays of funerary objects.

Zhao Ling is the ninth of the Ming Tombs and was opened to visitors in 1989. This is the tomb of Emperor Longqing, who died in 1572, and three of his wives.

The Beijing municipal government is trying to attract interest to the area with theme-park type attractions. New facilities include a golf course, the **Nine Dragons Amusement Park**, an archery and rifle range, shops, cafes, a 350-room hotel, swimming pool, aquarium, camp site, picnic area, fountain (with a 200m water jet), fishing pier (on the Shisanling Reservoir), racecourse, cross-country skiing area, helicopter rides, and even Mongolian yurts for use as a summer hotel!

MING TOMBS

1 Tai Ling
泰陵

2 Kang Ling
康陵

3 Mao Ling
茂陵

4 Yu Ling
裕陵

5 Qing Ling
庆陵

6 Xian Ling
献陵

7 Chang Ling
长陵

8 Jing Ling
景陵

9 Ding Ling
定陵

10 Zhao Ling
昭陵

11 International Friendship Forest
国际友谊林

12 Heliport
空中旅游机场

13 Yong Ling
永陵

14 De Ling
德陵

15 Beijing International Golf Club
北京国际高尔夫球俱乐部

16 Seven Arch Bridge
七孔桥

17 Si Ling
思陵

18 Small Palace Gate
小宫门

19 Lingxing Gate
棂星门

20 Stone Statues
石像生

21 Great Palace Gate
大宫门

22 Fairy Cave
仙人洞

23 Shisanling Reservoir Memorial
十三陵水库纪念碑

24 Stone Arch
石牌坊

25 Changping North Train Station
昌平北火车站

The **Ming Dynasty Waxworks Palace** (Míng Huáng Làxiàng Gōng) is the notorious wax museum that tourists are herded through if they book a Ming Tombs tour with a Chinese group. It is claimed to be the largest wax museum in the world. The wax figures are all well-known Chinese historical personages, and they will 'talk' to you thanks to some cleverly hidden speakers.

Just next door is the Qing dynasty's rejoinder, the **Ancient Beijing Mini-Landscape Park** (Lǎo Běijīng Wēisuō Jǐngguǎn). The park contains a scale model of old Beijing.

About 10km east of Changping at Xiaotangshan is the **China Aviation Museum** (Zhōngguó Hángkōng Bówùguǎn), which is also on some of the Great Wall Tour circuits (see Getting There & Away following). Chairman Mao's personal shuttle plane is on display here, but most of the aircraft on show were designed for destroying the Motherland's arch enemies.

Getting There & Away The tombs lie 50km north-west of Beijing and a few kilometres from the town of Changping. Tour buses usually combine them with a visit to the Great Wall at Badaling. Big tour buses leave from across the street from the southwest corner of Tiananmen Square between 6.30 and 10 am – for Y50 they'll bring you to the Great Wall at Badaling and the Ming Tombs (Chang Ling and Ding Ling). Smaller buses leave for the same destinations from the south end of Tiananmen Square (to the west of McDonald's) at 8 and 9.30 am ; Y40. Plan about nine hours for the whole trip. A tour bus (No 4) also leaves from Zhanlanguan, directly across the street from the entrance to the Zoo. Buses leave around 8 am and return around 6 pm and go to Badaling and Ding Ling (Ming Tombs). Cost is Y36, but the buses aren't as new and comfortable as the ones that leave from Qianmen.

If you don't want to combine the trip with Badaling and if you'd like to see tombs other than Chang Ling or Ding Ling, you can take minibus No 345 from Deshengmen to Changping. The mini-bus can be waved down just outside the Jishuitan subway exit. The trip to Changping is about an hour (Y6). Alternatively, you can take a large air-conditioned bus (No 845) from Xizhimen (just outside the Xizhimen subway stop) to Changping (Y7). From Changping you can hire a *miandi* (mini van), for Y60 for half a day. It's about a 10 minute ride from Changping to the entrance to the Ming Tombs. This is a good way to get around and explore the unrenovated tombs.

Western Qing Tombs
Qīng Xī Líng 清西陵

The Western Qing Tombs are in Yixian County, 110km south-west of Beijing. If you didn't see enough of Ding Ling, Yu Ling, Yong Ling and De Ling at the Ming Tombs, there's always Tai Ling, Chang Ling, Chong Ling and Mu Ling at the Western Qing Tombs.

The vast tomb area houses the mausoleums of emperors Yongzheng, Jiaqing, Daoguang and Guangxu, along with the tombs of empresses, princes, princesses and royal retainers, comprising over 70 tombs in all. The tomb of Emperor Guangxu (reigned 1875–1908), called Chong Ling, was the last of the imperial tombs. It was constructed between 1909 and 1915.

Unlike the Ming Tombs, there are two Qing Tomb sites, the result of Yongzheng's guilty conscience, or more likely fear of being buried next to his father, Emperor Kangxi: When Yongzheng's father appointed a younger son to ascend the throne, Yongzheng took matters into his own hands – killing his brothers and his father's ministers so that he could take his father's seat at the head of the empire.

Not many tours go to these tombs, so your only hope may be to share a chartered taxi. From Beijing it's a three-hour drive. You can also take a train part of the way to the tombs. From Beijing South station take a train to Gaobeidian, then change to a bus to the tombs from the long-distance bus station.

tting around the Beijing way – three million bicycles can't be wrong!

Wooden masks make unusual, if cumbersome, souvenirs.

Hamming it up at the Zhengyici, the oldest wooden theatre in China.

Bride for five minutes: a tourist takes a ride in a traditional wedding carriage.

Eastern Qing Tombs (Eastern Qing Tombs Map & Map 1)

Qīng Dōng Líng 清东陵

In Zunhua County, about 125km east of Beijing, the Eastern Qing Tombs valley offers a lot more to see than the Ming Tombs, although you may be a little jaded after the Forbidden City. In fact, it could be called Death Valley, housing as it does five emperors, 14 empresses and about 130 imperial consorts. In the surrounding mountains are buried princes, dukes, imperial nurses and so on.

The approach to the tomb area is a typical 'spirit way', similar to that of the Ming Tombs but with the addition of marble-arch bridges. The materials for the tombs came from all over China, including 20-tonne logs which were pulled over iced roads, and giant stone slabs.

Emperor Qianlong (reigned 1736–1795) started preparations for his inevitable demise when he was only 30, and by the time he was 88 had managed to spend 90 tonnes of his silver on the affairs of the hereafter.

Qianlong's resting place, Yu Ling, ended up covering about 500 sq metres. Some of the beamless stone chambers of the tomb are decorated with Tibetan and Sanskrit sutras, while the doors bear bas-relief Bodhisattvas.

Empress Dowager Cixi also got a head start. Her tomb, Dingdong, was completed some three decades before her death. The phoenix (the symbol of the empress) appears *above* that of the dragon (the symbol of the emperor) in the artwork at the front of the tomb. On other tombs, such symbols appear side by side. Sadly, both tombs were plundered in the 1920s.

These tombs have mostly been restored. However, as they see few visitors it makes a nice place for a picnic. Admission is Y55 (which gets you into nine tombs plus the exhibition centre).

Getting There & Away If you don't mind the long haul by public bus to the Eastern Qing Tombs, buses depart from Bawangfe bus station; look for the cluster of buses just east of the China World Trade Center off the Jingtong Expressway. Tour buses are considerably more comfortable than the local rattletraps and take 2½ hours to get there; you have about three hours on site. Hiring a car for the day from Beijing costs about Y400. Some people actually prefer to go from Tianjin.

DUIJIU VALLEY (MAP 1)

Duìjiù Yù

After you've dried out from the trip to the Ming Tombs, you might want to explore a scenic hiking area just 10km to the north. Duijiu (Mortar and Pestle) Valley is notable for its small river, waterfalls and pools set out among the boulders. Although the valley is well known to the Chinese and the area around the car park is crowded, few visitors venture very far up the gorge because the journey has to be made on foot. The upper end of the gorge becomes quite steep, but should be well within the capabilities of the average traveller.

To reach the entrance, take a taxi from the Ming Tombs. Once there, it costs Y10 to get in.

TANZHE TEMPLE (MAP 1)

Tánzhè Sì 潭柘寺

About 45km directly west of Beijing is Tanzhe Temple, the largest of all the Beijing temples, occupying an area 260m by 160m. The Buddhist complex has a long history dating as far back as the 3rd century (Jin dynasty). Structural modifications date from the Tang, Liao, Ming and Qing dynasties. The temple therefore has a number of features, such as dragon decorations, mythical animal sculptures and grimacing gods, which are no longer found in most temples in the capital.

Translated literally, Tanzhe means Pool Cudrania. The temple takes its name from its proximity to the **Dragon Pool** (Lóng Tán) and some rare Cudrania (*zhè*) trees. Locals come to the Dragon Pool to pray for rain during droughts. The Cudrania trees nourish silkworms and provide a striking yellow dye. The bark of the tree is believed to cure women of sterility, which may explain why there are so few of these trees left at the temple entrance.

EXCURSIONS

Compared to other temples in and around Beijing, Tanzhe Temple feels refreshingly tranquil. The long and narrow cobblestone path leading up to the temple is lined with locals selling dried fruits and nuts laid out on blankets. The temple grounds are covered with towering cypress and pine tress, many so old that their gangly limbs have to be supported by metal props. The best time to arrive is just before sunset, as the chant of resident monks floats through the temple.

The Tanzhe Temple complex is open to the public every day from 8.30 am until 6 pm. To get there, take bus No 15 from Zhanlanguan (across from the Zoo) and get off three stops later where it meets up with bus No 336. Take bus No 336 to Mengtougou, and from there you can hire a taxi. Alternatively, take the subway to Pingguoyuan, bus No 336 to Hetan and a numberless bus to the temple. Admission is Y30.

JIETAI TEMPLE (MAP 1)
Jiètái Sì 戒台寺
About 10km south-east of Tanzhe Temple is a similar but smaller compound. Jietai (Ordination Terrace) Temple was built around AD 622, during the Tang dynasty, with major improvements made by later tenants during the Ming dynasty. The main complex is dotted with ancient pine trees, all of which have been given quaint names. One of these, **Nine Dragon Pine**, is claimed to be over 1300 years old.

It is approximately 35km from Jietai Temple to Beijing, and the journey out here is usually combined with a visit to Tanzhe Temple.

BADACHU (MAP 1)
Bādàchù 八大处
Badachu is also known as Eight Great Temples (Bādà Sì) or Eight Great Sites. It has eight monasteries or temples scattered in wooded valleys. The Second Site has the

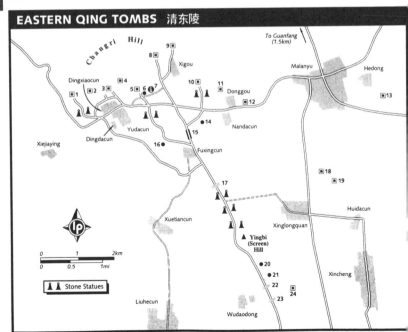

EASTERN QING TOMBS 清东陵

Buddha's Tooth Relic Pagoda, built to house the sacred tooth accidentally discovered when the Allied army demolished the place in 1900.

The mountain has numerous apricot trees, which makes for some cheerful and sweet-smelling scenery around April when the trees briefly bloom.

Since 1994, the ancient culture has been give a touch of excitement with an extravagant amusement park adventure: a terrifying roller-toboggan course. A chairlift will carry you up the hill to the top of the course, which stretches for 1700m and can send you hurtling downwards at speeds of up to 80 km/h.

Admission to Badachu (☎ 6887 5211) is Y5. The easiest way to reach it is by taking the east-west subway to Pingguoyuan and catching a taxi (Y10) from there. You can also take bus No 347, which runs from Badachu to Beijing Zoo; open 6 am to 6 pm daily.

FAHAI TEMPLE (MAP 1)
Fǎhǎi Sì 法海寺
The peaceful Fahai (Sea of the Law) Temple, on the western edge of Beijing, houses truly striking Buddhist murals dating to the Ming dynasty. The floor-to-ceiling **frescoes** depict in minute detail a gathering of Buddhist deities with a presiding 2m-high Guanyin. The well-preserved frescoes, reminiscent of the Mogao Caves in Gansu and the Yungang Caves near Datong, are worth the 20-minute ride to get here. Be sure to bring a flashlight, as the hall is dimly lit.

To get there, take the East-West subway line to the Pingguoyuan station. Then it's a Y10 miandi ride. The temple (☎ 6880 3976) is open from 9 am to 4.30 pm daily; admission is Y20.

STONE FLOWER CAVE (MAP 1)
Shí Huā Dòng
You can reach the Stone Flower Cave by following the same highway to Jietai Temple further westward. This is considered the most scenic set of caves in the Beijing area – so of course it's lit with coloured lights and has souvenir stands outside.

The cave (☎ 6031 2170) is located 55km south-west of central Beijing. From the Tianqiao bus station, take bus No 917 to Fangshan, from where you can get a tour bus or taxi. Admission to the caves is a whopping Y47.

EXCURSIONS

EASTERN QING TOMBS

1 Ding Ling 定陵	9 Xiaodong Ling 孝东陵	17 Longfeng (Dragon-Phoenix) Gate 龙凤门
2 Dingfei Ling 定妃陵	10 Jing Ling 景陵	
3 Dingdong Ling (Empress Cixi) 定东陵	11 Jingfei Ling 景妃陵	18 Huifei Ling 惠妃陵
4 Yufei Ling 裕妃陵	12 Taifei Ling (Two Concubines of Emperor Kangxi) 太妃陵	19 Huiling Ling 惠陵
5 Yu Ling (Emperor Qianlong) 乾隆裕陵	13 Princess Ling 公主陵	20 Stele Tower 石碑楼
6 Foreign Guest Reception Centre 外宾招待中心	14 Stele Tower 石碑楼	21 Robing Hall 理服廊
7 Tourist Office 旅游办事处	15 Seven-Arch Bridge 七孔桥	22 Great Palace Gate 大宫门
8 Xiao Ling 孝陵	16 Stele Tower 石碑楼	23 Stone Archway 石孔门
		24 Zhaoxi Ling 昭西陵

MARCO POLO BRIDGE (MAP 2)
Lúgōu Qiáo 卢沟桥

Publicised by the great traveller himself, the 260m-long Marco Polo Bridge (Lugou Bridge) is made of grey marble and has over 250 marble balustrades supporting 485 carved stone lions. The bridge was first built in 1192, but the original arches were washed away in the 17th century. The bridge is a composite of different eras and was widened in 1969. It spans the Yongding River near the little town of Wanping.

In 1751 Emperor Qianlong put his calligraphy to use and wrote some poetic tracts about Beijing's scenic wonders. His *Morning Moon Over Lugou Bridge* is now engraved into stone tablets and placed on steles next to the bridge. On the opposite bank is a monument to Qianlong's inspection of the Yongding River.

Despite the publicity campaign by Polo and Qianlong, the bridge wouldn't rate more than a footnote in Chinese history were it not for the famed 'Marco Polo Bridge Incident' which ignited a full-scale war with Japan.

On the night of 7 July 1937, Japanese troops illegally occupied a railway junction outside Wanping, which prompted Japanese and Chinese soldiers to start shooting at each other, and that gave Japan enough of an excuse to attack and occupy Beijing (then Peking). The Chinese were more than a little displeased by this, especially since Japan had already occupied Manchuria and Taiwan. The day of the Marco Polo Bridge Incident is considered by China watchers to be the day the Chinese became part of WWII.

A relatively recent addition to this ancient site is the **Memorial Hall of the War of Resistance Against Japan**, built in 1987. Also on the site is the Wanping Castle, the Daiwang Temple and a tourist hotel.

You can get to the bridge (☎ 8389 3919) by taking bus No 339 or 309 from Liulichang. Get off the bus at Taihuangchang, then hire a miandi the rest of the way for Y10. By bicycle it's about a 16km trip one way.

PEKING MAN SITE (MAP 1)
Zhōukǒudiàn 周口店

The old stamping ground of those primeval Chinese, the Peking men (and women, of course), Zhoukoudian Village is approximately 50km south-west of Beijing at the town of Fangshan.

Deemed a Unesco World Heritage Site, Zhoukoudian is the site where the remains of people who lived here half a million years ago have been excavated. In the 1920s and 1930s, a major archaeological excavation unearthed skull caps, stone tools and animal bones believed to be 230,000 to 500,000 years old. Unfortunately, research on Peking Man's skull was never carried out because the skull cap and other remains mysteriously disappeared on the eve of the Japanese invasion during an attempt to smuggle them to the USA. Subsequent digs have resulted in more remains, but sadly nothing as substantial as Peking Man.

> ## Skullduggery
>
> There is an interesting story behind the skull of the Peking Man. Early this century, villagers around Zhoukoudian found fossils in a local quarry and took them to the local medicine shop for sale as 'dragon bones'. This news got back to Beijing and archaeologists – foreign and Chinese – poured in for a dig.
>
> Many years later, a molar was found, and the hunt for a skull was on. It was finally found in the late afternoon of December 1929 – a complete skullcap of *Sinanthropus pekinensis*. The cap was believed to be over half a million years old; if so, it rates as one of the missing links in the evolutionary chain.
>
> Unfortunately, research on the skull was never carried out. When the Japanese invaded in 1937 the skull cap was packed away with other dig results and the whole lot swiftly vanished. The Chinese accused the Americans, the Americans accused the Japanese and the mystery remains. Other fragments surfaced from the site after 1949, but no comparable treasure was found.

Today there's not much to see here. There's an 'Apeman Cave' on a hillside above the village, several lesser caves and a number of archaeological dig sites. There is also a fossil exhibition hall with English explanations.

There are three distinct sections to the Peking Man exhibition hall: one dealing with pre-human history, one introducing the life and times of Peking Man, and the last dealing with recent anthropological research. Ceramic models, stone implements and the skeletons of several prehistoric creatures are on display. The exhibition hall is open from 8.30 am to 4.30 pm daily. Admission is Y20.

Getting There & Away
Zhoukoudian lies 48km south-west of Beijing. You can catch a bus No 917 from Tianqiao bus station (on the western side of Tiantan Park), which goes to Fangshan (one hour). From there you can catch a bus (No 2) or taxi to the site (6km). If combined with a trip to Tanzhe Temple and Marco Polo Bridge, approaching the site by taxi is not unreasonable.

SHIDU (SHIDU MAP & MAP 1)
Shídù 十渡

Shidu is Beijing's answer to Guilin. The pinnacle-shaped rock formations, small rivers and general beauty of the place make it a favourite spot with expatriate students, diplomats and business people.

Situated 110km south-west of central Beijing, Shidu means Ten Ferries or Ten Crossings. Before the new road and bridges were built, it was necessary to cross the Juma River 10 times while travelling along the gorge between Zhangfang and Shidu village.

Places to Stay
The gorge can be visited as a day trip, but it's really worth spending one night. The *Long-shan Hotel (Lóngshān Fàndiàn;* ☎ *6134 0912)* is a simple, family-run place opposite the train station. While foreigners aren't officially allowed to stay here, you might convince them to let you spend the night. In the town of Shidu, along the main road about 1.5km from the train station, is the **Yishu Lou Hotel** *(Yìshūlóu Fàndiàn;* ☎ *6134 9988)*. When you see a two-storey building with red lanterns in front you've found it. The hotel is on the 2nd floor, above the restaurant. Simple but clean rooms are Y40 per person.

Down near Jiudu (the 'ninth ferry'), next to the bungee-jumping platform, is the large **Shanguang Hotel** *(Shānguāng Lǔshi;* ☎ *6134 0762),* where rooms go for Y290. There's also a camping ground, conveniently located on a flood plain. In Liudu, nicely located on the river and away from any amusement facilities, is the **Dongzheng Hotel** *(Dōngzhèng Bīnguǎn;* ☎ *6134 0791),* where clean standard rooms are Y240.

Getting There & Away
Getting to Shidu is fastest by train, but there are only two departures daily, from the Beijing South (Yongdingmen) train station. If you take the morning train, the trip can be done in one day. See the schedule at the bottom of this page.

SHANGFANG MOUNTAINS (MAP 1)
Shàngfāng Shān 上方山

The scenic Shangfang Mountains are approximately 70km south-west of central Beijing, not far north of the highway between the Peking Man Site and Shidu.

Beijing-Shidu Train Schedule

no	from	to	depart	arrive
795	Yongdingmen	Shidu	6.38 am	8.49 am
897	Yongdingmen	Shidu	5.40 pm	8.11 pm
796	Shidu	Yongdingmen	7.40 pm	10.01 pm
898	Shidu	Yongdingmen	9.10 am	11.37 am

SHIDU

A major attraction is the **Yunshui Caves** (Yúnshuǐ Dòng). Don't expect to be the first human to explore these depths because you'll find coloured lights, souvenir shops and snack bars. About 1km to the east of the cave entrance is the Doulu Temple (Dōulù Sì), a large monastery complex in the foothills.

The best way to reach the mountains is to take a train from the Beijing South station and get off at Gushankou.

YUNJU TEMPLE (MAP 1)
Yúnjū Sì 云居寺
The Chinese have long built Buddhist shrines in caves, although the really legendary shrines (such as Datong, Luoyang and Dunhuang) are far from Beijing.

Just south of the Shangfang Mountains are some limestone hills riddled with small cave temples, some of which date back to the Sui dynasty (AD 589–618). The best-known cave temple in the area is the Yunju (Cloud Dwelling) Temple (☎ 6138 2101). China's state-controlled Buddhist association declared in 1987 that a box found in the temple contained two **bone fragments** that belonged to none other than Siddhartha Gautama (563–483 BC) himself, the founder of

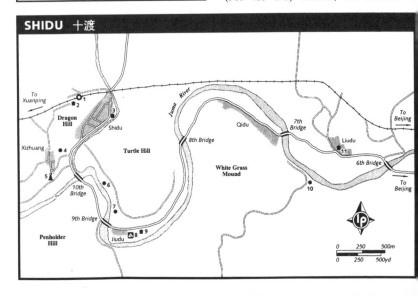

SHIDU 十渡

Buddhism. Of course, lacking a DNA analysis of the great Siddhartha, it would be rather difficult to prove or disprove this claim.

Although the two pieces of Siddhartha are in fact hardly bigger than a grain of sand, the 'discovery' has greatly changed the temple's fortunes. Money has poured into the temple's coffers from various overseas Buddhist associations, setting off quite a construction boom. In 1990 a new structure was erected to house more than 77,000 engraved wooden blocks containing the **Chinese Tripitaka** (Buddhist scriptures). This Tripitaka did not originate in Yunju Temple, but has been shipped in from other collections throughout China, such as the one at Beijing University. Only eight such sets of Tripitaka are known to exist in China.

To get there from Tianqiao bus station (west side of Tiantan Park) in Beijing, take bus No 917, which will bring you directly to the temple. It's open 8.30 am to 5.30 pm daily; admission is Y30.

KANGXI GRASSLANDS (MAP 1)
Kāngxī Cǎoyuán 康西草原

The grasslands are actually in a beautiful hilly region 80km north-west of the city. This is considered the best place in Beijing municipality for horse riding. It is also possible to spend the night here in a Mongolian yurt, but rug up and be prepared for surprisingly chilly nights, even in the summer. You can even arrange for a whole roast lamb for Y200 to Y300.

Unfortunately, the area is being dressed up for tourism and is rapidly developing a carnival atmosphere. There is already the gaudy City of the Three Kingdoms, as well as the Folklore Holiday Village, camel rides and a roller skating rink.

To get there you can take bus No 919 from the Deshengmen market. The Kangxi Grasslands is about 2½ hours drive from Beijing.

LONGQING GORGE (MAP 1)
Lóngqìngxiá 龙庆峡

About 90km north-west of Beijing is Longqing Gorge, a canyon in Yanqing County. The gorge was probably more scenic before the dam and reservoir flooded

the area. Rowing and hiking are the big attractions in summer.

From mid-December to the end of January this is the site of Beijing's deservedly famous **Ice Lantern Festival** (Bīngdōng Jié). The 'lanterns' are enormous ice carvings into which coloured electric lights are inserted. The effect (at least during the night) is quite stunning. Children (yes, including adult children) are welcome to amuse themselves to their chilled bottoms' content on the ice slide.

The ride from Beijing takes two hours one way. There are currently three hotels in Longqing Gorge and plenty more are on the drawing board.

HONGLUO TEMPLE (MAP 1)
Hóngluó Sì

About 65km north-east of central Beijing near Huairou is Hongluo (Red Conch Shell) Temple. The name derives from a legend that two conch shells emitted a red light here one evening.

The temple was built sometime during the Tang dynasty (AD 618–907) and it has since been rebuilt, renovated and renamed several times.

Hongluo Temple is large as far as such temples go, with several courtyards, halls and the quaint **Conch Shell Pagoda**. It was an important Buddhist pilgrimage site, even drawing the Tang, Ming and Qing emperors.

Adjacent to the temple is (get ready for it) the **Sino-Interest Mars Sports Centre** (☎ 6491 2233 ext 316), where weekenders go to play paintball (pītèbó).

To get there, take a bus from Dongzhimen bus station in north-east Beijing to Huairou, then change to a bus or taxi to Hongluo Temple. A visit to the temple can also be included on an excursion to the Great Wall at Mutianyu.

MIYUN RESERVOIR (MIYUN RESERVOIR MAP & MAP 1)
Mìyún Shuǐkù 密云水库

Some 90km north-east of Beijing is Miyun Reservoir, the city's water supply and largest lake in Beijing municipality. Since this is drinking water, swimming is prohibited, but the lake is impressive for its scenery.

MIYUN RESERVOIR

1 Fengjiayu
   冯家峪
2 Banchengzi
   半城子
3 Bulaotun
   不老屯
4 Taishitun
   太师屯
5 In Front of the Dam Park
   坝前公园
6 Xiwengzhuang
   溪翁庄
7 Miyun International
   Amusement Park
   密云国际游乐场
8 Miyun Train Station
   密云火车站
9 Mujiayu
   穆家峪
10 Dachengzi
   大城子

Chinese entrepreneurs know a good thing when they see it, and Miyun Reservoir has acquired a number of commercial recreation sites. Most important is the **Miyun International Amusement Park** (Mìyún Guójì Yóulè Cháng), not on the lake itself but 20km to the south-west, about 7km outside Miyun town. Facilities include a merry-go-round, monorail, car racing track and souvenir shops – just about everything you could possibly want in life.

If the carnival atmosphere gets to be too much, there are less touristy scenic sites around the reservoir. On the east side of the lake is **White Dragon Pool** (Báilóng Tán). While also being developed for tourism, White Dragon Pool retains much of its former charm. During the Qing dynasty, emperors on their way to Chengde would drop in for a visit, so the area is dotted with temples and pavilions that have been recently renovated.

MIYUN RESERVOIR 密云水库

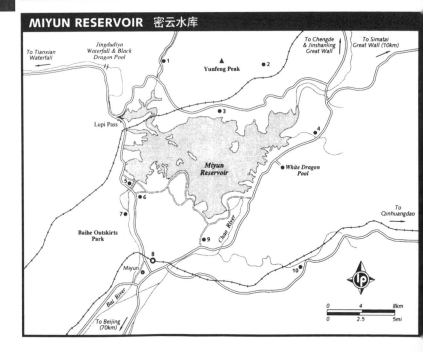

Believe it or not, right in front of the dam is the **In Front of the Dam Park** (Bàqián Gōngyuán), which is mainly just a place for tourists to get their pictures taken. On the shores of the reservoir itself is the *Yunhu Holiday Resort* (*Yúnhú Dùjiàcūn;* ☎ *6102 1991*), where you can stay for Y380.

North-west of Miyun Reservoir are the less visited scenic spots. These sights include **Black Dragon Pool** (Hēilóng Tán), **Jingdudiya Waterfall** (Jīngdūdìyā Pùbù) and **Tianxian Waterfall** (Tiānxiān Pùbù); due north is **Yunfeng Peak** (Yúnfēng Shān).

Trains running to Chengde stop at Miyun. Buses to Miyun depart from the Dongzhimen bus station.

YANQI LAKE (MAP 1)
Yànqí Hú

A small reservoir near Huairou (60km north-east of central Beijing), Yanqi Lake is perhaps Beijing municipality's best venue for water sports. Apart from swimming, paddle-boating and water-skiing, you can also go parasailing (towed by a speedboat while dangling from a parachute).

The main place to stay is the *Yanming Hotel* (*Yànmíng Lóu;* ☎ *6966 1124*), where standard twins are Y280. There is also a camping ground here.

Take a bus from Dongzhimen bus station to Huairou, then change to a bus or taxi to Yanqi Lake. The bus stop at Yanqi Lake is in front of the Yanming Hotel, and from there you can catch buses or taxis to Hongluo Temple and the Great Wall at Mutianyu.

HAIZI RESERVOIR (MAP 1)
Hǎizi Shuǐkù 海子水库

At the far eastern end of Beijing municipality is Haizi Reservoir, an artificial creation that is being promoted for tourism. The park around the lake is called **Jinhai Lake Park** (Jīnhǎi Hú Gōngyuán). The reservoir was the site of the aquatic sports during the 1990 Asian Games.

Because of the Games (which were poorly attended), the area has decent recreation facilities, though it's hard to say if everything will be kept in good condition.

Modern amenities include the *Jinhai Hotel* (*Jīnhǎi Bīnguǎn*) and the *Jinhai Restaurant* (*Jīnhǎi Cāntīng*). There is a pier where you can sometimes catch a cruise across the lake to the aquatic sports area (*shuǐshàng yùndòng chǎng*). The shore of the reservoir is dotted with some recently built pavilions to remind you that this is indeed China.

Buses going to the lake depart from Dongzhimen bus station.

TIANJIN (TIANJIN MAP, TIANJIN CENTRAL MAP & MAP 1)
Tiānjīn 天津

The fourth largest city in China, Tianjin is a major port about 2½ hours by bus to the south-east of Beijing. For centuries it has served as Beijing's outlet to the sea and has often been referred to as 'the Shanghai of the north'.

For the sea-dog Western nations of the 19th century, Tianjin was a trading bottleneck too good to be passed up. British gunboats persuaded the Chinese to sign the Treaty of Tianjin (1858) which opened the port to foreign trade. The Brits were soon joined by the French, Japanese, Germans, Austro-Hungarians, Italians and Belgians. Since 1949 Tianjin has been a focus for major industrialisation. But despite new high-rises, factories and a busy container port, much of Tianjin's old European architecture has been left intact – the city still has a good deal of charm and a very different flavour from Beijing.

For business people, the big event of the year is the Tianjin Export Commodities Fair held every March. It's for invited guests only – to get an invite, contact CITS or CTS well in advance.

Information
The Tianjin Tourism Bureau (☎ 2835 4860, fax 2835 2324) is at 18 Youyi Lu (almost opposite the Friendship Store). Just next door, at 22 Youyi Lu, is the China International Travel Service (CITS; Zhōngguó Guójì Lǚxíngshè; ☎ 2835 8499, fax 2835 2619).

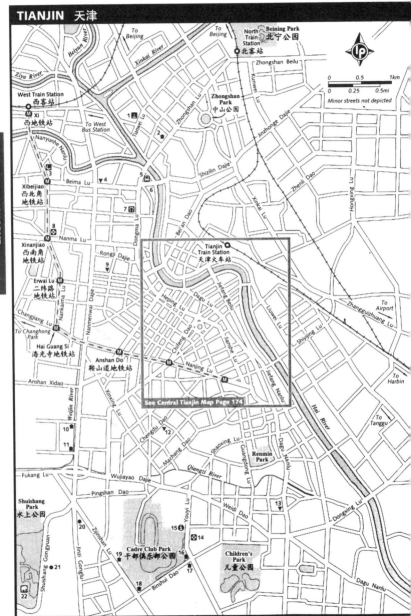

TIANJIN 天津

EXCURSIONS

To Beijing

To Beijing

North Train Station

Beining Park
北宁公园

北客站

Zhongshan Beilu

Beiyun River

Xinkai River

Ziya River

West Train Station
西客站

Xi
西地铁站

To West Bus Station

Nanyunhe Nanlu

Tianwei Lu

Zhongshan Lu

Zhongshan Park
中山公园

Kunwei Lu

Jinhonge Dajie

1

2

Xibeijiao
西北角
地铁站

Beima Lu

Dongma Lu

3

4

5

6

7

Shizilin Dajie

Xinkai Lu

Zhenli Dao

Hongxing Lu

8

Nanma Lu

Xinanjiao
西南角
地铁站

Rongji Dajie

9

Bei'an Dao

Tianjin Train Station
天津火车站

Erwai Lu
二纬路
地铁站

Nankaima Lu

Nanmenwai Dajie

Chengdu Dao

Heping Lu

Dagu Lu

Jiefang Beilu

Luwei Lu

To Airport

Changjiang Lu

To Changhong Park

Hai Guang Si
海光寺地铁站

Anshan Do
鞍山道地铁站

Chifeng Dao

Jianhe Lu

Jiefang Nanlu

Shuijing Lu

Zhangguizhuang Lu

To Harbin

Anshan Xidao

Wejia River

Nanjing Lu

See Central Tianjin Map Page 174

To Tanggu

Xining Lu

10

11

Chengdu Dao

12

Machang Dao

Shaoxing Lu

Guangdong Lu

Renmin Park
人民公园

Dagu Nanlu

Hai River

Fukang Lu

Wujiayao Dajie

Pingshan Dao

Qianzi River

Weidi Dao

13

Dongxing Lu

Shuishang Park
水上公园

Youyi Lu

20

15

14

Shuishang Gongyuan

Jinzi Gongfu

Zhumin Lu

Cadre Club Park
干部俱乐部公园

19

16

17

Children's Park
儿童公园

21

Binshui Dao

18

Dagu Nanlu

22

0   0.5   1km
0   0.25   0.5mi
Minor streets not depicted

Antique Market
Gǔwán Shìchǎng 古玩市场

The sheer size and variety of the Antique Market makes it fascinating to stroll through. Among the many items on sale are stamps, silver coins, silverware, porcelain, clocks, photos of Mao, Cultural Revolution exotica and old books.

The antique market is best on Sunday, when it expands enormously and spills out into side streets in every direction. On weekdays it occupies only a small section of Shenyang Dao in the centre of town. Operating hours are from 7.30 am until 3 pm – it's best to arrive around 8 am to get the widest selection.

Ancient Culture Street
Gǔ Wénhuà Jiē 古文化街

The Ancient Culture Street is a fair attempt to recreate the appearance of a Chinese city in times long gone. In addition to the traditional buildings, the street is home to vendors plugging every imaginable type of cultural memento from Chinese scrolls, paintings and name chops to the latest heavy metal sounds on CD. During public holidays street operas are often staged here as well.

Within the confines of the recreated street is the small Tianhou Temple (Tiānhòu Gōng). Tianhou (Heaven Queen) is the goddess of the sea, and is known by various names (such as Matsu in Taiwan and Tin Hau in Hong Kong). It is claimed that Tianjin's Tianhou Temple was built in 1326, but it has seen a bit of renovation since then.

Ancient Culture Street is a major drawcard for tourists, both foreigners and Chinese. The street is in the north-western part of town.

Confucius Temple
Wén Miào 文庙

On the northern side of Dongmen Nei Dajie, one block west of Ancient Culture Street, is Tianjin's Confucius Temple. It was originally built in 1463 during the Ming dynasty. The temple, and Confucianists in general, took quite a beating during the Cultural Revolution. By 1993, however, the buildings had been restored and opened to the public.

Grand Mosque
Qīngzhēn Sì 清真寺

Although it has a distinctly Chinese look, the Grand Mosque is an active place of worship for Tianjin's Muslims. The mosque is on Dafeng Lu, not far south of the West train station.

Dabei Monastery
Dàbēiyuàn 大悲院
This is one of the largest and best-preserved monasteries in the city. It was built between 1611 and 1644, expanded in 1940, battered during the Cultural Revolution and finally restored in 1980. The temple is on Tianwei Lu in the northern part of the city.

Catholic Church
Xīkāi Jiàotáng 西开教堂
This is one of the most bizarre-looking churches you'll ever see. Situated on the southern end of Binjiang Dao, the twin onion domes of the cathedral, also known as the Xikai Church, form a dramatic backdrop to the 'Coca-Cola Bridge' (a pedestrian overpass crossing Nanjing Lu). It's definitely worth a look. Church services are again permitted on Sunday, which is about the only time you'll have a chance to view the inside.

Earthquake Memorial
Kàngzhèn Jìniànbēi 抗震纪念碑
Just opposite the Friendship Hotel on Nanjing Lu there is a curious pyramid-shaped memorial. Although there's not much to see here, this Earthquake Memorial is a pointed reminder of the horrific events of 28 July 1976, when an earthquake registering eight on the Richter scale struck north-east China.

It was the greatest natural disaster of the decade. Tianjin was severely affected and the city was closed to tourists for two years. The epicentre was at nearby Tangshan – that city basically disappeared in a few minutes.

Hai River Park
Hǎihé Gōngyuán 海河公园
Stroll along the banks of the Hai River (a popular pastime with the locals) and see photo booths, fishing, early-morning *taiji*, rehearsing opera singers and old men toting bird cages. The esplanades of the Hai River Park have a peculiarly Parisian feel, as some of the railing and bridge work is French.

Tianjin's sewage has to go somewhere and the river water isn't so pure that you'd want to drink it. It's not Venice, but there are tourist boat cruises on the Hai River that start not far from the New World Astor Hotel.

TV Tower
Diànshìtái 电视台
In an attempt to whip the masses into patriotic fervour and prove that Tianjin is a modern metropolis, the TV Tower has been declared the great wonder of the city. Indeed, it's proven to be a major drawcard for domestic tourists. You can join in the fun by visiting the summit for a whopping Y100 fee and enjoy the warm feeling you get being atop the pride and joy of Tianjin. Views from the top aren't spectacular in the daytime, but things get better at night. The tower is also topped by a revolving restaurant.

You won't have any trouble locating the TV Tower – it dominates the skyline on the southern side of town.

Shuishang Park
Shuǐshàng Gōngyuán 水上公园
The large Shuishang Park is in the southwest corner of town, not far from the TV Tower. The Chinese name means Water Park and over half the surface area is a lake. The major activity here is renting rowboats and pedal boats.

It's one of the more relaxed places in busy Tianjin, except on weekends when the locals descend on it. The park features a Japanese-style floating garden and a decent zoo.

Getting to the park from the train station requires two buses. Take bus No 8 to the terminus and from there hop onto bus No 54, also to the terminus which is just outside the park entrance.

Art Museum
Yìshù Bówùguǎn 艺术博物馆
The Art Museum is easy to get to and pleasant to stroll around. Housed in an imposing rococo mansion, the museum houses a small but choice collection of paintings and calligraphy on the ground floor and some Tianjin folk art, including kites, clay figurines and posters, on the 2nd floor. On the top floor special displays are featured.

It's at 77 Jiefang Beilu, one stop from the main train station.

Zhou Enlai Memorial Hall
Zhōu Ēnlái Jìniàn Guǎn 周恩来纪念馆

Zhou Enlai is perhaps China's most respected revolutionary, in part because he tried to keep Mao's chaotic Cultural Revolution in check. Zhou grew up in Shaoxing in Zhejiang Province, but he attended school in Tianjin, so his classroom is enshrined and there are photos and other memorabilia from his time there (1913–17). The memorial is next to Shuishang Park in the south-western corner of town near the TV Tower. From the main train station, take bus No 8 to Balitai and then bus No 54 to the memorial hall. Admission is Y10.

Streetscapes
Far more engrossing than any of the preceding is Tianjin's European architecture from the turn of the 20th century. One minute you're in little Vienna, turn a corner and you could be in a London street; hop off a bus and you're looking at some vintage French wrought-iron gates or a neo-Gothic cathedral. Unfortunately, recent post-modern architectural horrors are starting to impact on Tianjin's skyline. Poking out of the post-earthquake shanty rubble is an ever-increasing number of high-rise castles of glass and steel. Nevertheless, the streets around Munan Dao, as well as Jiefang Lu, are particularly pleasant areas to stroll around.

If you're a connoisseur of architecture, Tianjin is a textbook of just about every style imaginable. Of course, things have been renamed, and anyone with a sense of humour will be amused by some of the uses to which the bastions of the European well-to-do have been put.

Places to Stay
The cheapest places open to foreigners are the guesthouses at Nankai and Tianjin universities. *Tianjin University Qinyuan Hotel* (*Tiānjīn Dàxué Zhuānjiā Lóu;* ☎ 2740 7711, fax 2335 8714) has very clean, well-kept doubles for Y166, including breakfast.

The *Tianjin University Foreign Students' Dormitory* (*Tiānjīn Dàxué Liúxuéshēng Lóu;* ☎ 2740 4373) also has rooms

starting at Y126. Not as well kept, but at similar prices, are the foreign students dormitories at Nankai University. There are two buildings offering accommodation. *Nankai University Building 2* (*Nánkāi Dàxué Yìyuánsùshè Èrhàolóu;* ☎ 2350 1832) has doubles on the grotty side for Y150, while the newer and better-kept *Building 4* (*Nánkāi Dàxué Yìyuánsùshè Sìhàolóu;* ☎ 2350 5335) has doubles for Y200.

Look no further than the *Imperial Palace Hotel* (*Tiānjīn Huánggōng Fàndiàn;* ☎ 2379 0888, fax 2379 0222, 177 Jiefang Beilu) for mid-range accommodation. This Singapore joint venture is housed in a beautiful and cosy building that was originally built by a British merchant in 1923 and recently renovated. It has a great Thai dinner buffet on Friday and Saturday for Y36. There's also the Sparkice Internet cafe open from 2 to 10 pm for Y20 per hour. The rooms start at Y581, including breakfast; during the low season a 45% discount isn't hard to get.

From here on it gets pricey. You can bask in luxury at the *Hyatt Hotel* (*Kǎiyuè Fàndiàn;* ☎ 2331 8888, fax 2331 1234, 219 Jiefang Beilu), where standard rooms are US$109, or US$90 on the weekends.

The *New World Astor Hotel* (*Lìshùndé Fàndiàn;* ☎ 2331 1688, fax 2331 6282, 33 Tai'erzhuang Lu) dates from early 20th century and retains the feel of foreign concession days (although it's been completely refurbished). Twins start at Y1105 and suites at Y1700.

Also ranked among Tianjin's most swanky hotels is the *Crystal Palace Hotel* (*Shuǐjīnggōng Fàndiàn;* ☎ 2835 6886, fax 2835 8886, 28 Youyi Lu). Facilities include a swimming pool, tennis court, health club and French restaurant. Standard rooms start at US$100.

The *Sheraton Hotel* (*Xǐláidēng Dàjiǔdiàn;* ☎ 2334 3388, fax 2335 8740, ✉ sheraton@mail.zlnet.com.cn, Zijinshan Lu) is in the southern part of Tianjin. It has 281 rooms priced between Y1500 and Y1750, plus 49 suites ranging from Y3125 to Y6250. To that, add another 15% surcharge, but if it helps the buffet breakfast is thrown in free. Guests also qualify for a free copy of the *South China Morning Post*.

In the vicinity of Ancient Culture Street, the *Tianjin Holiday Inn (Jiàrì Fàndiàn;* ☎ 2628 8888, fax 2628 6666, ✆ hotel@ mail.hitianjin.com, 288 Zhongshan Lu) has doubles starting at US$130.

One of the latest additions to Tianjin's collection of upmarket hotels is the *Ocean Hotel (Yuǎnyáng Bīnguǎn;* ☎ 2420 5518, fax 2420 5516, ✆ ohtj@ shell.tjvan.net.cn, 5 Ocean Square), located a short walk from the train station. Single rooms start at US$48 and doubles

at US$88 (although discounts bring rooms under Y500).

The *Dickson Hotel (Dàichéng Jiǔdiàn;* ☎ 2836 4888, fax 2836 5018, ✆ dickson@ shell.tjvan.net.cn, 18 Binshui Dao) is another reasonable upmarket hotel. Standard twins start at US$155.

The *Tianjin Grand Hotel (Tiānjīn Bīnguǎn;* ☎ 2835 9000, fax 2835 9822, Youyi Lu) is indeed grand and houses 1000 beds in two high-rise blocks. It has benefited from considerable renovation since it was first built in 1960, and prices have been hiked up to Y640 for twins.

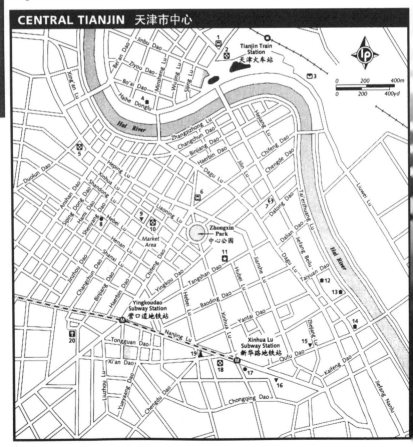

CENTRAL TIANJIN 天津市中心

Places to Eat

Popular with expats, the *Broadway Cafe* (*Guìbīnlóu Xīcāntīng;* ☎ *2330 0541 or 130-0130 7877, 74 Munan Dao*) serves steaks and other hearty Western fare. At the time of writing there were plans to move to a larger location on Ti Yuan Bei, near the TV Tower. An Irish pub, coffee bar and outdoor patio were also in the works for the new location.

The *City Slicker Saloon* (*Lǎowài Niúzǎi Cāntīng;* ☎ *2313 0278, 55 Nanjing Lu*) specialises in Tex-Mex, including fajitas, chilli dogs, barbecue ribs, nachos and salsa. The friendly owners will make you feel at home amid the bizarre country-and-western-style decor.

The place to go for Chinese food is *Food Street* (*Shípǐn Jiē*), a covered alley with two levels of restaurants. Old places close and new ones open all the time here, but there are approximately 40 to 50 restaurants on each level. You need to check prices – some of the food stalls are dirt cheap but a few upmarket restaurants are almost absurdly expensive. You can find some real exotica here, like snake (expensive), dog meat (cheap) and eels (mid-range). Food Street is a couple of blocks south of Nanma Lu, about 1km west of the city centre.

King of the dumpling shops is *Goubuli* (*Gǒubùlǐ;* ☎ *2730 2540*) at 77 Shandong Lu, between Changchun Dao and Binjiang Dao. The shop has a century-old history. The staple of the *maison* is a dough bun, filled with high-grade pork, spices and gravy. You can also get baozi with special fillings like chicken, shrimp or its delicious vegetarian mix (*shūcài bāozi*) – be prepared to wait 10 to 15 minutes. A set meal, including soup, pickled vegetables and eight dumplings is Y13 to Y18, depending on the filling. The baozi here truly are exceptional not only for the better quality ingredients but also because they aren't greasy (a rarity in these parts). Frozen versions of this product can be bought from grocery stores all over Tianjin. Goubuli has the alarming literal translation of 'dogs won't touch them' or 'dog doesn't care'. The most satisfying explanation of this seems to be that Goubuli was the nickname of the shop's founder, an unfortunate man with an outrageously ugly face – even dogs were said to be scared of him.

The *Eardrum Fried Spongecake Shop* (*Ěrduǒyǎn Zhágāo Diàn*) takes its extraordinary name from its proximity to Erduoyan (Eardrum) Lane. This shop

EXCURSIONS

CENTRAL TIANJIN

specialises in cakes made from rice powder, sugar and bean paste, all fried in sesame oil. These special cakes have been named (you guessed it) 'eardrum fried spongecake'. You can in fact find the cakes at various venues all around Tianjin, even at the train station.

Another Tianjin food speciality takes its name from its location at the *18th Street Dough-Twists Shop*. The dough-twists (*máhuā*) in question (made from sugar, sesame seeds, nuts and vanilla) aren't exclusive to this shop though – they can be bought all over town.

Kiessling's Bakery (Qǐshìlín Cāntīng), built by the Austrians back in foreign concession days (1911), is a Tianjin institution. It's at 33 Zhejiang Lu, in the same building as the Qishilin Hotel. Again, you needn't go to the shop as the cakes are distributed all around the city at various shops and restaurants.

Getting There & Away

Air If you like, you can even make your exit from China at Tianjin. Air China offers daily direct flights between Hong Kong and Tianjin. CAAC (☎ 2330 1556), of course, connects Tianjin with just about everywhere in China. It's at 113 Nanjing Lu. The International Building (*guójì dàshà*) at 75 Nanjing Lu has booking offices for Dragon Air and Korean Air. CITS can book tickets on most airlines.

Bus The opening of the Beijing-Tianjin Expressway has greatly reduced travel time between the two cities, with the journey taking about 1½ hours. Buses to Beijing depart from the front of Tianjin's main train station and cost Y30. From Beijing, catch the bus to Tianjin from the Zhaogongkou bus station on the southern side of town, but be careful you get a bus to Tianjin train station (Tiānjīn Huǒchē Zhàn) and not to the outlying districts of Kaifa or Tanggu (unless you want to go to Tanggu). Buses run about once every 15 minutes throughout the day.

There are four long-distance bus stations. Bus station No 1 (Yīlù Qìchē Zhàn), opposite the Bohai Hotel, has buses to Tanggu, Tianjin's port. From Tanggu you can catch a boat to South Korea or Japan.

Train For Beijing trains you'll want the Tianjin station in Tianjin. Some trains stop at both Tianjin and West, and some go only through the West station (particularly those originating in Beijing and heading south). Through trains to north-east China often stop at the North station.

Foreigners can avoid the horrible queues by purchasing tickets at the soft-seat ticket office on the 2nd floor of the departure hall in the train station.

Express trains take 1½ hours for the trip between Tianjin and Beijing. Local trains take about 2½ hours.

Boat Tianjin's harbour is Tanggu, 50km (30 minutes by train) from Tianjin proper. This is one of China's major ports, offering a number of possibilities for arriving and departing by boat. International passenger ferries ply the route between Tianjin and Inch'ŏn (South Korea), while another runs to Kobe, Japan. Tickets and schedules for these boats are available in Tianjin from CITS and other travel agencies (see the Getting There & Away chapter for more details).

THE GREAT WALL
Chángchéng 长城

Perhaps the most famous of all Beijing's nearby sights are the choice chunks of Great Wall that pass within about 100km of the capital and make for great day trips, or more intensive expeditions. It's no accident that some of the greatest wall restoration jobs have been carried out within spitting distance of Beijing, and the best of these are Badaling, Mutianyu, Simatai and (the more remote) Huanghua. See the following 'The Great Wall' section for all the details.

THE GREAT WALL

Also known to the Chinese as the '10,000 Li Wall', the Great Wall (Chángchéng) stretches from Shanhai Pass on the east coast to Jiayu Pass in the Gobi Desert.

Standard histories emphasise the unity of the wall. The 'original' wall was begun 2000 years ago during the Qin dynasty (221–207 BC), when China was unified under Emperor Qin Shihuang. Separate walls, constructed by independent kingdoms to keep out marauding nomads, were linked up. The effort required hundreds of thousands of workers, many of them political prisoners, and 10 years of hard labour under General Meng Tian. An estimated 180 million cubic metres of rammed earth were used to form the core of the original wall, and legend has it that one of the building materials used was the bodies of deceased workers.

The wall never really did perform its function as a defence line. As Genghis Khan supposedly said, 'The strength of a wall depends on the courage of those who defend it'. And sentries could be bribed. However, it did work very well as a kind of elevated highway, along which men and equipment could be transported across mountainous terrain. Its beacon tower system, using smoke signals generated by burning wolves' dung, transmitted news of enemy movements quickly back to the capital. To the west was Jiayu Pass, an important link on the Silk Road, where there was a customs post of sorts and where unwanted Chinese were ejected through the gates to face the terrifying wild west.

Right: With a past as long and twisted as its serpentine contours, the Great Wall has been a friend, foe and folktale to travellers for more than 2000 years. This view was recorded by Thomas Allom in the early 1800s.

During the Ming dynasty a determined effort was made to rehash the whole project, this time facing it with bricks and stone slabs – some 60 million cubic metres of them. This project took over 100 years, and the costs in human effort and resources were phenomenal.

The wall was largely forgotten after that. Lengthy sections of it have returned to dust and the wall might have disappeared totally had it not been rescued by the tourist industry. Several important sections have recently been rebuilt, fitted out with souvenir shops, restaurants and amusement park rides, and formally opened to the public. The most touristed area of the wall by far is Badaling. Also renovated but less touristed are Simatai and Jinshanling. But to truly appreciate the wall's magnificencé, seeing the wall *au naturel,* such as at Huanghua, is well worth the effort.

Badaling
Bādálǐng 八达岭

The majority of visitors see the Great Wall at Badaling, 70km north-west of Beijing at an elevation of 1000m. This section of the wall (called Bādálǐng Chángchéng) was restored in 1957, with the addition of guard rails. Since the 1980s Badaling has become exceedingly crowded so a cable car was added to smooth the flow of tourist traffic.

The **Great Wall Circle Vision Theatre** was opened in 1990. It is a 360° amphitheatre where 15-minute films about the Great Wall are shown.

There is an admission fee of Y25, which also gets you into the **China Great Wall Museum** (Zhōngguó Chángchéng Bówùguǎn). You can spend plenty more for a tacky 'I Climbed the Great Wall' T-shirt, a talking panda doll, a cuckoo clock that plays 'The East is Red' or a plastic reclining buddha statue with a light bulb in its mouth.

Getting There & Away CITS, CTS, big hotels and everyone else in the tourist business does a tour to Badaling. Prices border on the ridiculous, with some hotels asking over Y300 per person.

There are inexpensive Chinese tour buses to Badaling, although they usually combine Badaling with a visit to the Ming Tombs as well as a detour to a herbal medicine or souvenir shop. Big tour buses leave across the street from the south-west corner of Tiananmen Square between 6.30 and 10 am – for Y50 they'll bring you to the Great Wall at Bada-ling and the Ming Tombs. Smaller buses leave for the same destinations from the southern end of Tiananmen Square (to the west of McDonald's) at 8 and 9.30 am for Y40. Plan about nine hours for the whole trip. A tour bus (No 4) also leaves from Zhanlanguan, directly across the street from the entrance to the zoo. It leaves around 8 am and returns around 6 pm and goes to Badaling and the Ming Tombs. Cost is Y36, but the buses aren't as new and comfortable as the ones that leave from Qianmen. Probably the cheapest way to get to Badaling is to take minibus No 919 (Y10) from Deshengmen (next to the Jishuitan subway

THE GREAT WALL

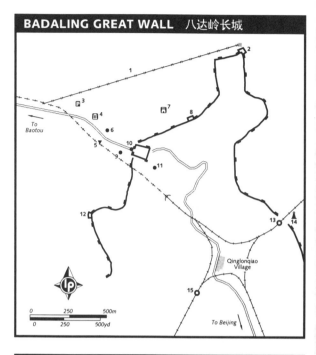

BADALING GREAT WALL 八达岭长城

To Baotou

Qinglonqiao Village

To Beijing

0   250   500m
0   250   500yd

BADALING GREAT WALL

1 Cable Car
  缆车
2 North No 8
  Tower
  北八楼
3 Car Park
  停车场
4 Great Wall Museum;
  Circle Vision Theatre
  长城博物馆、
  长城全周影院
5 Restaurants
  餐厅
6 Tourist Shop
  商店
7 Fort
  炮台
8 North No 4 Tower
  北四楼

9 Tourist Shop
  商店
10 North Gate
  Lock & Key
  北门锁钥
11 Former Outpost
  of Juyong Pass
  居庸外镇
12 South No 4
  Tower
  南四楼
13 Qinglongqiao
  Train Station
  青龙桥站
14 Zhan Tianyou
  Statue
  詹天佑像
15 Qinglongqiao New
  Train Station
  青龙桥新站

stop). Buses leave every 15 minutes (or as they fill up) starting from 5.30 am; the last bus leaves Badaling for Beijing at 6.30 pm.

A taxi to the wall and back will cost a minimum of Y400 for an eight-hour hire with a maximum of four passengers.

Mutianyu
Mùtiányù 慕田峪

To take some of the pressure off crowded Badaling, a second site for Great Wall viewing was opened at Mutianyu, 90km north-east of Beijing. It didn't take long before armadas of tour buses began to congregate around it, and today this part of the wall (called Mùtiányù Chángchéng) is almost as much of a carnival as Badaling. Admission here is Y20.

Getting There & Away From Dongzhimen bus station take bus No 916 to Huairou (Y4, one hour), from where you can change for a bus to Mutianyu.

Juyong Pass
Jūyōng Guān 居庸关

Originally constructed in the 5th century and rebuilt by the Ming, this section of the wall was considered one of the most strategically important because of its position as a link to Beijing. Now it has been thoroughly renovated to the point where you don't feel as if you're walking on a part of history. Still, if you're in a hurry, it's the closest section of the wall to Beijing. You can do the steep and somewhat strenuous circuit in under two hours.

Admission to the Great Wall at Juyong Pass is Y25.

Getting There & Away Approximately 50km north-west of Beijing, Juyong Pass is on the road to Badaling (Badaling is another fifteen minutes further down the road). Take minibus No 919 (Y10) from Deshengmen (next to the Jishuitan subway stop). Buses headed to Badaling leave every fifteen minutes (or as they fill up) starting from 5.30 am; be sure to let the bus driver know you want to be dropped off at Jūyōng Guān Chángchéng.

Simatai
Sīmǎtái 司马台

In sharp contrast to the over-restored wall at Badaling and Mutianyu is Simatai. This 19km section of wall largely retains its pristine crumbling condition. But things are changing. The first danger sign was the T-shirt vendors, who set up shop around 1994, followed by a loudspeaker which bellows music and 'nature sounds' to increase your enjoyment. In 1996 a cable car (Y40) was installed. Although many visitors complain of aggressive postcard hawkers, Simatai is still generally an enjoyable outing.

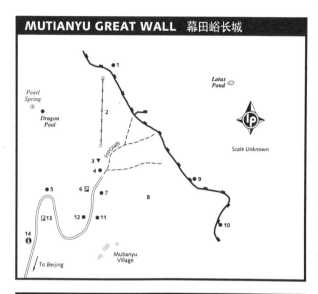

MUTIANYU GREAT WALL 幕田峪长城

Pearl Spring
Dragon Pool
Lotus Pond
Footpath
Scale Unknown
Mutianyu Village
To Beijing

MUTIANYU GREAT WALL

1 Beacon Tower
烽火台

2 Cable Car
缆车

3 Restaurants
餐厅

4 Yanjing Painting &
Calligraphy Studio
燕京书画社

5 Ticket Office
售票处

6 No 1 Car Park
第一停车场

7 Ticket Office
售票处

8 Toboggan
滑道

9 Zhengguan Tower
正关台

10 Stone Mortar
石臼

11 Guest-Welcoming
Pine Tree
迎宾松

12 Mandarin Duck Pine Tree
鸳鸯松

13 No 2 Car Park
第二停车场

14 Tourist Office
旅游区办事处

The Simatai section of the wall dates from the Ming dynasty and has some unusual features, like '**obstacle-walls**' – walls-within-walls used to defend against enemies who'd already scaled the Great Wall. There are 135 watchtowers at Simatai, the highest of which is Wangjing Lou. Small cannon have been discovered in this area, as well as evidence of rocket-type weapons such as flying knives and swords.

Simatai is not for the faint-hearted: this section of the wall is very steep. A few slopes have a 70° incline and you need both hands free, so bring a day-pack to hold your camera and other essentials. One narrow section of footpath has a 500m drop, so it's no place for acrophobes. The steepness and sheer drops, however, do help keep out the riffraff.

In the early 1970s a nearby PLA unit destroyed about 3km of the wall to build barracks, setting an example for the locals who used stones from the wall to build houses. In 1979 the same unit was ordered to rebuild the section they tore down.

Admission to the site at Simatai costs Y20.

Getting There & Away Simatai is situated 110km north-east of Beijing. To get there, take a minibus to Miyun (Y6, 1¼ hours) from Dongzhimen bus station. From Miyun you can hire a *miandi* for Y70 return (about fifteen minutes one way) or you could hire the miandi for Y30 one way and try to catch a tour bus from Simatai back to Beijing (about Y30).

For budget travellers, the best deal around is offered through the Jinghua Hotel – Y60 for the return journey by minibus. Ring its booking office (☎ 6722 2211) for more details. Hiring a taxi from Beijing for the day costs about Y400.

Jinshanling
Jīnshānlǐng 金山岭

Though not as steep (and therefore not as impressive) as Simatai, the Great Wall at Jinshanling (Jīnshānlǐng Chángchéng) is considerably less developed than any of the sites previously mentioned. This section of the wall has been renovated and souvenir vendors have moved in, but so far there is no cable car and visitors are relatively few. Many of the tourists stopping here are on an excursion between Beijing and Chengde in Hebei, with Jinshanling thrown in as a brief stopoff.

Perhaps the most interesting thing about Jinshanling is that it's the starting point for a hike to Simatai (see under the Walking the Wild Wall section later). You can do the walk in the opposite direction, but getting a ride back to Beijing from Simatai is easier than from Jinshanling. Of course, getting a ride should be no problem if you've made arrangements with your driver to pick you up (and didn't pay him in advance). The distance between Jinshanling and Simatai is only about 10km, but it takes nearly four hours because the trail is steep and stony.

Admission to the Great Wall at Jinshanling costs Y30. For more information on Jinshanling, see the Jinshanling to Simatai section of 'Walking the Wild Wall'.

Getting There & Away From Dongzhimen bus station you can take a minibus to Miyun (Y6, 1¼ hours), and from Miyun hire a miandi for Y80 return (one hour each way).

Walking the Wild Wall

Away from the heavily touristed areas of the Great Wall, long sections stride across the region's lofty mountain ranges. This 'Wild Wall' is remote, lonely, unspoilt, overgrown and crumbling. There are no tickets, no signposts, no hassles from trinket-sellers, no coach parks or garbage to spoil the view. Travellers can trek up narrow footpaths winding uphill from tiny villages in Beijing's backwoods and discover what for many may turn out to be the ultimate China experience. Here are three walks, the first two from Huanghua, about 60km north of Beijing, and the third between Jinshanling and Simatai Village. The walks coincide at Zhuangdaokou Pass. See the relevant Getting There & Away sections for details about access.

Huanghua to Zhuangdaokou Pass (4km, Three-Hour Loop)

The obvious place to start this walk is at the point where the wall meets the road in Huanghua. However, since the wall is in quite a poor state there, it's easier to walk about 100m to the south. After passing a small, deep quarry and an old toilet, you'll see a well-trodden path leaving the roadside and heading up a creek. The path keeps to the left-hand side of the creek and is clear and easy to follow. After about 300m it starts to veer towards the wall, and fades among the terraces, but your first target is in sight.

Second Watchtower To get to this tower (the first, lower tower has collapsed) make your way to an arched entrance just past the tower itself. As you pass through the archway, straight ahead is an **engraved tablet** embedded in the wall. It details construction of a 150-*zhang* length of wall in the seventh year of the Wanli period (AD 1579) by a group of commanders and their work force. The name of the stonemason who carved the tablet, Wu Zongye, is in the bottom left-hand corner.

The tower itself has three windows along both its northern and southern faces. Locals describe towers by referring to the number of openings along one face, referring to them as *kēng* (holes) or *yǎn* (eyes). So this tower is a three-hole or three-eyed tower, *sān kēng lóu* or *sān yǎn lóu*. It once had a wooden roof which supported a second-storey, but its central area is now open to the sky. You can see holes in the course of brick (half a metre above archway apexes) where roof-to-floor beams were positioned.

Leaving the tower, make your way west along the ramparts towards a derelict tower. From this high point you get panoramic views of the area.

Derelict Tower Looking east, the **Huanghua Reservoir** (Huánghuā Shuǐkù) is in full view. Beyond the reservoir, four towers dot the wall on its lower slopes, while a roofless **battle platform** can be seen near the summit. The wall then turns north and plunges out of sight. It reappears with a side view of the inverted, U-shaped stretch of wall known as the Gaping Jaw. Further on, the wall can be seen snaking up the Huanghua ridge.

Looking north, a few seemingly solitary watchtowers can be seen in the vicinity of Fenghuangtuo Mountain (1530m). They are connected by walls, but they are small in scale and of inferior quality.

Looking south, you can see Huanghua town and the wide river valley leading towards Huanghuazhen. The view starkly illustrates the strategic nature of the pass between the mountains here.

From the corner tower the wall swings north, running level through conifer woods before turning west again and dropping to a three-eyed tower, notable for its stone ceiling.

Stone Ceiling Tower Large slabs of igneous rock have been incorporated into the ceiling of this tower. Normally, rock was used only in foundations, with bricks employed throughout the upper levels. Given that the slabs are almost 1m long and about 40cm wide, it's difficult to explain their use; the effort required to hoist such heavy slabs into position would have been considerable.

Leave the tower through the western door and follow the wall as it drops through a thick conifer plantation. The parapets around here are in poor condition and the wall's pavement is overgrown and, in some places, totally derelict.

After 200m and another three-eyed tower, the ramparts cross a small valley where a pass, or gate, in the wall once existed. In compensation for the condition of the ramparts here, the gate is in excellent condition.

Zhuangdaokou Pass This pass, a passageway through the wall, is about 2.5m wide. It is in the form of a brick archway founded on large igneous blocks. It is most striking for its **engraved tablets** which are different on either side of the archway. The tablet on the southern side features three large characters – *zhuang dao kou* – reading from right to left. The smaller characters record the name of the official who put the tablet in place, Liu Xun, and the date, in the fifth year of the Wanli reign (1577). Farmers continue to use this gate to reach terraced hillsides beyond the wall to tend their fruit trees or coppice conifers for firewood.

The tablet on the northern face, also dated 1577, bears three large characters which read, from right to left, Zhèn Lǔ Guān (Suppress Captives Pass).

Zhuangdaokou was originally fortified in 1404, during the early years of the Ming dynasty. It was one of three passes (along with Juyong Pass at Badaling and Gubeikou in the north-east) deemed to be critical in blocking large Mongol armies on horseback and preventing them from reaching the capital easily. Between these passes, where sturdy walls and towers were built, there were only lines of watchtowers and beacon towers. It was left to later dynasties to connect them with walls.

Zhuangdaokou Pass to Zhuangdaokou Village From the archway turn south and follow the path downhill. It is about 500m to the village of Zhuangdaokou, a marvellous little settlement half nestled within the walls of an ancient barracks. The path is as old as the pass itself, linking the barracks with the wall.

As you enter the village, the barracks is the large walled structure on the left; it's possible to climb its wall at the near corner. It averages seven courses of stone blocks in height, and the blocks are of the same provenance and shape as those used as foundations for the wall. About half the foundation of the structure remains; it now encloses some farmhouses.

From the top of its walls you can see carved granite **water spouts** protruding from inside. All other structures, and half the walls, have been removed – probably during the Cultural Revolution.

Village to Bus Stop or Restaurant Follow your nose down through the narrow alleyways (note the **Cultural Revolution slogans** in yellow and faded images of Mao's head on crumbling plaster walls) to the southern edge of the village, then turn left at the bank of the stream and follow the main road for 1km to a T-junction. Buses for Huairou and Changping leave from here. Turn left here if you want to return to the starting point, or refuel at the Shuang Long Zhu Jiu Jia restaurant (literally, Pair of Dragons Playing with a Pearl Alcohol House).

Huanghua to Gaping Jaw (4km, Four-Hour Loop)

From the restaurant walk north for 50m and cross the top of the dam holding back Huanghua Reservoir. The dam occupies the site of the main Huanghua Men – only the foundations of this once-glorious gate remain.

From the far end of the dam, climb up the footpath on the northern side and enter the **first tower** through one of its north-facing windows.

It is a short, steep climb to the **second tower**. Parapets have fallen down and locals have removed the bricks; they have also taken away bricks which topped the stone block foundations of the rampart. The wall drops in height before climbing to the **third tower**. This is a conventional shape – more of a quadrangle than an oblong – and is offset well to the north.

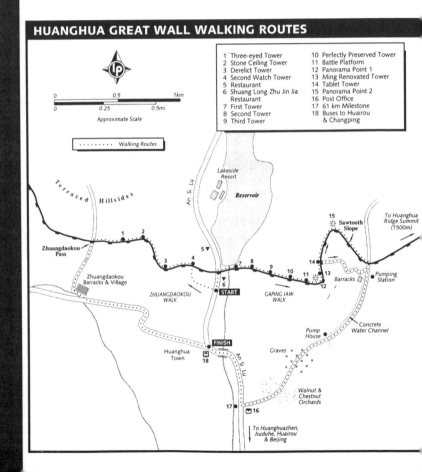

HUANGHUA GREAT WALL WALKING ROUTES

1 Three-eyed Tower
2 Stone Ceiling Tower
3 Derelict Tower
4 Second Watch Tower
5 Restaurant
6 Shuang Long Zhu Jin Jia Restaurant
7 First Tower
8 Second Tower
9 Third Tower
10 Perfectly Preserved Tower
11 Battle Platform
12 Panorama Point 1
13 Ming Renovated Tower
14 Tablet Tower
15 Panorama Point 2
16 Post Office
17 61 km Milestone
18 Buses to Huairou & Changping

.... Walking Routes

Perfectly Preserved Tower A gradual 200m climb takes you to the **fourth tower**. It is quite standard in shape, and is in exceptionally good condition. The ramparts before and beyond the tower are also in excellent condition (with parapets still standing and brickwork intact) as are its upper-storey battlements and loopholes.

The tower is a three-eyed structure with its central area open to the sky. On the floor of the tower is an **engraving** dating from the Longqing period (1567–72). At the time of writing, a wooden ladder in the tower gave access to the tower's top storey. Just outside the eastern door of the tower there's a flight of steps cut down into the ramparts and leading to a perfectly preserved **granite archway**. On the wall facing the archway is a gap that once housed a tablet.

Battle Platform Exiting the tower, the ramparts climb to a short steep section featuring small observation platforms in front of a large battle platform. This is like a roofless watchtower, asymmetrically offset to the north for observation and enfilading (flanking) fire. Within its parapets are two rows of loopholes, each topped with bricks of different designs. The platform, close to the summit, commands a strategic position for cannon fire to the valley below.

From the battle platform, the wall reaches the summit and then turns north to a tower which provides a fine place for views of the area.

Panorama Point 1 Looking north, you can see the distinctive shape of the section of the wall called Gaping Jaw. Looking east, the wall streaks up the Huanghua ridge towards the summit. From the south, the ridge profile looks like a camel's back and is called, 'The Camel's Back which Breaks the Wind'. Heading north, the ramparts lead to a well-preserved four-eyed tower.

Ming-Renovated Tower In good light, the colour of the top half-dozen courses of bricks, especially on the southern face of the tower, appears to differ from the rest. Inside, some parts of the brickwork seem to have been repaired with mortar of a different colour. These features suggest that the top of the tower was rebuilt and other parts inside were repaired. The reason why these efforts were made is open to debate. It is unlikely that the tower, in such a dominant, high position, was attacked and damaged. It is more likely that the tower dates from the early Ming and was repaired in the later Ming, or that it was damaged by an earthquake and repaired.

Tablet Tower About 100m downhill is another fine four-eyed tower. Just before the tower there are steps down from the wall leading through an archway off the wall and down the gully.

The second chamber on the right (south) houses an **engraved tablet** from the third year of the Longqing period (1570). It is etched with 206 characters and edged with a simple vine design.

You now have two options. The shorter route is to leave by the southern door, exit the wall via the steps and archway, and head down the gully path to the valley floor. This route is easy and reaches the valley via a small water-pumping station.

If you feel like a longer walk, leave the tower by the north door and walk around the Gaping Jaw and its steep eastern limb, called Sawtooth Slope. This option will appeal to those who enjoy a scramble as the Sawtooth Slope (named for its zigzag profile) is an extremely steep and slippery descent. It is possible to continue east along Huanghua ridge, but it's a tough hike that's very steep and challenging.

Barracks Both routes end up at the pumping station. From there you can walk about 50m south-west to a barracks. The structure's south-facing wall has an intact archway, and all four of its perimeter walls are standing. The barracks once housed up to 200 men stationed to guard this section of the wall, taking advantage of a sheltered position and a water source.

To the Main Road To return to the main road, walk south on the stony track that swings gradually to the west, crossing a concrete waterway after about 600m. There is a small pump house nearby on the right and a fork off and up a bank to the right (west). Avoid this and keep on the main track, passing conical grave mounds on either side of the track and walking through walnut and chestnut orchards.

The track swings right all the time and eventually hits the road by a post office and beside the 61km milestone of the An Si Lu. Head north to the bridge for transport to Huairou and Changping.

Getting There & Away

There is no direct bus to Huanghua, but there are two indirect routes. The first option is to take a public bus or minibus to Huairou from Dongzhimen long-distance bus station in Beijing (near the subway station of the same name). Bus No 916 leaves every 15 minutes from 5.30 am to 6.30 pm (Y4) and takes just over an hour to get to Huairou. Minibuses (Y5) have the same number (916), run the same route and are a little quicker. Let the bus driver know your intended destination

is Huánghuāchéng so he can tell you where to get off. From Huairou you can take a minibus directly to Huanghua (Y4, 40 minutes) or hire a *miandi* from Huairou to Huanghua for Y60 return. For an additional Y60 you can hire a miandi all the way back to Third Ring Rd in Beijing (most miandis are not allowed to enter Beijing).

Jinshanling to Simatai Village (9km, Five-Hour Loop)

In order to match the following descriptions with the actual features, it is *vital* to track your progress and know your tower number. To this end, a comment, minor or major, is made about all 30 towers on the hike.

Wall access is at Zhuanduokou Pass, at the top of an avenue of restaurants at Jinshanling. At the top of the street go straight ahead, passing in front of the quadrangular *siheyuan* (courtyard house), then toilets, on the right. It is 300m up to **Tower 30** in the dip. Turn left (east) towards Simatai and go several hundred metres uphill to the T-junction.

T-Junction Panorama Point A 150m spur or 'tail wall' that leads to the left (north) was built to command a ridge that provided attackers with an easy route up to the wall. On the hillside in the immediate foreground (east) are the low remains of the Northern Qi dynasty (AD 550–77) Great Wall. (More of the same wall can be seen at the end of this hike.)

Following the wall's route east, its watchtower-dotted outline can be seen snaking along the Jinshanling ridge and descending toward Simatai Reservoir in the valley. It then climbs further east up the Simatai ridge.

From the T-junction it's a short walk up to **Tower 29**, the highest on the first part of the hike. En route you pass through a series of *zhang qiang* (barrier walls). These are rebuilt – see the giveaway grey bricks – but ahead are many originals. They functioned as shields for guarding forces in the event of raiders mounting the wall.

Tower 29 is extensively reconstructed. Off to the right is a storehouse building now rented by local photographer Zhou Wanping, whose pictures are worth checking out.

Walk downhill to the shell-like ruins of **Tower 28**. Originally containing much wood, which had rotted, the structure collapsed. Look in the masonry for holes where wooden timbers and floorboards were once positioned.

KH

A further 100m downhill is a **battle platform** where cannon, installed on the wall from c. 1610, were positioned. There is a path off to the left leading back to the entrance.

Tower 27 has tubular archways, one of three internal tower styles found here. The others are angular chambers and domed structures.

Drainage En route to **Tower 26**, note the drainage system to channel water off the wall. Good drainage was vital to ensure that the fill's stones and mortar did not become saturated, act as a slurry and cause washouts. Channel bricks and damming stones guide rainfall toward pavement-level sluices, which also double as observation holes (loopholes). Under the sluice, bricks were carved to ease the water's passage down the wall.

Just before **Tower 26** are more barrier walls. The tower had a wooden roof structure, which, like others of the same material, has rotted, collapsed and become a derelict shell. **Tower 25** is perched on a large outcrop of bare rock.

Tower 24 is the type of brick-roofed structure that survives well. Outside, reconstruction ends and the wild wall begins. In **Tower 23** there are many timber holes and other impressions in the masonry where beams and posts were positioned. Between Tower 23 and **Tower 22** are eight barrier walls. Beyond Tower 22 are 15 more. The foot of the next slope has been completely washed out, leaving only the north-facing wall upright. This is a good place to view the wall in cross-section. Beyond is **Tower 21**, a derelict wooden structure. A further variation of loophole style can be seen in its parapets; this time they are of pyramidal shape.

Fifty metres out of Tower 21 is another major washout – a classic example of hydrostatic pressures causing the wall's collapse. **Tower 20** retains a rare trace of fossilised wood in its north-western corner. It is a very steep climb up to **Tower 19**.

Fossilised Wood & Pottery Fragments Tower 19 is brick-roofed with tubular archways. One hundred metres further on is **Tower 18**. In its north-west lower corner another fragment of fossilised wood is exposed. Fragments of pottery storage jars for water and grain, glazed and unglazed, can be found among the ruins here. The tower was probably used for foodstuffs.

There are more barrier walls between Towers 18 and 17. **Tower 17** is very derelict. Between Towers 17 and 16 on the inside (south-facing) wall are two gaps where engraved tablets were once positioned. **Tower 16** has good tubular arched ceilings and a fine granite archway entrance. **Tower 15** was a wooden structure; it has timber holes but little else of interest.

Tower 14 is a 'five-eyed tower', having five windows along its longest face. There are also fine bolt holes inside the door of its northwest entrance.

Dome Ceiling & Relief Tablet The floor of **Tower 13**'s central chamber is square while its roof is dome shaped, divided into eight segments with a small octagonal opening at its apex. Around the dome chamber are four tubular arched corridors. On the upper storey, but difficult to access, is a relief tablet depicting a *qilin*, a mythical beast symbolising good administration. This tower was used by a military official probably in command of the whole Jinshanling Wall.

Stamped Bricks Between Towers 13 and 12 are hundreds of *in situ* bricks stamped with characters contained within a long rectangular cartouche.

Quadrant Dome Tower Tower 12's central chamber is roofed with a fine dome divided into four quadrants. In its surrounding arched, tubular corridors is a stele base upon which an engraved tablet was once positioned. The tower's granite doorways and window sills, with hollows for hinges to turn, remain in good condition.

Between Towers 12 and 11 there are more stamped bricks on the inside of the ramparts. Through **Tower 11**, which is in fine condition with tubular arches, the ramparts en route to **Tower 10** have a gap on the inside of the north-facing parapet where a tablet was once positioned. Tower 10 has three tubular arches; the central one is much wider than the flanking two.

From Tower 10 it is a steep descent to **Tower 9**, which has a good granite doorway facing westward. Inside is yet another example of architectural design variation – the angular chamber. Also, while the central chamber is wide, flanking ones are narrow.

Out of Tower 9, parapets are broken down and the pavement is loose. Terraces to the south (right) of the wall contain its bricks. In the lower storey of **Tower 8** are cane mat marks imprinted on dark-brown mud. This 'plaster' was added for insulation in winter and indicates that those manning the wall were willing and allowed to make improvements to their frontier homes for the sake of comfort. About 5% of ceiling space is still 'insulated'.

Although it's a steep descent down to **Tower 7**, look out for stampings on the loose bricks. Tower 7 is a derelict shell structure, open to the sky.

One hundred metres out of Tower 7, on the south parapet, are a few solitary stamped bricks *in situ*. **Tower 6** was a wooden structure. Broken tiles from its roof can be found in the rubble. Out of Tower 6 is a steep downhill section that has resulted in a classic washout at the foot of the slope. Take the lower path on the southern side rather than threading your way along the narrow, crumbling wall-top path. From Tower 6, it is 150m downhill to the start of the rebuilt wall that leads from **Tower 5** eastwards.

View of Northern Qi Great Wall From **Tower 4**, further remains of the Northern Qi Great Wall can be seen on the mountain ridge to the south. The remains are most noticeable beyond (west of) the newly built road and two short telegraph poles. This mid-6th century wall stretched from north of Beijing to Datong in the west.

There is no way through **Tower 2**. Leave the wall before the tower and follow the footpath below. Rejoin the wall and continue down, leaving it again before **Tower 1**. Cross the bridge and follow the rocky road down to Simatai village.

William Lindesay

William Lindesay has walked the length of the Wall, from Jiayu Pass to Shanhai Pass. These walks are based on his second book about the Wall, Hiking on History: Exploring Beijing's Great Wall on Foot.

Right: The Great Wall snakes its way through the hills at Jinshanling.

The Great Wall

ROBYN ROSENFELDT

GLENN BEANLAND

Top: Napping in a turret, Simatai

Bottom: Mutianyu, one of the most popular sections of the Great Wall

Language

MANDARIN

A big plus for visitors to Beijing is that the dialect spoken there is also the official language of the PRC. It is usually referred to in the west as 'Mandarin', but the Chinese call it Putonghua – common speech. Putonghua is variously referred to as the 'Han language' *(hànyǔ)*, the 'national language' *(guóyǔ)* or simply 'Chinese' *(zhōngwén or zhōngguóhuà)*.

Writing System

Chinese is often referred to as a language of pictographs. Many of the basic Chinese characters are in fact highly stylised pictures of what they represent, but most Chinese characters (around 90%) are compounds of a 'meaning' element and a 'sound' element.

So just how many Chinese characters are there? It's possible to verify the existence of some 56,000 characters, but the vast majority of these are archaic. It is commonly felt that a well-educated, contemporary Chinese person might know and use between 6000 and 8000 characters. To read a Chinese newspaper you will need to know 2000 to 3000 characters, but 1200 to 1500 would be enough to get the gist.

Pronunciation

Most letters used in Pinyin are pronounced as in English, with the exception of the following:

Vowels

a	as in 'father'
ai	as in 'high'
ao	as the 'ow' in 'cow'
e	as the 'u' in 'fur'
ei	as the 'ei' in 'weigh'
i	as the 'ee' in 'meet' (or as the 'oo' in 'book' after c, ch, r, s, sh, z or zh)
ian	as in 'yen'
ie	as the English word 'yeah'
o	as in 'or'
ou	as the 'oa' in 'boat'
u	as in 'flute'
ui	as in the word 'way'
uo	like a 'w' followed by 'o'
yu	as in the German 'ü' – pucker your lips and try saying 'ee'
ü	as the German 'ü'

Consonants

c	as the 'ts' in 'bits'
ch	as in 'chop', but with the tongue curled back
h	as in 'hay', but articulated from farther back in the throat
q	as the 'ch' in 'cheese'
r	as the 's' in 'pleasure'
sh	as in 'ship', but with the tongue curled back
x	as in 'ship'
z	as the 'dz' in 'suds'
zh	as the 'j' in 'judge' but with the tongue curled back

The only consonants that occur at the end of a syllable are n, ng and r.

In Pinyin, apostrophes are occasionally used to separate syllables in order to prevent ambiguity, eg the word *píng'ān* can be written with an apostrophe after the 'g' to prevent it being pronounced as 'pín'gān'.

Tones

Chinese has a large number of words with the same pronunciation but a different meaning; what distinguishes these 'homophones' is their 'tonal' quality – the raising and lowering of pitch on certain syllables. Mandarin has four tones – high, rising, falling-rising and falling, plus a fifth 'neutral' tone which you can all but ignore. To illustrate, look at the word *ma* which has four different meanings according to tone:

high	*mā* (mother)
rising	*má* (hemp/numb)
falling-rising	*mǎ* (horse)
falling	*mà* (to scold/to swear)

Gestures

Hand signs are frequently used in China. The 'thumbs-up' sign has a long tradition as an indication of excellence. An alternative way to indicate excellence is to gently pull your earlobe between your thumb and index finger.

The Chinese have a system for counting on their hands. If you can't speak the language, it would be worth your while at least to learn Chinese finger counting (see the illustrations at the bottom of this page). One of the disadvantages of finger counting is that there are regional differences. The symbol for number 10 is to form a cross with the index fingers, but many Chinese just use a fist.

Phrasebooks

Phrasebooks are invaluable, but it's a better idea to copy out the appropriate phrases in Chinese rather than show someone the book – otherwise they may take it and read every page! Reading place names or street signs isn't difficult since the Chinese name is usually accompanied by the Pinyin form; if not you'll soon learn lots of characters just by repeated exposure. A small dictionary with English, Pinyin and Chinese characters is also useful for learning a few words.

For a more comprehensive guide to Mandarin, get a copy of the new edition of Lonely Planet's *Mandarin phrasebook*.

Pronouns

I		
	wǒ	我
you		
	nǐ	你
he, she, it		
	tā	他/她/它
we, us		
	wǒmen	我们
you (plural)		
	nǐmen	你们
they, them		
	tāmen	他们

Greetings & Civilities

Hello.		
	Nǐ hǎo.	你好
Goodbye.		
	Zàijiàn.	再见
Thank you.		
	Xièxie.	谢谢
You're welcome.		
	Búkèqi.	不客气
I'm sorry.		
	Duìbùqǐ.	对不起

Small Talk

May I ask your name?		
	Nín guìxìng?	您贵姓?
My (sur)name is ...		
	Wǒ xìng ...	我姓...

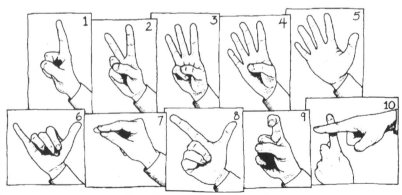

The Chinese system of finger-counting

No. (don't have)
   Méi yǒu.   没有
No. (not so)
   Búshì.   不是
I'm a foreign student.
   Wǒ shì liúxuéshēng. 我是留学生
What's to be done now?
   Zěnme bàn?   怎么办?
It doesn't matter.
   Méishì.   没事
I want ...
   Wǒ yào ...   我要
No, I don't want it.
   Búyào.   不要

Where are you from?
   Nǐ shì cōng nǎr 你是从哪儿
   láide?   来的?
I'm from ...
   Wǒ shì cōng ... láide. 我是从 ... 来的
Australia
   àodàlìyà   澳大利亚
Canada
   jiānádà   加拿大
Denmark
   dānmài   丹麦
France
   fǎguó   法国
Germany
   déguó   德国
Netherlands
   hélán   荷兰
New Zealand
   xīnxīlán   新西兰
Spain
   xībānyá   西班牙
Sweden
   ruìdiǎn   瑞典
Switzerland
   ruìshì   瑞士
UK
   yīngguó   英国
USA
   měiguó   美国

Language Difficulties

I understand.
   Wǒ tīngdedǒng. 我听得懂
I don't understand.
   Wǒ tīngbudǒng. 我听不懂

Do you understand?
   Dǒng ma?   懂吗?
Could you speak more slowly please?
   Qīng nǐ shuō màn yīdiǎn, hǎo ma?
请你说慢一点, 好吗?

Getting Around

I want to go to ...
   Wǒ yào qù ...   我要去 ...
I want to get off.
   Wǒ yào xiàchē. 我要下车
luggage
   xíngli   行李
left-luggage room
   jìcún chù   寄存处
one ticket
   yìzhāng piào   一张票
two tickets
   liǎngzhāng piào 两张票
What time does it depart?
   Jǐdiǎn kāi?   几点开?
What time does it arrive?
   Jǐdiǎn dào?   几点到?
How long does the trip take?
   Zhècì lǚxíng yào huā
   duōcháng shíjiān?
这次旅行要花多长时间?
buy a ticket
   mǎi piào   买票
refund a ticket
   tuì piào   退票
taxi
   chūzū chē   出租车
microbus ('bread') taxi
   miànbāo chē/ 面包车/
   miǎndī   面的
Please use the meter.
   Dǎ biǎo.   打表

Air

airport
   fēijīchǎng   飞机场
CAAC ticket office
   zhōngguó mínháng 中国民航售票处
   shòupiào chù
one way ticket
   dānchéng piào 单程票
round-trip ticket
   láihuí piào   来回票
boarding pass
   dēngjì kǎ   登机卡

Accommodation

hotel
 lǚguǎn 旅馆
tourist hotel
 bīnguǎn/fàndiàn/ 宾馆/饭店/
 jiǔdiàn 酒店
reception desk
 zǒng fúwù tái 总服务台
dormitory
 duōrénfáng 多人房
single room
 dānrénfáng 单人房
twin room
 shuāngrénfáng 双人房
bed
 chuángwèi 床位
economy room
(no bath)
 pǔtōngfáng 普通房
standard room
 biāozhǔn fángjiān 标准房间
deluxe suite
 háohuá tàofáng 豪华套房
book a whole room
 bāofáng 包房
Is there a room vacant?
 Yǒu méiyǒu kōng fángjiān?
 有没有空房间?
Yes, there is.
 Yǒu. 有
No, there isn't.
 Méiyǒu. 没有
Can I see the room?
 Wǒ néng kànkan fángjiān ma?
 我能看看房间吗?
I don't like this room.
 Wǒ bù xǐhuan zhèijiān fángjiān.
 我不喜欢这间房
Are there any messages for me?
 yǒu méiyǒu liú huà?
 有没有留话?
May I have a hotel namecard?
 yǒu méiyǒu lǚguǎn de míngpiàn?
 有没有旅馆的名片?
Could I have these clothes washed,
please?
 qǐng bǎ zhè xiē yīfú xǐ gānjìng, hǎo
ma?
 请把这些衣服洗干净, 好吗?

Visas & Documents
passport
 hùzhào 护照
visa
 qiānzhèng 签证
visa extension
 yáncháng qiānzhèng 延长签证
Public Security
Bureau (PSB)
 gōng'ān jú 公安局
Foreign Affairs Branch
 wài shì kē 外事科

Money

How much is it?
 Dūoshǎo qián? 多少钱?
Is there anything
cheaper?
 Yǒu piányi 有便宜
 yìdiǎn de ma? 一点的吗?
That's too expensive.
 Tài guìle. 太贵了
Bank of China
 zhōngguó yínháng 中国银行
change money
 huàn qián 换钱

Post

post office
 yóujú 邮局
letter
 xìn 信
envelope
 xìnfēng 信封
package
 bāoguǒ 包裹
air mail
 hángkōng xìn 航空信
surface mail
 píngyóu 平邮
stamps
 yóupiào 邮票
postcard
 míngxìnpiàn 明信片
aerogramme
 hángkōng xìnjiàn 航空信件
poste restante
 cúnjú hòulǐnglán 存局候领栏

reconfirm
  quèrèn   确认
cancel
  qǔxiāo   取消
bonded baggage
  cúnzhàn xínglǐ 存栈行李

Bus

bus
  gōnggòng qìchē
  公共汽车
minibus
  xiǎo gōnggòng qìchē
  小公共汽车
long-distance bus station
  chángtú qìchē zhàn
  长途汽车站
When is the first bus?
  Tóubān qìchē jǐdiǎn kāi?
  头班汽车几点开?
When is the last bus?
  Mòbān qìchē jǐdiǎn kāi?
  末班汽车几点开?
When is the next bus?
  Xià yìbān qìchē jǐdiǎn kāi?
  下一班汽车几点开?

Train

train
  huǒchē   火车
ticket office
  shòupiào chù   售票处
railway station
  huǒchē zhàn   火车站
hard-seat
  yìngxí, yìngzuò 硬席, 硬座
soft-seat
  ruǎnxí, ruǎnzuò 软席, 软座
hard-sleeper
  yìngwò   硬卧
soft-sleeper
  ruǎnwò   软卧
platform ticket
  zhàntái piào   站台票
Which platform?
  Dìjǐhào zhàntái? 第几号站台?
upgrade ticket
(after boarding)
  bǔpiào   补票

subway (underground)
  dìtiě   地铁
subway station
  dìtiě zhàn   地铁站

Bicycle

bicycle
  zìxíngchē
  自行车
I want to hire a bicycle.
  Wǒ yào zū yíliàng zìxíngchē.
  我要租一辆自行车
How much is it per day?
  Yìtiān duōshǎo qián? 一天多少钱?
How much is it per hour?
  Yíge xiǎoshí duōshǎo qián?
  一个小时多少钱?
How much is the deposit?
  Yājīn dūoshǎo qián?
  押金多少钱?

Directions

map
  dìtú   地图
Where is the ...?
  ... zài nǎlǐ?   ... 在哪里?
I'm lost.
  Wǒ mílùle.   我迷路了
Turn right.
  Yòu zhuǎn.   右转
Turn left.
  Zuǒ zhuǎn.   左转
Go straight ahead.
  Yìzhí zǒu.   一直走
Turn around.
  Wàng huí zǒu.   往回走
alley
  hútóng   胡同
lane
  xiàng   巷
road
  lù   路
boulevard
  dàdào   大道
section
  duàn   段
street
  jiē, dàjiē   街, 大街
No 21
  21 hào   21号

express mail (EMS)
yóuzhèng tèkuài
zhuāndì　邮政特快专递
registered mail
guà hào　挂号

Telecommunications

telephone
diànhuà　电话
telephone office
diànxùn dàlóu　电讯大楼
telephone card
diànhuà kǎ　电话卡
international call
guójì diànhuà　国际电话
collect call
duìfāng fùqián
diànhuà　对方付钱电话
direct-dial call
zhíbō diànhuà　直拨电话
fax
chuánzhēn　传真
computer
diànnǎo　电脑
email
diànzǐyóujiàn　电子邮件
(often called 'email')
internet
yīntè wǎng　因特网
hùlián wǎng　互联网
(more formal name)
online
shàng wǎng　上网
Where can I get
online?
Wǒ zài nǎr kěyǐ　我在哪儿
shàng wǎng?　可以上网？

Toilets

toilet (restroom)
cèsuǒ　厕所
toilet paper
wèishēng zhǐ　卫生纸
bathroom (washroom)
xǐshǒu jiān　洗手间

Health

I'm sick.
Wǒ shēngbìngle.　我生病了

I'm injured.
Wǒ shòushāngle.　我受伤了
hospital
yīyuàn　医院
laxative
xièyào　泻药
anti-diarrhoea
medicine
zhǐxièyào　止泻药
rehydration salts
shūwéizhí dīnàfā　舒维质低钠
pàodìng　发泡锭
aspirin
āsīpǐlín　阿斯匹林
antibiotics
kàngjùnsù　抗菌素
condom
bìyùn tào　避孕套
tampon
wèishēng mián tiáo　卫生棉条
sanitary napkin (Kotex)
wèishēng mián　卫生棉
sunscreen (UV) lotion
fáng shài yóu　防晒油
mosquito coils
wénxiāng　蚊香
mosquito pads
diàn wénxiāng　电蚊香

Time

What's the time?
Jǐ diǎn?　几点？
... hour ... minute
... diǎn ... fēn　... 点 ... 分
3.05
sān diǎn wǔ fēn　3点5分
now
xiànzài　现在
today
jīntiān　今天
tomorrow
míngtiān　明天
day after tomorrow
hòutiān　后天
three days from now
dàhòutiān　大后天
yesterday
zuótiān　昨天
Wait a moment.
Děng yī xià.　等一下

Numbers

0	*líng*	零
1	*yī, yāo*	一，幺
2	*èr, liǎng*	二，两
3	*sān*	三
4	*sì*	四
5	*wǔ*	五
6	*liù*	六
7	*qī*	七
8	*bā*	八
9	*jiǔ*	九
10	*shí*	十
11	*shíyī*	十一
12	*shí'èr*	十二
20	*èrshí*	二十
21	*èrshíyī*	二十一
100	*yìbǎi*	一百
200	*liǎngbǎi*	两百
1000	*yìqiān*	一千
2000	*liǎngqiān*	两千
10,000	*yíwàn*	一万
20,000	*liǎngwàn*	两万
100,000	*shíwàn*	十万
200,000	*èrshíwàn*	二十万

Emergencies

emergency
  jǐnjí qíngkuàng   紧急情况
hospital emergency
  room
  jízhěn shì   急诊室
police
  jǐngchá   警察
Fire!
  Zhǎohuǒ le!   着火了！
Help!
  Jiùmìng a!   救命啊！
Thief!
  Xiǎotōu!   小偷！
pickpocket
  páshǒu   扒手
rapist
  qiángjiānfàn   强奸犯

FOOD

At the Restaurant

restaurant
  cāntīng   餐厅

menu
  cài dān   菜单
bill (cheque)
  mǎi dān/jiézhàng   买单/结帐
set meal (no menu)
  tàocān   套餐
to eat/let's eat
  chī fàn   吃饭
chopsticks
  kuàizi   筷子
knife
  dàozi   刀子
fork
  chāzi   叉子
spoon
  sháozi   调羹/汤匙
Have you got any ...?
  Nǐ yǒu méiyǒu ...?
  你有没有 ...？
Please bring me one order of ...
  Qǐng nǐ chǎo yīpán ... gěi wǒ.
  请你炒一盘 ... 给我.
How much does this dish cost?
  Zhèzhǒng cài duōshǎo qián?
  这种菜多少钱？
What's the total cost for everything?
  Yígòng duōshǎo qián?
  一共多少钱？
I'm vegetarian.
  Wǒ chī sù.
  我吃素
I don't want MSG.
  Wǒ bù yào wèijng.
  我不要味精

Rice 饭

steamed white rice
  mǐfàn   米饭
watery rice porridge
  xīfàn   稀饭
rice noodles
  mǐfěn   米粉
fried rice (assorted)
  shíjǐn chǎofàn   什锦炒饭

fried rice Cantonese style
  guǎngzhōu chǎofàn 广州炒饭

Bread, Buns & Dumplings 面类
western-style bread
  miànbāo 面包
fried roll
  yínsī juǎn 银丝卷
steamed bun
  mántou 馒头
steamed meat bun
  bāozi 包子
fried bread stick
  yóutiáo 油条
dumplings
  jiǎozi 饺子
prawn cracker
  lóngxiā piàn 龙虾片

Vegetable Dishes 菜类
fried rice with vegetables
  shūcài chǎofàn 蔬菜炒饭
fried noodles with vegetables
  shūcài chǎomiàn 蔬菜炒面
spicy peanuts
  wǔxiāng huāshēng mǐ 五香花生米
fried peanuts
  yóuzhá huāshēng mǐ 油炸花生米
spiced cold vegetables
  liángbàn shíjǐn 凉拌什锦
Chinese salad
  jiācháng liángcài 家常凉菜
fried rape in oyster sauce
  háoyóu pácài dǎn 蚝油扒菜胆
fried rape with mushrooms
  dōnggū pácài dǎn 冬菇扒菜胆
fried bean curd in oyster sauce
  háoyóu dòufǔ 蚝油豆腐
spicy hot bean curd
  mápó dòufǔ 麻婆豆腐
bean curd casserole
  shāguō dòufǔ 沙锅豆腐
bean curd & mushrooms
  mógū dòufǔ 蘑菇豆腐
garlic & morning glory
  dàsuàn kōngxīn cài 大蒜空心菜
fried garlic
  sù chǎo dàsuàn 素炒大蒜
fried eggplant
  sùshāo qiézi 素烧茄子

fried beansprouts
  sù chǎo dòuyá 素炒豆芽
fried green vegetables
  sù chǎo qīngcài 素炒青菜
fried green beans
  sù chǎo biǎndòu 素炒扁豆
fried cauliflower & tomato
  chǎo fānqié càihuā 炒番茄菜花
broiled mushroom
  sù chǎo mógū 素炒蘑菇
black fungus & mushroom
  mù'ěr huákǒu mó 木耳滑口蘑
fried white radish patty
  luóbo gāo 萝卜糕
assorted hors d'oeuvre
  shíjǐn pīnpán 什锦拼盘
assorted vegetarian food
  sù shíjǐn 素什锦

Egg Dishes 蛋类
preserved egg
  sōnghuā dàn 松花蛋
fried rice with egg
  jīdàn chǎofàn 鸡蛋炒饭
fried tomatoes & eggs
  xīhóngshì chǎo jīdàn 西红柿炒鸡蛋
egg & flour omelette
  jiān bǐng 煎饼

Beef Dishes 牛肉类
fried rice with beef
  niúròusī chǎofàn 牛肉丝炒饭
noodles with beef (soupy)
  niúròu tāng miàn 牛肉汤面
spiced noodles with beef
  niúròu gān miàn 牛肉干面
fried noodles with beef
  niúròu chǎomiàn 牛肉炒面
beef with white rice
  niúròu fàn 牛肉饭
beef platter
  niúròu tiěbǎn 牛肉铁板
beef with oyster sauce
  háoyóu niúròu 蚝油牛肉
beef braised in soy sauce
  hóngshāo niúròu 红烧牛肉
beef with tomatoes
  fānqié niúròu piàn 番茄牛肉片

beef with green peppers
qīngjiāo niúròu piàn 青椒牛肉片
beef curry & rice
gālí niúròu fàn 咖喱牛肉饭
beef curry & noodles
gālí niúròu miàn 咖喱牛肉面

Chicken Dishes 鸡肉类
fried rice with chicken
jīsī chǎofàn 鸡丝炒饭
noodles with chicken (soupy)
jīsī tāng miàn 鸡丝汤面
fried noodles with chicken
jīsī chǎomiàn 鸡丝炒面
chicken leg with white rice
ītuǐ fàn 鸡腿饭
spicy hot chicken & peanuts
gōngbào jīdīng 宫爆鸡丁
fruit kernal with chicken
guǒwèi jīdīng 果味鸡丁
sweet & sour chicken
tángcù jīdīng 糖醋鸡丁
sauteed spicy chicken pieces
làzi jīdīng 辣子鸡丁
sauteed chicken with green peppers
jiàngbào jīdīng 酱爆鸡丁
chicken slices & tomato sauce
fānqié jīdīng 番茄鸡丁
mushrooms & chicken
cǎomó jīdīng 草蘑鸡丁
chicken pieces in oyster sauce
háoyóu jīdīng 蚝油鸡丁
chicken braised in soy sauce
hóngshāo jīkuài 红烧鸡块
sauteed chicken with water chestnuts
nánjiè jīpiàn 南芥鸡片
sliced chicken with crispy rice
jīpiàn guōbā 鸡片锅巴
chicken curry
gālí jīròu 咖喱鸡肉
chicken curry & rice
gālí jīròu fàn 咖喱鸡肉饭
chicken curry & noodles
gālí jīròu miàn 咖喱鸡肉面

Duck Dishes 鸭肉类
Beijing Duck
běijīng kǎoyā 北京烤鸭
duck with white rice
yāròu fàn 鸭肉饭

duck with noodles
yāròu miàn 鸭肉面
duck with fried noodles
yāròu chǎomiàn 鸭肉炒面

Pork Dishes 猪肉类
pork chop with white rice
páigǔ fàn 排骨饭
fried rice with pork
ròusī chǎofàn 肉丝炒饭
fried noodles with pork
ròusī chǎomiàn 肉丝炒面
pork & mustard greens
zhàcài ròusī 榨菜肉丝
noodles, pork & mustard greens
zhàcài ròusī miàn 榨菜肉丝面
pork with crispy rice
ròupiàn guōbā 肉片锅巴
sweet & sour pork fillet
tángcù zhūròu piàn 糖醋猪肉片
sweet & sour pork fillet
tángcù lǐjī 糖醋里脊
pork fillet with white sauce
huáliū lǐjī 滑溜里脊
shredded pork fillet
chǎo lǐjī sī 炒里脊丝
soft pork fillet
ruǎnzhá lǐjī 软炸里脊
spicy hot pork pieces
gōngbào ròudīng 宫爆肉丁
fried black pork pieces
yuánbào lǐjī 芫爆里脊
sauteed diced pork & soy sauce
jiàngbào ròudīng 酱爆肉丁
spicy pork cubelets
làzi ròudīng 辣子肉丁
pork cubelets & cucumber
huángguā ròudīng 黄瓜肉丁
golden pork slices
jīnyín ròusī 金银肉丝
sauteed shredded pork
qīngchǎo ròusī 清炒肉丝
shredded pork & hot sauce
yúxiāng ròusī 鱼香肉丝

shredded pork & green peppers
qīngjiāo ròusī 青椒肉丝

shredded pork & bamboo shoots
dōngsǔn ròusī 冬笋肉丝

shredded pork & green beans
biǎndòu ròusī 扁豆肉丝

pork with oyster sauce
háoyóu ròusī 蚝油肉丝

boiled pork slices
shuǐzhǔ ròupiàn 水煮肉片

pork, eggs & black fungus
mùxū ròu 木须肉

pork & fried onions
yángcōng chǎo 洋葱炒肉片
ròupiàn

Seafood Dishes 海鲜类

fried rice with shrimp
xiārén chǎofàn 虾仁炒饭

fried noodles with shrimp
xiārén chǎomiàn 虾仁炒面

diced shrimp with peanuts
gōngbào xiārén 宫爆虾仁

sauteed shrimp
qīngchǎo xiārén 清炒虾仁

deep-fried shrimp
zhá xiārén 炸虾仁

fried shrimp with mushroom
xiānmó xiārén 鲜蘑虾仁

squid with crispy rice
yóuyú guōbā 鱿鱼锅巴

sweet & sour squid roll
suānlà yóuyú juǎn 酸辣鱿鱼卷

fish braised in soy sauce
hóngshāo yú 红烧鱼

braised sea cucumber
hóngshāo hǎishēn 红烧海参

clams	*gé*	蛤
crab	*pángxiè*	螃蟹
lobster	*lóngxiā*	龙虾

Soup 汤类

three kinds seafood soup
sān xiān tāng 三鲜汤

squid soup
yóuyú tāng 鱿鱼汤

hot & sour soup
suānlà tāng 酸辣汤

tomato & egg soup
xīhóngshì dàn tāng 西红柿蛋汤

corn & egg thick soup
fènghuáng lìmǐ gēng 凤凰栗米羹

egg & vegetable soup
dànhuā tāng 蛋花汤

mushroom & egg soup
mógu dànhuā tāng 蘑菇蛋花汤

fresh fish soup
shēng yú tāng 生鱼汤

vegetable soup
shūcài tāng 蔬菜汤

cream of tomato soup
nǎiyóu fānqié tāng 奶油番茄汤

cream of mushroom soup
nǎiyóu xiānmó tāng 奶油鲜蘑汤

pickled mustard green soup
zhàcài tāng 榨菜汤

bean curd & vegetable soup
dòufu cài tāng 豆腐菜汤

wanton soup
húntùn tāng 馄饨汤

clear soup
qīng tāng 清汤

Miscellania & Exotica 其它

kebab
ròu chuàn 肉串

goat, mutton
yáng ròu 羊肉

dogmeat
gǒu ròu 狗肉

deermeat (venison)
lùròu 鹿肉

snake
shé ròu 蛇肉

ratmeat
lǎoshǔ ròu 老鼠肉

pangolin (armadillo-like mammal)
chuānshānjiǎ 穿山甲

frog
qīngwā 青蛙

eel
shàn yú 鳝鱼

turtle
hǎiguī 海龟

Mongolian hotpot
huǒguō 火锅

Condiments 香料

garlic	dàsuàn	大蒜
black pepper	hújiāo	胡椒
hot pepper	làjiāo	辣椒
hot sauce	làjiāo jiàng	辣椒酱
ketchup	fānqié jiàng	番茄酱
salt	yán	盐
MSG	wèijīng	味精
soy sauce	jiàng yóu	酱油
vinegar	cù	醋
sesame seed oil	zhīma yóu	芝麻油
butter	huáng yóu	黄油
sugar	táng	糖
jam	guǒ jiàng	果酱
honey	fēngmì	蜂蜜

Friut

apple	píngguǒ	苹果
banana	xiāngjiāo	香蕉
coconut	yēzi	椰子
longan	lóngyǎn	龙眼
loquat	pípa	枇杷
lychees	lìzhī	荔枝
mandarins	gānzi	柑子
mango	mángguǒ	芒果
pear	lízi	梨子
persimmon	shìzi	柿子
pineapple	bōluó	菠萝
pomelo	yòuzi	柚子
rambutan	hóngmáodān	红毛丹
sugar cane	gānzhé	甘蔗
tangerines	júzi	桔子

DRINKS

(bolied) water		
(kāi) shuǐ		开水
mineral water		
kuàng quán shuǐ		矿泉水
tea		
chá		茶
coffee		
kāfēi		咖啡

milk		
niúnǎi		牛奶
soybean milk		
dòujiāng		豆浆
coffee creamer		
nǎijīng		奶精
fizzy drink (soda)		
qìshuǐ		汽水
Coca-Cola		
kěkǒu kělè		可口可乐
fruit juice		
guǒzhī		果汁
coconut juice		
yézi zhī		椰子汁
orange juice		
liǔchéng zhī		柳橙汁
pineapple juice		
bōluó zhī		波萝汁
mango juice		
mángguǒ zhī		芒果汁
yoghurt		
suānnǎi		酸奶
Cheers!		
gānbēi!		干杯
(literally, 'dry glass')		
beer		
píjiǔ		啤酒
whisky		
wēishìjì jiǔ		威士忌酒
vodka		
fútèjiā jiǔ		伏特加酒
red grape wine		
hóng pútáo jiǔ		红葡萄酒
white grape wine		
bái pútáo jiǔ		白葡萄酒
rice wine		
mǐ jiǔ		米酒
hot		
rède		热的
ice cold		
bīngde		冰的
ice cube		
bīng kuài		冰块

Glossary

bei – north

CAAC – Civil Aviation Administration of China, which controls most of China's domestic and foreign airlines

CITS – China International Travel Service

concessions – small foreign colonies in all but name, commonly found in big eastern cities like Shanghai and Tianjin; all concessions were abolished when the Communists came to power in 1949

CTS – China Travel Service

Cultural Revolution – a massive revolutionary movement started by Mao Zedong in which people were encouraged to question and challenge all forms of traditional authority. It lasted from 1966 to 1976, causing enormous chaos and up to a million deaths.

CYTS – China Youth Travel Service

dajie – an avenue
dong – east

fengshui – an ancient form of divination based on the influence of geographical features

gongfu – a form of Chinese martial arts, usually called kung fu in the West; see also taijiquan

hutong – a narrow back street or alley

jie – a street
jin – Chinese unit of weight; one jin (jīn) equals 0.6kg (1.32lbs)

kaoyadian – Beijing duck; elaborately prepared roast, crisp-skin duck, a must-try in Beijing
Kuomintang – the Nationalist Party which controlled mainland China from 1911 to 1949 and still controls Taiwan

laobaixing – common people, the masses
laowai – foreigners

li – a Chinese unit of measure equal to approximately 540 metres
liang – Chinese unit of weight; one liang (liǎng) equals 37.5g (1.32oz); there are 16 liang to the jin (see earlier)
Little Red Book – the name commonly used in the West for the *Quotations of Chairman Mao Zedong,* the book universally read and studied in China before and during the Cultural Revolution
lu – road

Manchus – a non-Chinese ethnic group from Manchuria (present-day north-east China) which took over China and established the Qing dynasty (AD 1644–1911)
men – gate
miandi – 'bread taxi', yellow microbuses now banned in Beijing

nan – south

Peking – the spelling of 'Beijing' before the Communists adopted the Pinyin romanisation system in 1958
ping – Chinese unit of area; one ping equals 1.82 sq metres (19.6 sq feet)
Pinyin – the system of writing the Chinese language in the roman alphabet adopted by the Communist Party in 1958
PLA – People's Liberation Army
PRC – People's Republic of China, China's official name
PSB – Public Security Bureau, the police
putonghua – the standard form of the Chinese language used since the beginning of this century; it's based on the Beijing dialect

qigong – a variation of gongfu (see above), claimed to be capable of causing miracle cures

Red Guards – fanatical devotees of Mao Zedong during the Cultural Revolution
Renminbi – 'people's money', China's currency

ROC – Republic of China, China's official name from 1911 to 1949; Taiwan still uses this name

siheyuan – traditional Chinese courtyard house

stele – an upright slab or column of stone bearing images or inscriptions

taijiquan – a graceful, dance-like form of martial arts exercise, commonly seen around Beijing's parks in the mornings; usually shortened to taiji (called t'ai chi in the West)

Tripitaka – literally, the Three Baskets; the main body of Buddhist scriptures

xi – west

xiali – Beijing's most common and cheapest type of taxi; xiali is a brand name (the vehicle is a Sino-Japanese joint venture)

yuan – the main unit of Chinese currency

LONELY PLANET

ON THE ROAD

Travel Guides explore cities, regions and countries, and supply information on transport, restaurants and accommodation, covering all budgets. They come with reliable, easy-to-use maps, practical advice, cultural and historical facts and a rundown on attractions both on and off the beaten track. There are over 200 titles in this classic series, covering nearly every country in the world.

 Lonely Planet Upgrades extend the shelf life of existing travel guides by detailing any changes that may affect travel in a region since a book has been published. Upgrades can be downloaded for free from **www.lonelyplanet.com/upgrades**

For travellers with more time than money, **Shoestring** guides offer dependable, first-hand information with hundreds of detailed maps, plus insider tips for stretching money as far as possible. Covering entire continents in most cases, the six-volume shoestring guides are known around the world as 'backpackers bibles'.

For the discerning short-term visitor, **Condensed** guides highlight the best a destination has to offer in a full-colour, pocket-sized format designed for quick access. They include everything from top sights and walking tours to opinionated reviews of where to eat, stay, shop and have fun.

CitySync lets travellers use their Palm™ or Visor™ hand-held computers to guide them through a city with handy tips on transport, history, cultural life, major sights, and shopping and entertainment options. It can also quickly search and sort hundreds of reviews of hotels, restaurants and attractions, and pinpoint their location on scrollable street maps. CitySync can be downloaded from **www.citysync.com**

MAPS & ATLASES

Lonely Planet's **City Maps** feature downtown and metropolitan maps, as well as transit routes and walking tours. The maps come complete with an index of streets, a listing of sights and a plastic coat for extra durability.

Road Atlases are an essential navigation tool for serious travellers. Cross-referenced with the guidebooks, they also feature distance and climate charts and a complete site index.

LONELY PLANET

ESSENTIALS

Read This First books help new travellers to hit the road with confidence. These invaluable predeparture guides give step-by-step advice on preparing for a trip, budgeting, arranging a visa, planning an itinerary and staying safe while still getting off the beaten track.

Healthy Travel pocket guides offer a regional rundown on disease hot spots and practical advice on predeparture health measures, staying well on the road and what to do in emergencies. The guides come with a user-friendly design and helpful diagrams and tables.

Lonely Planet's **Phrasebooks** cover the essential words and phrases travellers need when they're strangers in a strange land. They come in a pocket-sized format with colour tabs for quick reference, extensive vocabulary lists, easy-to-follow pronunciation keys and two-way dictionaries.

Miffed by blurry photos of the Taj Mahal? Tired of the classic 'top of the head cut off' shot? **Travel Photography: A Guide to Taking Better Pictures** will help you turn ordinary holiday snaps into striking images and give you the know-how to capture every scene, from frenetic festivals to peaceful beach sunrises.

Lonely Planet's **Travel Journal** is a lightweight but sturdy travel diary for jotting down all those on-the-road observations and significant travel moments. It comes with a handy time-zone wheel, world maps and useful travel information.

Lonely Planet's eKno is an all-in-one communication service developed especially for travellers. It offers low-cost international calls and free email and voicemail so that you can keep in touch while on the road. Check it out on **www.ekno.lonelyplanet.com**

FOOD & RESTAURANT GUIDES

Lonely Planet's **Out to Eat** guides recommend the brightest and best places to eat and drink in top international cities. These gourmet companions are arranged by neighbourhood, packed with dependable maps, garnished with scene-setting photos and served with quirky features.

For people who live to eat, drink and travel, **World Food** guides explore the culinary culture of each country. Entertaining and adventurous, each guide is packed with detail on staples and specialities, regional cuisine and local markets, as well as sumptuous recipes, comprehensive culinary dictionaries and lavish photos good enough to eat.

LONELY PLANET

OUTDOOR GUIDES

For those who believe the best way to see the world is on foot, Lonely Planet's **Walking Guides** detail everything from family strolls to difficult treks, with 'when to go and how to do it' advice supplemented by reliable maps and essential travel information.

Cycling Guides map a destination's best bike tours, long and short, in day-by-day detail. They contain all the information a cyclist needs, including advice on bike maintenance, places to eat and stay, innovative maps with detailed cues to the rides, and elevation charts.

The **Watching Wildlife** series is perfect for travellers who want authoritative information but don't want to tote a heavy field guide. Packed with advice on where, when and how to view a region's wildlife, each title features photos of over 300 species and contains engaging comments on the local flora and fauna.

With underwater colour photos throughout, **Pisces Books** explore the world's best diving and snorkelling areas. Each book contains listings of diving services and dive resorts, detailed information on depth, visibility and difficulty of dives, and a roundup of the marine life you're likely to see through your mask.

OFF THE ROAD

Journeys, the travel literature series written by renowned travel authors, capture the spirit of a place or illuminate a culture with a journalist's attention to detail and a novelist's flair for words. These are tales to soak up while you're actually on the road or dip into as an at-home armchair indulgence.

The new range of lavishly illustrated **Pictorial** books is just the ticket for both travellers and dreamers. Off-beat tales and vivid photographs bring the adventure of travel to your doorstep long before the journey begins and long after it is over.

Lonely Planet **Videos** encourage the same independent, tough-minded approach as the guidebooks. Currently airing throughout the world, this award-winning series features innovative footage and an original soundtrack.

Yes, we know, work is tough, so do a little bit of deskside dreaming with the spiral-bound Lonely Planet **Diary**, the tearaway page-a-day **Day-to-Day Calendar** or a Lonely Planet **Wall Calendar**, filled with great photos from around the world.

TRAVELLERS NETWORK

Lonely Planet Online. Lonely Planet's award-winning Web site has insider information on hundreds of destinations, from Amsterdam to Zimbabwe, complete with interactive maps and relevant links. The site also offers the latest travel news, recent reports from travellers on the road, guidebook upgrades, a travel links site, an online book-buying option and a lively traveller's bulletin board. It can be viewed at **www.lonelyplanet.com** or AOL keyword: lp.

Planet Talk is a quarterly print newsletter, full of gossip, advice, anecdotes and author articles. It provides an antidote to the being-at-home blues and lets you plan and dream for the next trip. Contact the nearest Lonely Planet office for your free copy.

Comet, the free Lonely Planet newsletter, comes via email once a month. It's loaded with travel news, advice, dispatches from authors, travel competitions and letters from readers. To subscribe, click on the Comet subscription link on the front page of the Web site.

LONELY PLANET

Guides by Region

L onely Planet is known worldwide for publishing practical, reliable and no-nonsense travel information in our guides and on our Web site. The Lonely Planet list covers just about every accessible part of the world. Currently there are 16 series: Travel guides, Shoestring guides, Condensed guides, Phrasebooks, Read This First, Healthy Travel, Walking guides, Cycling guides, Watching Wildlife guides, Pisces Diving & Snorkeling guides, City Maps, Road Atlases, Out to Eat, World Food, Journeys travel literature and Pictorials.

AFRICA Africa on a shoestring • Cairo • Cape Town • Cape Town City Map • East Africa • Egypt • Egyptian Arabic phrasebook • Ethiopia, Eritrea & Djibouti • Ethiopian (Amharic) phrasebook • The Gambia & Senegal • Healthy Travel Africa • Kenya • Malawi • Morocco • Moroccan Arabic phrasebook • Mozambique • Read This First: Africa • South Africa, Lesotho & Swaziland • Southern Africa • Southern Africa Road Atlas • Swahili phrasebook • Tanzania, Zanzibar & Pemba • Trekking in East Africa • Tunisia • Watching Wildlife East Africa • Watching Wildlife Southern Africa • West Africa • World Food Morocco • Zimbabwe, Botswana & Namibia
Travel Literature: Mali Blues: Traveling to an African Beat • The Rainbird: A Central African Journey • Song to an African Sunset: A Zimbabwean Story

AUSTRALIA & THE PACIFIC Auckland • Australia • Australian phrasebook • Australia Road Atlas • Bush-walking in Australia •Cycling New Zealand • Fiji • Fijian phrasebook • Healthy Travel Australia, NZ and the Pacific • Islands of Australia's Great Barrier Reef • Melbourne • Melbourne City Map • Micronesia • New Caledonia • New South Wales & the ACT • New Zealand • Northern Territory • Outback Australia • Out to Eat – Melbourne • Out to Eat – Sydney • Papua New Guinea • Pidgin phrasebook • Queensland • Rarotonga & the Cook Islands • Samoa • Solomon Islands • South Australia • South Pacific • South Pacific phrasebook • Sydney • Sydney City Map • Sydney Condensed • Tahiti & French Polynesia • Tasmania • Tonga • Tramping in New Zealand • Vanuatu • Victoria • Watching Wildlife Australia • Western Australia
Travel Literature: Islands in the Clouds: Travels in the Highlands of New Guinea • Kiwi Tracks: A New Zealand Journey • Sean & David's Long Drive

CENTRAL AMERICA & THE CARIBBEAN Bahamas, Turks & Caicos • Baja California • Bermuda • Central America on a shoestring • Costa Rica • Costa Rica Spanish phrasebook • Cuba • Dominican Republic & Haiti • Eastern Caribbean • Guatemala • Guatemala, Belize & Yucatán: La Ruta Maya • Healthy Travel Central & South America • Jamaica • Mexico • Mexico City • Panama • Puerto Rico • Read This First: Central & South America • World Food Mexico • Yucatán
Travel Literature: Green Dreams: Travels in Central America

EUROPE Amsterdam • Amsterdam City Map • Amsterdam Condensed • Andalucía • Austria • Baltic States phrasebook • Barcelona • Barcelona City Map • Berlin • Berlin City Map • Britain • British phrasebook • Brussels, Bruges & Antwerp • Budapest • Budapest City Map • Canary Islands • Central Europe • Central Europe phrasebook • Corfu & the Ionians • Corsica • Crete • Crete Condensed • Croatia • Cycling Britain • Cycling France • Cyprus • Czech & Slovak Republics • Denmark • Dublin • Dublin City Map • Eastern Europe • Eastern Europe phrasebook • Edinburgh • Estonia, Latvia & Lithuania • Europe on a shoestring • Finland • Florence • France • Frankfurt Condensed • French phrasebook • Georgia, Armenia & Azerbaijan • Germany • German phrasebook • Greece • Greek Islands • Greek phrasebook • Hungary • Iceland, Greenland & the Faroe Islands • Ireland • Istanbul • Italian phrasebook • Italy • Krakow • Lisbon • The Loire • London • London City Map • London Condensed • Madrid • Malta • Mediterranean Europe • Mediterranean Europe phrasebook • Moscow • Munich • Norway • Out to Eat – London • Paris • Paris City Map • Paris Condensed • Poland • Portugal • Portuguese phrasebook • Prague • Prague City Map • Provence & the Côte d'Azur • Read This First: Europe • Romania & Moldova • Rome • Russia, Ukraine & Belarus • Russian phrasebook • Scandinavian & Baltic Europe • Scandinavian Europe phrasebook • Scotland • Sicily • Slovenia • South-West France • Spain • Spanish phrasebook • St Petersburg • St Petersburg City Map • Sweden • Switzerland • Trekking in Spain • Tuscany • Ukrainian phrasebook • Venice • Vienna • Walking in Britain • Walking in France • Walking in Ireland • Walking in Italy • Walking in Spain • Walking in Switzerland • Western Europe • Western Europe phrasebook • World Food France • World Food Ireland • World Food Italy • World Food Spain
Travel Literature: Love and War in the Apennines • The Olive Grove: Travels in Greece • On the Shores of the Mediterranean • Round Ireland in Low Gear • A Small Place in Italy

INDIAN SUBCONTINENT Bangladesh • Bengali phrasebook • Bhutan • Delhi • Goa • Healthy Travel Asia & India • Hindi & Urdu phrasebook • India • Indian Himalaya • Karakoram Highway • Kerala • Mumbai

LONELY PLANET

Mail Order

Lonely Planet products are distributed worldwide. They are also available by mail order from Lonely Planet, so if you have difficulty finding a title please write to us. North and South American residents should write to 150 Linden St, Oakland, CA 94607, USA; European and African residents should write to 10a Spring Place, London NW5 3BH, UK; and residents of other countries to Locked Bag 1, Footscray, Victoria 3011, Australia.

(Bombay) • Nepal • Nepali phrasebook • Pakistan • Rajasthan • Read This First: Asia & India • South India • Sri Lanka • Sri Lanka phrasebook • Tibet • Tibetan phrasebook • Trekking in the Indian Himalaya • Trekking in the Karakoram & Hindukush • Trekking in the Nepal Himalaya
Travel Literature: The Age of Kali: Indian Travels and Encounters • Hello Goodnight: A Life of Goa • In Rajasthan • A Season in Heaven: True Tales from the Road to Kathmandu • Shopping for Buddhas • A Short Walk in the Hindu Kush • Slowly Down the Ganges

ISLANDS OF THE INDIAN OCEAN Madagascar & Comoros • Maldives • Mauritius, Réunion & Seychelles

MIDDLE EAST & CENTRAL ASIA Bahrain, Kuwait & Qatar • Central Asia • Central Asia phrasebook • Dubai • Hebrew phrasebook • Iran • Israel & the Palestinian Territories • Istanbul • Istanbul City Map • Istanbul to Cairo on a shoestring • Jerusalem • Jerusalem City Map • Jordan • Lebanon • Middle East • Oman & the United Arab Emirates • Syria • Turkey • Turkish phrasebook • World Food Turkey • Yemen
Travel Literature: Black on Black: Iran Revisited • The Gates of Damascus • Kingdom of the Film Stars: Journey into Jordan

NORTH AMERICA Alaska • Boston • Boston City Map • California & Nevada • California Condensed • Canada • Chicago • Chicago City Map • Deep South • Florida • Hawaii • Hiking in Alaska • Hiking in the USA • Honolulu • Las Vegas • Los Angeles • Miami • Miami City Map • New England • New Orleans • New York City • New York City City Map • New York City Condensed • New York, New Jersey & Pennsylvania • Oahu • Out to Eat – San Francisco • Pacific Northwest • Puerto Rico • Rocky Mountains • San Francisco • San Francisco City Map • Seattle • Southwest • Texas • USA • USA phrasebook • Vancouver • Virginia & the Capital Region • Washington, DC City Map • World Food Deep South, USA
Travel Literature: Caught Inside: A Surfer's Year on the California Coast • Drive Thru America

NORTH-EAST ASIA Beijing • Cantonese phrasebook • China • Hiking in Japan • Hong Kong • Hong Kong City Map • Hong Kong Condensed • Hong Kong, Macau & Guangzhou • Japan • Japanese phrasebook • Korea • Korean phrasebook • Kyoto • Mandarin phrasebook • Mongolia • Mongolian phrasebook • Seoul • South-West China • Taiwan • Tokyo
Travel Literature: In Xanadu: A Quest • Lost Japan

SOUTH AMERICA Argentina, Uruguay & Paraguay • Bolivia • Brazil • Brazilian phrasebook • Buenos Aires • Chile & Easter Island • Colombia • Ecuador & the Galapagos Islands • Healthy Travel Central & South America • Latin American Spanish phrasebook • Peru • Quechua phrasebook • Read This First: Central & South America • Rio de Janeiro • Rio de Janeiro City Map • Santiago • South America on a shoestring • Trekking in the Patagonian Andes • Venezuela
Travel Literature: Full Circle: A South American Journey

SOUTH-EAST ASIA Bali & Lombok • Bangkok • Bangkok City Map • Burmese phrasebook • Cambodia • Hanoi • Healthy Travel Asia & India • Hill Tribes phrasebook • Ho Chi Minh City • Indonesia • Indonesian phrasebook • Indonesia's Eastern Islands • Jakarta • Java • Lao phrasebook • Laos • Malay phrasebook • Malaysia, Singapore & Brunei • Myanmar (Burma) • Philippines • Pilipino (Tagalog) phrasebook • Read This First: Asia & India • Singapore • Singapore City Map • South-East Asia on a shoestring • South-East Asia phrasebook • Thailand • Thailand's Islands & Beaches • Thailand, Vietnam, Laos & Cambodia Road Atlas • Thai phrasebook • Vietnam • Vietnamese phrasebook • World Food Thailand • World Food Vietnam

ALSO AVAILABLE: Antarctica • The Arctic • The Blue Man: Tales of Travel, Love and Coffee • Brief Encounters: Stories of Love, Sex & Travel • Chasing Rickshaws • The Last Grain Race • Lonely Planet Unpacked • Not the Only Planet: Science Fiction Travel Stories • On the Edge: Extreme Travel • Sacred India • Travel with Children • Travel Photography: A Guide to Taking Better Pictures

LONELY PLANET

You already know that Lonely Planet produces more than this one guidebook, but you might not be aware of the other products we have on this region. Here is a selection of titles which you may want to check out as well:

Read this First Asia & India
ISBN 1 86450 049 2
US$14.99 • UK£8.99 • 99FF

Healthy Travel Asia & India
ISBN 1 86450 051 4
US$5.95 • UK£3.99 • 39FF

Hong Kong, Macau & Guangzhou
ISBN 0 86442 584 8
US$15.95 • UK£9.99 • 120FF

Mandarin phrasebook
ISBN 0 86442 652 6
US$7.95 • UK£4.50 • 50FF

South-West China
ISBN 0 86442 596 1
US$19.95 • UK£12.99 • 160FF

China
ISBN 0 86442 755 7
US$29.99 • UK£17.99 • 199FF

Shanghai
ISBN 0 864442 507 4
US$15.99 • UK£9.99 • 119FF

Available wherever books are sold.

Index

Bold indicates maps.

Boxed Text

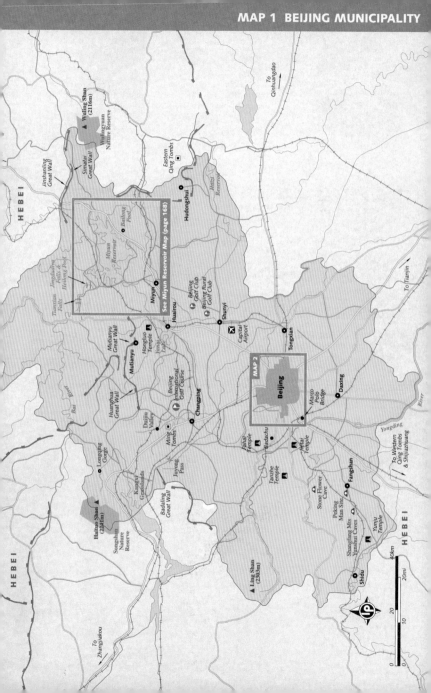

MAP 1 BEIJING MUNICIPALITY

HEBEI

Wuling Shan
(2116m) ▲

Wulingyuan
Nature Reserve

Jinshanling
Great Wall

Simatai
Great Wall

Eastern
Qing Tombs

Hudongshui

Jingshuihu
Falls &
Heilong Pool

Badong
Pool

Tianxian
Falls

Miyun
Reservoir

See Miyun Reservoir Map (page 168)

Haizi
Reservoir

Miyun

Huairou

Beijing
Golf Club

Beijing Rural
Golf Club

Shunyi

Tongxian

To Qinhuangdao

To Tianjin

Mutianyu
Great Wall

Hongluo
Temple

Yanxi
Lake

Mutianyu

Capital
Airport

MAP 2

Beijing

Daxing

Bai River

Huanghua
Great Wall

Beijing
International
Golf Course

Changping

Marco
Polo
Bridge

River

Dujiju
Valley

Ming
Tombs

Fahai
Temple

Jietai
Temple

Yongding

Longqing
Gorge

Juyong
Pass

Kangxi
Grasslands

Jietai
Temple

Tanzhe
Temple

Fangshan

To Western
Qing Tombs
& Shijiazhuang

Haituo Shan
(2241m) ▲

Songshan
Nature Reserve

Badaling
Great Wall

Stone Flower
Cave

Peking
Man Site

Yunju
Temple

Shangfang Mts
Yunshui Caves

HEBEI

▲ Ling Shan
(2303m)

Shidu

To
Zhangjiakou

40km

20mi

0   10   20

MAP 2 BEIJING

Xiangshan Botanic Gardens 香山植物园

Yuquanshan Lu 玉泉山路

Fragrant Hills Park 香山公园

Badachu Park 八大处公园

Kunming Lake

Yiheyuan 颐和园

Haidian Lu 海淀路

Zhongguancun Lu 中关

Shuangqing

Chen

Beisanhuan Xilu 北三环西路

Minzhuang Lu

Xiangshan Nanlu 香山南路

Reshuicun Lu 热水村路

Kunminghu Lu 昆明湖路

Wenquanhe Lu

Zhichun Lu

Haidian

Haidian Lu

Suzhou Lu

Xingshikou Lu

Kunming Nanlu

Wukesong Lu

Banjing Lu 板井路

Landianchang Nanlu

Wulu Train Station

Beijing Zoo 北京动物园

Map 3

Xisanhuan Beilu

Yuyuantan Park 玉渊潭公园

Shijingshan

Fifth Ring Road

Map 6

Fuximen Dajie

Shijingshan Lu 石景山路

Fuxing Lu 复兴路

复兴门大街 Fuxingmen Daji

To Guchenglu & Pingguoyuan Subway Stations

Bajiaocun 八角村地铁站

Babaoshan 八宝山地铁站

Yuquanlu 玉泉路地铁站

Wukesong 五棵松地铁站

Wanshoulu 万寿路地铁站

Xisanhuan Zhonglu

Beijing West Train Station 北京西火车站

Wujiacun Lu

Fengtai Lu

Third Ring Road 西三环中路

Fengtai

Beijing-Shijiazhuang Expressway 京石高速公路

Xisanhuan Nanlu

西三环南路

Fengtai Train Station 丰台站

Fengtai Donglu

Fengtai Lu

To Shijiazhuang

0   1   2km
0 0.5 1mi

MAP 2 BEIJING

Badaling Expressway
八达岭高速公路

To Airport &
Mövenpick Hotel

Guangshun Beidajie

Shoudujichang Expressway 首都机场高速公路

● 22

Beisihuan Zhonglu
北四环中路

● 23

Daliang Lu
大梁路

Fourth Ring Road

24   26

Anding Lu

Huixin Dongjie

Chaoyang

Beisihuan Donglu

● 28

Nanhugu Lu

Shuangyu Lu
双玉路

Huixindong Lu

北二环中路

20
21

25

Beisanhuan Zhonglu

Third Ring Road

27

Beisihuan Donglu
北四环东路

Map 4   Map 5

North
Train Station
北站火车站

Hepingli Train
Station

Beisanhuan Donglu

Liangmaqiao Lu

Xicheng

Second Ring Road

Dongcheng

Chaoyang
Park
朝阳公园

Second Ring
Road

Dongsanhuan Beilu 东三环北路

29   30

Nongzhanguan Nanlu
农展馆南路

● 31

Forbidden
City

Chaoyang Lu

Map 7

Chang'an Jie

Jianguomen Dajie

Jingtong Expressway 京通快速公路

Tiananmen
Square

Dawangqiao
大望桥地铁站

Sihuidong
四惠东地铁站

Second Ring Road

Beijing Train
Station
北京火车站

Dongsanhuan Zhonglu

Sihuixi
四惠西地铁站

Xuanwu

Chongwen

Guangqumen Nanbinhe Lu

Dongsanhuan Nanlu

Guangqu Lu

Tiantan
Park
天坛公园

Huagong Lu

nd View
arden
观园

Taoranting Park
陶然亭公园

Longtan
Park
龙潭公园

You'anmen Xibinhe Lu   You'anmen Dongbinhe Lu   Zuo'anmen Xibinhe Lu

Beijing South Train
Station (Yongdingmen)
北京南站永定门火车站

nshan Xilu

Nansanhuan Zhonglu

南三环东路 Nansanhuan Donglu

Beijing-Tianjin Expressway

Nansanhuan Zhonglu

36   35

34   33   32

Maliapu Dongjie
马家堡东街

Nanyuan Lu
南苑路

Dayangfang Lu

京津高速公路

Nanshan Lu

To
Tianjin

Beijing's modern skyline: Jianguomen Nei at sunrise

HILARY SMITH

The resplendent and soothing lines of the seventeen-arch bridge, Kunming Lake

Statue in the Old Summer Palace grounds

Imposing pavilions at Fragrant Hills Park offer a scenic setting for a stroll.

MAP 3 HAIDIAN & XICHENG

Wegongcun Lu

Xueyuan Nanlu

Haidian

Daluishu Lu

Dahuisi Lu

1

Minzuxueyuan Nanlu

Baishiqiao Lu

Gaoliangqiao Lu

高梁桥路

9

Zizhuyuan Park
紫竹院公园

4

2

3

English
Corner

Beijing Zoo
北京动物园

8

Zizhuyuan Lu

5

Xizhimen Wai Dajie

6

7

Xizhimen Wai Nanlu

Xisanhuan Beilu

西三环北路
(Third Ring Road)

Chegongzhuang Xilu 车公庄西路

Chegongzhuang Donglu 车公庄东路

Sanlihe Lu

Zhanlanguan Lu

28

Baiwanzhuang Xilu 百万庄西路

Baiwanzhuang Dajie

Xisanhuan Zhonglu

Fucheng Lu 阜成路

Sanlihe Lu

Sanlihe Donglu

29

西三环中路

Yuyuantan Park
玉渊潭公园

Yuetan Beijie

Yuyuan Lake

MAP 6

MAP 3 HAIDIAN & XICHENG

MAP 4

11

学院南路
Xueyuan Nanlu

Xitucheng Lu

Wulutong Jie

Xinde Jie

Rendinghu
Park
人定湖公园

Wenhuiyuan Beilu

Xinjiekou Wai Dajie

Deshengmen Wai Dajie

Wenhuiyuan Jie

Ande Lu

Sidaoku Lu

Xizhimen Bei Dajie

10

Jishuitan
积水潭地铁站

Deshengmen Dongdajie

Gulou Xidajie

Xizhimen
Train Station
西直门
火车站

德胜门西大街 Deshengmen Xi Dajie (Second Ring Road)

Xihai
Lake

Houhai Beiyan

13

Xinjiekou Beidajie

新街口北大街

12

Houhai
Lake

Deshengmen Nei Dajie

直门外大街

Xizhimen
西直门地铁站

Xizhemen Nei Dajie

Yangfang Hutong

14

Beishi Lu

Guan Park
官园公园

Baitasi Lu

Xinjiekou Nandajie

Liuyin Jie

15
16

Xicheng

18

Huguosi Jie 护国寺街

德胜门内大街

Longtoujing

17

-gongzhuang Donglu

Chegongzhuang
车公庄地铁站

Ping'anli Xidajie

19

Dianmen Xidajie

Chegongzhuang Donglu

Fuchengmen Beidajie

白塔寺路 Baitasi Lu

Xisi Beidajie

Xihuangchenggen Beijie

Xishiku Dajie

Beihai
Park
北海公园

Beilishi Lu

23

Fuchengmen
阜成门地铁站

26

25

24

22

20

Fuchengmen Nandajie

Fuchengmen Wai Dajie

-hengmen Wai Dajie

27

Fuchengmen Nei Dajie 阜成门内大街

Xi'anmen Jie

Wenjin Jie

Taipingqiao Dajie

Xisi Nandajie

Fuyou Jie

Yuetan
Park
月坛公园

Xidan Beidajie

21

MAP 6

MAP 3 HAIDIAN & XICHENG

GLENN BEANLAND

Men playing mahjong outside Tiantan Park

HILARY SMITH

Hui Muslim man outside lamb shop

The many faces of Beijing

HILARY SMITH

HILARY SMITH

GLENN BEANLAND

HILARY SMITH

HILARY SMITH

MAP 4 DONGCHENG

LP

MAP 3

Liuyin Park
柳荫公园

Huangsi Dajie

Hepingli Beijie 和平里北街

Andeli Beijie

Andeli Beijie 安德里北街

Qingnianhu Park
青年湖公园

Ditan
Park
地坛公园

Heping Dongjie

Gulou Wai Dajie

Jiugulou Wai Dajie

Ande Lu

Andingmen Wai Dajie

1

Xidajie

Andingmen
安定门地铁站

Yonghegong 雍和宫地铁站

Andingmen Dongdajie

Gulou
鼓楼地铁站

Andingmen Xidajie (Second Ring Road)

★ 2 安定门东大街

安定门西大街

Yonghegong Dajie

Dongzhimen Beixiaojie

3

6

Houhai Beiyan

Gulou Xidajie

Andingmen Nei Dajie

Guozijian Jie

Beiluogu Xiang

5 🛕 ▼ 4

雍和宫大街

Nanguan
Park
南馆公园

7

Gulou Dongdajie

鼓楼东大街

8

Jiaodaokou Dongdajie

Dongzhimen Nei Dajie

Nanluogu Xiang

9

10

Dongsi Beidajie

Jiaodaokou Nandajie 交道口南大街

Dongzhimen Namxiaojie

11

12

Dongcheng

Qianhai
Lake

13

东四北大街

Di'anmen Xidajie

Di'anmen Dongdajie

Zhanzi Zhonglu

Dongsishitao Lu

Beihai Park
北海公园

Di'anmen Wai Dajie

Meishuguan Houjie

Dongsi Beidajie

Chaoyangmen Beixiaojie

Beiheyan Dajie

Dongsi Nandajie

Beihai
Lake

Jingshan Houjie

Jingshan Dongjie

Dongfangchengzgen Beijie

14 Qianliang Hutong

Jingshan Xijie

Jingshan
Park
景山公园

15

Wusi Dajie 五四大街

Dongsi Xidajie

Chaoyangmen Nei Dajie

Jingshanqian Jie 景山府街

🏛 16

17 C

Beichang Jie 北长街

Beichizi Jie

Beiheyan Dajie

Donghuangchengzgen Nanjie

18

Dongsi Nandajie

Wangfujing Dajie (Bikes Prohibited)

Dongdan Beidajie

Forbidden
City
紫禁城

19

Qihelou Jie

20

Dengshikou Xijie

灯市口西街

21

22

Wangfujing Dajie

23

Zhong-
hai Lake

29

Donhuamen
Dajie

28

Dong'anmen Dajie

27

25

Jinyu Hutong

30

26

24

MAP 7

0 250 500m
0 250 500yd

MAP 4 DONGCHENG

PLACES TO STAY

6 Bamboo Garden Hotel
竹园宾馆

9 Youhao Guesthouse
友好宾馆

13 Lüsongyuan Hotel
侣松圆宾馆

18 Wangfujing
Grand Hotel
王府井大饭店

21 Fangyuan Hotel
芳园宾馆

23 Haoyuan Guesthouse
好园宾馆

24 Palace Hotel;
Roma Restaurant
王府饭店

25 Peace Hotel
和平宾馆

PLACES TO EAT

1 Tangenyuan
Restaurant
坛根院食坊

4 Mao Family
Restaurant
毛家菜饭店

10 Kaorouji Restaurant
北京烤肉季

11 Blue Lotus Cafe
蓝莲花咖啡馆

22 Green Angel
Vegetarian
Restaurant
绿天使素食馆

28 Dong'anmen
Night Market
东安门夜市

29 The Courtyard
四合轩

30 Purple Vine
Teahouse
紫藤庐

OTHER

2 PSB
(Visa Extensions)
公安局外事科

3 Lama Temple
雍和宫

5 Confucius Temple
孔庙

7 Bell Tower
钟楼

8 Drum Tower
鼓楼

12 Mao Dun Former
Residence
茅盾故居

14 Longfu Department
Store
隆福商业大厦

15 Star Cinema
明星电影院

16 China Art Gallery
中国美术馆

17 Dongsi Mosque
东四清真寺

19 Capital Theatre
首都剧场

20 Lao She Former
Residence
老舍故居

26 Xindong'an Plaza;
Donglaishun
(Hot Pot Restaurant)
新东安市场；
火锅店

27 Foreign Languages
Bookstore
外文书店

HILARY SMITH

Sunset behind the Forbidden City

Bicycles parked outside Hepingli Train Station

Sanlitun night life – Jam House Cafe

Whiling away the hours with mahjong

Making offerings at Dongyue Temple

MAP 5 CHAOYANG

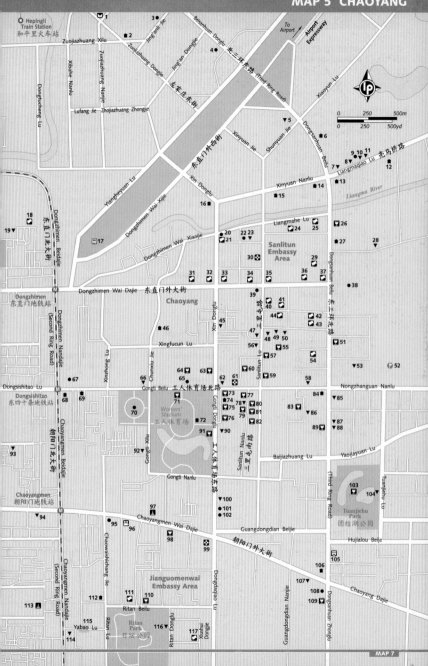

MAP 5 CHAOYANG

PLACES TO STAY

2 Radisson SAS Hotel
皇家大饭店

6 Hilton Hotel;
Sui Yan Restaurant
希尔顿饭店

12 21st Century Hotel;
Sino-Japanese Youth
Exchange Centre
二十一世纪饭店
中日青年交流中心

13 Kempinski Hotel;
Lufthansa Center;
Sorobol Restaurant;
Paulaner Brauhaus
凯宾斯基饭店；
燕沙商城

14 Kunlun Hotel
昆仑饭店

15 Huadu Hotel;
Full Moon Restaurant;
Friends
华都饭店

16 Yuyang Hotel
渔阳饭店

27 Great Wall Sheraton
长城饭店

46 Red House Hotel
瑞修宾馆

68 Swissôtel; Hong Kong-
Macau Centre;
瑞士酒店；
北京港澳中心

69 Beijing Asia Hotel
北京亚洲大酒店

72 Gongti Hotel
工体宾馆

74 City Hotel
城市宾馆

84 Zhaolong Hotel;
Zhaolong International
Youth Hostel
兆龙饭店
北京兆龙青年旅社

106 Jingguang
New World Hotel
京广新世界饭店

112 Ritan Hotel
日坛宾馆

PLACES TO EAT

5 Red Basil Thai
Restaurant
红罗勒泰国餐厅

7 Ban Cheng Xiang
Jiulou
半城香酒楼

8 Sansi Lang
三四郎

10 Adria
北京亚的里亚
餐饮有限公司

11 Golden Hill City
Restaurant
金山城重庆菜馆

19 The Baikul
贝加尔西餐厅

23 Green Tea House
绿茶舍

28 Peter Pan

45 Geng Wu Mess
庚午菜屋

47 Jenny Lou's

48 Bella's
贝拉餐厅

49 Serve the People
为人们服务

50 Golden Elephant
金象

53 La Galopin
巴黎皇家御膳房

56 Kebab Cafe
连衣餐厅

58 1,001 Nights
一千零一夜餐厅

62 Da Cheng
Yong He
大城永和

66 Ashanti
阿仙蒂

78 Rainbow
彩虹

85 Tuanjiehu Roast
Duck Restaurant
团结湖北京烤鸭店

86 Shanghai Moon
夜上海

87 Matsuko
松子日本料理

88 Asian Star
Restaurant
亚州之星新马印餐厅

90 Berena's Bistro
柏瑞娜酒家

92 Metro Cafe
意大利咖啡店

93 Red Capital Club
新红资俱乐部

94 Afanti
阿凡提

100 Schlotsky's Deli
斯乐斯基餐厅

104 Golden Cat
Dumpling City
金猫饺子城

107 Phrik Thai
京港泰式美食

114 Omar Khayyam
Restaurant
味美佳餐厅

116 Xihe Yaju
Restaurant
义和雅居餐厅

ENTERTAINMENT

26 Hard Rock Cafe
硬石餐厅

51 CD Cafe
CD咖啡

55 Jazzya;
Japanese Restaurant
李波餐厅

57 Public Space
公共场所

59 Boys & Girls
男孩子女孩子

60 Half & Half
海通酒家

63 Club Vogue
白房

64 Club Orange
橙街俱乐部

67 Poly Plaza
保利大厦

MAP 5 CHAOYANG

71 Havana Cafe
哈瓦纳咖啡屋

73 The Den
敦煌咖啡屋

75 Downtown Cafe;
Park Bar
城市咖啡；
公园酒吧

76 Frank's Place
万龙酒吧

77 Minder's
明大西餐馆

79 Jam House
芥茉房酒吧

80 Durty Nellie's
都伯临西餐厅

81 Nashville;
Hidden Tree
乡谣俱乐部；
隐蔽的树

82 Riders

83 The Loft
藏酷

89 TGI Friday's
星期五餐厅

91 Maggie's
麦姬酒吧

96 Ziguang Cinema
紫光电影院

98 Banana
巴那那

103 Island Club
中心岛俱乐部

105 Chaoyang Theatre
朝阳剧场

109 Hot Spot
热点俱乐部

110 Elephant Bar
大象酒吧

EMBASSIES
18 Russia
俄罗斯大使馆

21 Nepal
尼泊尔大使馆

24 Kazakstan
卡萨克斯坦大使馆

25 Singapore
新加坡大使馆

29 Pakistan
巴基斯坦大使馆

31 Australia
澳大利亚大使馆

32 Canada
加拿大大使馆

33 Germany
德国大使馆

34 Malaysia
马来西亚大使馆

35 Cambodia
柬埔寨大使馆

36 Sweden
瑞典大使馆

37 Myanmar
缅甸大使馆

40 UNICEF
联合国儿童基金会

41 Laos
老挝大使馆

42 South Korea
大韩民国大使馆

43 France
法国大使馆

44 Netherlands
荷兰大使馆

54 Italy
意大利大使馆

111 North Korea
北朝鲜大使馆

117 New Zealand
新西兰大使馆

OTHER
1 Post
Office
邮电局

3 China
International
Exhibition Centre
中国国际展览馆

4 China Travel
Service Tower
中旅大厦

9 Liangmaqiao Market
亮马桥市场

17 Dongzhimen Bus Station
长途东直门中心站

20 Tayuan Diplomatic
Building
塔园外交办公楼

22 Dreamweavers
织锦绣时装

30 Friendship Supermarket
友谊超级商场

38 Agricultural Exhibition
Centre
农业展览馆

39 Red Phoenix
红凤凰

52 Chaoyang Golf Club
朝阳高尔夫球具乐部

61 Kylin Plaza
麒麟大厦

65 Tibet Dipper Photo
Service
西藏北斗星图片总社

70 Workers'
Gymnasium
工人体育场

95 Full Link Plaza
丰联广场

97 Dongyue Temple
东岳庙

99 Landao
Department Store
(Dongdaqiao)
蓝岛大厦

101 Extreme Beyond
探险•芬坝•登山装备
专卖店

102 Bing Bing
严冰冰服装工作室

108 PLA Military
Supply Shop
解放军队第3501工厂
第1经销部

113 Zhihua Temple
智化寺

115 Yabao Lu
(Clothing Market)
雅宝路

MAP 6 FENGTAI & XUANWU

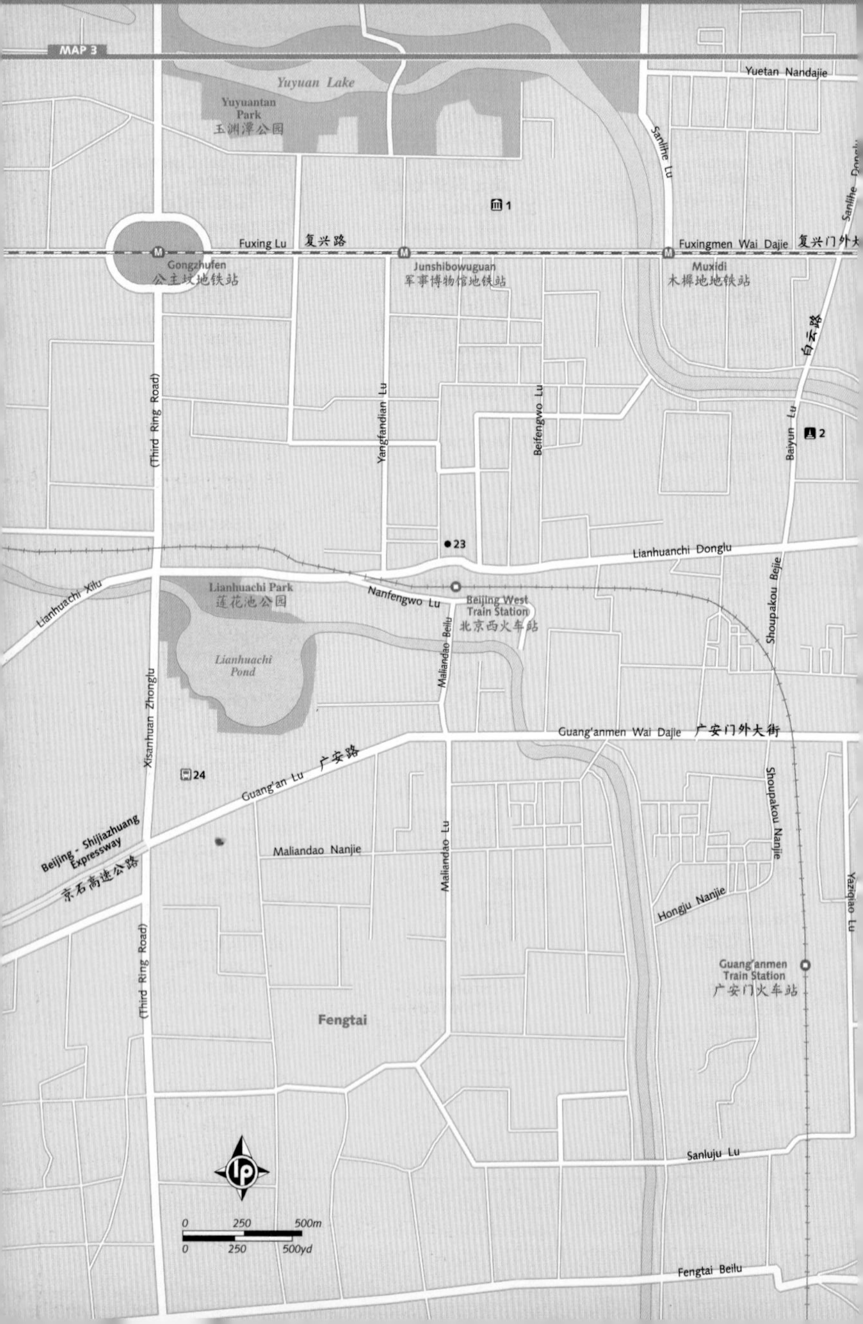

MAP 3

Yuyuan Lake

Yuetan Nandajie

Yuyuantan
Park
玉渊潭公园

Sanlihe Lu

Sanlihe Donglu

🏛1

Fuxing Lu 复兴路

Fuxingmen Wai Dajie 复兴门外大

Ⓜ Gongzhufen
公主坟地铁站

Ⓜ Junshibowuguan
军事博物馆地铁站

Ⓜ Muxidi
木樨地地铁站

Baiyun Lu

(Third Ring Road)

Yangfangdian Lu

Beifengwo Lu

Baiyun Lu

🏛2

Lianhuachi Donglu

●23

Shoupakou Beijie

Lianhuachi Xilu

Lianhuachi Park
莲花池公园

Nanfengwo Lu

Beijing West
Train Station
北京西火车站

Lianhuachi
Pond

Maliandao Beilu

Xisanhuan Zhonglu

Guang'anmen Wai Dajie 广安门外大街

Shoupakou Nanjie

🏛24

Guang'an Lu 广安路

Beijing - Shijiazhuang
Expressway
京石高速公路

Maliandao Nanjie

Maliandao Lu

Hongju Nanjie

(Third - Ring Road)

Guang'anmen
Train Station
广安门火车站

Yazhuang Lu

Fengtai

Sanluju Lu

0   250   500m
0   250   500yd

Fengtai Beilu

MAP 6 FENGTAI & XUANWU

MAP 3

MAP 7

Nanhai Lake
南海

Nanlishi Lu
南礼士路

Fuxingmen Beidajie
复兴门北大街

Narishikou Beijie

Xidan Beidajie

Xidan
西单

Foyou Jie

Xibianmen Nei Dajie

Fuxingmen Nei Dajie 复兴门内大街

3 ⊗

6 ● 7 ●

8 ● 9 ●

Xichang'an Jie

Nanlishilu
南礼士路
地铁站

Fuxingmen
复兴门
地铁站

5 ●

Xidan
西单地铁站

10

Guang'anmen Beibinhe Lu

Naoshikou Zhongjie

Xinwenhua Jie

Xuanwumen Nei Dajie
宣武门内大街

Tongjingge Lu

Xirongxian Hutong

Beixinhua Jie

4 ●

Naoshikou Nanjie

Changchun Jie

Xuanwumen Xidajie

19

Xuanwumen Dongdajie

Shangxi Jie

Xuanwumen
宣武门地铁站

Hepingmen
和平门地铁站

11

18

Xuanwu
Art Garden
宣武艺园

Changchun Jie

Xiaxie Jie

Xuanwumen Wai Dajie
宣武门外大街

Liulichang Xijie
琉璃厂西街

Liulichang
Dongjie

12

Guangyi Jie

13

Nanxinhua Jie
南新华街

14

15

Guang'anmen Nei Dajie

广安门内大街

Luomashi Dajie

Changchun Jie

Jiaozi Hutong

Lanman Hutong

Mishi Hutong

Fengfanghu Jie

17

Yong'an Lu

16

Hufang Lu

Guang'anmen Nanshuncheng Jie

Niu Jie

20

Baiguang Lu

Nanheng Xijie

Nanheng Dongjie 南横东街

21

Beiwei Lu

Xuanwu
宣武

Perter Hutong

Haiyaochang Jie

Wanshou
Park
万寿公园

Baizhifang Xijie

Baizhifang Jie 白纸坊街

Liren Jie

You'anmen Nei Dajie

Nancyuan Jie

Taoranting
Park
陶然亭公园

Grand View
Garden
大观园

Taiping Jie

You'anmen Xibinhe Lu 右安门西滨河路

22 ●

MAP 6 FENGTAI & XUANWU

Dragons and other mythical beasts are common themes in Chinese architecture.

DAMIEN SIMONIS

GLENN BEANLAND

OLIVIER CIRENDINI

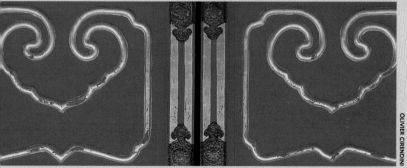

OLIVIER CIRENDINI

Door details from the Forbidden City

MAP 7 CHONGWEN & CHAOYANG

MAP 7 CHONGWEN & CHAOYANG

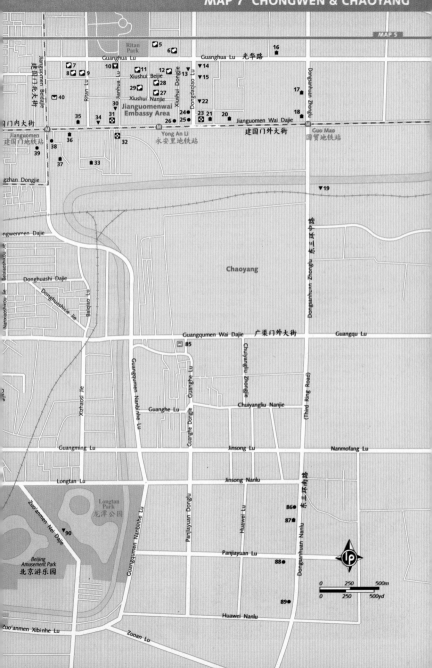

MAP 5

Ritan Park

Guanghua Lu

Guanghua Lu 光华路

Jianguomen Beidajie
建国门北大街

Ritan Lu

Jianhua Lu

Xiushui Beijie

Xiushui Nanjie

Dongdaqiao Lu

Xiushui Dongjie

Dongsanhuan Zhonglu

Jianguomenwai
Embassy Area

门内大街

Jianguomen Wai Dajie 建国门外大街

Jianguomen
建国门地铁站

Guo Mao
国贸地铁站

Yong An Li
永安里地铁站

gzhan Dongjie

ngwenmen Dajie

Donghuashi Dajie

Nankiaoshikou Jie

Donghuashixie Jie

Baiqiao Lu

Chaoyang

Dongsanhuan Zhonglu
东三环中路

Guangqumen Wai Dajie 广渠门外大街

Guangqu Lu

Xizhaosi Jie

Guangqumen Nanbinhe Lu

Guanghe Lu

Guanghe Dongjie

Chuiyangliu Zhongjie

Chuiyangliu Nanjie

Guanghe Lu

Jinsong Lu

(Third Ring Road)

Nanmofang Lu

Guangming Lu

Longtan Lu

Zuo'anmen Nei Dajie

Longtan
Park
龙潭公园

Jinsong Nanlu

Panjiayuan Dongjie

Huawei Lu

Dongsanhuan Nanlu

东三环南路

Beijing
Amusement Park
北京游乐园

Panjiayuan Nanbinhe Lu

Panjiayuan Lu

Zuo'anmen Xibinhe Lu

Zuoan Lu

Huawei Nanlu

0   250   500m
0   250   500yd

Dajie

ngzhao Jie

MAP 7 CHONGWEN & CHAOYANG

Tiananmen Gate

DAMIEN SIMONIS

'Antiques' at Panjiayuan Market

CAROLINE LIOU

MAP 7 CHONGWEN & CHAOYANG

11 Vietnam
越南大使馆

12 USA
美国大使馆

27 Ireland
爱尔兰大使馆

28 USA
美国大使馆

29 Mongolia
蒙古大使馆

OTHER

1 Beijing Department Store
北京百货大楼

3 Beijing Union Hospital
协和医院

4 Dahua Cinema
大华电影院

10 John Bull Pub
地道的英式酒吧

23 Guiyou Department Store
贵友商场

24 Dragon House
御龙阁

25 Empire Quick Prints
英派尔快印
北京有限公司

26 Xiushui Silk Market
秀水东街

31 Friendship Store
友谊商店

32 Scitech Plaza
赛特购物中心

38 BTG (formerly CITS);
Tourism Building
北京国际旅行社
（旅游大厦）

39 Ancient Observatory
古观象台

40 International Post Office
国际邮店局

42 Cofco Plaza

43 Chang'an Grand Theatre
长安大剧场

44 Oriental Plaza
东方广场

45 Beijing Arts and Crafts Central Store;
Food Court
北京工艺美术服务部

48 Imperial Archives Museum (Wan Fung Gallery)
皇史城

49 Tiananmen
天安门

50 Great Hall of the People
人民大会堂

51 Monument to the People's Heroes
人民英雄纪念碑

52 Chinese Revolution History Museum
中国革命历史博物馆

53 Mao Zedong Mausoleum
毛主席纪念堂

54 CITS
中国青年旅行社

56 Entrance to Underground City
地下城门口
（西打磨厂街62号）

58 Qianmen
正阳门（前门）

59 Qianmen Tour Bus Station
前门，旅游车发车站

60 Lao She Teahouse
老舍茶馆

80 Hongqiao Market/ Pearl Market
红桥市场/珍珠市场

83 Yihong Carpet Factory
艺虹地毯厂

84 Qianmen Carpet Factory
前门地毯厂

85 Majuan Long-Distance Bus Station
马圈(马甸)长途汽车

86 Zhaojia Chaowai Market
朝外市场

88 Panjiayuan Market
潘家园市场

89 Curio City
北京古玩城

91 Beijing International Tennis Centre
北京国际网球中心

92 Yuan Long (Silk Store)
元隆顾绣绸缎商行

The Monument to the People's Heroes, Tiananmen Square, and (right) a detail

MAP LEGEND

CITY ROUTES

Freeway	Freeway
Highway	Primary Road
Road	Secondary Road
Street	Street
Lane	Lane
	On/Off Ramp

	Unsealed Road
	One Way Street
	Pedestrian Street
	Stepped Street
	Tunnel
	Footbridge

REGIONAL ROUTES

	Tollway, Freeway
	Primary Road
	Secondary Road
	Minor Road

BOUNDARIES

	International
	State
	Disputed
	Fortified Wall

HYDROGRAPHY

	River, Creek
	Canal
	Lake

	Dry Lake; Salt Lake
	Spring; Rapids
	Waterfalls

TRANSPORT ROUTES & STATIONS

	Local Railway
	Underground Rlwy
	Disused Railway
	Subway, Station
	Lightrail Tram

	Cable Car, Chairlift
	Ferry
	Walking Trail
	Walking Tour
	Path

AREA FEATURES

	Building
	Park, Gardens

	Market
	Sports Ground

	Beach
	Cemetery

	Campus
	Hotel

POPULATION SYMBOLS

CAPITAL	National Capital	City	City
CAPITAL	Provincial Capital	Town	Town

Village	Village		
	Urban Area		

MAP SYMBOLS

Place to Stay	Place to Eat	Point of Interest

Airport	Fountain	National Park
Bank	Golf Course	Pagoda
Bus Terminal	Hospital	Parking
Castle	Internet Cafe	Police Station
Chalet	Lookout	Post Office
Church	Monument	Pub or Bar
Cycling	Museum	Ruins

Stately Home
Shopping Centre
Telephone
Temple, Buddhist
Tomb
Tourist Information
Zoo

Note: not all symbols displayed above appear in this book

LONELY PLANET OFFICES

Australia
Locked Bag 1, Footscray, Victoria 3011
☎ 03 9689 4666 fax 03 9689 6833
email: talk2us@lonelyplanet.com.au

USA
150 Linden St, Oakland, CA 94607
☎ 510 893 8555 TOLL FREE: 800 275 8555
fax 510 893 8572
email: info@lonelyplanet.com

UK
10a Spring Place, London NW5 3BH
☎ 020 7428 4800 fax 020 7428 4828
email: go@lonelyplanet.co.uk

France
1 rue du Dahomey, 75011 Paris
☎ 01 55 25 33 00 fax 01 55 25 33 01
email: bip@lonelyplanet.fr
www.lonelyplanet.fr

World Wide Web: www.lonelyplanet.com *or* AOL keyword: lp
Lonely Planet Images: lpi@lonelyplanet.com.au